CASE STUDIES
IN
CONTRACTING
AND
ORGANIZATION

Randy Beuttltt

CASE STUDIES IN CONTRACTING AND ORGANIZATION

Scott E. Masten, *Editor*

New York   Oxford
OXFORD UNIVERSITY PRESS
1996

OXFORD UNIVERSITY PRESS

Oxford   New York
Athens   Auckland   Bangkok   Bombay
Calcutta   Cape Town   Dar es Salaam   Delhi
Florence   Hong Kong   Istanbul   Karachi
Kuala Lumpur   Madras   Madrid   Melbourne
Mexico City   Nairobi   Paris   Singapore
Taipei   Tokyo   Toronto

  and associated companies in

Berlin   Ibadan

Library of Congress Cataloging-in-Publication Data

Case studies in contracting and organization/Scott E. Masten,
    editor.
      p.   cm.
    Includes bibliographical references and index.
    ISBN 0-19-509251-1; 0-19-509252-X (pbk)
      1. Industrial organization (Economic theory)—Case studies.
      2. Contracts—Economic aspects—Case studies.
I. Masten, Scott E., 1955–.
HD2326.C378   1996
381—dc20   95-7971
                                                      CIP

9 8 7 6 5 4 3 2 1

Printed in the United States of America

on acid-free paper

To
Kathy, Callie, and Ted

PREFACE

In his 1972 remarks before the National Bureau of Economic Research, Ronald Coase offered a rather bleak assessment of the state of industrial organization. "Industrial organization," he complained, "has become the study of the pricing and output policies of firms, especially in oligopolistic situations" (1972: 62) when the central issues in the organization of economic activity concern the allocation of activities among firms, the structure of contractual arrangements between firms, and the effects of changes in the law on organizational form. What was needed, Coase maintained, was "a more direct approach to the problem" of organization (73), a change he felt "was most likely to come through the stimulus provided by the patterns, puzzles, and anomalies revealed by systematic data-gathering" (71). Echoes of Coase's lament could still be heard almost twenty years later in Sam Peltzman's (1991) and Alvin Klevorick's (1991) reviews of the *Handbook of Industrial Organization* (Schmalensee and Willig, 1989): Resonant themes include mainstream industrial organization's (over)emphasis on oligopolistic interactions, the wide gulf and imbalance between theory and empirical work, and the need for greater attention to the legal environment in which transactions take place.

Although it has yet to be fully incorporated into the industrial organization curriculum, a substantial literature on the organization of business transactions that is responsive to Coase's concerns has emerged and continues to grow. Spurred in part by developments in the analysis of firms and contracting practices beginning in the 1970s, researchers began to explore in much greater detail the activities of and relations among commercial transactors. Rather than stress strategic pricing and output decisions, these studies emphasize transactors' efforts to discover and adopt organizational arrangements that constrain strategic behavior and facilitate mutually beneficial transactions, efforts whose success depends in important ways on the content, operation, and limitations of the legal system. But the feature that most distinguishes this literature from the mainstream is its empirical content and, especially, the progress researchers have made identifying and collecting detailed transaction-level information on organizational practices and the nature and attributes of transactions.

The purpose of this book is to introduce the empirical literature on contracting and organization to a wider audience. Although much of this literature has appeared in top academic journals, the range of industries and organization practices analyzed and the principles of economic organization illuminated by that research are still not widely appreciated. My aim in assembling the readings in this book is to facilitate access to this research and thereby increase awareness and appreciation of its contributions to our understanding of the purposes and implications of organizational choices.

In selecting readings, my primary criteria were the overall quality of the study and the goal of covering as wide a range of industries, practices, and principles as possible. Hence, with the exceptions of chapters 8 and 9, both of which analyze—albeit in different ways—vertical integration in the automotive industry, each chapter examines a different industry. But more important than either the specific industries or practices represented is that each application illustrates important principles of organization that generalize to commercial transactions in other settings.

To keep the readings accessible to a broad audience, I also chose to exclude some of the more technical studies contained in the literature. As a result, very few equations and diagrams appear in the book. The most technical material remaining describes econometric techniques that readers without appropriate backgrounds should be able to skim without serious loss of appreciation. Unfortunately, accommodating these criteria and the substantial length of several of the studies meant omitting some excellent contributions, many of which are referred to in the readings and listed in the bibliography at the end of the book. More comprehensive lists can be found in a pair of recent surveys (Klein and Shelanski, 1994; Crocker and Masten, 1995).

With two exceptions, all of the material in this collection has been previously published. Edward Gallick's study of tuna harvesting, excerpted in chapter 11, has appeared previously only as a Federal Trade Commission report and, consequently, has not had the exposure it deserves. The other exception is the introduction (chapter 1). Although most of the readings are self-contained and their central lessons accessible with relatively little background, some familiarity with the terminology and framework employed in the readings and the problem of economic organization more generally is likely to be helpful. Toward that end, chapter 1 provides an introduction to the theory and concepts of transaction cost economics, followed by an overview of each study's principal contributions to our understanding of organization.

The readings themselves have been reproduced with only minor alterations. To enhance readability, I have deleted some of the large number of purely documentary footnotes contained in the originals and, where appropriate, have abbreviated and moved references from footnotes to the text. Remaining footnotes have been renumbered and complete references compiled in a single bibliography at the end of the book. Minor modifications in section and table numbering have also been made for purposes of consistency in style. The permission of the publishers and authors to reprint their articles is greatly appreciated.

Because of the relatively nontechnical nature of the readings, the book should be accessible to business and law students as well as to advanced undergraduate and graduate students in economics. While the widest potential classroom application for the book is as a supplementary reading in industrial organization courses, its most direct application would be in the growing number of courses on the economics of organization and institutions.

Another potential application is in business economics or strategic management courses on contracting and organization. Unlike standard business-school cases, the studies contained in this book are not mere accounts of observed business practices but seek to provide systematic analyses of variations in organizational forms and practices over time and across transactions. The book, for instance, might serve as a useful complement to Paul Milgrom and John Roberts textbook, *Economics, Organization and Management*. Finally, the readings could also serve as a supplement to law school courses on contracting and commercial transactions as a way of exposing future lawyers and legal academics to the factors that influence actual business practices.

Ann Arbor   S. E. M.
September 1995

CONTENTS

OR – Awkward style

P A R T III

HYBRIDS

CASE STUDIES
IN
CONTRACTING
AND
ORGANIZATION

C h a p t e r

1

INTRODUCTION

This book is about the ways in which businesses organize production and exchange and, particularly, about why relationships between commercial transactors take the forms they do. Why do manufacturers buy some components and make others? What influences the duration and structure of contractual agreements? When will a company distribute its products through an independent distribution network rather than use commissioned employees? Why has franchising become such an important organizational form in the retail sector? These are just a few of the broad questions that even a casual look at modern business transactions raises. Closer scrutiny of business dealings reveals a complex of clever, sometimes subtle, organizational solutions to the diverse problems commercial transactors confront procuring, producing, and distributing goods and services.

The study of contracting and organization is important for several reasons. First, the activities a firm chooses to engage in and the structure of its relations with other businesses are important strategic decisions for business firms. Pursuing the wrong mix of activities or failing to fashion appropriate links with suppliers and distributors can increase costs and put a firm at a disadvantage relative to its competitors. Business histories offer abundant testimony of the role of organizational innovations in the success of particular businesses and industries: The development and adoption of the multidivisional corporate form by General Motors and Dupont during the 1920s (Chandler, 1966) and Swift's successful forward integration in meat-packing during the 1880s (Porter and Livesay, 1971; Chandler, 1977) are but two examples.

Organizational form has also been a critical, if not the decisive, factor in everything from the success of Japanese firms during the 1980s to the collapse and disintegration of central planning in Eastern Europe. Recent attempts to quantify the relation between organizational form and economic performance suggest that the implications of governance choice and design are indeed substantial. A study of the effects of legislation restricting the rights of franchisors to terminate franchisees, for example, found that the loss of this single contractual instrument significantly reduced the use of franchising in states that adopted such laws and decreased the value of franchisors operating in those states by an average of 6.4 percent, or $2 million for the median firm (Brickley, Dark, and Weisbach, 1991b). Estimates from a study of naval construction put the costs of choosing the wrong procurement mode for a typical component at between 12 and 25 percent of its value (Masten, Meehan, and Snyder, 1991). Contrary to Herbert Simon's assertion that organizations are in a sort of "neutral equilibrium" in which changes in organizational form, one way or another, matter little (1991: 28), the available evidence is that organizational form matters a great deal. With so much at stake, business decision makers would be well advised to choose and design organizational arrangements carefully.

Understanding why businesses organize as they do is also important for the development of sound public policies toward business organization. The most obvious implications concern antitrust policy. Aside from pricing practices such as collusion and predation, the chief concerns of the antitrust laws involve organizational issues such as mergers, integration, and vertical contract restrictions like exclusive dealing arrangements and product tie-ins and bundling. Several of the studies in this book, in fact, had their origins in antitrust cases (chapters 4, 11, 12, and 13). As these studies illustrate, an improved understanding of the role and performance implications of contracting and organization reduces the likelihood that business practices that serve legitimate economic functions will be misconstrued as anticompetitive.[1]

Finally, the study of actual contracting practices stands to inform lawyers and judges about the goals of commercial contractors and the sources of contractual failures. For courts, such knowledge is crucial to the formulation of appropriate legal rules and their application in individual cases. For lawyers, the study of contracting can provide insights with which to help clients design more effective agreements.

The perspective on contracting and organization employed by the readings in this book is known as *transaction cost economics*, which is, in turn, a part of the *new institutional economics*, a body of research that seeks to explain the variety of institutional and organizational arrangements societies adopt to govern economic activity. The central tenet of transaction cost economics is that the efficiency of alternative organizational arrangements turns on a comparison of the costs of transacting under each. Although the origins of transaction cost economics can be traced to developments in law, economics, and organization theory as early as the 1930s (see Williamson, 1985: 1–12), the logical foundation for analyzing problems of organization in transaction cost terms derives from the insight, due originally to Ronald Coase (1960), that all potential gains from trade would be realized but for the costs of reaching and enforcing agreements. Hence, in assessing the relative merits of alternative organizational arrangements, the focus of attention becomes the nature and size of the frictions preventing transactors from securing those gains.

While Coase provided the underlying logic, the substantive contributions of transaction cost economics derive from two subsequent developments. The first consisted of efforts, initiated and most forcefully articulated by Oliver Williamson (e.g., 1971; 1979a), to "operationalize" the theory, that

---

[1] George Bittlingmeyer (1993) has gone so far as to argue that changes over time in the content and enforcement of antitrust laws have been a major cause of business cycles.

is, to relate transaction costs to institutional arrangements and observable attributes of transactions in ways that would permit hypotheses about organizational form to be formulated and tested. The second was the emergence of a body of empirical research examining in detail the problems and organizational practices of commercial transactors. The latter provided evidence on the validity of transaction cost propositions and also identified a host of new organizational problems and phenomena in need of systematic analysis.

The studies contained in this book offer a sample of the empirical research on contracting and organization that has arisen over the past fifteen or so years. The readings in part I explore the role of contracts in governing exchange and the factors influencing the design and duration of contractual agreements; those in part II consider vertical integration as an alternative to market exchange and the conditions likely to prompt transactors to forsake contracting in favor of internal organization; while part III's readings examine intermediate or "hybrid" organizational forms such as franchising and leasing that exhibit features associated with both contracting and internal organization. Although each study focuses on a particular industry, the principles of contracting and organization they illustrate apply broadly.

The remainder of this chapter is divided into two sections. The first provides an introduction to the problem of economic organization and to the theory and concepts employed in the readings. This is followed by an overview of each study and its relation to the theory.

1. THE PROBLEM OF ECONOMIC ORGANIZATION

Problems of organization arise wherever the benefits of specialization lead to trade. As Richard Nelson observed, "Robinson Crusoe had an economic problem but (ignoring Friday) not one that posed issues of economic organization" (1981: 96). Thus, while Crusoe had to decide how to allocate his time between fishing, harvesting coconuts, and building shelter—an economic problem of allocating scarce resources among competing uses—he did not, at least until Friday came along, have to coordinate his activity with anyone else and therefore did not have to consider the manner in which his interactions with others would be governed.

With trade, however, comes the need to coordinate. Though economists have traditionally emphasized the role of the price system in performing that function, the price system is only one among many ways that coordination is accomplished in any complex economy. Individuals and, more specifically, commercial transactors may negotiate price and other aspects of performance transaction by transaction, or they may set the terms of current trade and provide for future adjustments to those terms in a long-term contract. Alternatively, transactors may decide to integrate production and exchange and govern their activities "internally." A range of hybrid or intermediate forms of organization, such as franchising and joint ventures, provides still additional alternatives.

While the persistence of diverse organizational forms suggests that no single organizational form is ideal for every transaction, the advantages that derive from organizing one way instead of another are not self-evident: Benefits to cooperating exist regardless of the particular organizational arrangement governing a transaction. As long as there are gains from trade, parties have an incentive to negotiate a deal that realizes those gains. Ronald Coase's critical discernment was that organizational form matters only to the extent that (1) there exist impediments to reaching and enforcing agreements, and (2) those impediments differ from one mode of organization to another.

1.1. The Nature and Sources of Transaction Costs

Transaction costs is the term used to describe the impediments to reaching and enforcing agreements. They have been described as "the costs of running the economic system" (Arrow, 1969: 60) and are associated with such activities as bargaining, contracting, and monitoring performance, activities that are not directly productive but which are engaged in only as a consequence of the need to coordinate activities among transactors.

The existence of transaction costs can be traced to two attributes of human nature (Williamson, 1975, 1985). The first, *bounded rationality*, refers to fact that, although individuals intend to act in a rational manner, their ability to realize those intentions is hampered by their limited knowledge, foresight, skill, and time (Simon, 1957, 1961). Because of bounded rationality, individuals cannot solve complex problems instantaneously or anticipate all possible future events; nor can they always devise and effectively communicate appropriate responses to contingencies they do foresee. Moreover, because everyone suffers such limitations, there exist no omniscient third parties capable of resolving disagreements accurately and cheaply to whom transactors can appeal for assistance.

Second, potential gains from trade may be sacrificed because of the propensity of at least some individuals to behave opportunistically (Williamson, 1975, 1979). Although cooperation enhances the value of exchange, every transaction also contains a source of potential conflict: each transactor will wish to appropriate for himself as large a share of the gains from trade as possible. *Opportunism* refers to the willingness of transactors to renege on promises, cheat on agreements, shirk responsibilities, circumvent rules, search out loopholes, or otherwise exploit the vulnerabilities of a trading partner in hopes of eliciting a more favorable distribution of the rents accruing to exchange. (Not everyone is so unprincipled, of course, but bounded rationality makes it difficult to distinguish the trustworthy from the unscrupulous, making guarding against opportunism the prudent course.)

Opportunistic behavior can be divided into two principal types: (1)

deviations from joint-surplus maximizing behavior that produce a de facto redistribution of gains from trade *within* the terms of an existing agreement, and (2) efforts designed to exact more favorable terms at the outset or to force a renegotiation and thus a de jure modification of terms previously agreed to (compare Klein, 1992: 154; Masten, 1988c: 184, 186–87).

The first type of opportunism, which is a response to price signals contained in a contract, is what economists commonly refer to as moral hazard. Shirking, cutting corners, or debasing quality in some undetectable (or unactionable) fashion or in dimensions that have been left unspecified or poorly defined are examples of such behavior. In deviating from joint-maximizing effort levels, the shirker seeks not to alter the express terms of the contract but to take advantage of existing terms or lapses in specification and enforceability. Ideally, the transgressor would like his behavior to go undetected by both the courts and his trading partner.

The second form of opportunism consists of efforts to "hold up" a trading partner and involves actions taken to set new terms rather than in reaction to existing ones. Opportunism of this second type is not limited to actions that directly benefit a transactor but also includes the possibility of expending resources in activities undertaken solely to impose costs on a trading partner in hopes of eliciting concessions. At the contract formation stage, such activities include haggling and strikes. During contract execution, they may entail suing for trivial deviations, making false claims of dissatisfaction, "working to rule," or withholding relevant information in hopes of inducing a breach.[2] Because such tactics often cost the initiator as well as their recipient, they are profitable to engage in only if they succeed in making the status quo so disagreeable that a trading partner finds it less onerous to accede to a renegotiation than to insist on the current terms.

Opportunistic behavior is costly both because efforts to hold up a trading partner—long with that party's attempts to counteract them—consume resources directly, and because the failure of transactors to reach agreements or take appropriate actions leaves gains from trade unrealized. To the extent transactors can devise organizational arrangements that reduce the probability or cost of conflicts over the distribution of gains, the surplus available to distribute between them rises. The problem is that efforts to constrain opportunism, whether by attempting to devise more elaborate contractual protections ex ante or through greater monitoring and oversight ex post, inevitably place additional demands on bounded rationality. Consequently, in choosing among and designing organizational arrangements, transactors confront a constant tension between "economizing on bounded rationality" and "safeguarding against the hazards of opportunism" (Williamson, 1985: 32).

---

[2] For more extensive lists and further discussion, see Muris (1981), Goetz and Scott (1983), and Goldberg (1985). See also Williamson (1983: 526) and Masten (1988c).

1.2. Adaptation as the Central Problem of Organization

Organization, even in the presence of bounded rationality and opportunism, would pose few serious problems in a static world. "So long as things continue as before, or at least as they were expected to, there arise no new problems requiring a decision, no need to form a new plan" (Hayek, 1945: 523). In the presence of change and uncertainty, however, transactors need to plan, monitor, and continually adjust their behavior, activities that demand attention and cooperation if the benefits of trade are to be realized (Williamson, 1985, 1991). Inasmuch as change and uncertainty are ubiquitous elements of the economic environment, *adaptation* to unfolding events becomes the central problem of economic organization (Hayek, 1945: 523–24; Williamson, 1991: 277–78). By altering the processes through which adjustments to changing circumstances are anticipated and effected, institutional and organizational arrangements influence the cost and accuracy of adaptations.

An Illustration: Efficient Breach

The relation between institutions and adaptation processes can be usefully illuminated by considering the problem of efficient breach of contract. Because of changes in the opportunity cost of performance, one or the other party to a contract may turn out to regret having entered the contract and wish to breach the agreement. Whether proceeding with the transaction is efficient, however, depends on the realized value of performance to *both* parties: As long as the value the buyer places on performance exceeds the value of the seller's assets in their next best alternative application, performance of the contract remains efficient even though one of the parties takes a loss under the prevailing terms.

The standard economic approach treats contract breach as an incentive problem, that of defining appropriately scaled damages to induce efficient performance (see, for instance, Shavell, 1980). A legal rule requiring specific performance of each contract, it is argued, would prevent breach even when nonperformance is efficient and thus cause parties to trade too often relative to the optimum. Requiring the breaching party to pay expectation damages or "lost profits," in contrast, would induce him to breach only when doing so would leave him better off, even after compensating the other party, and would therefore lead to breach only when efficient.

The fallacy—as Ian Macneil (1982) has termed it—in the theory of efficient breach stems from the fact that buyers and sellers are free to negotiate mutually advantageous adjustments, regardless of the legal rule governing breach, whenever nonperformance is the desired result. Thus, under a specific performance rule, if exchange with a third party were the efficient thing to do, that result could be achieved by, for instance, the seller negotiating a release from his contractual obligation to the original buyer; if the new trade is in fact efficient, the surplus generated by the new opportunity will be sufficient to allow the seller to "buy out" of the contract and still be better off.

An implicit assumption of the efficient breach literature is thus that such negotiated adjustments are costly. But, while that assumption is reasonable, the validity of the corollary assumption that the costs generated in such negotiations necessarily exceed the costs of determining fault and assessing damages under a damage rule is less evident. Ultimately, the relative efficiency of alternative rules for contract breach turn on a comparison of the costs of accomplishing adjustments under each.

The point of this illustration is that the efficient or "substantively rational" (Simon, 1978) response to change is the same regardless of whether specific performance or damages is the legal rule. What varies with the rule adopted is the process or procedures—and the corresponding tactics and strategies—through which the transactors can seek to effect adaptations. Since differences in the processes and associated costs of achieving desired adjustments are what determines the efficiency of alternative legal rules, processes as well as outcomes matter.

1.3. Legal Rules and Organizational Forms

The logic that makes process concerns central to analyzing the efficiency of alternative legal rules also applies to the analysis of organizational forms. Given the same technology, information, and actors, anything that could be accomplished within a firm, for example, could in principle also be accomplished with a contract, and vice versa. What varies as transactions are relocated from one organizational form to another are the duties, procedures, and sanctions available to the transactors and, hence, the tactics they can employ and the processes through which adaptations are realized. Since it is the legal system that regulates those duties and delimits and enforces sanctions, distinctions among organizational forms find their ultimate basis in the law (see Williamson, 1979, 1991; Masten, 1988b).

Discrete Market Transactions

The legal system affords independent firms or individuals engaged in discrete market transactions considerable autonomy and flexibility in the periods both leading up to and following the actual transaction (Macneil 1974; Williamson, 1979, 1991). In discrete transactions, parties are generally free to bargain or not bargain as they please. Moreover, once a transaction is consummated, the parties have relatively few ongoing obligations and may, for example, use or dispose of the items procured in whatever manner they choose.[3] The relative latitude afforded transactors in simple exchanges provides them both the ability and the incentive to adapt their behavior to events and information as they arise.

That latitude, however, also provides transactors a tactic to extract rents. Parties to a simple exchange may haggle, stall, or walk away from the deal

---

[3] The existence of product liability and implied warranty obligations are exceptions to this generalization.

altogether if they are dissatisfied with the terms currently tendered; courts rarely intervene to force the parties to come to terms. Similarly, in the absence of concrete agreements by the parties themselves, courts generally refrain from regulating the post-exchange behavior of the transactors, even if that behavior imposes costs on other parties to the transaction.[4] Thus, although flexible, market transactions are relatively exposed to the potential for holdups and reneging.

Contracting

The essence of a contract is to move beyond mere promises, which transactors alert to the propensity toward opportunism will wisely discount. By entering a contract, transactors hope to delimit the range of acceptable behavior and reduce the prospect of costly repetitive bargaining. In support of those objectives, the legal system restricts the ability of one party to extort concessions from the other by unilaterally refusing to deal or threatening not to perform, assesses damages or employs other remedies for breach, and, perhaps most important, provides an explicit and detailed set of rules and procedures for resolving disputes.

Contracting, however, is also subject to a variety of well-known hazards and limitations. First, contracts that cover the full range of possible contingencies are prohibitively expensive to write. Contractual agreements may be incomplete "because of the inability to identify uncertain future conditions or because of inability to characterize complex adaptations even when the contingencies themselves can be identified in advance" (Goetz and Scott, 1981: 2).

Second, courts are not the reliable enforcers of contractors' intentions sometimes portrayed in both the law and economics literatures. Even when the intent of the parties is clear, judges and juries may be unable (because of bounded rationality and the opportunistic representations of the litigants) to determine whether those intentions have been fulfilled. The inability to define the precise obligations of each party in response to changing events in ways that can be enforced in a low-cost fashion means that contracts will, on the one hand, tend to be inflexible and, on the other, leave considerable opportunity to cheat on the agreement or to redistribute contractual surpluses by forcing an explicit renegotiation of the terms of trade. In that regard, contracts do not so much define the terms of trade as establish the framework within which future negotiations over the terms of trade will take place.

Vertical Integration

Vertical integration represents an alternative to contracting where the hazards of market exchange are severe. The advantages accruing to integration,

---

[4] An example might be a computer manufacturer's decision to discontinue a product line without regard for the effect of that decision on the resale value of earlier customers' equipment or the value of hardware and software designed and produced by third parties specifically for that line.

and even the properties that distinguish internal from market organization, have been the subject of much debate, however. Some commentators on the theory of the firm deny that integration possesses any unique governance advantages. As these scholars correctly note, integration by itself changes neither human nature nor the technological or informational environment confronting transactors (see Evans and Grossman, 1983). Nor, they argue, does integration alter the authority of transactors to direct production or settle disputes: employers have no authority or disciplining power beyond that available to a consumer seeking to direct or discipline his grocer. All either can do is "fire or sue" (Alchian and Demsetz, 1972: 777). For these economists, the firm represents little more than a collection or "nexus" of otherwise ordinary contractual relationships.

Although termination and legal sanctions are, as Alchian and Demsetz argued, the only options ultimately available, *when* you can fire and *what* you can sue for vary with the mode of organization adopted. As discussed earlier, differences among organizational forms originate in distinctions established by the legal system. In the case of integration, the legal system occasions both ownership and governance distinctions. Of the two, ownership is the most direct way to integrate. By allocating residual rights of control over the use and disposition of assets, ownership restricts the ability of nonowners to withhold assets from production and thus limits hold-up opportunities. In effect, ownership avoids holdups by eliminating the second transactor.[5]

Integration may also be effected, either separately or in conjunction with ownership, through the internalization of production. Whereas ownership alters the legal relationship of transactors to assets, internalizing production alters the legal relationships of transactors to each other. First, the law places greater burdens on employees (vis-à-vis independent contractors) to obey directives, disclose information, and otherwise act in the interests of an employer (see Clark, 1985; Masten, 1988). Second, and arguably more important, the law governing internal transactions is characterized by "judicial forbearance": "whereas courts routinely grant standing to firm should there be disputes over prices, the damages to be ascribed to delays, failures of quality and the like, courts will refuse to hear disputes between one internal division and another over identical technical issues" (Williamson, 1991: 274). While independent contractors can appeal to courts to resolve disputes, top management exercises ultimate authority in disputes between internal divisions; it is its own court of last resort. Differences in the responsibilities, sanctions, and procedures applying to internal and market transactions thus seem to support the greater discretion and control and superior access to information generally associated with internal organization.

The benefits of integration are limited, however, by the bureaucratic

---

[5] Klein, chapter 8. See also Klein, Crawford, and Alchian (1978) and Grossman and Hart (1986).

inefficiencies that inevitably plague large organizations. Although, in principle, a newly integrated firm should be able to operate at least as efficiently as the two independent firms from which it was formed simply by allowing each division of the combined firm to operate independently as it had before and only intervening where net benefits were likely to be realized, the management of the combined enterprise will be unable, given the law governing internal transactions, to commit to intervening only in such a selective fashion (Williamson, 1991). Without effective assurances that owners will not appropriate performance enhancements, the incentives of division managers to innovate, maintain assets, acquire and utilize information, and otherwise invest in the efficient operation of the division will be compromised. In their place, the firm is forced to substitute weaker, indirect incentives dependent on managerial oversight (Williamson, 1985, chapter 6).[6] The loss of incentive intensity, combined with the limited capacity of management to administer additional transactions, ultimately undermines the efficacy of internal organization and thereby limit firm size.

Hybrids

The term hybrid does not refer to a distinct category of organizational forms but to a diverse collection of relationships that either combine contracting and vertical integration or lie somewhere between markets and hierarchy in terms of incentive intensity, adaptability, and bureaucratic costs (Williamson, 1991: 280–81). Thus, joint ventures and arrangements in which one contractor (or both) holds a partial equity interest in the other blend elements of both contracting and ownership. Meanwhile, the degree of control afforded franchisors under franchise agreements, though legally contracts between two independent entities, is often thought to give franchising "firmlike" properties (see, for example, Rubin, 1978; Alchian and Woodward 1987). Given the variety of hybrid forms, the nature of hybrids, their advantages and disadvantages, and the rules that influence their form must be assessed on a case-by-case basis.

1.4. Matching

Once the properties that distinguish organizational forms from one another have been identified, the remaining task is to match organizations and transactions or, more specifically, to "align transactions (which differ in their attributes) with governance structures (the costs and competencies of which differ) in a discriminating (mainly, transaction cost economizing) way" (Williamson, 1988: 73). The most important conceptual contribution of transaction cost reasoning to the study of economic organization has been

---

[6] Employee obligations to disclose information to employers and employer liability for harms to third parties caused by employees in the course of performing their jobs also stand to weaken employee incentives to use initiative and exercise care, increasing the need for managerial oversight (see Masten, 1988b).

in identifying the critical dimensions that influence the relative efficiency of various organizational forms.

Asset Specificity

The scope for opportunism is limited where transactors can easily turn to alternative trading partners if one seeks to gain at the expense of the other. Often, however, realization of cost economies or design benefits requires investment in relationship-specific assets, assets that are specifically designed or located for a particular user. Because relationship-specific investments have a discretely lower value in their next best application, such investments isolate the parties from alternative trading opportunities and generate appropriable quasi rents—the difference between the value of the assets in their intended and next best use—the distribution of which may become a source of contention between the parties.

This "fundamental transformation" from a situation of ex ante competition to small numbers bargaining when investments are relationship specific is one of the primary forces motivating the adoption of specialized governance structures (Williamson, 1985). The more difficult it is to find substitute performance or to redeploy investments to alternative uses, the larger the appropriable quasi rents, and the greater the incentive to engage in behavior designed to appropriate a larger share of those gains.

Asset specificity can take at least four forms (Williamson, 1983):

1. Physical-asset specificity, which involves investments in equipment such as tooling or dies specially designed to serve a particular customer.
2. Site or location specificity, which occurs when a buyer or seller locates his facilities next to the other to economize on transportation costs.
3. Human-asset specificity, which arises when a transactor develops skills or knowledge valuable only when dealing with a particular trading partner.
4. Dedicated assets, which are investments made to support exchange with a particular customer that, though not specific to that customer, would result in substantial excess capacity were the customer to discontinue purchases.

In addition, the threat of holdups or opportunism may also arise or be exacerbated where the timing of performance is critical. "Temporal specificity" may arise because a product's value is inherently time dependent, like newspapers; because of the serial nature of production, as in construction projects; because the product is perishable, as is the case with agricultural commodities; or because, like natural gas and electricity, the product is costly to store. In such circumstances, delay may become an effective strategy for eliciting price concessions because of the difficulty of arranging substitute performance on short notice.

The hazards of trading in the presence of durable, relationship-specific investments are likely to be particularly acute in discrete market transactions. The ability of parties to haggle, stall, or walk away from a deal leaves relationship-specific investments entirely unprotected. As described earlier, contracts and vertical integration alter the strategies transactors can employ in pursuit of appropriable quasi rents and offer some, albeit imperfect, protection against opportunism.

Complexity and Uncertainty

Both the design of contractual agreements and the choice between contracting and integration depend in part on the degree of complexity and uncertainty associated with the transaction. The more complex the transaction, the harder it becomes to describe fully and accurately the responsibilities of each party in a contract, and the more difficult it will be for courts to assess whether those obligations have been fulfilled. Greater uncertainty, meanwhile, makes it harder to write complete agreements and more likely that the parties either will fail to adapt to changing conditions or will find it profitable to engage in costly efforts to evade performance.

Transactors may respond to the inability to write complete contracts in two ways. First, as the transaction becomes more complex or uncertain, contracts are likely to become more "relational" in character. Rather than attempting to lay out a detailed specification of the terms of the agreement, relational contracts attempt simply to establish the process through which future terms of trade will be determined—"the establishment, in effect, of a constitution governing the ongoing relationship" (Goldberg, 1976: 428; see also Williamson, 1979a). In designing those terms, contracting parties will wish to adopt contract provisions that avoid the need for costly adjudication while maintaining incentives for appropriate adaptation. The problem is finding contract structures that encourage rent-increasing adaptations (flexibility) but discourage rent-dissipating efforts to redistribute existing surpluses (opportunism).

Where uncertainty or complexity is particularly severe, vertical integration may offer advantages over contracting. Although complexity and uncertainty are likely to increase the costs of internal administration as well—complex transactions are more difficult to manage, while the need to keep track of and respond to changing circumstances places greater demand on management's limited attention—the differential effect of complexity and uncertainty on the costs of contracting and internal organization is likely to favor the latter: whereas contracting demands prior anticipation of potential problems, internal organization facilitates adaptation to changing circumstances as they unfold (Williamson, 1975: 25).

Measurement Costs

Contract designs may also be influenced by the desire to reduce excessive or duplicative sorting, searching, and measurement costs. Problems of wasteful sorting and searching arise in situations where obtaining information about the characteristics of a good or about likely future conditions stands to alter the distribution of gains from trade—and is therefore privately valuable—but does not improve the allocation of goods and services or otherwise increase the surplus available. Examples include such products as first-run movies and uncut diamonds, both of which have the property that their values vary substantially and are difficult both for producers to control and for purchasers and producers to ascertain (Kenney and Klein, 1983). The difficulty and expense of pricing each item individually makes it profitable for each theater owner and diamond merchant to search for undervalued items and reject overpriced ones. Organizational arrangements that reduce the time and effort expended in redundant search and repricing leave more gains from trade to be divided among the transactors (see Goldberg and Erickson, chapter 4; Gallick, chapter 11; and Leffler and Rucker, 1991).

Reputation

The prospect of repeated and ongoing interactions often tempers the propensity to behave opportunistically. In such settings, the long-run loss of confidence of one's current or potential future trading partners tends to outweigh the short-run gains from cheating a trading partner (Telser, 1980). The effectiveness of reputation as a constraint on opportunism depends on a variety of factors, however, among them (1) value of future cooperation; (2) the ease of detecting opportunistic behavior. (3) the time it takes to respond to cheating once detected; and (4) the ability of other potential trading partners to observe and communicate instances of opportunism. Where reputation is insufficient to deter opportunism, parties are more likely to turn to contracts and court ordering to govern transactions. But even where conditions are favorable, reputation may require institutional supports to be fully effective.

The Role of Risk Aversion

Conspicuously absent from the readings in this collection, and in the transaction cost literature more generally, is any analysis of the implications of risk aversion.[7] While it is certainly the case that organizational arrangements affect the allocation of risk among transactors, transaction cost economists have offered several justifications for putting aside risk preference considerations when analyzing organizational form (Goldberg, 1990b; Williamson, 1985: 388–89; and Klein, 1983: 370; also see Mayers and Smith, 1982). First, most of the literature on organization, like the readings in this book, is concerned with trade in intermediate products between commercial transactors whose owners can typically diversify their financial holdings to mitigate the effects of risk. Second, the relative risk preferences of individuals, like tastes more generally, cannot be observed directly and

---

[7] Risk preferences concern people's attitudes toward risky choices. A risk-averse person, for instance, is one who would prefer a certain gain of $100 to a 50:50 chance of receiving $200 or nothing.

so must be inferred from observed behavior, inviting rationalization and circular arguments. Relatedly, the ability to rationalize organizational forms on the basis of assumptions about relative risk aversion has tended to preempt efforts to develop other explanations for observed practices.

Finally, even where risk aversion is at issue, the governance of risk transfers, like other transactions, can be accomplished in a variety of ways: in addition to forward contracts and vertical integration, risk may be transferred through futures markets and various forms of third-party insurance, among other arrangements. The choice of institutions to govern risk transfers involves issues of measurement and appropriability identical to those arising in the governance of product and service transactions and calls for a comparative institutional analysis of the type used to analyze those transactions.

2. THE READINGS

2.1. Contracting

Because use of the legal system to resolve disputes is costly, parties have incentives to resolve disputes themselves and to invoke court adjudication only as a last resort. Robert Ellickson's study of informal rules governing disputes over the ownership of harvested whales during the late eighteenth and nineteenth centuries deals with the governance of trade in what might be called a precontractual setting. Despite abundant opportunities for disagreements over rights to captured whales to arise, the number of disputes litigated during the "heyday" of the whaling industry were negligible. Ellickson attributes this to the efficacy of the private norms the whaling community developed to resolve conflicting claims (relative, implicitly, to the costs and limitations of formal, legal dispute resolution). Ellickson argues, first, that the repeated interaction and social contacts among whalers afforded members of the whaling community the information and power to enforce the community's norms without having to resort to courts. He then hypothesizes that the content of the informal rules whalers developed should reflect the desire to minimize the sum of transaction costs and deadweight losses associated with failing to exploit gains from trade: Rules that provide the strongest incentives for whalers to cooperate during pursuit and capture tend to be vague and difficult to administer, while clear, bright-line rules offering lower transaction costs tend to elicit inadequate cooperation.

Ellickson's analysis of the historical record reveals that actual whaling norms struck a balance between providing incentives to pursue whales and the transaction costs of administering the rule. In particular, the rules adopted to cover different fishing grounds varied with the predominant species of whales and the associated harvesting technology in a way consistent with his wealth-maximization hypothesis.

An indication of the success of these informal norms and sanctions in supporting an environment conducive to whaling is, as one observer put it, "the extent of the industry which has grown up under it" (93). That "success," however, eventually resulted in the depletion of the world's whale stocks and the decline of the whaling industry. As the close-knit whaling communities subsequently began to unravel, litigation over contested whales increased. Ellickson's account thus offers testimony to the conditions important to the emergence and survival of informal dispute resolution and, conversely, the circumstances in which informal mechanisms are likely to break down and necessitate formal, third-party adjudication of disputes.

Whereas Ellickson analyzes an industry that voluntarily adopted and relied on informal rules, Thomas Palay's study of modern rail freight contracting considers a setting in which regulatory barriers to formal contracting forced transactors to resort to informal arrangements. At the time of Palay's study, the Interstate Commerce Act, which regulated interstate rail carriage, restricted the prices and other terms under which railroads and shippers could contract for rail services. In particular, the nondiscrimination requirements of the ICA prohibited shippers and railroads from negotiating special prices for special services and made contractual protections such as minimum shipping requirements unenforceable. These restrictions posed problems especially for the shipment of cargoes requiring specialized or shipper-specific railcars. Without guarantees that shippers would use the carrier to transport their products, rail carriers were reluctant to invest in cars that had limited alternative uses. Shippers, despite their interest in assuring that railroads were equipped to meet their transport needs, were unable to make volume commitments within the framework established by the ICA.

Palay describes how railroads and shippers responded to carrier reluctance to invest in shipper-specific railcars and to the special needs of shippers through the use of informal, legally unenforceable agreements. As Palay carefully documents, the manner of enforcing agreements, attitudes toward requests for adjustments, willingness to negotiate adaptations, and the propensity to exchange information for long-term and structural planning all varied with the specificity of investments underlying the transaction.

Palay's account of rail-freight agreements also portrays the importance of personal relations to the formation and maintenance of informal agreements and the disruptive effect that personnel changes can have on those relations (see also Palay, 1985). Where personal relations arise naturally or spontaneously, as was apparently the case in the whaling communities of the eighteenth century, informal norms may constitute an effective alternative to costly legal dispute resolution. In other contexts, however, personal relations may be costly to establish and preserve. Indeed, the expansion of the opportunities for trade beyond those with whom we have personal relations is one of the great benefits a well-functioning system of commercial law confers on society. In principle, at least, the legal system enables parties to make commitments and provides a set of procedures for resolving disputes where community norms and reputation considerations, though never entirely absent, provide inadequate supports.

In contrast to agreements among rail carriers and shippers, the petroleum coke contracts Victor Goldberg and John Erickson study were at least nominally enforceable. Goldberg and Erickson trace the adoption of long-term contracts for petroleum coke (a byproduct of oil refining) to the site specificity of coke production and processing facilities. Given coke's bulky and hazardous nature and the small number of feasible alternative customers, a coke producer was exposed to substantial costs of either storage or interrupted production if its primary customer failed to remove coke from the refinery on a timely basis. To encourage refiners to invest in new coking capacity, the contracts either required that the customer remove all of the refinery's coke output immediately or, when the refiner was the customer's sole source of coke, contained price schedules that discouraged the customer from reducing its purchases.

Although the quantity requirements in the petroleum coke contracts created legally actionable obligations, inevitable gaps and ambiguities in contracts and the imperfect and costly nature of judicial enforcement left, as always, scope for opportunism. After considering alternative explanations for the pricing provisions contained in petroleum coke contracts, Goldberg and Erickson conclude that the most plausible rationale was the desire to reduce the costs of precontract search and postagreement jockeying over the terms of trade. Their analysis thus supports an interpretation of contracting in terms of the mitigation of relational frictions over one emphasizing moral hazard considerations.

Among the many contracting issues that Goldberg and Erickson raise is the fact that interactions among contract terms often make the interpretation of particular provisions dependent on the rest of the agreement—detail that is often accessible only through intensive case analysis. The advantage of case studies in this respect must be balanced, however, against the greater generality and confidence that more formal statistical analyses provide. Empirical researchers have therefore sought to gain insights into the nature and purposes of contracts by testing contracting theories using data on large numbers of contracts.

In our analysis of the governance of natural gas transactions, Keith Crocker and I use a sample of nearly 300 contracts to explore the role and incidence of "take-or-pay" requirements. Natural-gas producers faced the problem that, once they had incurred the cost of drilling a well and attaching it to a gas pipeline, the pipeline company had an incentive to seek price concessions by refusing to take deliveries of gas. Contracts, it turned out, offered only limited protection against such holdups; in early cases, courts ruled that the difficulty of determining whether and how much gas had been drained away by other producers or by natural seepage precluded determining damages for breach of contract at a level of certainty sufficient to meet common law standards (e.g., *Red Jacket Oil & Gas Co.* v. *United Fuel Gas Co.*, 58 F. Supp. 367 [1943]; 146 F.2d 651 [1944]). Crocker and I hypothesized that take-or-pay provisions, which require buyers to pay for a prespecified minimum quantity of output even it that quantity is not taken, represented a private-ordering response to the problems of court determination of contract damages. Supporting this contention, our analysis showed that the magnitude of take-or-pay provisions varied with the alternative value of gas covered by each contract in a way consistent with the goal of encouraging efficient adaptations to changing circumstances.

The use of long-term contracts in the natural-gas industry is consistent with the relationship-specific investment argument described earlier. Natural-gas production and transmission require large, durable, location-specific investments in facilities and equipment. Paul Joskow's study of the duration of contracts between coal mines and electric generating companies provides more systematic evidence on the relation between specific investments and contracting. Building on an earlier case study (Joskow, 1985), Joskow describes how regional differences in the characteristics of coal and in transportation distances and alternatives affect the physical- and site-specificity of generators and coal mines across the United States. His findings that coal contracts tend to be longer for mine-mouth plants, in the western and midwestern United States than in the East, and the greater the annual contract quantity are all consistent with the prediction that repeated ex post bargaining becomes more expensive relative to designing and administering long-term contracts as investments become more relationship specific.

The relationship-specific investment rationale that seems to account for the use of long-term contracts in petroleum coke, natural gas, and coal transactions appears, at first glance, to founder in the context of ocean shipping. As Craig Pirrong points out, transportation of bulk cargo in ships is governed under an array of organizational alternatives, including long-term contracts and vertical integration. But ships are clearly redeployable geographically and therefore not site specific under the standard definition. And although ships may be specially designed to carry a particular type of cargo, they are not—unlike some of the rail cars discussed by Palay—specific to a particular shipper. Finally, human capital required for ocean shipping involves marine and cargo-handling skills specific neither to shippers nor carriers.

Pirrong attributes the use of long-term contracts and vertical integration in shipping to temporal specificities that arise because of the difficulty of arranging alternative shipping services for some commodities on short notice and relates the extent of timing difficulties to (1) contracting practices in the market for the commodity being shipped, (2) the thickness of the shipping market, and (3) whether the commodity is most efficiently shipped aboard specialized or general-purpose tonnage. His investigation of fourteen bulk shipping markets shows that the duration of shipping contracts and the incidence of vertical integration align with these factors as predicted. In addition to its substantive contributions, Pirrong's analysis highlights the need for detailed knowledge of transactions. Although the conditions of bounded rationality and opportunism that generate transactional frictions may be universal, the manifestations of those frictions and the factors that influence their incidence vary in ways that often become apparent only with intensive knowledge of the industry.

2.2. Vertical Integration

In "Vertical Integration as Organizational Ownership: The Fisher Body–General Motors Relationship Revisited," Benjamin Klein elaborates on what has come to be a classic illustration (originally sketched in Klein, Crawford, and Alchian, 1978) of the role of relationship-specific investments in the decision to integrate. In response partly to Ronald Coase's skepticism about the importance of relationship-specific investments for economic organization, Klein describes the limitations of reputation and contracting as constraints on opportunism and how, as in GM's experience with Fisher Body, "contracts may actually create, rather than solve, hold-up problems" (203): With the shift from labor-intensive wood automobile bodies to metal bodies around 1919 came the need to make large relationship-specific investments in giant presses and in dies for stamping body parts. Despite efforts to craft appropriate protections, the long-term, exclusive-dealing contract under which GM initially sought to procure metal bodies afforded the Fisher brothers an enormous opportunity to hold up GM when demand for closed metal automobile bodies soared unexpectedly in the early years of the contract, Ultimately, the tensions between the two became so great that GM integrated Fisher Body. Klein's account of the evolution of the relationship between GM and Fisher provides a rare look at the dynamics of the transformation process and the hazards of choosing the wrong organizational form.

Klein then uses GM's integration of Fisher Body to address the debate over the distinctions between firm and market organization. Specifically, Klein argues that the acquisition of "organizational capital" through vertical integration reduces the potential for holdups where relationship-specific human assets are at stake. Even though Klein questions the importance of legal differences between employment and independent contractor relationships in defining the firm, he attributes the advantages of "organizational ownership" to the fact that "telling all of the employees to leave [one company] and show up on Monday morning at a new address" is not "legally possible." Hence, the only issue is which and not whether legal rules distinguish firm and market transactions.

Kirk Monteverde and David Teece's study of integration of automotive components presents statistical evidence corroborating Klein's anecdotal account of the role of relationship-specific investments in the procurement decisions of automotive manufacturers. Monteverde and Teece argue that the specialized know-how that arises in the development of new automotive components and the difficulty of transferring skills and know-how make it costly to switch suppliers once applications engineering has been completed; company-specific components and those whose development involve a greater amount of applications engineering effort pose a greater risk of opportunism and are thus more likely to be integrated. Their statistical analysis, employing qualitative rankings of the level of engineering effort and of the specificity of automotive components, supports the importance of asset specificity—especially investments in relationship-specific *human* capital—in integration decisions in the automotive industry (see also Monteverde and Teece, 1982b; Walker and Weber, 1984, 1987; and Masten, Meehan, and Snyder, 1989).

My 1984 article examining the determinants of make-or-buy decisions in an aerospace program provides additional evidence of the importance of relationship-specific investments in the governance of vertical relations. Components that were specifically designed for use in the aerospace system studied were significantly more likely to be produced internally. The study also shows, however, that the effect of component specificity on the probability of integration is greatest for relatively complex components, supporting the argument that contracting hazards grow relative to the costs of internal administration as the obligations of the parties become more difficult to define. Government procurement regulations and practices also align with transaction cost prescriptions.

2.3. Hybrids

Inasmuch as hybrids represent attempts to achieve a balance between the benefits of market and integrated governance, we might expect hybrids to be associated with intermediate levels of relationship-specific investments (Williamson, 1991: 283). The diversity of hybrid forms, however, suggests that the factors and circumstances leading to the adoption and design of hybrid relationships are themselves diverse. Thus, although relationship-specific investments play some role in most of the studies in this section, measurement cost considerations seem to be the more salient concern in the design of hybrid relations. Indeed, the viability of some forms, such as equipment leasing and franchising, may actually depend on assets being redeployable at low cost (Masten and Snyder, chapter 12).

Edward Gallick examines the nature and evolution of governance arrangements between tuna fishermen and tuna processors. As Gallick describes, the principal governance problem facing tuna harvesters and processors was that of oversearch. Even though a given tuna had the same value to any tuna processor, differences in the size, species, and freshness of tuna created the incentives for harvesters, processors, or both to engage in prepurchase inspection and sorting of tuna in search of the most valuable fish. Since sorting of tuna did not enhance but only potentially redistributed the value of a catch, governance arrangements that reduced the amount of sorting, such as the exclusive dealing arrangements adopted by American tuna captains and processors, stood to increase efficiency. This contrasts with the auctioning of tuna in Japanese and other foreign markets where sales of raw, as opposed to canned, tuna dominate and make sorting socially valuable.

A side effect of the exclusive dealing contracts employed in the United States, however, was to transform tuna boats and harvests into relationship-specific assets, exposing captains to the threat of opportunism on the part of processors, who could threaten to delay unloading the tuna unless tuna captains acceded to price concessions. In the period of "bait boats," small catches and frequent stops in port restrained processors' incentives to hold up harvesters. The conversion to mechanized "purse-seine," vessels in the late 1960s, however, resulted in much larger boats making less frequent deliveries, reducing the effectiveness of reputation as a device for constraining the incentives for processors to holdup captains. In response, harvesters and processors made a number of organizational adjustments designed to increase the cost and reduce the benefits of processor holdups, including joint ownership of tuna boats by captains and processors (where boats had previously been independently owned by captains). The need to leave captains the incentive to exercise care and judgment in the use of boats and choice of fishing grounds, however, weighed against full integration, given the difficulty of monitoring performance over the 10,000-mile range and up to three month-periods these ships were at sea.

Equipment leasing represents a form of partial or quasi integration intermediate between contractual sales and full integration, in that the manufacturer of the equipment retains ownership of assets that independent downstream firms use in production. In our study of United Shoe Machinery Corporation's leasing practices, Edward Snyder and I examined the role of leasing as an alternative to both sales with contractual warranties and integration as means of promoting the development, production, and servicing of complex machinery and the supply of advice and information supporting the productive use of that equipment. Problems inherent in the transfer of information, plus the difficulty of adequately describing machine performance and the obligations of the transactors in the event of failures, would have exposed contractual guarantees to endless disputes over the adequacy of advice, culpability for breakdowns, and timing of repairs. Forward integration into shoe production by shoe-machinery manufacturers, meanwhile, would have forfeited the high-powered incentives that production by a large number of independent shoe manufacturers engendered. Leasing surmounts these problems by making the manufacturer's revenue from machinery transactions dependent on the realized value of machines, thus encouraging the performance of any activity that increases the value of the leased good.

Leasing also has drawbacks and limitations, however. For one, leasing reduces the incentive of the customer to use and maintain machines with appropriate care. And since the benefits of leasing depend on the ability to return or repossess machines, leasing will not be effective where equipment is specific to a particular customer. Snyder and I show that United Shoe Machinery employed leasing selectively to reflect these considerations, leasing only those machines where the hazards of contractual warranties relative to leasing were most acute. We also discuss how the structure of

United's leases sought to promote the efficient use and retention of shoe machines while economizing on the costs of governing exchange and resolving disputes.

The motives for and design of United Shoe Machinery's leases share a number of features with another familiar hybrid form: franchising. Among the similarities are the need for downstream production by a large number of geographically dispersed outlets that makes integration of all outlets impractical; the existence of a stock of know-how and business practices (and, in the case of franchising, a brand name) that is extendable to a large number of producers; and the existence of a range of ongoing services, information transfers, and free-riding problems that make outright sale or comprehensive licensing of brand names and information ineffective devices for controlling opportunism.

Timothy Muris, David Scheffman, and Pablo Spiller examine the traditional use of franchising for the manufacturing and bottling of soft drinks and discuss recent changes in the industry underlying the trend toward integration of those operations by soft-drink concentrate manufacturers. The efficiency of geographically dispersed production and bottling of soft drinks arose because of cost economies associated with shipping concentrate relative to bottled soft drinks. Centralized control of such widely scattered operations was made impractical by the difficulty of monitoring and communicating with those operations, particularly in the early decades of the industry. The franchised bottling system arose to provide bottlers high-powered incentives to operate efficiently and promote the product locally.

Although the system worked reasonably well for more than fifty years, both major concentrate manufacturers began to consolidate and integrate bottling operations in the 1970s. Muris, Scheffman, and Spiller attribute these developments to changes in the way soft drinks were produced and marketed. Among these were (1) an increase in the efficient size of bottling operations resulting from the demise of returnable bottles, decreases in transportation costs, and innovations in bottling technology; and (2) the emergence of giant supermarket chains and other large customers spanning the territories of multiple bottlers, which increased complexity and the need for coordination between concentrate manufacturers and distributors. The larger size of bottlers, combined with the greater complexity of the industry and the increased importance of "spillovers" across territories, aggravated frictions between manufacturers and bottlers at the same time that improvements in communication and transportation and the consolidation of operations were lowering the costs of centralized control. Muris, Scheffman, and Spiller's analysis of the performance of Coca-Cola Co. and PepsiCo. indicates that, given the new conditions in the soft-drink market, integration indeed improved efficiency.

Early soft-drink manufacturing and bottling differs from most modern franchise settings in terms of both the relative simplicity of the product and the separability and compatibility of franchisor and franchisee interests. In typical franchise settings, quality and consistency considerations tend to be more prominent. Franchise contracts attempt to balance the need for high-powered incentives against the risks of opportunism in a variety of ways. Giving franchisees claims on the residual earnings of their outlets provides incentives to operate outlets efficiently, while royalty payments serve to motivate franchisors to support the value of the franchise through advertising and policing of franchisees. The ability of franchisors to terminate franchisees under most franchise agreements, meanwhile, represents an important incentive mechanism: To the extent that franchisees earn rents on their operations, the threat of termination constitutes a major deterrent to franchisee opportunism.

The reading by Kaufmann and Lafontaine examines the earnings of franchisees at what many regard as the quintessential franchisor, to determine whether McDonald's franchise contracts do, in fact, leave economic rents with franchisees. After detailed analysis, Kaufmann and Lafontaine conclude that Mcdonald's franchisees do earn substantial ex post rents and earn sizable ex ante rents as well. The question of why McDonald's does not attempt to appropriate more of the future profits of its franchise operations leads Kaufmann and Lafontaine to consider a variety of issues related to the structure and timing of payments under franchise agreements and their relation to opportunism, reputation, and franchisee liquidity. Their verdict that the existence of ex ante rents reflects the scarcity of potential franchisees with adequate capital raises important questions about the relation among wealth, organization, and economic performance that have only begun to receive systematic attention (see Demsetz, 1995).

3. CONCLUSION

Despite their depth and scope, the readings in this book only scratch the surface of the problems businesses and individuals encounter in the course of their affairs and the organizational solutions they devise to deal with them. Although no single theory is likely ever to explain fully all of the reasons why people organize as they do, the readings assembled here confirm that an economic approach to contracting that emphasizes the efforts of individuals to organize their affairs so as to economize on the costs of transacting provides numerous insights into the ways that, in Victor Goldberg and John Erickson's words, "reasonably clever businessmen and lawyers cope with problems scholars might consider intractable."

The comparative institutional orientation employed by the authors of the readings in this book to analyze private organization is also rapidly being extended to analyze the broader political, legal, and regulatory institutions that form the institutional environment within which private transactions take place. Among these are analyses of the organization of Congress (Weingast and Marshall, 1988), the role and evolution of constitutions (North and Weingast, 1989), and the effects of the institutional structure of government on the exercise of political power (Gely and Spiller, 1990). New insights into relations between the character of a country's political and legal institutions and private governance are also beginning to emerge (Williamson, 1991; and Levy and Spiller, 1994). Unifying those efforts is the recognition that all institutions have limitations and that discriminating alignment of institutions and transactions requires attention to the costs of transacting.

P A R T

1

CONTRACTING

C h a p t e r
2

A HYPOTHESIS OF WEALTH-MAXIMIZING NORMS: EVIDENCE FROM THE WHALING INDUSTRY

Robert C. Ellickson

This essay analyzes the rules that high-seas whalers used during the heyday of their industry to resolve disputes over the ownership of harvested whales. The evidence presented sheds light on two important theoretical issues of property rights.

The first issue is the source or sources of property rights. According to what Williamson calls the "legal-centralist" view (1983: 520), the state is the exclusive creator of property rights. Many scholars, including Thomas Hobbes (1909: 97–98), Garrett Hardin (1968), and Guido Calabresi (Calabresi and Melamed, 1972: 1090–91), have at times succumbed to legal-centralist thinking. An opposing view holds that property rights may emerge from sources other than the state—in particular, from the workings of non-hierarchical social forces. The whaling evidence refutes legal-centralism and strongly supports the proposition that property rights may arise anarchically out of social custom.[1]

Reprinted from the Journal of Law, Economics, and Organization vol. 5, no. 1 (Spring 1989) © 1989 by Yale University. All rights reserved. ISSN 8756-6222. Reprinted with the permission of Oxford University Press.

Robert C. Ellickson is Walter E. Meyer Professor of Property and Urban Law, Yale University. This is part of a larger project published by Harvard University Press as a book entitled *Order without Law* (1991). The book more fully develops the hypothesis and presents a wider range of evidence relevant to it.

I thank Debbie Sivas for exceptional research assistance, and, for their constructive suggestions, Richard Craswell, Geoffrey Miller, Richard Posner, Roberta Romano, and participants in faculty workshops at the Stanford Business School and the Harvard, Yale, and University of Chicago Law Schools.

[1] For more evidence to this effect, and also a taxonomy of alternative systems of social control, see Ellickson (1987). Perhaps the classic description of the emergence of informal property rights in a relatively anarchic environment is Umbeck (1977), a study of mining claims during the early years of the California gold rush.

The second theoretical issue is whether one can predict the content of informal property rights (norms) that informal social forces generate. This essay advances the hypothesis that when people are situated in a close-knit group, they will tend to develop for the ordinary run of problems norms that are wealth-maximizing. A group is "close-knit" when its members are entwined in continuing relationships that provide each with power and information sufficient to exercise informal social control.[2] A norm is "wealth-maximizing" when it operates to minimize the members' objective sum of (1) transaction costs and (2) deadweight losses arising from failures to exploit potential gains from trade. This theory of the content of norms is proffered as the most parsimonious explanation of variations among whaling rules.

1. THE PROBLEM OF CONTESTED WHALES

Especially during the period from 1750 to 1870, whales were an extraordinarily valuable source of oil, bone, and other products.[3] Whalers therefore had powerful incentives to develop rules for peaceably resolving rival claims to the ownership of a whale. In *Moby-Dick*, Melville explained why these norms were needed:

> It frequently happens that when several ships are cruising in company, a whale may be struck by one vessel, then escape, and be finally killed and captured by another vessel . . . . [Or] after a weary and perilous chase and capture of a whale, the body may get loose from the ship by reason of a violent storm; and drifting far away to leeward, be retaken by a second whaler, who, in a calm, snugly tows it alongside, without risk of life or line. Thus the most vexatious and violent disputes would often arise between the fishermen, were there not some written, universal, undisputed law applicable to all cases . . . .
>
> The American fishermen have been their own legislators and lawyers in this matter. (1851: 504–5)

Melville's last sentence might prompt the inference that whalers had some sort of formal trade association that established rules governing the

---

[2] Close-knittedness enables a member to monitor others and to use informal means of self-help against deviants. In my 1991 book I investigate more fully the linkage between this social condition and the emergence of wealth-maximizing norms. For some glimpses of social control among the close-knit, see Acheson (1988), a description of the customs of Maine lobstermen, and Ellickson (1986), an account of how close-knit rural residents in California informally discipline ranchers who carelessly manage cattle. The present article contains one scrap of evidence that the loss of close-knittedness makes informal cooperation more difficult: American whalers increasingly turned to litigation when their industry began to decline, a trend that would make them see their relationships as less enduring. See n. 39.

[3] Mid- to late-nineteenth-century judicial opinions recorded the value of single whales (of unreported species) caught in the Sea of Okhotsk, located north of Japan, at over $2,000: *Swift v. Gifford*, 23 Fed. Cas. 558 (D. Mass. 1872) (No. 13,696), $3,000; *Taber v. Jenny*, 23 Fed. Cas. 605 (D. Mass. 1856) (No. 13,720), $2,350. In the latter part of the nineteenth century, mean family income in the United States was on the order of $600 to $800 per year. See Bureau of the Census, 1 *Historical Statistics of the United States: Colonial Times to 1970*, at 322 (1975).

ownership of contested whales. There is no evidence, however, that this was so. Anglo-American whaling norms seem to have emerged spontaneously, not from decrees handed down by either organizational or governmental authorities.[4] In fact, whalers' norms not only did not mimic law; they *created* law. In the dozen reported Anglo-American cases in which ownership of a whale carcass was contested, judges invariably held proven whalers' usages to be reasonable and deferred to those rules.[5]

2. THE WHALING INDUSTRY

At first blush it might be thought that whalers would be too dispersed to constitute the membership of a close-knit social group. During the industry's peak in the nineteenth century, for example, whaling ships from ports in several nations were hunting their prey in remote seas of every ocean. In fact, however, the entire international whaling community was a tight one, primarily because whaling ships commonly encountered one another at sea, and because whalers' home and layover ports were few, intimate, and socially interlinked. The scant evidence available suggests that whalers' norms of capture were internationally binding.[6]

The Greenland fishery was the first important international whaling ground. The Dutch were the leaders there during the period around 1700, but later encountered increasing competition from French, British, and American whaling vessels. After 1800, ships from the two English-speaking nations became dominant both in Greenland and elsewhere. By the mid-1800s the United States, a fledgling international power, had emerged as the preeminent whaling nation.[7]

American whalers were concentrated in a handful of small ports in southern New England. Nantucket, the dominant North American whaling port in the eighteenth century, was home to over half the New England

---

[4] Melville (1851: 505) asserted that the only formal whaling code was one legislatively decreed in Holland in 1695. The code's contents evoked no description from Melville and also drew no mention in the subsequent Anglo-American case reports.

[5] See, for example, *Addison & Sons* v. *Row*, 3 Paton 339 (1794); *Swift* v. *Gifford*, 23 Fed. Cas. 558 (D. Mass. 1872) (No. 13,696); see generally Holmes (1881: 212). But compare *Taber* v. *Jenny*, 23 Fed. Cas. 605 (D. Mass. 1856) (No. 13,720) (holding for plaintiff on the basis of general common law regarding abandoned property, despite defendant's [doubtful] assertion that the usage was otherwise).

[6] A dictum in *Fennings* v. *Lord Grenville*, 1 Taunt. 241, 127 Eng. Rep. 825, 828 (Ct. Comm. Pleas 1808), asserts that the fast-fish "usage in Greenland is regarded as binding on persons of all nations." The loneliness of the high seas prompted whalers of different backgrounds to interact with one another. Melville, in chapter 81, provides a fictional account of a mid-Pacific meeting in which the *Jungfrau* of Bremen hailed the *Pequod* of Nantucket in order to obtain needed lamp oil. An actual high-seas trade between a British and a New England ship is described in n. 11.

[7] See Ashley (1938: 23–29); Hohman (1928: 5–6, 20–22). The U.S. industry peaked in about 1846, when its whaling fleet consisted of over 700 vessels. At that same time the combined whaling fleets of all other nations totaled 230 ships (Stackpole, 1953: 473).

whaling fleet in 1774 (Stackpole, 1953: 53–54). New Bedford, which during the 1820s finally supplanted Nantucket as the leading American whaling center, in 1857 berthed half the whaling ships in the United States (Hohman, 1928: 9). Life within these specialized ports centered on the whaling trade. Because of its remote island location and strong Quaker influence, Nantucket was particularly close-knit. "There is no finer example in history of communal enterprise than the Nantucket Whale Fishery. The inhabitants were uniquely situated for united effort.... Through intermarriage they were generally related to one another, and in fact were more like a large family than a civic community.... The people were so law-abiding that there was little or no government in evidence on the Island" (Ashley, 1938: 31). Many Nantucketers shifted to New Bedford when it emerged as the leading whaling center. There whaling also became a "neighborhood affair."[8]

The captains who commanded the whaling ships occupied pivotal positions in the development and enforcement of whaling norms. Two captains based in the same small whaling port were unquestionably members of a close-knit group and would be vulnerable, for example, to gossip about misconduct at sea. The captains' social circles tended, moreover, to extend well beyond their home ports. Migrants from Nantucket, the world's wellspring of whaling talent, became influential not only in other New England ports but also in foreign whaling nations. By 1812, for example, 149 Nantucketers had commanded British whaling ships.[9]

Even whalers sailing from distant ports tended to socialize at sea. Herman Melville, who in *Moby-Dick* portrays eight meetings between the *Pequod* and other whaling vessels, devotes a chapter to the gam (1851: chap. 53). The gam was a friendly meeting between the officers of two whaling ships that had encountered each other at sea. Typically, the two captains would meet for several hours or more on one ship, and the two chief mates on the other. One reason for the gam was to obtain whaling intelligence. ("Have ye seen the White Whale?") In addition, whaling ships might be on the high seas for three or more years at a stretch. More than most seamen, whalers were eager to pass on letters to or from home[10] and to trade to replenish supplies.[11] Although the gam was hardly a mandatory ritual among whalers, only they, and no other seamen, engaged in the practice.[12]

---

[8] Ashley (1938: 99). Byers (1987) provides a comprehensive history of early Nantucket. The hypothesis offered here takes social conditions as exogenous. A more ambitious theory might attempt to attribute the close-knittedness of the whalers' home ports to their recognition that a tight land-based social structure would abet cooperation at sea.

[9] Ashley (1938: 26). See generally Stackpole (1953: 133–44, 390).

[10] Melville (1851: 341); Hohman (1928: 87).

[11] See, for example, Chatterton (1926: 111) quoting the 1836 journal of Samuel Joy, a New England whaling captain: "I got an anchor from an English ship for 40 lbs tobacco and a steering oar."

[12] "So then, we see that of all ships separately sailing the sea, the whalers have most reason to be sociable—and they are so" (Melville, 1851: 342). See also Ashley (1938: 103–4), Hohman (1928: 16), Morison (1921: 325).

Whalers also congregated in specialized layover ports. When the Pacific fisheries developed, for instance, the Maui port of Lahaina emerged as a whalers' hangout in the Hawaiian Islands.

3. THE CALCULUS OF WEALTH MAXIMIZATION

Wealth-maximizing norms are those that minimize the sum of transaction costs and deadweight losses that the members of a group objectively incur. By hypothesis, whalers would implicitly follow this calculus when developing norms to resolve the ownership of contested whales. As a first cut, this calculus would call for a whaling ship's fraction of ownership to equal its fractional contribution to a capture. For example, a ship that had objectively contributed one-half the total value of work would be entitled to a one-half share. In the absence of this rule, opportunistic ships might decline to contribute cost-justified but underrewarded work, leading to deadweight losses.[13]

This first cut is too simple, however, because utilitarian whalers would be concerned with the transaction costs associated with their rules. They would tend to prefer, for example, bright-line rules that would eliminate arguments to fuzzy rules that would prolong disputes, Finding a cost-minimizing solution to whaling disputes is vexing because there is no ready measure of the relative value of separate contributions to a joint harvest. Any fine-tuning of incentives aimed at reducing deadweight losses is therefore certain to increase transaction costs.

4. HYPOTHETICAL WHALING NORMS

In no fishery did whalers adopt as norms any of a variety of rules that are transparently poor candidates for minimizing the sum of deadweight losses and transaction costs. An easily administered rule would be one that made the possession of a whale carcass normatively decisive. According to this rule, if ship A had a wounded or dead whale on a line, ship B would be entitled to attach a stronger line and pull the whale away. A possession-decides rule of this sort would threaten severe deadweight losses, however, because it would encourage a ship to sit back like a vulture and freeload on others' efforts in the early stages of a hunt. Whalers never used this norm.

Equally perverse would be a rule that a whale should belong entirely to the ship whose crew had killed it. Besides risking ambiguities about the cause of a whale's demise, this rule would create inadequate incentives for

---

[13] The present discussion assumes that wealth-maximizing whalers would ignore the risk that their actions might excessively deplete the stocks of whales. This assumption will be examined in section 6.

whalers both to inflict nonmortal wounds and to harvest dead whales that had been lost or abandoned by the ships that had slain them.

To reward early participation in a hunt, whalers might have developed a norm that the first ship to lower a boat to pursue a whale had an exclusive right to capture, so long as it remained in fresh pursuit. This particular rule would create numerous other difficulties, however. Besides being ambiguous in some contexts, it would create strong incentives for the premature launch of boats and might work to bestow an exclusive opportunity to capture on a party less able than others to exploit that opportunity.[14]

Somewhat more responsive to incentive issues would be a rule that a whale belonged to a ship whose crew had first obtained a "reasonable prospect" of capturing it and thereafter remained in fresh pursuit.[15] This rule would reward good performance during the early stages of a hunt and would also free up lost or abandoned whales to later takers. A reasonable-prospect standard, however, is by far the most ambiguous of those yet mentioned, invites transaction costs, and, like the other rules so far discussed, was not employed by whalers.

5. ACTUAL WHALING NORMS

Whalers developed an array of norms more utilitarian than any of these hypothetical ones. Evidence of the details of whaling usages is fragmentary. The best sources are the court reports in which evidence of usages was admitted, especially when the contesting whalers agreed on the usage and disputed only its application.[16] Seamen's journals, literary works such as *Moby-Dick*, and historical accounts provide additional glimpses of the rules in use.

Whaling norms were not tidy, certainly less tidy than Melville asserted in *Moby-Dick* (1851; chap. 89). Whalers developed three basic norms, each of which was adapted to its particular context. As will be evident, each of the three norms was sensitive to the need to avoid deadweight losses because each not only rewarded the ship that had sunk the first harpoon, but also

---

[14] According to Bockstoce (1986: 61), whalers in the western Arctic had informally agreed to defer to the first boat in the water but tended to ignore this agreement when whales were scarce. Bockstoce's authority for this proposition is thin. He apparently relies on Williams (1964: 368), an old man's remembrance of a whaling voyage taken at age fifteen. The incident that prompted Williains's mention of this purported practice was one in which the ships that chose to defer to another's lowered boats were "too far off to take any interest in the affair." More probative would have been an incident in which a ship nearer to a whale had deferred to prior lowering by a more distant ship.

[15] In his dissent in the staple Property casebook decision, *Pierson* v. *Post*, 3 Cai. R. 175, 2 Am. Dec. 264 (Sup. Ct. N.Y. 1805). Judge Livingston argued that a fox hunter with a "reasonable prospect of taking" his prey should prevail over the actual taker.

[16] See *Hogarth* v. *Jackson*, 1 Moody & M. 58 (1827) (parties agreed that the fast-fish rule prevailed in the Greenland fisherv); *Swift* v. *Gifford*, 23 Fed. Cas. 558 (D. Mass. 1872) (No. 13,696) (parties stipulated that New England whalers honored the first-iron rule).

enabled others to harvest dead or wounded whales that had seemingly been abandoned by their prior assailants. All three norms were also sensitive to the problem of transaction costs. In particular, norms that bestowed an exclusive temporary right to capture on a whaling ship tended to be shaped so as to provide relatively clear starting and ending points for the time period of that entitlement.

5.1. Fast-Fish, Loose-Fish

Prior to 1800, the British whalers operating in the Greenland fishery established the usage that a claimant owned a whale, dead or alive, so long as the whale was fastened by line or otherwise to the claimant's boat or ship.[17] This fast-fish rule was well suited to this fishery. The prey hunted off Greenland was the right whale.[18] Right whales, compared to the sperm whales that later became American whalers' preferred prey are both slow swimmers and mild antagonists.[19] The British hunted them from heavy, and sturdy whaling boats. Upon nearing one, a harpooner would throw a harpoon with line attached; the trailing end of the line was tied to the boat.[20] So long as the harpoon held fast to the whale and remained connected by the line to the boat, the fast-fish norm entitled the harpooning boat to an exclusive claim of ownership as against subsequent harpooners. If the whale happened to break free, either dead or alive, it was then regarded as a loose-fish and was again up for grabs. Although whalers might occasionally dispute whether a whale had indeed been fast,[21] the fast-fish rule usually provided sharp beginning and ending points for a whaler's exclusive entitlement to capture and thus promised to limit the trans-action costs involved in dispute resolution.

The fast-fish rule created incentives well adapted to the Britishers' situation in Greenland. Because right whales are relatively slow and docile, a whale on a line was not likely to capsize the harpooning boat, break the line, or sound to such a depth that the boatsmen had to relinquish the line. Thus the fast-fish rule was in practice likely to reward the first harpooner, who

---

[17] *Addison & Sons* v. *Row*, 3 Paton 339 (1794): *Hogarth* v. *Jackson*, 1 Moody & M. 58 (1827). Melville (1851: chap. 89) identified the fast-fish, loose-fish distinction as the governing principle among American whalers. He also noted at several points, however, that an American whaler who had merely placed a waif on a dead whale owned it so long as he evinced an intent and ability to return (1851: 500, 505). The evident tension between these two rules drew no comment from Melville.

[18] The ambiguous term *right whale* is used here to refer to a family of closely related species of baleen whales. The two most commonly hunted species were the Biscayan right whale and the Greenland right whale (or bowhead).

[19] Ashley (1938: 65); Hohman (1928: 180): Jackson (1978: 3–11). Some whaling crews, "though intelligent and courageous enough in offering battle to the Greenland or Right whale, would perhaps—either from professional inexperience, or incompetency or timidity, decline a contest with the Sperm whale" (Melville, 1851: 279). Melville's fictional and ferocious Moby-Dick was, needless to say, a sperm whale.

[20] See Ashley (1938: 93).

[21] See *Hogarth* v. *Jackson*, 1 Moody & M. 58 (1827) (a whale merely entangled in a line is fast).

had performed the hardest part of the hunt, as opposed to free riders waiting in the wings. Not uncommonly, however, a right whale sinks shortly after death, an event that requires the boatsmen to cut their lines.[22] After a few days a sunken whale bloats and resurfaces. At that point the fast-fish rule entitled a subsequent finder to seize the carcass as a loose-fish, a utilitarian result because the ship that had killed the whale might then be far distant. In sum, the fast-fish rule was a bright-line rule that created incentives for both first pursuers of live whales and final takers of lost dead whales.

5.2. Iron-Holds-the-Whale

Especially in fisheries where the more vigorous sperm whales predominated, whalers tended to shift away from the fast-fish rule. The evidence on whalers' usage is too fragmentary to allow any confident assertion about when and where this occurred. The fast-fish rule's main alternative—the rule that iron-holds-the-whale—also provided incentives to perform the hardest part of the hunt. Stated in its broadest form, this norm conferred an exclusive right to capture upon the whaler who had first affixed a harpoon or other whaling craft to the body of the whale. The iron-holds-the-whale rule differed from the fast-fish rule in that the iron did not have to be connected by a line or otherwise to the claimant. The normmakers had to create a termination point for the exclusive right to capture, however, because it would be foolish for a Moby-Dick to belong to an Ahab who had sunk an ineffectual harpoon days or years before. Whalers therefore allowed an iron to hold a whale for only so long as the claimant remained in fresh pursuit of the iron-bearing animal. In some contexts, the iron-affixing claimant also had to assert the claim before a subsequent taker had begun to "cut in" (strip the blubber from) the carcass.[23]

American whalers tended to adopt the iron-holds-the-whale rule wherever it was a utilitarian response to how and what they hunted.[24] Following

---

[22] Hohman (1928: 165n). Melville (1851: 468) asserted that twenty slain right whales sink for every sperm whale that does.

[23] Although the phrase "fresh pursuit" does not appear in whaling lore, it nicely expresses the notion that the crew of the first ship to affix a harpoon had rights only so long as it both intended to take the whale and had a good chance of accomplishing that feat.

[24] "The parties filed a written stipulation that witnesses of competent experience would testify, that, during the whole time of memory of the eldest masters of whaling ships, the usage had been uniform in the whole fishery of Nantucket and New Bedford that a whale belonged to the vessel whose iron first remained in it, provided claim was made before cutting in" (*Swift* v. *Gifford*, 23 Fed. Cas. 558, 558 [D. Mass. 1872] [No. 13,696]). The *Swift* opinion also cited *Bourne* v. *Ashley*, 3 Fed. Cas. 1002 (D. Mass. 1863) (No. 1698), to the effect that the usage of the first iron had been proven to exist as far back as 1800. *Swift* held that this usage was a reasonable one and was applicable to a dispute over a whale caught in the Sea of Okhotsk, located east of Siberia and north of Japan.

It is highly doubtful, however, that the usage of the first iron was as universal among New Englanders as the parties had stipulated in *Swift*. The *Swift* opinion itself mentioned British cases that described other usages in effect among the international community of whalers in the Greenland and mid-Pacific fisheries. See also Melville (1851: 505) for the irreconcilable assertion that the fast-fish rule was the overriding one among American whalers.

Native American practices, some early New England seamen employed devices called drogues to catch whales. A drogue was a float, perhaps two feet square, to which the trailing end of a harpoon line was attached. The drogue was thrown overboard from a whaling boat after the harpoon had been cast into the whale. This device served both to tire the animal and also to mark its location, thus setting up the final kill.[25] Because a whale towing a drogue was not connected to the harpooning boat, the fast-fish rule provided no protection to the crew that had attached the drogue. By contrast, the iron-holds-the-whale rule, coupled with a fresh-pursuit requirement, created incentives suitable for drogue fishing.[26]

This rule had particular advantages to whalers hunting sperm whales. Because sperm whales swim faster, dive deeper, and fight more viciously than right whales do, they were more suitable targets for drogue-fishing. New Englanders eventually did learn how to hunt sperm whales with harpoons attached by lines to boats (Ashley, 1938: 65-66, 92-99). The vigor of the sperm whale compared to the right whale, however, increased the chance that a line would not hold or would have to be cut to save the boat. A "fastness" requirement would thus materially reduce the incentives of competing boatsmen to make the first strike. The iron-holds-the-whale rule, in contrast, was a relatively bright-line way of rewarding whoever won the race to accomplish the major feat of sinking the first harpoon into a sperm whale. It also rewarded only the persistent and skillful because it conferred its benefits only so long as fresh pursuit was being maintained.

Most important, unlike right whales, sperm whales are social animals that tend to swim in schools (Ashley, 1938: 75; Melville, 1851: chap. 88). To maximize the total catch, when whalers discovered a school their norms had to encourage boatsmen to kill or mortally wound as many animals as quickly as possible, without pausing to secure the stricken whales to the mother ship.[27] Fettering whales with drogues was an adaptive technology in these situations. The haste that the schooling of whales prompted among hunters also encouraged the related usage that a waif holds a whale. A waif is a pole with a small flag atop. Planting a waif into a dead whale came to signify that the whaler who had planted the waif claimed the whale, was nearby, and intended soon to return. When those conditions were met, the usages of American whalers in the Pacific allowed a waif to hold a whale.[28]

[25] See Ashley (1938: 89–93); Melville (1851: 495). The barrels used to slow the great white shark in the film *Jaws* are modern equivalents of drogues.

[26] In *Aberdeen Arctic Co*, v. *Sutter*, 4 Macq. 355, 3 Eng. Ruling Cas. 93 (1862), the defendant had seized in the Greenland fishery a whale that the plaintiff, Eskimo employees had previously fettered with a drogue. The court held for the defendant, finding that no exception to the fast-fish usage, well established for the Greenland fishery, had been proven.

[27] In two instances in the Galápagos fishery single ships came upon schools of sperm whales and singlehandedly killed ten or more in one day (Stackpole, 1953: 401).

[28] In two cases arising in the Sea of Okhotsk, the defendants had slaughtered whales that the plaintiffs had waited and anchored on the previous day. The plaintiffs prevailed in both. See *Barlett* v. *Budd*, 2 Fed. Cas. 966 (D. Mass. 1868) (No. 1,075) (plaintiff, who proved the usage

(continued)

Because a ship might lose track of a whale it had harpooned or waifed, whaling norms could not allow a whaling iron to hold a whale forever, When a mere harpoon (or lance) had been attached, and thus it was not certain that the harpooning party had ever fully controlled the whale, the harpooning party had to be in fresh pursuit and also had to assert the claim before a subsequent taker had begun to cut in.[29] On the other hand, when a waif, anchor, or other evidence of certain prior control had been planted, the planting party had to be given a reasonable period of time to retake the whale and hence might prevail even after the subsequent taker had completed cutting in.[30]

Because the iron-holds-the-whale usage required determinations of the freshness of pursuit and sometimes of the reasonableness of the elapsed time period, it was inherently more ambiguous than the fast-fish norm was. By hypothesis, this is why the whalers who pursued right whales off Greenland preferred the fast-fish rule. The rule that iron-holds-the-whale, however, provided better-tailored incentives in situations where drogues were the best whaling technology and where whales tended to swim in schools. In these contexts, according to the theory, whalers switched to iron-holds-the-whale because they saw that its potential for reducing deadweight losses outweighed its transaction-cost disadvantages.

5.3. Split Ownership

In a few contexts whaling usages called for the value of the carcass to be split between the first harpooner and the ultimate seizer.[31] According to

that a waif holds a whale, was independently entitled to recover as a matter of property law); *Taber* v. *Jenny*, 23 Fed. Cas, 605 (D. Mass, 1856) (No. 13,720) (plaintiff, who had a high probability of retaking the whale, should prevail as a matter of property law over defendant, who should have known from the appearance of the whale that it had been killed within the previous twelve hours).

[29] See *Heppingstone* v. *Mammen*, 2 Hawaii 707, 712 (1863): *Swift* v. *Gifford*, 23 Fed. Cas. 558, 558–59 (D. Mass. 1872) (No. 13,696). Hohman (1928: 166) asserted, without citing authority, that a subsequent taker of a sperm whale–bearing whaling craft also had to give the owner of the craft a reasonable length of time to retake the whale.

Cutting-in was a laborious process that involved all hands for as long as a day or more. It could not be begun until after the crew had chained the whale to the ship and rigged up special slaughtering equipment. See Melville (1851: chaps. 66–67); Hohman (1928: 167). Hohman (1928: 166) has alleged that if the first vessel to have attached a harpoon or lance were to come upon a subsequent taker that had justifiably begun to cut in, the first vessel remained entitled to any blubber still in the water.

[30] See *Bartlett* v. *Budd*, 2 Fed. Cas. 966 (D. Mass. 1968) (No. 1,075) (defendant had cut in on the day after the plaintiff's Crew had killed, anchored, and waifed the whale); see also Hohman (1928: 166); "Thus a carcass containing the 'waif' of a vessel believed to be in the general vicinity was never disturbed by another whaler."

[31] A fact-specific example of this solution is *Heppingstone* v. *Mammen*, 2 Hawaii 707, (1863), where the court split a whale fifty-fifty between the owner of the first iron and the ultimate taker. The crew of the *Oregon* had badly wounded the whale but was on the brink of losing it when it was caught and killed by the crew of the *Richmond*. The *Richmond* then surrendered the carcass to the *Oregon*, whose captin refused the *Richmond*'s request for a half share. In light of the uncertainty that the *Oregon* would have retaken the whale, the court rendered the Solomonic solution that the *Richmond*'s captain had proposed.

an English decision, in the fishery around the Galápagos Islands a whaler who had fettered a sperm whale with a drogue shared the carcass fifty-fifty with the ultimate taker.[32] The court offered no explanation for why a different norm had emerged in this context, although it seemed aware that sperm whales were often found in large schools in that fishery. The utilitarian division of labor in harvesting a school of whales is different than that for a single whale. The first whaling ship to come upon a large school should fetter as many animals as possible with drogues and relegate to later-arriving ships the task of capturing and killing the encumbered animals.[33] The Galápagos norm enabled this division of labor. It also showed sensitivity to transaction costs because it adopted the simplest focal point for a split: fifty-fifty.

Better documented is the New England coastal tradition of splitting a beached or floating dead whale between its killer and the person who finally found it. The best known of the American judicial decisions on whales, *Ghen* v. *Rich*,[34] involved a dispute over the ownership of a dead finback whale beached in eastern Cape Cod. Because finback whales are exceptionally fast swimmers, whalers of the late nineteenth century slew them from afar with bomb-lances. A finback whale killed in this way immediately sank to the bottom and typically washed up on shore some days later. The plaintiff in *Ghen* had killed a finback whale with a bomb-lance. When the whale later washed up on the beach, a stranger found it and sold it to the defendant tryworks. The trial judge held a hearing that convinced him that there existed a usage on the far reaches of Cape Cod that entitled the bomb-lancer to have the carcass of the dead animal, provided in the usual case that the lancer pay a small amount (a "reasonable salvage") to the stranger who had found the carcass on the beach. As was typical in whaling litigation, the court deferred to this usage and held the tryworks liable for damages: "Unless it is sustained, this branch of industry must necessarily cease, for no person would engage in it if the fruits of his labor could be appropriated by any chance finder.... That the rule works well in practice is shown by the extent of the industry which has grown up under it, and the general acquiescence of a whole community interested to dispute it."

The norm enforced in *Ghen* divided ownership of a beached finback whale roughly according to the opportunity costs of the labor that the whaler and finder had expended. It thus ingeniously enabled distant and unsupervised specialized laborers with complementary skills to coordinate with one another by implicit social contract. The remote location and small population of eastern Cape Cod fostered close-knit social conditions that the theory supposes were conductive to the evolution of utilitarian norms. Under those intimate circumstances, offshore whalers were apparently able to use their

---

[32] *Fennings* v. *Lord Grenville*, 1 Taunt. 241, 127 Eng. Rep. 825 (Ct. Comm. Pleas 1808).

[33] In *Fennings* the plaintiff had in fact left the drogued whale in order to pursue another.

[34] 8 Fed. 159 (D. Mass. 1881).

general community ties to obtain informal control over beachcombers who were not connected to the whaling industry.[35]

The choice between entitling an ultimate seizer to a preestablished fraction of the whale, such as the half awarded in the Galápagos, or to a "reasonable reward," as on Cape Cod, is a typical rule/standard conundrum. "Reasonableness" standards allow consideration of the exact relative contributions of the claimants. Compared to rules, however, standards are more likely to provoke disputes about proper application. For low-level norms, the hypothesis of wealth-maximizing norms supposes that norm makers, seeing that rules best reduce transaction costs and that standards best reduce deadweight losses, make a utilitrarian stab at picking the cost-minimizing alternative.[36]

6. CONCLUDING REMARKS

The example of the high-seas whalers illustrates, contrary to the legal-centralist view, that informal social networks are capable of creating rules that establish property rights. Whalers had little use for law or litigation.[37] The five reported American cases resolving the ownership of whales at sea all arose out of the Sea of Okhotsk. With the exception of an 1872 decision,[38] in which the year of the whale's capture is not indicated, all involved whales caught during the period 1852 to 1862. The lack of litigation over whale ownership prior to that time is remarkable for two reasons. First, it suggests that for more than a century American whalers had been able to resolve their disputes without any reassurance from American courts. Second, whalers succeeded in doing this during a time period in which all British decisions on whale ownership supported norms other than the iron-holds-the-whale rule that the Americans were increasingly adopting.[39]

[35] Two centuries before *Ghen* New Englanders had enacted ordinances to solve an analogous problem. The seventeenth-century hunters of right whales in the near-shore Gulf Stream were better at killing them than at controlling their carcasses. In 1688 the Plymouth colony had rules that called for whalers to place identifying marks on their lances and that specified how many shillings a finder who towed a dead whale ashore was to receive from the lancer. See Dow (1925: 9–10). Long Island laws of the same period called for the killer and the finder of a dead whale at sea to split it equally and also entitled the finder of a whale carcass on a beach to receive a reward (*id.* at 15).

[36] The seminal works on choices between *legal* rules and standards are Ehrlich and Posner (1974) and Kennedy (1976: 1687–88). See also Diver (1983).

[37] Maine lobstermen continue this New England maritime tradition. Informal "harbor gangs" use self-help, not law, to police lobstering territories. See Acheson (1988: 73–77).

[38] *Swift* v. *Gifford*, 23 Fed. Cas. 358 (D. Mass. 1872) (No. 13,696).

[39] Why litigation burst forth from incidents in the Sea of Okhotsk in the 1850s is unclear. One possibility is suggested by the fact that most of the whales found in that vicinity were bowheads, a relatively passive species (Bockstoce, 1986: 28–29). For these baleen whales it may have been utilitarian for whalers to revert from the first-iron rule to the fast-fish rule. American

Because informal norms are in many contexts an important source of rules, analysts should be interested in their content. This essay has offered and defended the hypothesis that members of a close-knit group define their low-level property rights so as to maximize their joint objective wealth. A hypothesis of this sort is most persuasively supported through successful ex ante predictions, not ex post explanations such as those just provided.

An analyst equipped with the hypothesis of wealth-maximizing norms might be unable to predict the precise whaling norms that would develop in a particular fishery. Information about costs and benefits is inevitably fuzzy, both to the normmakers themselves and to analysts. An analyst, however, could confidently identify a large set of norms that would *not* be observed, such as, in the whaling case, "possession decides," "the first boat in the water," or "a reasonable prospect of capture." The content of the three basic norms the whaling community developed tends to support the hypothesis because all three were consistently sensitive to both production incentives and transactions costs and varied in utilitarian fashion with conditions prevailing in different fisheries.

Any post hoc explanation risks being too pat, and this one is no exception. A critic might question the analysis on a number of grounds. First, the discussion suggests that whalers might have been wise to use the first-iron rule for sperm whales, and the fast-fish rule for right whales. They did not, and instead varied their rules according to the location of the fishery, not according to species. Perhaps whalers anticipated that species-specific rules would engender more administrative complications than their fishery-specific rules did. It is relevant that there are dozens of whale species other than sperm and right whales. In light of that fact, it may have been simplest to apply to all species of whales in a fishery the rule of capture best suited to the most commercially valuable species found there. In addition, a cruising whaling ship had to have its boats and harpoons at the ready (Chatterton, 1926: 140). Richard Craswell has suggested to me that this necessity of prearming may have limited the whalers' ability to vary their capture techniques according to the species encountered.

Second, a critic could assert that the whalers' norms described were too short-sighted to be wealth-maximizing. By abetting cooperation among small clusters of competing hunters, the norms aggravated the risk of overwhaling. The nineteenth-century whalers in fact depleted their fisheries so rapidly that they were impelled to seek whales in ever more remote seas. Had they

---

whalers, accustomed to hunting sperm whales in the Pacific, may have had trouble making this switch.

A more straightforward explanation is that the New England whaling community was becoming less close-knit when this spate of litigation occurred. The American whaling industry had begun to decline during the 1850s and was then decimated during the Civil War when several of these cases were being litigated (Hohman, 1928: 290–92, 302). The deviant whalers involved in the litigated cases, seeing themselves nearing their last periods of play, may have decided to defect. In two of the five reported cases arising out of the Sea of Okhotsk (*Swift* and *Bourne*), both litigants even operated out of the same port, New Bedford. When the whalers' informal system of social control began to unravel apparently even its core was vulnerable.

developed norms that set quotas on catches, or that protected young or female whales, they might have been able to keep whaling stocks at levels that would support sustainable yields.

The arguments that respond to this second criticism point up some shortcomings of the informal system of social control, as compared to other methods of human coordination. Establishment of an accurate quota system for whale fishing requires both a sophisticated scientific understanding of whale breeding and an international system for monitoring worldwide catches. For a technically difficult and administratively complicated task such as this, a hierarchical organization, such as a formal trade association or a legal system, would likely outperform the diffuse social forces that make norms. Whalers who recognized the risk of overfishing thus could rationally ignore that risk when making norms on the ground that normmakers could make no cost-justified contribution to its solution.

Whalers might rationally have risked overwhaling for another reason. Even if overwhaling was not wealth-maximizing from a global perspective, the rapid depletion of whaling stocks may well have been in the interests of the club of whalers centered in southern New England. From their parochial perspective, grabbing as many of the world's whales as quickly as possible was a plausibly wealth-maximizing strategy. These New Englanders might have feared entry into whaling by mariners based in the southern United States, Japan, or other ports that could prove to be beyond their control. Given this risk of hostile entry, even if the New Englanders could have created norms to stem their own depletion of world whaling stocks, they might have concluded that a quick kill was more to their advantage. The whaling saga is thus a reminder that norms that enrich one group's members may impoverish, to a greater extent, those outside the group.

COMPARATIVE INSTITUTIONAL ECONOMICS: THE GOVERNANCE OF RAIL FREIGHT CONTRACTING

Thomas M. Palay

1. INTRODUCTION

In recent years both economists[1] and lawyers[2] have studied the factors that lead private parties to adopt a particular institutional framework for their voluntary transactions. Their inquiry has been into the question of "governance choice." The term governance is a shorthand expression for the institutional framework in which contracts are initiated, negotiated, monitored, adapted, enforced, and terminated.[3] To date, however, the literature on the subject has been largely conceptual. One of its central theoretical propositions, attributable to both Williamson and Klein, Crawford, and Alchian, is that the most significant factor affecting the

Reprinted from the Journal of Legal Studies, vol. XIII (June 1984) by permission of the University of Chicago Press. © 1984 by The University of Chicago. All rights reserved.

Thomas M. Palay is Professor of Law, University of Wisconsin—Madison. This paper has benefited from the helpful criticisms and suggestions of Oliver Williamson, Yoram Ben-Porath, Peter Carstensen, Bill Clune, Victor Goldberg, Henry Hansmann, Neil Komesar, Rick Lempert, Ted Schneyer, Bill Whitford, and Richard Zerbe. An earlier draft was presented at the 1983 meeting of the Law and Society Association in Denver, Colorado. I have had almost as many financial backers as readers and I want to thank the Brookings Institution, the School of Public and Urban Policy of the University of Pennsylvania, and the Law School of the University of Wisconsin for their support.

[1] See, for example Williamson (1979); Klein, Crawford, and Alchian (1978); Goldberg (1976); and Monteverde and Teece (1982b).

[2] See, for example, Komesar (1981); and Macaulay (1963).

[3] As far as I can discern, the term *governance* was first used in this context by Williamson (1979).

governance choice is the extent to which the parties have made idiosyncratic investments in support of their transaction. Their reasoning is straightforward and familiar.[4] The more specialized the investment, the lower its value in its next best use. This heightens the risk of opportunistic behavior during both the performance and renegotiation of the contract.[5] Both sides, therefore, are willing to make increased expenditures to protect themselves against the possibility that the other party will act to obtain potentially appropriable quasi rents.[6]

This paper empirically tests the theory of governance choice within the context of real-world contracting between rail freight carriers and their shippers. These transactions are particularly interesting, as the contracts in question are often used to avoid regulatory constraints and are thereby made unenforceable in a court of law (Palay, 1985). The study examines the effect of variation in the character of investment on the adaptation, monitoring, and informal enforcement of contracts. In broad outline it supports the basic proposition that as investment characteristics become more transaction specific, the associated institutional structure becomes increasingly unique to the parties and transactions it supports.

Section 2 briefly describes the data set and how the transactions were classified. Section 3 provides a short sketch of the contracts that were used. Section 4 details the governance structure that supported the various types of transactions. The final section makes some concluding remarks.

2. THE DATA

The data are to two types: case studies and tabulations. The former involve a detailed description of particular transactions and their associated governance structures. The latter contain the summarization and cross-classification of the interview responses.

The data base was developed from a series of thirty-five field interviews held between October and December 1979 with rail carriers and their

---

[4] As Williamson (1979) argues: "The crucial investment distinction is this: to what degree are transaction-specific (nonmarketable) expenses incurred. Items that are unspecialized among users pose few hazards, since buyers in these circumstances can easily turn to alternative sources, and suppliers can sell output intended for one order to other buyers without difficulty" (239).

[5] Opportunistic behavior refers to the proclivity of individuals to exploit the advantages to be attained from (1) the making of false or empty—that is, self-disbelieved—threats and promises concerning future conduct, or (2) the selective or distorted disclosure of information. Thus, related to the so-called moral hazard problem, it goes beyond, expanding the rational egoist characterization of economic actors to encompass varying degrees of strategic, myopic, and guileful behavior. Williamson (1975).

[6] Klein, Crawford, and Alchian define the quasi-rent value of an asset as "the excess of its value over its salvage value, that is, its value in its next best *use* to another renter. The potentially appropriable specialized portion of the quasi rent is that portion, if any, in excess of its value to the second highest-valuing *user*" (298).

shippers.[7] The carrier interviews were held with the marketing and sales departments of three railroads, all of which were chosen for their willingness to be interviewed and their geographic proximity to Washington, D.C.[8] The shippers were, in general, matched to the carriers.[9] Though they were chosen because they moved a significant volume of their product on one of the three designated carriers, it proved infeasible in all cases to restrict their discussions to those railroads. Most of the shippers market nationwide and thus problems existed about the interviewees' personal familiarity with the details of the specific transaction I had discussed with the rail carrier. In addition, in order to maintain my promise to keep interviews confidential, it was impossible to tell shippers that I had talked with a particular carrier about a given transaction. Nevertheless, by choosing the interviews carefully I was fortunate enough to have many interviewees discuss transactions with the appropriate carriers and, in some instances, relate their answers to precisely the same transaction the carrier had described.

The interviews generated detailed discussions of fifty-one transactions, which may be broken into the following commodity groups:[10] finished automobiles (two shipper, six carrier); automobile parts (two shipper, seven carrier); aluminum (five shipper, three carrier); paper (two shipper, five carrier); steel (four shipper, six carrier); scrap (three shipper, two carrier); and chemicals (one shipper, three carrier). By concentrating on a small number of commodity groups I was able both to control somewhat for the type of investment that was undertaken and to develop some limited expertise in the transportation of these particular goods. This facilitated comparisons across transactions.

Conceptually, testing the hypothesis that governance structures vary systematically with the characteristics of the capital supporting the transaction is straightforward: identify the relevant classifications of investment characteristics and cross-classify these with the apparent form of the supporting governance structure. Three classifications of investment are used: nonspecific, moderately idiosyncratic, and highly idiosyncratic. While

[7] Unfortunately, seven of these had to be discarded because they were incomplete, the parties proved to be less than cooperative, or only one side of the transaction could be investigated.

[8] It is important to note that while only three railroads were used, each of the carriers consciously divided their sales and marketing functions into semi-autonomous commodity or car groups. That is, aluminum, steel, scrap, paper products, automobiles, and chemicals were generally handled by separate market managers located within semi-independent profit centers. Shippers who dealt with more than one marketing department of a given railroad often complained of the lack of coordination this system seemed to foster.

[9] That is, the rail users were chosen because their shipping needs required that they use one of the interviewed railroads. Although geographic proximity was not as important a consideration, limited interviewing resources precluded my seeing shippers located west of the Mississippi River, and most were situated in the northeastern United States. The willingness of the companies to provide access to highly confidential material and to their corporate traffic department, without my having to use the public affairs office, played an important role in the selection process.

[10] The numbers in parentheses represent the number of transactions described from the perspective of the shipper and the carrier, respectively.

investment characteristics really form a more or less continuous spectrum running from perfectly fungible to perfectly idiosyncratic, little is lost by reducing the spectrum to these three discrete bands.[11]

Nonspecific investment involves capital that is easily transferable between users and uses. Alternative sources of supply, or alternative uses, for physical and human capital are readily available to the parties. Thus the identity of the party currently providing or receiving the benefit from the capital is irrelevant, for substitutes can be obtained at little (if any) additional cost. In the rail freight industry the movement of pulpboard, pulpwood, scrap, alumina, finished steel, iron ore, and sanitary tissue paper were each supported by nonspecialized capital. Standard boxcars, covered hoppers, or gondolas were used in each instance. Little was done in the way of transaction-specific planning or coordination.

The other two categories of investment both involve capital for which ex post alternative sources of purchase or supply are limited by the specialized requirements of the transaction. At the moderately idiosyncratic end of the interval are those transactions for which substitution, though not impossible, certainly is more difficult and involves more costly adaptations than does nonspecialized investment. The movements of semifinished aluminum, semi-finished steel, and automobile parts fall in this category. For example, both semifinished metals are transferred in covered coil cars or specially designed and fitted boxcars. These cars can be shifted between shippers of semifinished metals, but their value is significantly reduced outside the movement of coils and sheet.

TABLE 3.1
Type of Capital

Type of capital	Number
Nonspecific	
Pulpboard and sanitary paper	5
Pulpwood	2
Scrap metal	5
Alumina	4
Finished steel	3
Iron ore	2
Moderately idiosyncratic	
Automobile parts	9
Semifinished steel	5
Semifinished aluminum	4
Highly idiosyncratic	
Finished automobiles	8
Chemicals	4

[11] These correspond to Williamson's categories: nonspecific, mixed, and idiosyncratic (Williamson, 1979: 238–45).

Transactions at the highly idiosyncratic end of the spectrum entail capital for which alternative sources of supply and use are even more restricted. Included here are the movements of chemicals and finished automobiles. The latter, for instance, are moved in auto racks, which have but one use—the movement of finished automobiles. Once built, their worth in their next best use is roughly equivalent to their scrap value. What is more, the configuration of the decks and tie-downs makes it virtually impossible to transfer the railcars either between manufacturers or across models without substantial modification.

The fifty-one transactions examined, therefore, fall into the categories presented in Table 3.1.

3. THE CONTRACTS

The contracts discussed here generally involved a mixture of formally and informally derived terms. The formal elements, particularly the price term, were found in the published rate tariffs. Under the antidiscrimination provisions of the Interstate Commerce Act as it existed at the time of this study, the filed tariff constituted the entire agreement between the parties.[12] Thus the form of the agreement was supposed to be that of a long-term, incomplete contract completed on a spot or a short-term, nonrecurrent basis. In addition, substantive restrictions were placed on both price and service terms.

The informal elements of the agreement were used to supplement and complete the rate tariffs. In the cases that I studied they generally were negotiated and renegotiated on a short-term recurrent, or a long-term incomplete basis, though occasionally spot contracts were used. The informal terms tended to involve (1) the number of cars the carrier would procure for, and dedicate to, the move; (2) the round-trip transit time between origin and destination; (33) specific service standards; and (4) the volume that shipper would guarantee carrier. These aspects of the agreement were not included in the tariff. To the extent that the resulting contracts violated the constraints imposed by the regulatory scheme they were unenforceable before either the Interstate Commerce Commission or a court of law.[13]

4. THE GOVERNANCE STRUCTURES

The investment characteristics discussed in section 2 can be cross-classified by governance structures. I identify five elements of governance structures that I expect to vary as investment characteristics vary: (1) the expected

---

[12] 49 U.S.C. § 11903 and 49 U.S.C. § 10761–62 (Supp. V, 1982). See also Guandolo (1979: 689–721) for a discussion of the Elkins Act.

[13] For more details of these contracts, see Palay (1985).

method of enforcement, (2) adaptations to changed circumstances, (3) the types of adjustments effectuated, (4) whether information for long-term planning was exchanged, and (5) whether structural planning was attempted. These were derived from a synthesis of the somewhat longer lists of Macneil (1974) and Wachter and Williamson (1978). Each aspect is discussed in turn.

4.1. Enforcement

The issue uppermost in the minds of the parties was how they were to obtain the performance promised when the contract in question was not enforceable in a court of law. Specifically, I was interested in how parties believed they ultimately would be protected from opportunistic behavior. The emphasis is not so much on how parties force their contracting opposites to provide specific performance, but on how they ensure that they receive what they are entitled to under the agreement. After all, the issue is not really *who* provides the service, but *whether* the precise service bargained for is ultimately delivered.

To compile a set of data on this issue I asked the interviewees to respond to four questions:

1. What, if anything, keeps [the other party] from backing out of his commitments to you?
2. What ultimately protects you from his not keeping his promises and his side of the understanding?
3. What permits you to rely on his promises and representations? That is, how can you afford to make commitments or do things in reliance upon the agreement that you have with _____?
4. If he does fail to live up to his side of the understanding, do you have viable alternatives?

The technique required sacrificing the precision that might be obtained with a formal questionnaire, but two offsetting advantages made the course of action desirable. First, the informal conversational tone encouraged the interviewees, who were suspicious of academic interviews and concerned with the confidentiality of proprietary information, to be more open about important matters of institutional detail. Second, the absence of a formal questionnaire made it possible to proceed with the interviews without having to clear them through the firm's public affairs department.

The responses on enforcement were grouped by common features. Five subgroups were distinguished. They are cross-classified with investment characteristics in Table 3.2. There is an obvious pattern to this table. Where the investment is standardized, the enforcement mechanism tends to be market oriented. However, as the investment becomes more idiosyncratic, the means of ensuring enforcement tends, as predicted, to be transaction specific.

TABLE 3.2
Enforcement and Investment Characteristics

Investment characteristics	Type of enforcement					Row total
	e_1	e_2	e_3	e_4	e_5	
Nonspecific investment	14	4	2	1	0	21
Moderately idiosyncratic investment	0	0	7	11	0	18
Highly idiosyncratic investment	0	0	1	7	4	12
Column total	14	4	10	19	4	51

The first grouping described governance structures premised on the existence of potential or readily available substitutes (e_1). In particular, fourteen interviewees (nine railroad and five shipper) felt that their ultimate protection derived from their ability to exit from existing relations and easily procure alternative uses or sources of service for their equipment. The emphasis was on fulfilling the terms of the agreement by turning to substitutes rather than on enforcing the existing agreement. Cross-classifying the responses with investment characteristics yields the first column in Table 3.2.

For example, carrier R moved sanitary tissue paper for shipper K. To do so, the railroad invested heavily in both physical and human capital. But the investment involved little specialized equipment. The rolling stock tended to be free-running general service rail cars that were easily transferable among shippers, carriers, and uses. Either the fifty-foot/seventy-ton or the sixty-foot/one-hundred-ton boxcar was used. At the time of the interview each cost between $35,000 and $55,000. Neither the character of the product nor the nature of the transaction dictated any need for specialized handling or coordination. Carrier was particularly concerned that shipper K might use the cars on another railroad's routes. Rates were calculated on a ton-per-mile basis and shipper believed that the equipment per diem neither covered the cost of the cars nor contributed anything to fixed overhead. The railroad indicated that its primary protection from shipper's ability to take advantage of him at the renegotiation or recontracting phase was market related. If shipper failed to live up to the agreement, carrier could transfer its cars to some other user. When it came right down it it, R's willingness to bind its future to K was premised on its knowledge that it did not have to trust shipper to fulfill its end of the bargain. If K failed to deliver on its promise, R would suffer only momentary losses and could stop delivering equipment. As R's market manager stated:

> I don't have to trust what he tells me. We've got plenty of uses for fifty-foot boxes. If we provide [shipper] with cars and they use them to move paper over someone else's routes, it'll be a long time before I provide them with anything

other than the bare minimum that I can get away with. The next time I'll be plenty wary about committing cars to them on a long-term basis. They'll sweat for them, and they're not going to be the best we've got.

Similarly, it was clear that carrier appreciated the constraints imposed on it because shipper had alternative means of transporting its sanitary paper to final customers. As carrier stated, "[c]ompetition from trucks is what keeps us from raising our prices too high. Our costs, and competition from other railroads, keeps us from setting them too low." The last sentence refers to the possibility that other railroads (competing either in carrier's market or in some other market of shipper) might protest a rate that is set below either fully allocated costs or variable cost.

Four of the fourteen e_1 transactions believed that it was the fear of exit that ultimately forced the parties to live up to their agreements. Interests were secured because of the existence of potential alternatives and not necessarily because of actual recourse to those substitutes. Shipper K, involved with R in the movement of sanitary tissue paper, described its primary protection from opportunistic conduct in these terms. Shipper K believed that its interests were ultimately secured by carrier R's reluctance to act in ways that would tempt K to "take its business elsewhere." It emphasized the *potential* for exiting rather than the act of doing so. In a sense, K's interests were secured by its ability to project a credible threat. With respect to the agreement on volume and equipment, K stated:

> When I or any one of our people promise some guy ten or fifteen carloads per day, we expect them to deliver the cars. If they won't, they know I'll use someone else. I've done it before.
>
> All bets are off when [carrier] stops sending me the cars. If he can't provide the equipment, then he knows I'm only going to dilly dally around so long. I can get service from [other carrier] or from trucks if I have to. I prefer to use rail and [carrier] has been good to us, but I work for [shipper], and my job is to deliver to our customers.

K argued that the rates were similarly constrained. It agreed that it was carrier's perception of the competition from trucks that guaranteed bargaining parity at the recontracting or renegotiating stage. The characteristics of the capital involved did not lock in either party once the initial contract was set. But shipper believed that its protection from opportunistic price increases did not come from actively seeking other suppliers of rail services. Rather, it was carrier's *concern* that shipper might do so that shipper relied upon for its protection.[14]

Common to the four transactions of the second group (e_2) (one railroad and three shipper) was the belief that opportunistic tendencies were controlled by a combination of actual alternatives and the implicit threat

---

[14] Shipper indicated with respect to price that there is always the possibility of "going to the Commission," but while that alternative is available, recourse to it is relatively rare. Moreover, the commission only rarely "sets" prices. In general it simply approves or disapproves a protested rate.

to withdraw any future service or volume. The premise was that parties would act to ensure the continuance not only of present contracts, but of future, expected ones as well.

The line between this category and the first is somewhat more pronounced than may be apparent at first glance.[15] Concern over future withdrawal of business will induce someone to refrain from opportunistic behavior today only if that part has, a priori, a nontrivial expectation that the future service or volume will materialize. In the instant cases, that expectation was created by one party's promise to the other. A, for instance, might say to B, "If you provide me with ten cars per day to carry widgets today, I promise to provide you with at least 50 percent of the whatsits produced at our new plant next year."

The parties were doing something in exchange for future consideration. They would not know whether the other party would fulfill the promise until much later. To premise enforcement upon concern over the continuance of future contracts requires a degree of trust in one's trading partners that goes beyond the mere existence of actual and potential substitutes. Thus, the governance structure described by the respondents in group 2 combined both existence of alternatives (present and future) and, subtly, the presence of some degree of trust. The data are cross-classified with investment characteristics in Table 3.2, column 2.

A good example of this type of enforcement involves shipper H, a major user of iron ore. H produced finished steel and required rail transportation at three stages of its production process. By far its heaviest use of rail capacity was in the movement of raw materials—coal, coke, lime, and iron ore—which amounted to somewhere between forty and fifty million tons per year. The iron ore was mined in the northern Midwest where it was generally transformed into pellets, sinter, or reduced ore. It was then transported by ship to one of two ports. From the port it had to be moved by rail car two hundred miles to the mill site at destination.

The plant at destination was equipped solely for rail delivery. It was serviced directly by two railroads and had access to a third through reciprocal switching agreements. Rates from the ports were virtually identical and the question usually was which carrier could provide H the best service to the mills. The heavy density of iron ore pellets required that they be transported in either open-top hoppers or gondolas. Neither the hopper nor the gondola car was outfitted with equipment specific to the iron ore traffic. Hoppers are heavily used in the coal, grain, and alumina markets. Gondolas are also employed to transport machinery, lumber, clay, gravel, and metal scrap. Both cars, then, have significant alternative uses.

Though the transaction was relatively standardized, potential difficulties arose when H delivered the ore to port. Once there the ore was virtually assured to carrier X. Any other option involved nontrivial storage and inventory costs or additional transportation expenses (Palay, 1981). The

---

[15] I am indebted to Stewart Macaulay for helping to make this point clear to me.

railroad could breach with current impunity the promise to provide the cars necessary for timely service. The existence of possible future business, though, kept the potential current problems—while significant—short-term. Shipper H believed that its protection came ultimately from its ability to threaten to withhold future business from an offending railroad. It was also confident that carrier knew that it could count on H's future business if it acted in good faith. As H stated: "It's nothing that has to be said. I don't call up [X] and say 'if you don't do this you'll never see another pellet of ore again.' I don't have to. They know that if they produce the cars we'll keep giving them our business. Screw around with me, and that's the last trainload of ore they'll get—until we get desperate."

The third group (e_3) comprises ten respondents (six railroad and four shipper) who described the basis for protection as some combination of the elements cited by groups e_1 and e_4 or e_5. These answers are cross-classified with investment in column 3 of Table 3.2. In each case the parties talked of the existence of alternatives and said that the parties with whom they dealt had a reputation for fair dealing. Neither party was able, or willing, to say which of the two elements figured more prominently.

For instance, carrier T moved large quantities of aluminum sheet and plate to fabricating facilities located at various destinations throughout the United States. The transaction involved moderately idiosyncratic investment and the contract entailed trading volume for specified service standards and a guarantee of railcars. When asked to describe what it was that held the informal contractual relations together, T equivocated. In one breath it clearly mentioned and talked about trust and realized mutuality of interest. "We've been dealing with [shipper D] from the beginning. When they located and designed their plant they knew we'd be one of their primary carriers. I believe what they tell us. They know how we operate; that we're an honest bunch of people. Neither one of us plays games. I like dealing with them." Nevertheless, in the next breath carrier T was careful to point out its potential market alternatives: "We work very hard to maintain our image of integrity and fair play. We're very business-like. But I guarantee you that [shipper D] knows that if he pushes me once too often he'll find himself sitting around with a lot of aluminum sheet and no cars. Alternatively, we could stop investing money in new equipment for him."

In the fourth subgrouping (e_4) of nineteen transactions (thirteen railroad and six shipper),[16] opportunistic conduct was attenuated by a realized mutuality of interest, manifested in the parties' apparent reluctance to exploit short-term advantages to the detriment of long-run relations. These responses are cross-classified in column 4 of Table 3.2.

Before investors make expenditures on idiosyncratic capital, their expectations must be reasonably secure. To facilitate the process both shippers and carriers felt it crucial to maintain reputations for honesty, integrity,

---

[16] The ratio of railroads to shippers found in this category is virtually identical to the ratio of railroads (twenty-one) to shippers (nine) contained in the sample of idiosyncratic transactions.

and trustworthiness. Opportunistic conduct could destroy any established reputation effects. Concern over appearing honest, therefore, seems to have forced the parties to be so. In order to maintain reputations, shippers and carriers simply did not take advantage of the ex post small-numbers bargaining conditions. Instead, trust relations developed.

For instance, carrier X and shipper A were involved in the movement of finished automobiles which involved highly idiosyncratic investment. Each was asked to describe what, if anything, kept the other party from backing out of its commitments. Both parties indicated that "we need them as much as they need us," and the "business-like" behavior of the other. The parties had developed a relationship that, as carrier admitted, was both envied and suspected by the other divisions of railroad X. Shipper, though, was careful to describe the situation as being "strictly a good faith" relation, "honest and business-like, but not social."

Both shipper and carrier apparently were reluctant to exploit short-term advantages if it would lead to harm in the long-run relation. For example, amortization agreements were used to offset the risk that slumping auto sales, an auto industry strike, or a major design change might render the existing auto racks useless. Neither party, though, believed that the rack-car amortization agreements were legally enforceable. The understandings primarily were used to reduce ambiguity, to reinforce shipper's "moral commitment" to share the risk of idiosyncratic investment, and to reduce the unease of some of carrier's operations (as opposed to marketing) people.

Despite the legal unenforceability of these agreements, shipper had several times paid off the unamortized portion of cars when it discontinued use. Both parties pointed to the example of the "Epsilon" railcar, produced exclusively to move shipper's Epsilon model automobile. Shipper was initially quite taken with the concept and encouraged carrier to purchase a specified number of the railcars. Unfortunately, some time after the railcars went into service, shipper drastically altered the design of the Epsilon automobile, rendering carrier's equipment obsolete. The automobile manufacturer subsequently reimbursed carrier slightly more than $1 million for the unamortized portion of the investment. Shipper felt that it was "in our best interest" to honor the agreement. As the director of transportation put it: "We've got to keep them healthy, viable and happy to guarantee that we'll get the equipment we need, when we need it."

The realized mutuality of interest also was manifested in an apparent willingness to undertake nonmandatory tasks that helped to facilitate and improve the working relationship itself. These investments in "transactional capital" often did not have an immediate or obvious return. Take, for instance, carrier X's willingness to accommodate shipper A by fully absorbing the cost of "switching" shipper's cars. The issue was not really the money, but rather the fact that this practice caused accounting and bureaucratic headaches for shipper. Upon learning of the problem, carrier unilaterally changed its policy on the issue to shipper's advantage. Carrier thought that the incident probably cost it about $50,000, but that the "investment" would pay for itself over time by strengthening the relationship with shipper. Carrier felt confident that the effort would be more than reciprocated.

The development of these relations takes both real resources and time. However, once the relations are successfully developed, both parties have the ability to make credible requests, reject inadequate offers, and make long-term commitments. Two years prior to the interview, for instance, "Richard Roe" at shipper A requested that railroad Y purchase thirty-five enclosed multilevel racks for a movement of finished automobiles from origin to destination. After confirming that thirty-five cars were in fact needed for the move and that a proper return would be realized if the promised volume materialized, the investment was made. Not so much as a letter promising the given volume of traffic was exchanged.[17] Y's explanation for going ahead with an investment valued between $1.5 and $2 million was the trust relations developed at both the individual and firm level. "As long as I have been here [shipper A] has never backed out of a commitment. They have a policy that when they promise something they follow through. [Richard Roe] is a real gentleman. I believe that he would never purposely hurt me."

Two different trust relations are critical in this last class of cases. The first is between individuals or departments, the second between firms. Where only the former exists the other parties can never be certain that a decision by an individual or a department will be backed up throughout the organization. Where both exist the parties have the further advantage of being able to believe that actions will not be overruled, which helps both in making and in justifying decisions.

There appears to be no special formula for developing the necessary trust relations. "John Smith" at carrier X insisted that reputations of this nature simply develop from a policy of always being "straight with the customer." Each of the division heads under Smith used similar phrases to describe how they developed the reputations of their sections. Both indicated that in their section it was Smith's policy that "you tell the customer no tales."

Carrier X also gave shipper A a good deal of credit for having developed excellent relations at both the individual and firm level. Of the four major automobile producers, shipper A was the only one that carrier felt would deliver most of what it promised. Carrier said, for example, that the actual commitment of finished vehicles to the railroad was roughly 90 percent of the volume shipper promised.

The fifth category of enforcement (e_5) reduced opportunistic tendencies by combining the realized mutuality of interest described above with vertical integration. Involved here were four transactions (three railroad and one shipper), all of which entailed the movement of chemicals. In each instance, shipper owned its own rolling stock and rented track access and locomotive

---

[17] Concededly there was an amortization agreement. However, as indicated, such understandings were little more than a written record of the particular agreement. They were, according to all the parties, unenforceable.

power from the carrier. The responses are cross-classified with investment characteristics in column 5 of Table 3.2.

A good example of this type of enforcement involves shipper E, a major producer of chemical products. Of those chemicals that were moved by rail, most traveled in tank cars or in covered hoppers. The former were among the most specialized cars in general use. They usually were constructed to be substance-specific. Glass or rubber linings, specialized pressure valves, and damage control equipment are but a few examples of the unique equipment employed. Quality control and safety concerns prevented the transfer of cars across products or manufacturers. Utilization patterns simply made it too costly to attempt to modify a car to handle a new product after each trip, and cleaning involved expensive facilities and technologies. In addition, shipper used carrier in a pipeline capacity. Thus specialized coordination and handling were required to maintain a constant flow.

To guarantee safety and quality control, shipper employed a governance structure premised on vertical integration. It owned in excess of ten thousand rail cars. To enforce the other aspects of any agreement realized mutuality of interest was employed. The chemical industry is, in the words of one market manager, a "handshake industry, where your word is your bond." Shipper E, for instance, wanted to move a million tons of a substance from origin to destination. Carrier X offered to transport the substance at a price of 69 cents per hundredweight. Carrier Y, however, offered to publish a rate of 65 cents per hundredweight. E readily accepted X's offer because (1) it felt it to be more realistic, but, more important, (2) it knew that when X's representative promised a particular rate that price would be in force for a significant period. Even after Y changed its filed rate to 75 cents per hundredweight, carrier X did not raise its price. As carrier X's chemical manager stated: "It's far more important that they believe I'm reliable than that we jack the price up on them. Maybe I could have gotten more out of them, but now I have them on the hook. Besides, they believe me when I come calling." E could have accepted Y's initial offer and then switched to X if the former raised its price. However, it was unable to accept the performance losses associated with any switch over. In addition, shipper was concerned that switching to railroad Y would create the impression that it was willing to deal "fast and loose" with the railroads.

4.2. Adjustments

The manner in which parties attempt to adjust contracts to changed circumstances is also a key element of a governance structure. The interviews were organized first to elicit the response of the parties to hypothetical changes in circumstances that might call for contractual modification. These preliminary responses set the stage for the more specific inquiries that follow. I therefore have data on two issues: the general reaction of parties to requests for adjustments and the nature of any adjustments that were made.

Attitude toward Adjustments

The parties responded to requests for adjustments in one of two ways: holding to original terms (a_1) or flexibility (a_2). The responses tended to correspond to the type of investment used to support the transaction. They are cross-classified with investment characteristics in Table 3.3.

The responses of eighteen nonspecific and two idiosyncratic transactions indicated an interest in holding the other party to the original negotiated terms. Two types of responses were classified in this manner. The first were those who denied the request as long as possible and who tried to enforce the initial contract term as originally negotiated. Thirteen of the transactions supported by nonspecific capital responded in this way. These parties assumed that the other side was, or should have been, able to project enough of the relevant future into the present to make appropriate risk-bearing or sharing decisions from the outset.

Shipper G's reaction to carrier's request for an increase in price is not atypical of this approach. G is a major producer of finished steel. It employed rail transportation at all three stages of its production process. At the finished steel to consignee stage it moved approximately 45 percent of its total tonnage by rail. The finished steel was usually shipped in standard fifty- and sixty-foot boxcars, though some was moved in regular and covered gondolas. Most of this equipment was nonspecialized. All of it had a significant number of alternative uses. With the exception of covered gondolas, readily accessible substitutes were available.

The finished steel was sold on a price-absorbed basis. That is, it was purchased FOB nearest mill to customer. Therefore, the buyer (consignee) paid the freight bill from the mill nearest destination and the shipper paid the remainder. Technically the steel customer had the right to choose the route and negotiations should have taken place between the carrier and the consignee. The sheer number of customers, though, made it difficult for the railroad to deal separately with each steel consignee. In addition, the relative lack of bargaining power of the users of finished steel (vis-à-vis the railroads) had made it desirable for them to use shipper as their agent. Typically,

TABLE 3.3
Attitude toward Adjustments and Investment Characteristics

Investment characteristics	Attitude toward adjustments		Row total
	a_1	a_2	
Nonspecific investment	18	3	21
Moderately idiosyncratic investment	2	16	18
Highly idiosyncratic investment	0	12	12
Column total	20	31	51

therefore, the railroad's first approach on the price increase—before going to the consignee—was to the steel producer's traffic department. The theory was that if carrier could not get shipper's support for the price adjustment, the railroad was likely to be unsuccessful with the consignee.

In this instance, the proposed rate increase came on top of a recent general price increase. Shipper G's first formal notice was a letter indicating carrier's intention to raise the rate and requesting shipper's support. Though no specific mention was made of any preliminary informal discussions of the proposed increase, shipper indicated that it was not surprised at the request. This probably indicated either that it had received prior notice of the request or that it anticipated carrier's revenue problem at the time of the initial rate negotiation. Whatever the reason, shipper's initial formal response was negative. Carrier's representative requested a meeting between shipper's traffic department and carrier's marketing, pricing, and sales offices. After the conference shipper decided to reject carrier's request for support. They indicated that while there might be some merit to the request, carrier would have to live with the terms it had negotiated. As shipper's traffic manager asserted, the railroad, "like anyone else," had obligated itself for the long term to do something—in this case, to ship finished steel to destination—at "the negotiated rate," and any attempt to renegotiate the price because of a failure to anticipate future circumstances properly would meet stiff resistance.

The chances of the parties resolving those issues between themselves, shipper believed, were relatively slim. Carrier was not sure that it was prepared to take the matter all the way to the Interstate Commerce Commission. It believed that if the consignees ultimately lost before the ICC, they might switch to truck. G predicted that the most likely scenario would see the railroad pushing the issue to the point where the consignees began negotiating seriously with some trucking firms. If at that point shipper was still unwilling to back carrier's position, it would withdraw the proposal. If shipper were to back the proposal carrier would have to submit its figures to independent (from the railroad) verification. It would also have to be prepared to prove that the original price proposal was in fact "a mistake" rather than a calculated strategic move to attempt to lock the traffic in to carrier.

A second set of responses was also classified as indicating an interest in holding the other party to the original contract. The three nonspecific and two moderately idiosyncratic transactions of this group tended to characterize their reaction to requests for adjustments in terms of hesitancy rather than absolute resistance. They were willing to adjust initial under-standings only if doing so would place their firm in a clearly superior position to that originally negotiated. There was more discussion of flexibility here than with the first group. However, when questioned further, they indicated only a theoretic flexibility. Only when more favorable terms could be worked out was there a true willingness to make adjustments. Initial terms were preferred unless concessions could be obtained that left the parties better off then they had been under the original contract.

The governance structure supporting the movement of sanitary paper exhibited this type of adjustment. Carrier described how shipper K had sought an adjustment in the number of boxcars assigned to movements originating at K's plant. Originally the agreement specified that carrier would provide shipper with a certain number of cars as long as shipper met specified volume commitments. Carrier anticipated that the agreement would run for "years." During my interview, carrier had first argued that its ultimate decision to permit the change was proof of its flexible attitude. But further questioning revealed that carrier's initial response to shipper K—in fact, its first several responses—had been to deny the request. At that time, shipper had proposed that carrier increase the number of cars assigned to the origin plant in exchange for a proportionate increase in the amount of pulpboard shipped with R. Carrier's reaction was to reject the proposal. As R explained: "The numbers just weren't there. The [initial understanding] was nothing special and their [new] offer didn't advance it any."

Several more attempts were made by shipper to increase its pool of available cars. Each was resisted by carrier in favor of the original terms of agreement. Finally, carrier offered to provide shipper with a number of boxcars above and beyond the present pool. K, in turn, would have to agree not to contest a rate increase on the traffic. When asked to describe why it now was willing to make the adjustment, carrier responded: "It makes sense dollar-wise. The return's there. Our revenue on that movement is drastically increased."

Twenty-eight of the responses indicated an attitude toward adjustments that was a good deal more flexible. Sixteen of the moderately idiosyncratic and twelve of the highly idiosyncratic transactions were predisposed toward acting favorably upon the requests of their contracting partners. The possibility that they were being taken advantage of apparently did not worry them. On the contrary, the ability to change agreements in the face of problems or altered circumstances was perceived as essential to the preservation of their investments. For instance, both shipper A and carrier X, involved in the movement of finished autos, indicated that the parties were favorably predisposed toward making (or potentially having to make) adjustments in initial contract terms. Shipper in particular reiterated its basic policy of keeping carrier, and for that matter all railroads, "viable."

Types of Adjustments

The third facet of governance concerned the form of the contractual adjustments if and when they were made. Two types of adjustments were identified: unilateral (n_1) and negotiated (n_2). The data are summarized in Table 3.4 and indicate a tendency toward negotiated adjustments as the degree of idiosyncrasy increased. In addition, as investment became more transaction specific, there was a greater willingness to trade present adjustments for future consideration. Slightly more than half of the transactions did not involve a major adjustment, so that a third category—no adjustments attempted (n_3)—appears to, but does not, vary systematically with investment characteristics.

TABLE 3.4
Types of Adjustments and Investment Characteristics

| Investment characteristics | n_1 | Types of adjustments | | | |
| | | n_2 | | n_3 | Row total |
		Present tit-for-tat	Future consideration		
Nonspecific investment	4	7	0	10	21
Moderately idiosyncratic investment	0	4	4	10	18
Highly idiosyncratic investment	0	1	4	7	12
Column total	4	12	8	27	51

Unilateral adjustments involved one party's announcement of a change without consulting the other. Negotiations were not seriously pursued. The initiating party cared little whether the relation itself was impaired. Five transactions involved adjustments of this nature. Four involved nonspecific investment, while one was supported by idiosyncratic capital. Railroad X, for instance, decided that the movement of pulpboard, which is transported in standardized equipment, was no longer compensatory. To rectify the situation, X announced a surcharge of S dollars per car, effective shortly after the announcement was made. No attempt was made to notify customers or encourage negotiations. In fact, on the day of the announcement executives from one of the large paper concerns were in the office of railroad X's market manager for forest products to discuss matters related to the price of pulpboard movements. No mention of the impending surcharge announcement was made. As X explained, "If you get people involved in a negotiation process, the whole thing can drag on for months." This is in marked contrast to the types of adjustments discussed below that were made by the same railroad (though a different marketing section) with respect to the movement of finished automobiles.

The alternative method of making adjustments was through negotiation. Two types of negotiated changes were evident. The first found the parties agreeing to change terms in exchange for fully compensatory, *present* consideration. Seven of the eleven nonspecific and five of the thirteen idiosyncratic transactions where adjustments were witnessed involved negotiations of this nature. Shipper A and carrier X, involved in the movement of finished automobiles, negotiated adjustments in this manner. Unilateral action was not seriously considered and the renegotiations generally involved an immediate quid pro quo.

One example illustrates the pattern, Despite their size and weight, finished automobiles are highly susceptible to damage from the environment, vandalism, and theft while in transit to final destinations. To reduce these losses, auto shipper A in the mid-1970s encouraged carrier to switch from open to enclosed auto racks. The change necessitated two types of investment in physical capital. First, there was the considerable cost either of enclosing the open equipment or of purchasing new, fully enclosed cars. Second, the fully enclosed auto rack is roughly nineteen feet high, while the standard clearance (bridge and tunnel heights) on carrier's route is much lower, requiring investments in higher clearances to complete the conversion. Many railroads, feeling that it was essential to accommodate the auto shipper, immediately began to increase their clearances, procure the necessary equipment, and renegotiate the rates. Carrier X, for a variety of strategic and financial reasons, refused to do so and continued to use the old cars.

During this same period, X renewed an old complaint. For many years it had been troubled by what it felt were noncompensatory movements of finished vehicles, especially the carloads of automobiles interchanged with railroads located in a particular region of the country. For reasons that had to do with the formula for splitting revenue on "foreign" (interchanged) movements, carrier believed that the routes were losing money. Carrier insisted that to make the routes compensatory it needed an increase of roughly S dollars per carload. The usual practice called for X to split its rate increase with all foreign lines. Carrier wanted to prevent payments to third parties whose share was already compensatory. Carrier X, therefore, proposed to shipper that in exchange for partially enclosing the auto racks, a fixed surcharge payable only to carrier be placed on each carload of automobiles. While this represented a radical departure from existing pricing practices, shipper eventually agreed despite the problems this might cause in its relations with other carriers.

Shipper attributed at least part of its willingness to accept the surcharge to carrier's careful preparation of its case. Unlike other divisions at carrier that faced similar problems, the automobile transportation section was very careful not to surprise or antagonize shipper. The groundwork for the surcharges had been laid months in advance, and A was carefully kept apprised of the situation. In the end, A even supported X's proposal before the ICC. Both shipper and carrier felt that a large part of the credit for the maintenance of cordial relations, even in the face of the price increases, could be given to "John Smith" at carrier, who handled the situation in a "very business-like" manner.

The second type of negotiated adjustments were made in return for some implicit or explicit future consideration. Eight of the thirteen idiosyncratic transactions where adjustments were witnessed involved negotiations of this nature. For instance, railroad D indicated that it might provide additional cars to a steel mill for movements of semifinished steel, to increase its chances of receiving a lucrative movement at some point in the future. Alternatively, the carrier might provide needed equipment to preserve or enhance its reputation or to develop goodwill. On the shipper side, auto company G almost always approved a proposed rate increase. Its argument was, in effect, that by providing needed revenues to the railroads today it would help to guarantee that specialized investment would be undertaken in the future.

TABLE 3.5
Long-Term Planning and Investment Characteristics

Investment characteristics	Information for long-term planning		
	h_1 (No)	h_2 (Yes)	Row total
Nonspecific investment	13	8	21
Moderately idiosyncratic investment	5	13	18
Highly idiosyncratic investment	1	11	12
Column total	19	32	51

4.3. Information for Long-Term Planning

To be effective, any governance structure must entail exchanges of information for short-term, specific planning (Macneil, 1974). But the exchange of information for long-term forecasting as well as the sharing of proprietary and impacted data evidences a different attitude toward governing the transaction.[18] Thus, the fourth facet of governance explored with the parties was whether they exchanged long-term forecasting, proprietary, or impacted information with their contracting partners (h_1 = no, h_2 = yes). There is some indication from the data that parties to idiosyncratic transactions were more likely to be involved in exchanges of information for long-term forecasting than were the parties to nonspecific transactions. The data are summarized in Table 3.5.

4.4. Information for Structural Planning

Even more interesting in terms of the type of information exchanged is the fifth element of governance. The parties were asked whether the information necessary for structural planning was shared (s_1 = no, s_2 = yes). Structural planning involves the development of rules or procedures for dealing with long-term problems or unforeseen contingencies. Where markets were relied upon as the primary governance mechanism, little joint structural planning was evident. Nonspecific investments, therefore, tended to generate only infrequent exchanges of information for the purpose of structural planning.

With idiosyncratic transactions, in contrast, the data indicate that the parties were more likely to engage in exchanges of information for structural planning. Both formal and informal procedures for dealing with problems were established, and conversations were held to discuss the future course of

[18] Williamson (1975) defines impacted data as "mainly attributable to the pairing of uncertainty with opportunism. It exists in circumstances in which one of the parties to an exchange is much better informed than is the other regarding underlying conditions germane to the trade, and the second party cannot achieve information parity except at great cost—because he cannot rely on the first party to disclose the information in a fully candid manner" (14).

TABLE 3.6
Structural Planning and Investment Characteristics

Investment characteristics	Information for structural planning		Row total
	s_1 (No)	s_2 (Yes)	
Nonspecific investment	19	2	21
Moderately idiosyncratic investment	8	8	16
Highly idiosyncratic investment	1	10	11
Column total	28	20	48[a]

[a] Three interviewees provided insufficient data to permit an unambiguous classification.

the transaction. Many of the automobile transactions in particular involved regular conversations of this nature. For instance, automobile shipper B moved automobile parts with carrier Z. Because B maintained short inventories at its various assembly plants, it was crucial that Z provide consistent, on-time service. Shipper's procedures for dealing with carrier over these issues were relatively formalized. Each month shipper requested that a representative from each of the railroads with the most troublesome routes come to Detroit. At these discussions, B's traffic people would provide the railroads with a detailed analysis of the problems. They also made requests for improvements. If after thirty days carrier still was meeting its schedule less than 70 percent of the time, shipper would begin testing new routes. This might, as B put it, "mean spending a few more dollars," but it conveyed additional information to the railroad. If after sixty days carrier was still performing below standard, shipper might switch some traffic to another railroad. At all stages of the process the matter was handled in a reasonably formal manner, but with "plenty of give and take." As shipper put it: "We will make every effort to help them correct their problems. Usually the problem is legitimate and usually they fix it. If they can't, I want them to know that I don't like having to switch on them, but that I have to. We can't afford to have a plant close down. But I want the whole thing handled very business-like, with the minimum of bruised egos."

The data for idiosyncratic and nonspecific transactions are summarized in Table 3-6. It indicates that as investment becomes more idiosyncratic there is a greater likelihood that the exchanges of information necessary for structural planning will be made.

5. CONCLUSION

A consistent pattern emerges from this study. In this paper I have examined data on contractual enforcement, adaptations, and long-term planning. In each instance the predictions made by the general theory have been borne

TABLE 3.7
Governance Structure and Investment Characteristics

Investment characteristics	Governance structure			
	Market (g_1)	Mixed (g_2)	Relational (g_3)	Row total
Nonspecific investment	13	7	1	21
Moderately idiosyncratic investment	0	10	8	18
Highly idiosyncratic investment	0	2	10	12
Column total	13	19	19	51

out by the data. Indeed, the combined force of the data is, if anything, more powerful than its component parts. Some rough measure of that force is suggested by showing the correlation between the increased use of long-term relational contracting devices and the existence of highly idiosyncratic investments by the parties, as is done in Table 3.7.[19] The qualitative data make it difficult to test these conclusions with precise statistical techniques. Inspection of the data, though, suggests that they tend to confirm the theoretical hypothesis advanced by institutional economists; namely, that the form of the institutional structure used to support contractual relations depends upon the character of the transaction being effected. Where the transaction involves idiosyncratic investment the governance mechanism is apt to be bilateral and unique to the parties. Conversely, as the investments become more standardized a concomitant reduction governance specialization results.

[19] Table 3.7 is derived by aggregating the data presented in Tables 3.2–3.6. Category g_1 is made up of those parties classified as e_1, a_1, n_1, h_1, and s_1. Category g_3 is made up of those classified as e_4 or e_5, a_2, n_2, h_2, and s_2. Category g_2 is defined as any combination of the five elements described above, other than those defined as g_1 or g_3. Included among the governance mechanisms classified as "mixed" are the three ambiguous responses concerning the use of structural planning. In each instance, the governance structure would have been classified as mixed even if the responses had been unambiguous.

QUANTITY AND PRICE ADJUSTMENT IN LONG-TERM CONTRACTS: A CASE STUDY OF PETROLEUM COKE

Victor P. Goldberg and John R. Erickson

1. INTRODUCTION

Much economic activity takes place within a framework of complex, long-term contracts. While economists have shown increased interest in these contracts, surprisingly little is known about them, or, indeed, about how to analyze the contracting activity of private economic actors. A case study of the actual contracts used in one industry could provide sorely needed data about the way in which reasonably clever businessmen and lawyers cope with problems scholars might consider intractable. In this article, we provide such an analysis of contracts concerning a particular product—petroleum coke. We focus on the problems of quantity and price adjustment. We do not deal, except in passing, with the question of why the parties chose long-term contracts rather than short-term agreements or vertical integration by contract rather than by ownership.

In 1964, the Federal Trade Commission (FTC) launched an investigation into the possible anticompetitive effect of the long-term contracts under which eight oil refineries sold petroleum coke to the Great Lakes Carbon Corporation (GLC). The investigation culminated in a 1973 decision that

Reprinted from the Journal of Law and Economics, vol. XXX (October 1987) by permission of the University of Chicago Press. © 1987 by The University of Chicago. All rights reserved.

Victor P. Goldberg is the Thomas J. Macioce Professor of Law and Co-Director of the Center for Law and Economic Studies, Columbia University; John R. Erickson is Professor of Finance, California State University at Fullerton. Part of Goldberg's research was funded by a grant from Northwestern University School of Law. Part of Erickson's research was funded by a grant from the Great Lakes Carbon Company. The paper benefited from comments at seminars at UCLA (Economics), Toronto (Law), Stanford (Law), Virginia (Law), and Northwestern (Law).

these contracts violated the antitrust statutes.[1] The contracts collected by the commission in its investigation are our primary source of data. The *Great Lakes Carbon* record and the FTC's nonpublic files included about ninety contracts, which account for about 80 percent of all the domestic petroleum coke contracts written between 1946 and 1973.[2] In addition, the FTC's Compliance Files provided us with a number of post-1973 contracts, while industry sources supplied us with a few more.

Long-term contracts enable economic actors to coordinate behavior, while stopping short of full, formal vertical integration. These contracts reflect the problems posed by the human characteristics of the transactors (their limited ability to process information, their propensity for strategic or opportunistic behavior); by the physical characteristics of the subject matter of the transaction (that is, problems with defining and monitoring quality, the production technology, the ease of access to alternative buyers or sellers, the relation-specific nature of the physical plant, and so forth), and by the reliability of external enforcement (legal enforcement or good will). These contracts embody the particular solutions developed by the contracting parties. Our working assumption here is that the solutions are correct—that is, that the contracts are "efficient" adaptations.[3] On the basis of this assumption, we can then work backward and ask why particular contract terms (or patterns of terms) might be efficient.[4]

Two caveats are in order. First, a written contract is at best an imperfect representation of the underlying economic relation. A written document is typically an incomplete specification of the terms and conditions. Moreover, even the terms and conditions explicitly included in the contract can be changed or suspended; indeed, adjustments to changed conditions are frequently made without consulting the written contracts (see Macaulay, 1963). The documents will reflect the concerns of the parties as filtered

---

[1] In the Matter of Great Lakes Carbon Corporation, et al., 82 F.T.C. 1529 (1973). The record of this case and the FTC's file serve as our primary source of information. The commission's internal classification of the case is 8805, and this number is used in referencing the location of documents. Complainants' exhibits are designated by CX. Exhibits by the defendants are designated by GLCX (Great Lakes Carbon), TX (Texaco), and MOX (Mobil). Proposed Findings of Fact and Conclusions of Law are found at 8805-1-3-2; these are denoted by the party's abbreviation followed by an F (for example, Complaint Counsel's Findings are CF). Documents introduced as evidence are designated by their FTC file number. Files were usually not paginated.

[2] The contracts were written by thirty different sellers of petroleum coke at forty-four different refineries. (In 1970, there were thirty-five refiners operating fifty-three coke-producing refineries.) The nature of the contracts varies considerably. Some are formal documents over twenty pages long, while others are two-paragraph letters saying that the parties renew their previous agreement with no changes. In a number of contracts, some confidential information (often concerning price) was deleted by the FTC.

[3] We have in mind a very narrow meaning of efficiency. The adaptations are efficient for the parties, not necessarily for any larger group (such as society as a whole).

[4] The theoretical framework for analyzing complex institutional arrangements in general, and long-term contracts in particular, has been developing over the last decade or so. See Goldberg (1980); Klein, Crawford, and Alchian (1978); Williamson (1985); and Putterman (1986).

through their lawyers and conditioned by their expectations regarding the reasonableness of the opposite party in adjusting to unspecified contingencies. Second, our working assumption is only a research strategy, not an article of faith. People do stupid things, and, in some instances, the best explanation of why a particular term was adopted is that the parties made a mistake. There are two countervailing forces influencing the likelihood that petroleum coke contracts would embody mistakes. On the one hand, considerable time and effort went into designing the contracts; contract terms were not simply lifted off the shelf. On the other hand, the long terms and the infrequent participation in the market by most of the buyers and sellers[5] meant that contract terms were not necessarily "equilibrium" terms—that is, the results of market forces rewarding winners and penalizing losers. The contract terms meet only the weak test of birth, not the stronger test of survival.

We have chosen not to rely on three common explanations: (*a*) the contract terms are imposed by the big and powerful on the small and weak; (*b*) the terms facilitate anticompetitive behavior;[6] and (*c*) the contracts reflect the risk preferences of the parties. We are not asserting that any of these propositions is false; we are simply trying to see how far we can go in explaining contract structure without invoking these three arguments. This research strategy was not, of course, adopted on a whim. It reflects our view that these propositions will not be of much help in explaining the structure of these, or most other, long-term economic relations. Indeed, we can go a step further and suggest that these propositions can impede (and have impeded) research on complex exchange by providing superficially appealing answers that have discouraged search along more fruitful lines.

In the next section, we provide some background on the petroleum coke industry. Section 3 analyzes the structure of coke contracts, emphasizing the duration, ease of termination, locus of decisions as to quantity, and the use of commission pricing. Section 4 focuses on the price-adjustment mechanisms used in the coke contracts.

2. PETROLEUM COKE: ITS PRODUCTION, PROCESSING, AND USE

Petroleum coking is a process that takes the heavy residual oils left over from the initial distillation of crude oil and, through the application of high temperatures, produces gas oil and petroleum coke (often referred to as "green coke"). The former can be further processed into lighter distillate fuels, such as gasoline, turbine and diesel fuels, and light fuel oil. Coke accounts

---

[5] Some of the aluminum company buyers, for example, entered into a contract with only one coke supplier.

[6] This was, of course, the FTC's presumption in *Great Lakes*. For a complete analysis of the antitrust case, it would obviously be necessary to consider whether the contracts had a possible anticompetitive purpose or effect; that is the subject of a separate paper.

for less than 3 percent of the value of a barrel of oil. If not coked, the residual oil would be processed into heavy fuel oil or turned into asphalt. Thus, coking permits a low-value residual to be upgraded to more valuable light and middle distillate fuels. In 1970, fifty-three cokers were in operation in the United States. About 15 percent of the crude oil refined in the United States was coked (Goldberg and Erickson, 1982).

The principal constituent of green coke is carbon, which makes up from 82 percent to 92 percent of the total weight. It also contains volatile matter, ash, sulphur, and trace metals. The amounts of sulphur and metals in coke depend directly on the origin of the crude oil from which it comes, and the amounts present determine the use to which it is put. High-sulphur coke, which is less valuable, is used primarily for fuel in utility boilers and cement kilns.

Most low-sulphur coke—about 40 percent of all green coke—is calcined. Calcining converts the coke from a hydrocarbon to a pure carbon. This eliminates the volatile elements, increases its hardness, and makes it an excellent conductor of electricity. At the same time, calcining reduces coke's suitability for use as fuel. Most calcined coke is used for the production of anodes for the electrolytic cell reduction of alumina to aluminum.[7] Calcining reduces the weight of coke by 15–30 percent and raises its value substantially. In 1970, a ton of low-sulphur green coke sold for around $10, while a ton of calcined coke sold for around $30. Production of one pound of aluminum requires approximately 0.5 pounds of green coke (or about 0.4 pounds of calcined coke). About 3 percent of the cost of aluminum can be attributed to calcined coke.[8]

The GLC is the largest producer of calcined coke. Great Lakes' calciners, their initial dates of operation, and their capacity as of 1964, are shown in Table 4.1.[9] Twelve other firms operate twenty-one additional calciners, with a total capacity about twice that of Great Lakes.

Great Lakes served as a middleman, selling both green and calcined coke to end users. Other calcining firms also served as middlemen. In 1959, Kaiser Aluminum and Chemical Company became the first end user to build a calciner. In subsequent years, Kaiser added five additional calciners, and three other aluminum companies also built calciners. Although the major part of their calciner output was for their own anode production, the aluminum companies did sell some calcined coke to other final users. While there has been a substantial amount of backward integration into calcining

---

[7] In the 1970s about 75–80 percent of the calcined coke produced in the United States was used for aluminum anodes, about half being sold to foreign users.

[8] Aluminum prices in the late 1960s were about 25 cents per pound. Green coke sold for about $10 per ton and calcined coke for about $30. At the conversion rates noted in the text, the shares of the aluminum price attributable to green and calcined coke were 1 percent and 2.4 percent, respectively.

[9] According to industry sources, since 1964 capacity at the Port Arthur and Wilmington plants has roughly doubled, and at the Enid plant it has tripled. At the Chicago plant, it has been halved.

TABLE 4.1
Calcining Plants Owned by Great Lakes Carbon, 1964

Location	Capacity (tons/month)
Port Arthur, Texas	
Started calcining operations 1935	3,000
Added second calciner 1938	9,000
Added third calciner 1952	18,000
Total	30,000
Calumet plant, Chicago, Illinois	
Started calcining operations 1942	18,000
Added second and third units 1948	10,000
Added fourth unit 1959	8,000
Total	36,000
Wilmington plant, Wilmington, California	
Started calcining operations 1940	12,000
Added second unit 1952	18,000
Total	30,000
Enid plant, Enid, Oklahoma: started November 1964	15,000
Casper plant, Casper, Wyoming	
Started processing 1956	2,500
Added second unit 1964	2,500
Total	5,000
Lockport, Lockport, Illinois: started 1937; abandoned 1958	7,500

Source: F.T.C. 8805-4-2-1-1.

by aluminum companies, there has been very little forward integration by refiners. Continental Oil installed a calciner in 1956, but, by 1970, only four of the thirty-five coking refiners had installed calciners.[10]

Because coke is a low-value, bulky product, transportation costs play a significant role in the economics of coking. Unless a coker has access to ocean ports, or to a calciner within a radius of fifty miles, shipping by rail is the cheapest alternative. As an indication of the magnitude of these costs, we regressed 1968 rail freight rates against distance:[11]

$$F = 5.41 + 0.0038D, \qquad R^2 = 0.77, N = 0.85$$
$$(7.6)$$

where F is freight rate per ton, and D is distance in miles. That is, shipping

---

[10] More recently Arco and Gulf have built large calciners.

[11] The data are from 8805-4-2-2, pp. 276–78. The t-statistic is in parentheses.

costs independent of distance were about $5 per ton, and shipping coke 1,000 miles costs about $4 more. At the time, high-quality coke sold for about $10 per ton freight on board (f.o.b.), while low-quality coke sold for about half that. Because calcined coke had a considerably higher value per pound, producers had an incentive to locate calciners near the source of supply and to transport calcined coke to the location of the end user. If a coker was located near a calciner, trucking was a reasonably inexpensive method of transport. In eleven instances, cokers and calciners were physically adjacent, so that no transportation (other than to or from the inventory pile) was necessary. Proximate location drastically reduced transportation costs, but other costs were likely to be higher. For example, it might require sacrificing economies of scale in the coking or calcining process. In addition, it could increase the contracting parties' vulnerability to opportunistic behavior by their counterparts.

The bulkiness of coke makes it expensive to store. Coke is also a fire hazard and a source of pollution unless it is put in covered storage. The costs of storing coke include both the direct costs of preparing land and of providing railroad spurs, water sprays, bulldozers, and loading equipment and the opportunity cost of the land employed for storage. It also must include the possible costs arising from an accumulation of inventory, an accumulation that may cause a disruption in the refinery's operations.[12] Some of these costs arise regardless of whether the coke is stored at the refinery or elsewhere. But others, notably the opportunity cost of land, depend crucially on where the coke is stored. Economizing on inventory costs requires rapid processing to keep the total inventory low and rapid removal of inventory to lower-value storage areas. As we shall see in the next section, the latter is of particular importance in explaining the variation in the structure of coke contracts.

3. STRUCTURE OF THE CONTRACTS

The parties to a long-term contract have a mutual interest in designing a contract that maximizes its value to both parties. They also, however, have a selfish interest in achieving a large individual share, even if doing so results in a reduced overall value. If the parties could costlessly constrain their non-cooperative, opportunistic behavior, contracting would not be very difficult —or interesting. Much of the structure of contracts reflects the attempts of parties to constrain their noncooperative behavior in order to increase the total pie. In our discussion, we will emphasize the pie-increasing motives; but it should be understood that the opportunism problem is omnipresent.

In the long run, the parties involved want to assure the continuation of their relation while still maintaining enough flexibility to adapt the relation

---

[12] The production of coke has a "vast potential to disrupt the entire operation of the refinery due to its rapid accumulation" (MOF at p. 22).

to changed circumstances. The more vulnerable a party is to termination, ceteris paribus, the greater the protection it would want. Thus, a coker with ample storage space and easy access to the sea would have little reason to rely on a particular customer, and it would not insist on a very long contract term with large penalties for early termination. On the other hand, a calciner built adjacent to a coker and with poor access to alternative coke suppliers would opt for greater protection.

The parties also face a short-run coordination problem. The coker's costs depend on the rate at which coke is removed from the refinery. If coke is removed too slowly, the coker is faced with a number of costly options. It could accelerate the search for new customers, reduce the selling price, add to inventory if storage space is available, reduce the production rate, or, in the limit, shut down its coking operation. The opportunity cost of refinery products not produced is a significant element of the cost of untimely removal. Because oil companies can substitute output from noncoking operations, the cost is related to the difference between the net returns from coking and the refiner's next best alternative. The buyer also faces costs if the rate of delivery deviates from the optimal rate. If too much coke arrives, the firm would have to store it or otherwise dispose of it. If too little, then the calciner must draw down inventory, acquire coke from an alternative supplier, produce at an inefficiently low rate, or, in the limit, shut down.

As integrated firm would face the same problem of balancing these various costs. The problems are compounded, however, when the decisions are to be made by independent firms. To facilitate coordinated, adaptive, sequential decision making, the parties could establish channels for conveying exchange-related information or set up procedures to deal with disputes, for example, arbitration. They could also build into the contract incentives for controlling the costs arising from miscoordination. Our primary focus will be on the locus of responsibility and on the incentive structures. In the remainder of this section we will focus on the means by which the contracts dealt with the long- and short-run coordination problems.

To facilitate exposition, we have divided the contracts into four groups: (1) sales of coke to Great Lakes Carbon for calcining (this covers most of the GLC contracts in the sample), (2) sales to aluminum companies, (3) commission contracts, and (4) the remainder. In an earlier draft, we included a large number of specific contract terms in the text. Most readers found that this impeded the flow of the argument. We, have, therefore, decided to omit the specific contract language and instead to paraphrase. For readers interested in the precise language, the contract terms are available separately as an appendix.[13]

Great Lakes' Calcining Contracts

A number of features common to most of the GLC contracts influenced their basic structure. The coker's capacity was usually considerably less than

---

[13] A copy of the appendix is on file at the editorial offices of the *Journal of Law and Economics*.

GLC's calciner capacity; for example, in 1963 GLC's Port Arthur calciner purchased at least 15,000 tons of coke from eight refiners, and its Calumet calciner purchased a similar amount from six. Moreover, GLC maintained more than 250 acres for coke storage at ten different locations. The storage capacity was about 3 million tons; in 1963 and 1964, its average inventory was about 2 million tons, which was equal to about one year's purchases.[14] Consequently, GLC was not particularly vulnerable to variations in the flow of coke from any single source. Sellers, on the other hand, generally had little storage capacity. If inventory was allowed to accumulate on the premises, the coker would have to shut down the coking operations. The cokers could have bought additional land—at a price—for storing coke inventory at the refinery and could have controlled—also at a price—the nuisance damages arising from storing coke at the refinery. We infer that the price for doing so was too high; on net, it was more profitable for most of these refiners to have the inventory moved away from the refinery.[15]

Almost all the GLC contracts were full output/immediate removal contracts with GLC bearing all the risks of changes in the rate of coke output. The coker was obligated to sell only if it produced. The decision to produce was entirely in the hands of the coker. The coker could terminate without legal obligation if it ceased production of coke at the refinery. Termination for the purpose of selling to another buyer would, however, constitute a breach of contract. The contract was asymmetrical in that GLC did not have the option of ceasing performance without being liable for damages. Indeed, GLC typically agreed to provide immediate removal of the coke, so that a failure to remove coke rapidly enough would constitute a breach of its obligations. GLC's nonperformance would be excused legally only for specified conditions having to do with changes in the coke's quality or for circumstances beyond the parties' control.[16]

The GLC contracts were generally of long duration, especially when a new coker was involved. Nine of the ten contracts written between 1946 and 1961 involving new cokers were for a period of at least ten yesrs.[17] Contract length is, to be sure, a slippery concept. A contract might permit termination without penalty at a certain date prior to the stated termination date. For

---

[14] 8805-4-2-1-1-. GLC's inventory was unusually high in those years.

[15] Conceivably, the refiner could have shipped the coke itself, rather than relying on GLC. It could have maintained the distant stockpiles or shipped the coke to stockpiles owned by others (including GLC). Thus, GLC's 1974 contract with Mobil's Beaumont, Texas, refinery gave Mobil, in the event the contract were terminated, the right to store up to 400,000 tons of coke at GLC's Port Arthur facility; the agreement was for one year, with the option on a second year as well; prices for handling Mobil's inventory were specified in the contract. This was the only instance of such a term in the contracts. It seems quite certain that forward integration into inventory removal and storage by refiners was more costly than backward integration into removal and storage by calciners.

[16] Suspension or termination of the contract for failure to meet quality standards is discussed in Goldberg and Erickson (1982: 30–39).

[17] The one exception was a five-year contract with Skelly Oil in 1958 (8805-4-2-1-1, p. 30). Skelly had considerable space available for inventory storage.

example, GLC's twenty-year agreement with American Oil gave each party the privilege of terminating with six months' notice at the end of the tenth and fifteenth years. The stated twenty-year term does, nonetheless, convey some information. There would be a greater presumption of renewal at the tenth anniversary than for a straight ten-year agreement; a party terminating at the reopening date would have to meet a higher standard of reasonableness to maintain its reputation with the trade.[18]

The primary determinant of contract length was the coker's need to protect its reliance interest. The small number of feasible alternative outlets for the coker mean that the value of the coker's investment would fall substantially if the relation were terminated. GLC's ample storage capacity and its multiple sources made it relatively less vulnerable.[19]

The Aluminum Contracts

Ten contracts between coking refiners and aluminum producers were included in the record. Some significant features of the these agreements are summarized in Table 4.2. Only the La Gloria-Alcoa contracts did not involve construction of either a new coker or a calciner. These agreements, not surprisingly, were for a much shorter period than the others. At three locations, the contracting parties were engaged in the simultaneous construction of an adjacent new coker and calciner.

The aluminum contracts differed considerably from the GLC agreements. Whereas, in the Great Lakes Carbon contracts, the refiner was responsible for determining whether, and how much, coke should be produced, in the aluminum contracts, the decision was in the hands of the buyer. All the contracts specified a minimum level of output. In no case did the buyer agree to take all the coker's output, even though in all but three instances the contract quantity was close to the coker's capacity. Moreover, in nine of the agreements, the coking refiner could not refuse to produce coke without being liable for damages.[20]

Six of the contracts allowed the buyer to reduce its purchases below the contract quantity under certain conditions. However, to provide some protection for the coker, the contracts included nonlinear pricing rules to

---

[18] A variant was a contract for three successive three-year terms. The contract stated that the parties could not terminate solely because the price was unsatisfactory without first engaging in good faith negotiation on the price.

[19] Two of GLC's calciners were built in close proximity to a single coker that supplied all its needs. The small calciner (50,000 tons per year) at Casper, Wyoming, had facilities to store one year's coke. The Wilmington, Calfornia, calciner was built near Mobil's large Torrance coker (coke output of about 500,000 tons per year). The calciner had storage capacity of about eight months (8805-4-2-1-1). Moreover, Mobil had additional storage capacity for coke in the event GLC's facilities were full (CX 5). In addition, GLC had access to the ocean and shipped most of the coke to Japan; in 1964, it sold 378,000 tons to Japan, about one-third of which was calcined (CX 1305).

[20] The one exception was the Humble-Kaiser agreement (CX 68). Because Humble had already accumulated a coke stockpile of 200,000 tons that could supply Kaiser's needs for four years, the cost to Kaiser of granting Humble discretion on production of coke was obviously not great.

TABLE 4.2
Aluminum Contracts

Refinery	Buyer	Exhibit number	Contract date	New coker	New calciner	Quantity close to coker capacity	Contract length (in years)	Calciner adjacent
Gulf	Alcoa	CX 30	May 13, 1960	✓	—[e]	✓	10	—
Champlin	Swiss Aluminum	CX 20	June 2, 1960	✓	—	✓	11.5	—
Humble	Reynolds	CX 31	September 7, 1961	✓	✓	✓	10	✓
LaGloria	Alcoa	CX 34	January 23, 1962	—	—[e]	—	3	—
Humble	Kaiser	CX 68	April 1, 1963	—	✓	✓	8	—[d]
LaGloria	Alcoa	CX 35	January 11, 1964	—	—[e]	—	3[b]	—
Cities Service	Swiss Aluminum	CX 25	February 1, 1964	✓	✓	—	8	—
Shell	Kaiser	CX 38	June 11, 1964	✓	✓	—	8	✓
Atlantic-Richfield	Harvey	CX 17	December 22, 1965	✓	✓	✓	15	✓
Humble	Reynolds	CX 418	March 1, 1967	✓[a]	✓[a]	✓	10[c]	✓

[a] Expansion of coker and calciner roughly doubled capacity.
[b] Renewal of CX 34.
[c] Revision of CX 31.
[d] Kaiser's calciner at Mead, Washington, was built specifically to process the high-sulphur coke produced by Humble's Billings, Montana, coker.
[e] The coke in these contracts is calcined for the aluminum company by Great Lakes Carbon.

discourage such reductions. The form these pricing rules took differed considerably. The differences are of less importance than the fact that nonlinear pricing rules were common. Nonlinear pricing was only used in contracts in which the buyer had some discretion as to how much of the output it required.

Alcoa's contract involving Gulf's new coker gave Gulf the right to shut down the coker if inventory at the refinery reached 10,000 tons (twenty days' output). Alcoa would have to pay a "standby" charge during the shutdown period of $75,000 per month. With the contract price at $12 (before escalation) and the contract quantity 500 tons per day, Alcoa in effect paid for about 40 percent of the coke, whether or not it took any. Moreover, if Alcoa did not take most of the contracted amount, inventory would accumulate and the inventory constraint would quickly become binding. Alcoa could take coke at below the contract rate only if Gulf chose to produce at a reduced rate. Thus, Gulf was assured that Alcoa would have to take its interests into account when determining how much coke to take. Alcoa's contracts with LaGloria gave the coker less protection, although they still included nonlinear pricing. The price for the first 10,000 tons (35 percent of the contract quantity) was $14 per ton, while the price for the remainder was only $11.25.

Two large cokers were constructed in conjunction with new calciners by Humble (with Reynolds) and Richfield (with Harvey). The Humble-Reynolds contract was entered into in September 1961, and the coker and calciner were in operation by spring 1963.[21] Reynolds agreed to take a minimum of 330,000 tons of coke per year, a quantity that it would either use itself or resell. Reynolds had the right to reduce its obligation if its estimated domestic aluminum primary ingot production were to fall below 420,000 tons per year. Since this output level would require only about 210,000 tons of petroleum coke, Reynolds in effect agreed that, in the event of a decline in demand for its aluminum, it would be fully responsible for disposing of the 120,000 tons of coke not needed for its own operations. For each ton by which Reynolds's projected aluminum production fell below 420,000, Reynolds was relieved by taking 0.78 tons.[22] Since its own coke usage would decrease by 0.5 tons, Reynolds's obligation to sell coke on the open market was reduced by 0.28 tons. Reynolds was obliged to pay 50 percent of the contract price whether or not the coke was produced.

In 1967, the contract was revised since "Reynolds, because of the projected need for additional green . . . coke, has requested Humble to increase the quantity of green . . . coke supplied by it to Reynolds."[23] The new agreement was for 600,000 tons. The arrangement for dealing with a reduced demand for Reynolds aluminum was carried over to the new contract with only minor

---

[21] See CX 31. The contract was for ten years from the date of first delivery with two five-year renewal periods.

[22] The minimum obligation was (330,000/420,000) times the projected aluminum output.

[23] CX 418. The contract was to run until the end of December 1978; it also had two five-year renewal periods.

changes in the numbers. This contract added a new wrinkle by reducing the marginal price; the first 430,000 tons each year cost \$12.50 while the price for the remainder was \$10.50.

Since Reynolds's projected coke requirements for the early 1970s were only about 500,000 tons per year, the contract committed Reynolds to becoming a serious marketer of calcined coke. Vertical integration into marketing enabled Reynolds to provide additional assurance to Humble that it stood ready to remove Humble's coke. This arrangement enabled Humble to achieve greater economies of scale than would have been possible if Reynolds were the only buyer and if is had agreed to take a smaller amount that was closer to its actual needs, or if it had agreed to a requirements contract.[24]

Alternatively, the parties could have set the quantity at the calciner's capacity and relied on other middlemen to remove the remaining coke. This is, in effect, what Richfield and Harvey did. Harvey agreed to construct, on land leased from Richfield and adjacent to Richfield's Watson, California, refinery, a calciner capable of handling about one-fourth the refinery's coke output. Richfield agreed to maintain a sufficient inventory of coke to assure a constant monthly flow of coke to keep Harvey's calciner operating at full capacity.

The Richfield-Harvey contract period was fifteen years; however, under certain circumstances the contract could be terminated after only eight years (with two years' notice). The lease established a schedule of payments that was unrelated to the quantity of coke. Thus, by charging one price for the land and a second price per ton of coke, the parties established a two-part pricing system. The contract price of \$3.10 per ton was only about one-quarter the current market price of equivalent quality coke, while the rental fee was above the fair market rate.

Richfield had two other buyers of coke from the Watson refinery. Mitsui had a one-year, renewable, fixed-price contract for 50,000–70,000 metric tons per year for sale to Japan; Mitsui had the exclusive right to sell Richfield's coke in Japan and agreed not to sell coke outside Japan without Richfield's consent. Wilson Carbon had an exclusive right under a six-year commission contract to sell Richfield's coke anywhere in the world other than to Harvey or in Japan. Wilson agreed to take a minimum of 200,000 short tons. Thus, in the three contracts combined, Richfield had firm commitments to remove about two-thirds the coker's capacity. For the remaining one-third, Wilson had the first option, but Richfield reserved the right to determine whether the additional coke should be produced. Mitsui and Harvey had lesser claims on coke beyond their contract maximum. Mitsui would be able to buy coke that Richfield had available at the contract price. Harvey's contract terms did not carry forward to any additional sales.[25]

---

[24] A requirements contract would have imposed all the risks of demand fluctuations on Humble and would have drastically reduced the protection of its reliance interest.

[25] Cities Service's coker at Lake Charles, Louisiana, also allowed for achieving scale economies in coking by having the coker contract with additional marketers.

Commission Pricing

Only two GLC contracts and none of the aluminum contracts utilized commission pricing. In contrast, nearly half the contracts involving other middlemen set the contract price as a fraction of the buyer's resale price. Other things being equal, commission pricing is more attractive the less the buyer does to the coke before reselling it. That is, commission pricing is easier to arrange and police if the reseller simply takes the order and arranges to ship the coke out of stockpiles maintained by the refinery than if he stores the coke, combining it with coke from other producers, or processes the coke (for example, calcining it).

Commission pricing was the standard for low-quality (high-sulphur) coke. The price to the middleman was usually 95 percent of the price at which the coke was resold. The contracts often covered the entire coker output, but they differed from GLC's contracts by allowing for intermediate storage. Cokers promised to provide in advance an approximate schedule of coke production to facilitate the buyer's planning, but they refused to be bound by that schedule. The contracts were for a much shorter duration than those involving calcinable coke. Contracts were typically for less than five years and termination was on relatively short notice.

Commission pricing has a number of desirable properties. It provides, as a side effect, an automatic mechanism for adjusting prices over the life of the agreement. (The advantage of price adjustment will be discussed in the following section.) It also reduces the refiner's incentive to "cheat" in the quality dimension; the parties could therefore devote fewer resources to specifying quality and monitoring performance. Indeed, most of these contracts did not specify quality.[26]

Contracting parties can avoid some of the ex ante costs of gathering information by using commission pricing. With a fixed-price contract, the middleman has an incentive to line up resale contracts before negotiating the initial price. The coker also has an incentive to acquire information on the resale market lest the middleman use the additional information to extract the lion's share of the rewards. Commission pricing reduces the value of special price information and, therefore, permits the parties to develop the information in a more timely, less costly manner.[27]

One problem with commission pricing is that it impairs the middleman's incentive to search for customers willing to pay a high price. The reseller would be indifferent between price/effort combinations that yielded the same expected profit. The refiner, however, would not be indifferent since its compensation would depend on the resale price. It would prefer the

---

[26] Most contracts not using commission pricing did specify quality standards. They also spelled out the procedures for measurement and dispute settlement and established rules for dealing with coke that did not meet the quality standards. See Goldberg and Erickson (1982: 30–38).

[27] For similar arguments on the benefits of constraining "oversearching," see Kenney and Klein (1983); Barzel (1977, 1982). The same basic argument is used in the following section to explain why parties might find price-adjustment mechanisms to be mutually beneficial.

high-price/high-effort combination. To guard against the reseller's choosing the "quiet life," the commission contracts typically included a ceiling on inventory accumulation and a minimum average price. The minimum price was renegotiated frequently (often quarterly), and, if the parties could not agree on a minimum price, the contract would be terminable on short notice (often thirty days). However, the seller agreed not to offer to sell coke at or below the price offered by the reseller—the reseller could, in effect, match any outside offer.

Great Lakes Carbon's two commission contracts nicely illustrate the complications that arise when the reseller does more than simply take orders for shipment from a stockpile maintained by the coker. Both involved new cokers being constructed in the Los Angeles area in the late 1960s. Each coker could hold up to two months of inventory, so that timely removal, while desirable, was not as critical as it was for other cokers dealing with GLC. The coke had a low sulphur content, but there was not sufficient calcining capacity in the Los Angeles region to process it. This coke was destined for shipment outside the region; primarily to Japan.

The term of these contracts was substantially shorter than the other contracts involving new cokers—(three and five years, respectively). This shorter term reflects the coker's lesser reliance on a single purchaser. GLC had an advantage over other middlemen when the initial contracts were signed, since it already had extensive customer contacts in Japan, as well as ample storage capacity on the West Coast.[28] However, performance of the contract tended to erode its advantages vis-à-vis potential competitors. Because information developed by GLC regarding the existence of customers was revealed to the coker, GLC's market development effort was made available to potential competitors.[29] Indeed, both contracts were subsequently lost to competitors.

The inventory constraint meant that coke had to be removed even if it had not yet been sold. Therefore, the price to GLC was not set as a percentage of the f.o.b. price; it was set at 90 percent of the net resale price—resale price minus the costs incurred by GLC in reselling the coke if these costs had not been reimbursed by the customer.[30] This is similar to f.o.b. pricing, except that the costs of reselling are paid in what amounts to a cost-plus arrangement. The contracts included complex variants on the minimum average price arrangement of other commission contracts. If the costs of

---

[28] In 1965, GLC exported 192,000 tons of noncalcined, high-quality (low-sulphur) coke to Japan; this was about 80 percent of the coke in this category exported by American firms. It accounted for about 90 percent of the calcined coke exported to Japan. See CX 1307.

[29] Because the price paid by GLC depended on GLC's selling price and its selling costs, the contract required that GLC make all materials related to costs available to the coker.

[30] The costs included (a) all freight and other transportation charges, (b) all handling and storage charges, (c) the cost of any sizing of coke which in GLC's opinion increased the total market value of the coke more than the cost of processing, (d) bona fide selling commissions paid to third parties, and (e) taxes (CX 14).

resale exceeded the price, the coker would refund the excess to GLC. In that event, however, the coker would have the option of suspending deliveries to GLC.[31] The importance to the coker of removing inventory meant that it would be willing to accept a minimum average price of zero.

The coke covered by these agreements was either shipped directly to Japan or moved to GLC's storage facilities, where it was commingled with coke from other sources for subsequent shipment to Japan. If commission rates differed, or if some of the coke in GLC's inventory were purchased at a fixed price, then GLC would have an incentive to act opportunistically in designating the source of a particular shipment. The contracts provided a mechanism for constraining such behavior. If the average net price for a calendar year exceeded the average net price of all "Western Coke" sold by GLC in that year, then GLC would have to repay the excess multiplied by the number of tons delivered under the contract during the year, GLC was responsible for determining the average selling price, but the seller had the right to require an audit, the cost of the audit being borne equally by the two firms.[32]

Other Contracts

Union Oil and Collier entered into two contracts involving construction of an adjacent calciner and coker at two California locations—Oleum and Santa Maria. The agreements (CX 43, CX 66) illustrate nicely some of the points made above. The contracts were similar in a number of respects. Both were for full output of the coker and gave Union Oil the option of suspending, reducing, or discontinuing production of coke. Both were for long periods—the Oleum contract was for ten years[33] and the Santa Maria contract for twelve. However, there were significant differences, which stemmed largely from the availability of inventory storage capacity at the two sites. The Oleum site could store less than six months of coke output, while the Santa Maria site had a two-year capacity.

At Santa Maria, the stockpile was Collier's only protection from supply disruptions. At Oleum, the contract included a very elaborate package that provided Collier with considerably more assurance of a continued supply. It also provided less assurance of removal than did the Santa Maria or GLC contracts.[34] The contract called for a minimum quantity of 1 million tons over ten years—approximately 40 percent of the coker's capacity. In the event that Union's production at the Oleum plant was reduced or discontinued (so that the minimum would not otherwise be obtained), it agreed

---

[31] The two contracts treated this slightly differently.

[32] In both contracts, an independent third party would determine the average selling price if the parties disagreed.

[33] The contract was amended after two years and extended for an additional one-and-a-half years (CX 44).

[34] Collier received less assurance of a continued supply than did the aluminum companies. It also undertook a greater commitment to remove coke than did the aluminum companies.

to make up the deficiency with coke of similar quality from other sources at the contract price.

If inventory at the Oleum coker reached 50,000 tons (three months' output), Union could either offer it for sale (giving Collier the option to take the coke at a price 10 percent below the outside offer) or require Collier to remove the coke. In the latter event, Collier would pay only 50 percent of the contract price. Thus, when there was external evidence of slack demand (inventory accumulation) and Union had confirmed this evidence through its inability to find buyers at prices below the contract price, Union would then share the cost of the demand reduction.

Carbon product producers were typically content to purchase their coke from middlemen. However, in some instances such producers chose to contract directly with a coker. The coker generally had more than one customer for its coke and was capable of carrying a reasonable amount of inventory; it was not purchasing removal services. As a result, the contracts typically gave very little protection to the reliance interest of either the buyer or the seller.

The carbon product contracts were either requirements contracts or for a fixed quantity.[35] The seller was obligated to deliver coke only if it produced. It had the right to determine whether, or how much, to produce. If the seller did not produce sufficient coke, the buyer would be free to meet its needs elsewhere and would have the option of terminating the contract on short notice. The term of the contracts was short—from one to five years. Moreover, in some of the agreements, the buyer had the right to shop for a better price. If the seller did not elect to meet lower price, the contract could be terminated on short notice.[36]

4. PRICE ADJUSTMENT

The parties did not enter into multiyear contracts in order to make bets on the future course of prices. Rather, they entered into these agreements for the reasons developed in Section 3. Having done so, they had to make some decisions regarding the price during the life of the agreement.[37] While they could simply establish a single price or a schedule of future prices that would be in force for the entire period, they also had the option of providing some

[35] Air Reduction accounted for all three of the requirements contracts (CX 23, CX 39, CX 420).

[36] The three Air Reduction contracts fixed price for a period, after which the buyer could search for a lower price. In the 1962 agreement, the initial price was firm for eighteen months, but this dropped to nine months in 1964 and zero months in 1967. In a letter to the commission, a Union Carbide executive noted regarding one of its agreements with Cities Service: "Carbide ascertained it could procure comparable coke at a lower price. As the Carbide contract with Cities Service included a price protection clause, and Cities Service indicated it was unwilling to meet the lower offer made to Carbide, the contract was terminated according to its terms" (8805-4-2-1-4).

[37] This does not mean that price problems have no effect on the structure of the contracts. As we show below, the increased rate of price change post-1973 did influence contract structure.

mechanism for adjusting prices in light of changed circumstances. Nearly 90 percent of the pre-1973 contracts and all of the post-1973 contracts did provide some price flexibility.

Indexing is the most obvious price-adjustment mechanism, but there are others as well. The parties could simply agree to renegotiate price either at fixed dates (for example, quarterly or annually) or at one side's request. A hybrid mechanism involving indexing and negotiation utilizes an index with a maximum-minimum limitation. If the indexed price falls outside the predetermined range, the parties can either continue at the ceiling (or floor) price or renegotiate the agreement. Another way of adjusting to changing market conditions is to allow the parties to solicit outside offers and then permit the other party to match the offer. Commission pricing, by its very nature, automatically links the contract price to external market conditions.

Indexing has the obvious advantage of being easy to implement and beyond the control (usually) of the parties involved. It also has the obvious disadvantage of not tracking changing conditions perfectly. Ceteris paribus, the lower the correlation between an index and the "correct" current price, the less attractive will indexing be. Renegotiation has the advantage of allowing the parties to use accurate, current information in revising the contract. It also, of course, suffers from the fact that reopening the contract can result in strategic behavior, especially if one of the parties is vulnerable to a threat of nonrenewal. Other things being equal, the greater this vulnerability, the less attractive would be the prospect of renegotiating.

Given that price adjustment can be difficult and costly, why bother? What are the benefits to risk-neutral firms? We will suggest three reasons for incorporating a price-adjustment mechanism into a contract; only the last two, we believe, are apposite in the case of coke contracts.

First, adjusting the price to keep it in line with current market prices gives the parties the proper short-run price signals. If the parties have much discretion regarding the short-run quantity of coke, this could be important. However, for most coke, this is not the case. Coke is a by-product for the coking refiner; the buyer—especially Great Lakes Carbon—often bought the coker's entire output. Quantity was determined by the demand for the refiner's lighter distillates, not for coke. Indexing a coke price to the market for this reason would be similar to indexing a home mortgage to the current rental rate so that homeowners could better take into account the opportunity cost of being their own tenants.

Two alternative reasons appear to be more plausible for explaining the usage of price adjustment mechanisms in petroleum coke contracts: reduction of precontract search and postagreement incentives to breach or behave opportunistically.[38] In both these explanations, the success of price adjustment depends on its ability to reduce the variance of outcomes. The reduced

---

[38] This argument is developed in Goldberg (1985).

variance is not, however, valued for itself. Rather, it enables the parties to curtail behavior that is mutually harmful, thereby increasing the value of the agreement to both parties.

A party contemplating entering into a contract has an incentive to increase its expected share of the gains from trade by expending resources to improve its information on the future course of costs and prices. The more each spends to achieve an informational advantage, the smaller the pie. Ceteris paribus, the larger the variance of the outcomes, the more resources would be devoted to this effort. The parties have an incentive to incorporate into the initial agreement a device that would discourage this wasteful searching. By reducing the value of special information, price-adjustment mechanisms can do precisely that.

If, after the firms enter into a long-term agreement, the contract price differs substantially from the market price, then the loser could be reluctant to continue the agreement. In this event, the loser could breach and suffer the legal and reputational consequences. There are, however, a number of less severe alternatives to willing compliance. A buyer could, for example, insist on strict compliance with the quality standards; he could remove coke from inventory at a slower pace than otherwise; or he could read the contract literally—"working to the rules" as often happens in labor disputes or in centrally planned economies. If the probability of such wasteful behavior increases as the divergence between contract and market price widens, rules that narrow the gap—price-adjustment rules—become increasingly attractive.

The Pre-1973 Contracts

None of the pre-1973 contracts was indexed specifically to changes in the aggregate price level.[39] Only five used a broad-based measure of inflation— one utilizing the Wholesale Price Index (WPI) and the other four the WPI for other than farm products and food (and three of these four adjusted prices only on an annual basis).

Over half the pre-1973 GLC contracts utilized a price index, and all except two of these had a maximum-minimum limitation. In all but one, the index was based on the price of the crude oil supplied to the refinery, with the price being adjusted either whenever the posted crude price changed or at monthly or quarterly intervals. Four of these contracts supplemented the crude oil index with an index of wages of oil refinery workers and one also included an adjustment for the WPI nonfarm component.[40] The actual maximum-minimum limitations were deleted by the FTC in most instances,

---

[39] Since changes in costs or in the market price concern changes in nominal values, adjustments for them implicitly involve some adjustment to changes in the overall price level. In this sense, all of the coke contracts that provided some price flexibility contain some mechanism for adjusting, albeit imperfectly, to changes in the overall price level.

[40] The three contracts that adjusted for crude oil and wages weighted the two equally (CX 1, CX 2, CX 6); the contract which indexed for crude, wages, and the WPI component weighted the three .75, .15, and .10, respectively.

TABLE 4.3
Maximum-Minimum Price Limitations for Great Lakes Carbon Contracts, Pre-1973

Seller	Exhibit number	Contract date	Base ($)	Maximum ($)	Minimum ($)
Sunray DX	CX 9	March 1, 1957	—	15	8
CRA	CX 408	January 18, 1957	—	15	8
CRA	CX 409	March 7, 1963	—	15	8
NCRA	CX 410	March 19, 1957	—	10	4
NCRA	CX 411	January 29, 1963	—	10	4
NCRA	CX 412	July 22, 1963	—	10	4
Ucan	8805-4-2-1-6	March 1, 1957	10	15	8
Derby	8805-4-99-1	April 30, 1968	10.50	15	7
LaGloria	CX 34[a]	January 23, 1962	12.00[b]	10.50	7.50
LaGloria	CX 35[a]	February 11, 1964	11.25[c]	18.50	7.50

[a] LaGloria sold to Alcoa. Most of the coke was shipped directly to Great Lakes' calciner at Port Arthur for calcining on Alcoa's account.

[b] The base price of coke shipped directly to Alcoa was $14.75.

[c] The base price of coke shipped directly to Alcoa was $14.00.

and all that remains is shown in Table 4.3. This skimpy evidence suggests that the price could diverge from the base by around 20–50 percent before reaching the ceiling (or floor).

GLC renegotiated rather than indexed at only three cokers prior to 1966. However, from 1966 through 1973, only three of the fourteen contracts included a price index. Of the remainder, two contracts utilized commission pricing (which implicitly indexes to the market price), and two were for one year or less. In the other seven contracts, price adjustment was accomplished by negotiation.

These contracts typically invoked the intentions of the parties to continue the agreement; negotiations were to be undertaken in "good faith," and in the event that negotiations failed, the current price would continue for a period of time—usually six to eighteen months—after which the agreement would terminate.

Prices could be revised even if the contract did not explicitly provide for changes. The record contains numerous examples of price reductions to Great Lakes Carbon (and to others) during the slump in 1962–65. Letters from two of GLC's suppliers give an indication of the nature of the revisions:

> As we explained to you this price increase to the March 19, 1957, contract level was requested and made only after the most careful consideration of all factors involved. As you know, we have now been on the reduced price basis for two years. We have been happy to work with Great Lakes throughout the years even to the extent of granting price relief when requested by your people. (CX 413)
>
> This is to confirm our discussion of June 17 at which time we agreed to abrogate the terms of our contract covering petroleum coke produced at our El Dorado Refinery for six months starting July 1, 1965. This is a contract dated June 27,

1956 as amended January 31, 1957 and October 2, 1959. In order to give you some assistance in your marketing program, we will invoice all shipments of El Dorado coke production between July 1, 1965 and December 31, 1965 at _____ per ton, F.O.B. El Dorado. It is understood that this revised price will apply only to the production during the indicated six months and that the other terms and conditions of the basic contract are unchanged. In the absence of any subsequent agreements, the price will revert to the contract schedule of _____ per ton, effective January 1, 1966. (CX 53)

These nonmandated price reductions were undoubtedly a factor in the increased reliance on renegotiation in the 1966–73 contracts. The favorable experience with voluntary renegotiation indicated that the costs associated with opportunistic behavior when the contract price is renegotiated need not be prohibitively high.[41] Moreover, the voluntary reductions reflected the failure of the price index to track market conditions accurately. That is, the expected costs of renegotiation fell at the same time that the expected benefits of indexing declined.

Most of the non-GLC middleman contracts either were commission contracts or utilized a simple price index. In only three instances did the parties explicitly state that price adjustment would be accomplished by negotiation, and one of these was not quite an arm's-length agreement.[42]

Where aluminum companies constructed new calciners in reliance on supply by a particular coker, the contract price was typically fixed for a substantial period (see Table 4.4). The only instance in which this was not so was the first Humble-Reynolds agreement. When that was revised, however, the parties eliminated the elaborate indexing formula (which covered over two pages in the 1961 agreement) and instead fixed the price for ten years. A similar adjustment was made in the arrangement between Mobil and Union Carbide (rows 6 and 7 of Table 4.4). The parties abandoned monthly indexing and instead agreed on a fixed price for the duration of the contract.

The substantial length of the period over which prices remain fixed in these contracts stands in sharp contrast to what existed in other petroleum coke contracts. The fixed price agreements all date to the period in which GLC was making the transition from indexing to negotiated price adjustment and most likely are response to the same underlying factors —namely the poor correlation between available indexes and market conditions. Why was there a more extreme response in the aluminum contracts?

The aluminum contracts generally entailed greater insulation from current market conditions. Reopening a contract would mean that the parties would haggle over how to share the pie. The more the parties are isolated from

---

[41] Contrast this to the aluminum contracts discussed below.

[42] 8805-4-99-2, 8805-3-4, and CX 41. The last contract was between a coker and a joint venture of which the coker owned 50 percent.

TABLE 4.4
Price Adjustment in Contracts Involving End-User's New Calciners

Coker	Calciner	Contract	Date	Term of contract (in years)	Period until first revision (in years)	Index period	Indexed to
Humble	Reynolds[a]	CX 31	1961	10	1	Annual	Wages in petroleum refining, WPI, all commodities except farm and food, Bunker C fuel oil price
Humble	Reynolds[a]	CX 418	1967	10	10		
Humble	Kaiser[a]	CX 68	1963	8	8		
Shell	Kaiser[a]	CX 38	1964	8	8		
Richfield	Harvey[a]	CX 17	1965	15	5	Every three years	Bunker C fuel oil
Mobil	Union Carbide[b]	CX 404	1960	5	2	Monthly	Calcined coke sold to aluminum industry
Mobil	Union Carbide[b]	CX 405	1963	$3\frac{3}{4}$	$3\frac{3}{4}$		

[a] Aluminum company.
[b] Mobil's contract was with General Carbon, but Union Carbide guaranteed payment (CX 406); Union Carbide also contracted with Marathon (CX 36), but that price clause was deleted from the record.

alternative trading partners, the larger the size of the pie to be shared. The larger the pie, the more resources the parties would devote to pursuing it. That is, the higher reliance interest in the aluminum contracts would result in higher renegotiation costs, making frequent renegotiation relatively less attractive.

Moreover, the "good will" sanction would be a less effective constraint on negotiations for aluminum producers than for GLC. The past track record of GLC enhanced the coker's confidence that it would negotiate price adjustment in good faith, and its continued dealings with a large number of suppliers made maintenance of this good reputation worthwhile. The aluminum companies had neither the track record nor a large incentive to maintain their reputation for fair dealing in this market. Reynolds and Harvey, for example, had no other contracts.

The Post-1973 Contracts

The petroleum coke industry was subjected to two major shocks in 1973. On June 5, the FTC handed down its decision finding Great Lakes Carbon's long-term contracts in violation of the antitrust laws. The remedy required that GLC amend all its existing contracts so that they would extend for a period no longer than three years and all new GLC contracts be for a maximum of three years.[43] The remedy also restricted the length of the contracting period for the eight oil company respondents. The restrictions on contract length did not apply to other buyers or sellers of coke. The other shock was a tremendous increase in volatility in both the crude oil and the aluminum markets. Between 1973 and 1979, green coke prices rose from about $13 to $60, while calcined coke prices rose from about $30 to $120.[44]

Our ability to trace the effect of the post-1973 changes in the structure of petroleum coke contracts is limited by the availability of data. We have twenty-nine Great Lakes contracts,[45] but we have had access to only a handful of contracts involving other buyers. After analyzing the GLC contracts, we will discuss briefly the changes in the contracts involving aluminum companies.

Most of the GLC contracts contained a clause that reflected the restrictions imposed by the Commission's decision. The term was three years, and the parties could not extend the term of the contract prior to six months

---

[43] There were three exceptions: (a) if a new coker or calciner were involved, the maximum contract length was five years; (b) the limitation applied if only GLC took more than 50 percent of the coker's output (which had always been the case for its long-term contracts); (c) it could offer a longer term if it were meeting a competitive offer in good faith (so long as the offer was not from a new entrant).

[44] See Goldberg and Erickson (1982: tables 9 and 10).

[45] Twelve of the contracts were from the Compliance File, 8805-3-3-2; the remainder were made available to one of the authors by Great Lakes' counsel. Some of the contracts were amended to increase prices. The commission's restrictions on renewal prevented the parties from extending the term of the agreement. If these amendments are not counted as "contracts" then the number of contracts falls to 25.

before the date at which the contract would expire.[46] The only contracts that were not for three years were a series of one-year contracts with Continental and a one-year contract with Midland in 1974 (which was succeeded by a three-year agreement). In both cases, GLC's last contract with the refinery prior to the FTC's decision was for only nine months, so the short term of the postdecision contracts at these refineries was not related to the changed circumstances in the petroleum coke market. It is clear, then, that the three-year restriction imposed by the commission was binding.

The three-year duration is misleading, however, since almost all the contracts could be terminated on fairly short notice. About two-thirds of the contracts could be terminated on three to six months' notice if the parties failed to agree on a new price. Only two contracts—both with Mobil—allowed for termination without cause by either party (three months' notice was required).[47]

The salient feature of the post-1973 contracts is, not surprisingly, the focus on the problem of price adjustment. The response to the increased variability of prices was a substantial decrease in the period between price changes. The contracts split approximately evenly between those relying on indexing and those relying on renegotiation. Through the beginning of 1976 the price of crude oil was the basis for indexing.[48] From July 1976 onward, however, if the contract provided for indexing, the only external price utilized was that of calcined coke.

The purpose of indexing in this period of high volatility was very different from its purpose in the previous period. There was no intention to ensure automatic price adjustment for the life of the contract. Rather it functioned as part of the renegotiation process. The index was only expected to be in force for short periods. Thus, half the contracts with prices indexed to crude oil called for renegotiation at a fixed interval of three to six months. The other half did not set a fixed date for renegotiation. Instead, they established a maximum and minimum (about 15 percent above and below the base price.) If the calculated price fell outside this range, one party could request price renegotiation. If the parties failed to agree on a new price, the contract would terminate in three months. Thus, indexing only provided a point of reference for renegotiation. That is, if one party did not accept the calculated price, it could request renegotiation, and, if the other party refused, it could terminate the agreement. If the indexed price is expected to be closer to the

[46] The six-month renewal period was also mandated by the Commission: "It is further ordered, that respondent Great Lakes Carbon Corporation, its successors and assigns, shall not renew or extend any existing contract for the purchase or marketing of an amount in excess of fifty percent (50%) of the estimated annual production of petroleum coke at any refinery more than six (6) months prior to termination of the contract being renewed or extended" (82 F.T.C. 1529, 1672–73).

[47] A 1976 contract with Atlantic Richfield could be terminated after one year with 120 days notice.

[48] Eight contracts utilized indexes; all included the cost of crude oil; one added wages, and another added wages and refinery fuel costs and electricity (crude oil had a weight of 93 percent in this agreement).

market price than is the base price, then indexing would have reduced the rewards of opportunism associated with renegotiating the price.

Nine of the post-1973 GLC contracts were with Texaco—three contracts at three different sites. All nine contacts gave Texaco the right to terminate the agreement if it received a bona fide offer above the contract price; however, GLC could continue the agreement by matching the higher price. This arrangement was adopted to adjust the contract price to rapidly changing market conditions, not to facilitate termination. Rapid adjustment to objectively determined information meant that the parties were less likely to engage in bickering and similar behavior that would reduce the probability of their renewing the contract. The Texaco contracts also utilized one other form of price adjustment that relied on the continuation of the long-term relationship between the two firms—ex post pricing. In 1974 and 1975, when Texaco and GLC could not reach an agreement on price by the contractually determined deadline, they agreed to extend the negotiating period for a stated period. In the interim, they continued to perform with GLC paying at the preexisting price. When agreement was finally reached, the new price was applied retroactively. Thus, two 1974 contracts were effective as of January 1 even though they were not signed until August 26.

In 1973, aluminum producers were performing under minimum quantity, fixed-price contracts. The fixed-price contracts provided the aluminum companies with an unanticipated windfall. Rather than simply accepting the windfall until the contract expired, the aluminum companies had the option of trading off part of the windfall to enhance their future access. Access could, of course, be achieved in other ways. The aluminum company could acquire nearby land for storing inventory, or it could find alternative suppliers. A new coker could be constructed at a convenient location before the existing contract expired. Our discussions with industry sources suggest that, with one notable exception (discussed below), contract prices were renegotiated upward.

The new prices were not, however, necessarily tied to a formal extension of the contract. Kaiser, which had the most coke contracts, did not extend its agreements; rather, it shifted to three-year contracts. Moreover, the new Kaiser contracts included price-adjustment mechanisms similar to those of GLC. Contract price was typically indexed, but prices could be renegotiated if the indexed contract price was out of line. In the GLC agreements, renegotiation was triggered by mechanical rules. The price could be re-negotiated if the indexed price hit the ceiling or floor, or if sufficient time had passed. Kaiser's trigger was an announcement by either party that the current price was unacceptable. In that event, the parties would have a short period (about three months) to renegotiate a price; if they failed, the contract would terminate after another three months.

Kaiser's willingness to accept such a renegotiation arrangement appears surprising given its vulnerability to opportunistic behavior by its suppliers. The increased volatility made tracking of current price more valuable than in the pre-1973 period, but we would have expected the parties to choose a less manipulable rule; for example, price could have been indexed to external prices (such as crude oil or calcined coke) and the parties could have been given the right to solicit outside offers, with their counterpart having the right of first refusal. Kaiser's willingness to go further than this might be explained by two factors. First, Kaiser had become increasingly less vulnerable to the loss of a single coke supplier; it operated six calciners, with the largest accounting for approximately one-fourth its capacity. Moreover, its calcined coke output had grown so that it now substantially exceeded Kaiser's internal needs. Kaiser looked more like a middleman than an aluminum company end user. Second, Kaiser's renegotiation of the fixed price, pre-1973 contracts might be viewed as an indication of its good faith; ceteris paribus, the more trust, the more viable the price renegotiation.

Kaiser's earlier contracts were indexed to crude oil, but most of the more recent ones were based on calcined coke prices. GLC's posted price of calcined coke was first used, but this proved unsatisfactory when GLC maintained the posted price in the early 1980s in the face of a price decline of about 30–40 percent (Fasallo, Tarrillion, and Matson, 1982). Kaiser shifted to a measure based on actual Kaiser transaction prices that, although more subject to manipulation, better tracked the price of green coke.

The one exception regarding renegotiation was Richfield's contract with Harvey (subsequently Martin Marietta). The failure to renegotiate price led to considerable ill will, and the contract was allowed to expire in its fifteenth year. Richfield exercised its option to have the land returned and the calciner removed, although it did permit Marietta to operate the calciner after the agreement expired (until Marietta's new calciner came on line). Marietta was supplied by a new coker built by Champlin Oil; the new calciner, a joint venture with Champlin, was located adjacent to the coker. It is generally believed in the industry that the demolition of the calciner was an unnecessary and costly result of the decision not to renegotiate prices.

5. CONCLUDING REMARKS

The substantial amount of contractual detail we have provided indicates some of the ingenious solutions parties have devised for resolving some apparently intractable problems of coordination across organizational boundaries. We will not provide a full summary of all the features of the contracts. Instead, we will confine attention to a few points deserving special emphasis.

A refiner has to determine how much freedom it is willing to sacrifice in setting its rate of coke output, while a buyer must determine how much responsibility for accepting a given amount of coke it will bear. Since coke is a low-value by-product accounting for less than 3 percent of the value of refined oil, the coker would prefer to decide how much coke it should produce on the basis of conditions in the oil market. Moreover, the less storage capacity available at the refinery, the more the refiner would value a buyer's promise to promptly remove whatever coke the refinery happens to produce.

The full-output, immediate removal contracts that Great Lakes Carbon usually entered into provided the coker with this assurance. Nevertheless, when a coker entered into a contract in which it was to be the sole supplier of a calciner, it would almost invariably give up most of its freedom to determine its output rate in order to provide the buyer with sufficient assurance.

One of the most surprising findings was the frequent use of multipart, or nonlinear, prices to protect the seller's reliance. We must emphasize that considerable effort was necessary to reinterpret the contract language in a manner that would reveal the nonlinear pricing—this was not an easily observable fact that cried out for an explantion. We suspect that our efforts here will put subsequent researchers on guard and will result in the discovery of numerous other nonlinear pricing arrangements that had hitherto gone unnoticed.

Virtually all the GLC contracts that indexed to crude oil prices imposed maximum-minimum limits. However, while the maximum (minimum) was about 40–50 percent above (below) the base price in the low-inflation 1960s, it was only about 15 percent above (below) the base in the high-inflation 1970s. It would seem contrary to intuition that the limits would shrink as the rate of inflation rises. The apparent paradox is resolved by recognizing that the limitations served a completely different function in the two periods. In the former, the index was in force for the life of the contract. The limits came into play only if some major unanticipated change occurred, at which time the parties would then be forced to renegotiate in order to take the new circumstances into account. The limits would be reached only under rather extraordinary circumstances. In the latter case, indexing provided a point of reference for renegotiation. Frequent renegotiation, which kept the contract price in line with current market conditions, could be triggered either by setting fixed dates to renegotiate (for example, at quarterly intervals) or by setting narrow boundaries on an indexed price—boundaries that the parties expected would routinely be reached.

Increased price volatility resulted in contracts that were of shorter duration and easier to terminate. This is, of course, inconsistent with the notion that the parties would enter into long-term contracts to protect themselves from price fluctuations. It appears that the increased price volatility raises the costs of long-term contracts relative to both short-term contracts and integration by ownership.

We have had reasonable success explaining the structure of the petroleum coke contracts without invoking power, anticompetitive behavior, or risk preferences. Instead, we have focused on long-term reliance, short-term coordination, the costs of acquiring information, and other "relational" concepts. While a single case study may not prove anything, it can suggest which research strategies are more likely to prove fruitful. Furthermore, since the economic theory of contracts has heretofore largely ignored the empirical data, case studies of this sort should lead to a reshaping of the theorists' research agenda—a reshaping that would give more weight to the sorts of issues that prove to be important in this market.

C h a p t e r

5

EFFICIENT ADAPTATION IN LONG-TERM CONTRACTS: TAKE-OR-PAY PROVISIONS FOR NATURAL GAS

Scott E. Masten and Keith J. Crocker

To avoid repeated bargaining in transactions supported by durable, transaction-specific investments, parties may decide to specify the terms of future trade in a long-term contract at the outset of the relationship (see, for example, Klein, Crawford, and Alchian, 1978; and Williamson, 1979a). A principal limitation of long-term contracting, however, is its inflexibility in the face of fluctuations in supply and demand: although contingent claims contracts permit adaptation to changing circumstances, contingent performance is costly to stipulate and even more difficult for courts to administer. To mitigate these hazards, parties will therefore wish to choose contract terms that minimize the need for costly adjudication while maintaining incentives for appropriate adaption.

This paper examines the incidence of "take-or-pay" provisions in contracts between natural gas producers and pipelines from this perspective. Take-or-pay clauses require pruchasers to pay for a contractually specified minimum quantity of output, even if delivery is not taken. The existence of such provisions and efforts by pipelines to have them abrogated in the face of

Reprinted with permission from the American Economic Review vol. 75, no. 5 (December 1985). © 1985 by the American Economic Association.

Scott E. Masten is Professor of Business Economics and Public Policy, the University of Michigan; Keith J. Crocker is Professor of Economics, the Pennsylvania State University. This paper was presented at the Third Annual Conference of the Rutgers University Advanced Workshop in Public Utility Economics and Regulation, May 1984. We thank Michael Canes, Maxim Engers, Matt Gelfand, Richard Higgins, Douglas Kinney, Jonathan Skinner, the University of Virginia Microeconomics Workshop, and an anonymous referee for helpful suggestions. Financial support was provided by the Federal Trade Commission. The views presented are our own, not those of the Commission, individual commissioners, or staff.

declining demand during the most recent recession have generated a debate regarding the role such terms play in allocating gas resources. A common perception has been that take-or-pay provisions are an artifact of wellhead price regulation: by assuring a minimum payment, take obligations raise the expected value of a contract to a producer and thereby circumvent the effect of the price ceiling. To the extent that producers of high-cost gas were able to command higher obligations, some pipelines have been induced to purchase and sell more expensive gas to end users while leaving lower-cost supplies with smaller take requirements in the ground. The implication of this view is that take provisions are anomalies that distort market incentives and should therefore be nullified, permitting pipelines to adjust purchases in a more appropriate manner.

The problem with this explanation is that the incidence of take provisions is not limited to regulated gas supplies, but is also a feature of contracts covering unregulated pre-1954 interstate and pre-1978 intrastate gas, as well as of recently deregulated categories of new "high-cost" gas.[1] Moreover, take-or-pay clauses are also encountered in contracts for coal and other unregulated commodities.[2] In view of this, both H. G. Broadman and M. A. Toman, and M. E. Canes and D. A. Norman have suggested that take obligations might be a means of allocating risk between producers and pipelines. High take provisions reduce risk for producers by guaranteeing a minimum return on investments in well capacity. Unfortunately, such arguments do not provide a practical basis upon which to evaluate observed contractual arrangements without knowledge of the relative risk preferences of the parties involved.

This paper offers an interpretation of take-or-pay provisions that relies on neither risk aversion nor the existence of regulatory price ceilings. Instead, we argue that take obligations can be viewed as a mechanism for effecting appropriate incentives for contractual performance, and show that efficient breach considerations define an optimal take percentage as a function of characteristics of the transaction. These incentives are distorted, however, by the existence of regulated price ceilings, causing the adoption of take

---

[1] See Broadman and Toman (1983); and Canes and Norman (1983). Take provisions were also an integral part of producer-pipeline contracts throughout the essentially unregulated period before area pricing was adopted in 1960. The *Phillips* decision in 1954 gave the Federal Power Commission jurisdiction to regulate wellhead prices of gas sold in interstate commerce. The initial regulatory efforts, however, sought to institute cost-based rates on a well-by-well basis. Using this approach, the commission never progressed beyond regulating the parties to the original decision. The result was a prodigious case backlog. According to Paul MacAvoy and Robert Pindyck, "... The Commission itself forecast that it would not finish its 1960 case load until the year 2043" (1975: 13). Area rates, which effectively froze prices at the market levels of 1958–9, were an attempt to lend tractability to the regulatory process.

[2] As Canes and Norman note, E. M. Carney (1978) discusses the use of take-or-pay provisions in coal contracts. Similar arrangements also appear in other contracts as minimum bill provisions.

obligations *in excess* of optimal levels.[3] Whether a policy to reduce "excessive" take provisions to ex post optimal levels can be justified on the basis of regulatory interference depends on the regulatory environment expected to govern the development of future gas reserves.

Section 1 develops these arguments and applies them to contracting in the natural gas industry. Section 2 presents an empirical test of the model employing actual data on producer-pipeline contracts and well characteristics.

1. PERFORMANCE INCENTIVES IN LONG-TERM CONTRACTS

Once a transaction-specific investment has been made, only imperfect market alternatives exist and both the buyer and seller are locked into a bilateral monopoly relationship. To prevent contention over the resulting quasi rents from dissipating too large a portion of the gains from trade, the parties may try to secure a mutually advantageous distribution through a contract, the duration of which will depend in part on the durability of the associated investments. In industries with particularly durable capital, it is not uncommon to observe contractual agreements that extend for ten years or more.[4]

Over such long horizons, the need for adaptation to changing circumstances, and hence the desire for flexible arrangements, may be substantial. But a tradeoff generally exists between the flexibility provided for in a contract and the ease with which it can be implemented: a single contractual stipulation is relatively straightforward for courts to enforce in comparison to multiple contingent claims which require that both the parties and the courts establish the state that has actually transpired. The more provisions stipulated, the greater the scope for both honest misinterpretation and intentional deception, and thus the greater the likelihood of a dispute requiring costly adjudication.

To minimize these costs, the parties will wish to stipulate terms that do not require court verification of exogenous events. Accordingly, contracts usually employ unilateral options rather than contingent clauses to accommodate adaptation.[5] The goal is to design contracts in ways

---

[3] Except where explicitly noted, we will be referring throughout the paper to private optimality in exchange between a buyer and a seller. The social efficiency of any contractual provision depends upon whether private valuations are distorted from social valuations by the existence of externalities or other factors. We show here that the presence of price regulation does not in and of itself justify the abrogation of take-or-pay obligations.

[4] Goldberg and Erickson, for instance, note that in their sample, "Nine of ten contracts... involving new [petroleum] cokers were for a period of at least ten years" (1982: 10). Coal contracts are of similar duration (Carney: 197). Also see below.

[5] The notion of a unilateral option is analogous to the self-selection behavior often observed in theoretical models of bargaining in an environment of asymmetric information (see, for example, Harris and Townsend, 1981).

that reconcile the exercise of such options with joint profit-maximizing behavior.[6]

The adoption of take-or-pay provisions in long-term contracts can be usefully interpreted in this light. Fluctuations in demand or costs may make it unprofitable or even inefficient to carry out the original objectives of a contract. By altering incentives to accept or reject delivery, take provisions can induce buyers to release investments to their alternative uses only when it is efficient to do so.

1.1. Natural Gas Production and Contracting

These considerations bear directly on the organization of production and exchange in the natural gas industry. Most natural gas is purchased by pipelines from independent producers for distribution to customers in regional markets. Like oil production, the extraction of gas requires large, durable, location-specific investments in facilities and equipment. However, unlike the field market for oil, which is characterized by a functioning spot market, gas sales tend to be governed by extended contracts averaging fifteen to twenty years in length. This disparity in contractual structures governing commodities that are so closely related in production technologies may be traced to differences in transmission alternatives. Whereas pipelines represent virtually the only economically feasible form of transportation for gas, oil may be transported by truck or barge as well as by pipeline, thereby reducing the extent to which oil producers are locked into a bilateral relationship.[7]

Uncertainty regarding future market conditions can make it hazardous to commit resources contractually to a particular application, however. For example, in the face of a decline in gas demand, it may become more economic to sell gas to an alternative pipeline (if the decline is regional) or to store it for future use (if the decline is economy-wide). Since uncertainty increases with the distance of the relevant horizon, the need to provide for adaptation is most acute in longer term agreements. The prevalence of take-or-pay clauses in both long-term coal and gas contracts is consistent with this reasoning. Take obligations encourage efficient adaptation by relating the payment schedule in a contract to the alternative

---

[6] That joint profit-maximizing behavior does not always coincide with the private incentives of the parties to an exchange is a familiar proposition:

> ... joined as they are in an idiosyncratic condition of bilateral monopoly, both the buyer and seller are strategically situated to bargain over the disposition of any incremental gain whenever a proposal to adapt is made by the other party. Although both have a long-term interest in effecting adaptations of a joint profit-maximizing kind, each also has an interest in appropriating as much of the gain as he can on each occasion to adapt. Efficient adaptions which would otherwise be made thus result in costly haggling or even go unmentioned, lest the gains be dissipated in costly subgoal pursuit (Williamson, 1979a: 242).

[7] A more complete discussion of oil field markets and how they differ from those of gas is given in McDonald (1971).

values of the resources either in sale to alternative customers or in storage for future use.

Alternative sale values of a product in transaction-specific relationships are limited by the design and location of specialized investments. For natural gas, the most important determinant of that value is the number and proximity of alternative pipelines. The fewer the connections to pipelines, the less likely that a producer will be able to dispose of gas at a price comparable to that in the original contract. In the extreme, the sale of gas to an alternative customer may require the construction of costly new transmission facilities.[8]

Because of this, and the fact that the demand for energy resources often fluctuates on a nationwide basis, the best alternative employment for both coal and gas is often to store it for future use. Since the product can usually be left in the field, storage is generally less costly for the producer than the customer. The resource value of stored gas may be diminished, however, by the proximity of other wells: gas not extracted may be drained away by other producers operating in the same field. To attenuate the problem of competitive extraction and protect landowners from drainage, the primary gas-producing states have instituted well-spacing rules and prorationing of output among the wells in a field.[9] The prorationing formulas generally used assign each producer an interest in the field based on surface ownership and well deliverability. Gas demand is divided among the various producers by the assignment of production allowables based on each producer's interest in the field.

But such intervention, while mitigating the drainage problem, does not eliminate it. The formulae are, at best, imprecise rule-of-thumb estimates of gas location relative to surface ownership. Moreover, a production allowable conveys only the *opportunity*, not the guarantee, to produce a given amount of gas in a specified period of time. An operator who is unwilling or unable to produce his allowable faces the prospect of drainage to those who do.[10] Consequently, most gas production remains governed by the *Rule of Capture*: "Possession of the land... is not necessarily possession of the gas. If an

---

[8] Alternative sale possibilities are sometimes governed by the particulars of the supply contract between a producer and a pipeline. Often, the contract governs only a portion of the well's output, which is sold to the contracting pipeline on a first refusal basis. In other cases, particularly when the field is served by a single pipeline, the entire output of a well is "dedicated" to a particular pipeline for the life of the contract. When gas demand is low, however, pipelines have little incentive to enforce these dedication clauses. Indeed, given the present surplus, many pipelines are attempting to renegotiate their purchase obligations downward and would welcome sale to alternative buyers (see Norman, 1984).

[9] Gas and oil prorationing differ in several significant respects, reflecting the greater importance of extraction rates on the amount of oil that is ultimately recoverable. For a more complete discussion, see Sullivan (1955).

[10] Both Texas and Oklahoma have attempted to ensure that producers are equally able to sell their allowables by requiring pipelines to purchase ratably (according to each producer's interest) from their suppliers in a field. However, other states do not require ratable take (Sullivan: 348), nor does this approach preclude disproportionate purchases by different pipelines.

adjoining, or even distant, owner drills on his own land, and taps your gas, so that it comes into his well and under his control, it is no longer yours, but his."[11]

In general, the desirability of reallocating resources away from their intended use depends critically on their value in alternative applications. In the case of gas, the appropriate take obligation in each instance will depend on the nature of the well and its relation to other wells, pipelines, and markets.

1.2. Take-or-Pay and Breach of Contract

To illustrate these concerns, consider the relationship between a pipeline (or buyer) and producer (or seller) of natural gas, both of whom are assumed to be risk neutral. After gas has been discovered but prior to investing in production and transmission facilities, the parties write a contract specifying a capacity level and the terms under which the product is to be exchanged in subsequent periods. The value of this capacity to the pipeline depends upon such things as weather patterns, economic fluctuations, and the prices of alternate fuels, all of which are uncertain at the time the contract is written and the well drilled. If we let θ represent this uncertainty, and define

$v(\theta)$ = the value of the well to the pipeline, net of transmission costs and gross of payments to the producer; and

y = the payment made by the pipeline to the producer for a contractually specified quantity of gas;

then, once θ is revealed, the pipeline and the producer would receive $v(\theta) - y$ and y, respectively—if the exchange takes place: for low values of θ, and hence of v, the pipeline would wish to breach the contract with the producer. Specifically, the pipeline would wish to discontinue deliveries whenever $v(\theta) < y$.[12] Were this to occur, the pipeline would then earn no net return,[13] and the producer would seek the next highest value of his capacity, $s(\alpha)$, which is a function of well attributes, α.

---

[11] *Westmoreland and Cambria Natural Gas Company* v. *Dewitt*, 130 Pa. St. 235, 18A, 724, 725 (1889).

[12] For analytical tractability, we consider a model in which gas deliveries are discontinued in a discrete fashion; i.e., the purchaser either "takes" the gas at the contract price, or else "pays" the contractually specified percentage of the full obligation and releases all of the gas contracted for to its alternative use. With a few exceptions, the continuous analog to this model in which the buyer may gradually decrease the quantity of gas taken from the producer yields the same qualitative results.

[13] By no net return, we mean zero revenues. Note that a pipeline's willingness to fulfill the terms of a contract may also depend on the opportunity to purchase alternative low-cost gas supplies. In that case, his return in the event of breach would be $\max\{0, \bar{v}\}$ where $\bar{v}$ is his net revenue from the alternative purchases. This possibility does not affect the optimal breach penalty discussed below.

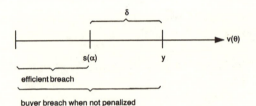

Figure 5.1

Since efficiency requires that gas be used in its highest value, breach would in fact be efficient if $s(\alpha) > v(\theta)$. But for $s(\alpha) < v(\theta) < y$, the pipeline would wish to breach, even though it would be inefficient to do so. Figure 5.1 depicts the ranges of $v(\theta)$ for which the buyer would wish to breach and for which breach would be efficient. In general, there is a tendency, as illustrated in the diagram, for breach to occur too frequently in unsecured agreements.

The pipeline could, however, be induced to reject delivery efficiently by imposing a penalty for nonperformance, $\delta = y - s(\alpha)$. This penalty, known as "expectation damages," is commonly employed by the courts and would normally apply to gas contracts in the absence of a stipulated take obligation.[14] If the courts always and unerringly chose this award, there would be little need to stipulate damages in the contract. But the uncertainty associated with judical rulings encourages costly litigation. By stipulating damages, the parties avoid the costly process of determing the appropriate penalty in the courts, and rejection of deliveries becomes an option that may be unilaterally invoked by the purchaser.

Since the optimal penalty for breach declines as a well is depleted, gas contracts usually express the penalty for refusing delivery as a fraction of reserves or deliverable capacity. In that way, the penalty obtaining in each successive period covered by the contract adjusts automatically to the declining level of remaining reserves. Written as a percentage, γ, of the contractually specified payment, the penalty described above becomes

$$\gamma = 1 - \frac{s(\alpha)}{y} \tag{1}$$

Since y must be at least as great as $s(\alpha)$ to cover the fixed costs of production and induce the producer to enter the contract with the pipeline,

[14] The efficiency of the expectation damage has been demonstrated elsewhere; see, in particular, Barton (1972), and Shavell (1980). Pierce (1983) has noted that, under the Uniform Commercial Code, a pipeline would be liable to a producer for "the difference between the market price and the contract price of the gas available but not taken" (79), precisely the penalty described above. Note that take provisions address only the problem of buyer breach, and as such are adopted only where the principal source of uncertainty is on the demand side of the transaction, a condition true of both coal and gas production. In practice, parties must base their choice of δ on the conditional expectation of $s(\alpha)$ in the event of breach.

the optimal take percentage will be nonnegative. As a rule, $s(\alpha)$ will equal y only when the producer can sell his output to another pipeline that comparably values the gas, which is unlikely unless the producer is already connected to several pipelines. At the other extreme, where gas has no alternative value to the producer, the optimal take percentage is 100 percent, which would be the case, for example, were all of the gas drained away by nearby wells if not extracted by the producer himself.

1.3. The Effects of Regulation

In general, contract terms perform two functions. First, they permit parties to establish a division of the gains from trade that allows both to cover fixed costs; and second, they determine the performance incentives in force during execution of the agreement. When contract terms are freely set, transfers between the parties prevent distributional considerations from interfering with the choice of incentive structures.

Thus far we have seen that take obligations serve the second of these functions, and that buyers and sellers may have an incentive to specify such terms even in the absence of regulation and risk aversion. The presence of price controls, however, may distort those incentives. In the case of natural gas, wellhead price restrictions prohibit certain divisions of gains and create an excess demand for gas production capacity. As a result, producers may engage in nonprice competition for capacity through the choice of contract terms. In that regard, raising take obligations will, ceteris paribus, increase the amount the seller receives when the buyer rejects delivery, thereby raising the expected value of the contract to the seller.[15] By setting a take percentage greater than the optimal level, the parties in effect sacrifice some efficiency in performance incentives in order to achieve a higher level of investment. The take percentage that would be chosen in a regulated transaction becomes

$$\gamma = 1 - \frac{s(\alpha)}{y} + D \tag{2}$$

where $D > 0$ reflects the excess demand induced by the presence of binding price constraints.[16]

---

[15] Because an increase in γ both raises the amount paid in the event of breach and reduces the number of states in which breach occurs, it is possible that beyond some point an increase in γ could, depending on the distribution of θ, reduce the expected value of the contract to the seller. In equilibrium, however, more restrictive price ceilings lead unequivocally to higher take percentages on the margin (see our 1984 working paper).

[16] The additive form of equation (2) follows directly from the model in our earlier paper where we characterize efficient contracts between a producer and a pipeline. The choice of γ in an efficient contract is shown to be a second-best response to the existence of a regulatory price ceiling.

2. EMPIRICAL RESULTS

Here we employ data on natural gas producer-pipeline contracts and associated well attributes to test the relationship characterized by equation (2), which we rewrite for estimation purposes as

$$\gamma_i = 1 - \frac{s(\alpha_i)}{\gamma_i} + \xi D_i \tag{3}$$

where ξ is a coefficient measuring the effects of excess demand, D_i, on take percentages. Prior to estimating this relationship, we describe the data used in the estimation and construct a proxy for D_i.

2.1. Gas Contracts and Well Characteristics

The data used for this study were obtained from several sources. Information regarding price and take obligations was obtained from a survey (EIA-758) conducted by the Energy Information Administration (EIA) in 1982. Through this survey, the EIA obtained detailed data on 659 contracts governing the interstate sale of natural gas from 615 wells located in the lower 48 states. The contracts included in the survey were randomly selected from post-1978 wells which qualified for incentive pricing under Sections 102, 103, 107, and 108 of the Natural Gas Policy Act (NGPA, 1978).[17] Since the data were obtained in disaggregated form, we were able to examine the relationship between take obligations and well characteristics on a well-by-well basis.

Information on the characteristics of the wells governed by these contracts was obtained independently from records at the EIA. Data availability reduced the sample to approximately 300 contracts governing onshore gas priced under NGPA sections 102 ("new" natural gas), 103 ("new" onshore production wells), and 107 ("high cost" gas from deep wells, tight sands, Devonian shales or geopressurized brine).

The variables employed in the estimations are:

γ_i = the contractually specified take percentage for a contract covering gas produced from well i;

$\bar{p}_i$ = the applicable price ceiling (if any) for this gas in October 1981;

p_i^0 = the actual contract price for the gas in October 1981;

D_i = a measure of excess demand for gas from well i;

$DEPTH_i$ = the depth in feet of well i;

$BUYERS_i$ = the number of independent pipelines serving the gas field tapped by well i;

$SELLERS_i$ = the number of independent producers operating in the corresponding field;

---

[17] For a more complete explanation of the survey methodology, see U.S. Dept. of Energy, EIA, (1982a).

$HERF_i$ = the Herfindahl numbers equivalent for the concentration of pipelines in the FERC gas region corresponding to well i,

$$= \left[\sum_i \left(\frac{R_{it}}{T_i} \right)^2 \right]^{-1}$$

where R_{it} is the dedicated reserves of interstate pipeline t in FERC gas area i, T_i is the total amount of reserves dedicated to interstate pipelines in the gas area, and the summation is taken over all of the interstate pipelines with reserves in the gas area.[18]

2.2. Excess Demand

As a proxy for the effect of a price ceiling on the demand for gas, let

$$D_i = p_i^* - \bar{p}_i \quad \text{if} \quad p_i^0 = \bar{p}_i$$
$$= 0 \quad \text{if} \quad p_i^0 < \bar{p}_i$$

where p_i^* is the price that would have obtained for well i in the absence of price constraints, and $\bar{p}_i$ is the applicable price ceiling. Thus, if the constraint on price is not binding, $D_i = 0$, and γ is affected only by $s(\alpha)$. If the ceiling is binding, however, D measures the difference between the unconstrained and ceiling prices.

Since p_i^* cannot be observed for $p_i^* \geq \bar{p}_i$, we employ maximum likelihood techniques to construct an estimate for this variable. Where the observations of the dependent variable are truncated, as is the case here, Tobit is an appropriate estimation procedure.[19] In particular, suppose that $p_i^* = aW_i + e_i$, where W_i is a vector of well characteristics affecting p_i^*, and e_i is normally distributed with zero mean and variance σ^2. Then the observed price in a contract covering well i would be

$$p_i^0 = p_i^*, \quad \text{if} \quad p_i^* < \bar{p}_i$$
$$= \bar{p}_i, \quad \text{if} \quad p_i^* \geq \bar{p}_i$$

The likelihood function of the ith observation is

$$L_i = f(aW_i) \quad \text{if} \quad p_i^0 < \bar{p}_i$$
$$= 1 - F(aW_i) \quad \text{if} \quad p_i^0 = \bar{p}_i$$

[18] In order to construct a pipeline, the Natural Gas Act (1938) requires that the transmission company obtain a certificate of public convenience and necessity from FERC. One requirement is that the transmission company demonstrate "adequacy of reserves," i.e., a sufficient supply of gas to keep the pipeline in operation. As a result, gas reserves are often contractually "dedicated" to individual pipelines. Thus one indicator of the proximity and capacity of pipelines in a geographical region is the number of pipelines that have dedicated reserves in the area and the relative size of those reserves. The information used to compute this measure was obtained from U.S. Dept. of Energy, EIA, *Gas Supplies of Interstate Natural Gas Pipeline Companies–1980*, (1982).

[19] See, for example, Maddala (1983).

TABLE 5.1
Estimation of p^*

Variable	Coefficient	T-Ratio	Mean
CONSTANT	1.0623	10.890	1.000
DEPTH	0.27465×10^{-3}	4.4689[a]	10368
HERF	0.35661	2.7472[a]	4.8687
BUYERS	0.34237	2.6665[a]	4.5709
SELLERS	−0.06202	−2.4156[b]	9.3041

χ^2: 403.333 with 4 degrees of freedom[c]
Number of observations: 296
Proportion of observations for which $p^0 < \bar{p}$: .1757

[a] Indicates significance beyond the .01 level.
[b] Indicates significance beyond the .05 level.
[c] Indicates significance beyond the .001 level.

Estimates for p_i^* are derived by maximizing the likelihood function,

$$\Lambda_i = \prod_1^N L_i$$

with respect to a and σ^2.

Results of the estimation of p_i^* are reported in Table 5.1. The price at which gas is exchanged in an unregulated transaction depends upon the costs of drilling and connecting the well to a pipeline, as well as on the relative bargaining positions of the transactors. In general, one would expect drilling costs, and hence price, to be positively related to the depth of the well. Also, a large number of buyers and sellers in a particular gas field would tend to undermine the respective group's bargaining position, with corresponding effects on price. In addition, to the extent that connection costs are reduced by the proximity of transmission lines, increases in the concentration of pipelines serving an area should also raise the value of the transaction. The availability of alternative pipelines depends both on their number and transmission capabilities. The Herfindahl measure defined above provides a proxy for the proximity of pipeline capacity to a particular well.

As can be seen from Table 5.1, the coefficient on each of the variables has the expected sign and is significant beyond the .05 level.

2.3. Take-or-Pay Percentages

We may now turn to estimating the effects of alternative values and excess demand on take percentages. To derive an estimate of $s(\alpha)$, the alternative value of a well, recall that this value will be the maximum of two alternatives: the resource value, which is the discounted value of the gas if left in the ground to be sold at a later date less losses due to drainage by other wells; and the sale value, which is the net value of the gas from sale to another pipeline.

Letting X_i be a vector of attributes affecting the resource value and Z_i a vector affecting the sale value, the expected value of the gas in an alternative use may be represented as

$$s(\alpha_i) = (\beta_1 X_i + \beta_2 Z_i)q_i$$

where q_i is the capacity of well i, and β_1 and β_2 are coefficient vectors.[20]

Substituting into equation (3) and adding an error term, ε_i, yields

$$\gamma_i = 1 - \beta_1 \frac{X_i}{p_i^0} - \beta_2 \frac{Z_i}{p_i^0} + \xi D_i + \varepsilon_i \qquad (3')$$

The theory of the preceding section predicts that well characteristics, X and Z, which raise (lower) the alternative value of developed capacity should lead to a decrease (increase) in the size of take obligations, and thus implies negative (positive) values of the corresponding coefficients in β_1 and β_2. Meanwhile, we would expect that the more constraining the price ceiling, that is, the greater $p_i^* - \bar{p}_i$, the larger should be γ_i, implying $\xi > 0$.

In determining the resource value of the gas, the larger the number of sellers in a field, the greater the drainage that would occur if a producer were forced to "shut in" his supplies, and hence, the lower this alternative value. The alternative sale value in turn would be expected to increase with the availability of alternative purchasers as measured by the number of buyers in the field and the number of pipelines in the region. Hence, *BUYERS* and *HERF* should both raise the expected alternative value of a well, implying a lower take percentage, and *SELLERS* should reduce $s(\alpha)$ and raise γ.

The ordinary least square (*OLS*) estimates of (3') are presented in Table 5.2. (The prefix S on a variable indicates that it has been divided by price; see equation (3'). Also note that γ is expressed in percentage terms rather than as a fraction.) Each of the coefficients in this regression has the predicted sign and is statistically significant beyond the 10 percent level. The evidence is thus consistent with the hypothesis that take percentages are designed to influence adaptation in long-term contracts and, in particular, are negatively related to the alternative value of gas reserves. Moreover, price ceilings seem to have the predicted effect on take provisions, raising the percentage paid for nondelivery. The findings indicate that, at the mean, a 1 percent decrease in the price ceiling will lead to a 6 percent increase in the take obligation. For the mean values of the independent variables, the regulatory price ceiling increases the predicted take obligations from 79 to 85 percent.

---

[20] It would be possible to estimate $s(\alpha)$ as the maximum of its resource and sale values using switching regression techniques (see Maddala). We have chosen instead to let well characteristics affect the *expected* value of $s(\alpha)$ additively for its relative computational ease.

TABLE 5.2
Estimation of Take Obligations

Variable	Coefficient	T-Ratio	Mean
CONSTANT	82.0822	43.6650	1.000
SSELLERS	0.4833	2.0927[a]	3.9819
SBUYERS	−1.3136	−1.7589[b]	2.1080
SHERF	−0.8646	−1.7929[b]	2.3270
REGCONST(D)	1.85132	3.9956[c]	2.8897

F: 13.24079 with 4 and 294 degrees of freedom[c]
Number of observations: 299
$R^2 = 0.1526$

[a] Indicates significance beyond the .05 level.
[b] Indicates significance beyond the .1 level.
[c] Indicates significance beyond the .001 level.

3. CONCLUSIONS

The results of this paper suggest that the incentive to provide flexibility in long-term contracts is an important consideration in the design of contract terms, and that the nature of those terms can be predicted on the basis of characteristics of the transaction. In particular, we have identified an efficiency motivation for the inclusion of take-or-pay provisions in long-term agreements: take obligations induce purchasers to release output to alternative uses only when it is efficient to do so. These incentives may be distored, however, by the existence of regulated price ceilings. In the case of natural gas, government regulation of wellhead prices appears to have caused nonprice competition in take obligations leading to higher percentages than would prevail in the absence of such regulation.

Empirical tests presented in the paper support the hypotheses of the model. Take percentages are significantly lower for wells associated with small numbers of sellers and large numbers of buyers, each of which raise the alternative value of the gas, a result which seems to apply more generally: E. M. Carney, for example, has noted that, in coal contracts, "If . . . the coal mine has no access to other markets, the seller obviously has more need for a take or pay clause than he would otherwise"; while, on the other hand, "If the seller can get his product to other markets, the take or pay provision is often tempered to reflect that fact" (226).

The evidence presented here refutes the common perception that take-or-pay provisions are solely an artifact of wellhead price regulation and hence serve no useful purpose in the absence of regulation. Providing that externalities do not result in a divergence of private and social valuations,[21]

---

[21] Where a field is exploited by a single producer, the gas production process involves no obvious externalities. With more than one operator, however, gas not sold by one producer may be captured and profitably marketed by other producers in the same field. In that event, the social value of "shut in" gas is apt to exceed the value of that gas to the original

take obligations contained in contracts written in unregulated environments provide for efficient adaption to changing circumstances in long-term contractual relationships. Whether a policy to reduce excessive take provisions to ex post optimal levels should be advocated on the basis of regulatory interference depends upon both the current regulatory status of the gas covered by the contract and the regulatory environment expected to govern the sale of gas discovered in the future. For example, if the gas under consideration has been deregulated and deregulation is expected to continue in the future, the possibility of private bilateral renegotiation obviates the need for intervention. With the removal of the price ceiling, the efficiency gains arising from the reduction of take obligations can be distributed between the buyer and seller through price adjustments, effecting a true Pareto improvement.[22]

Contract terms should also be upheld for categories of gas that currently remain regulated if price regulation is expected to be extended into the future: the precedent established by a reduction of take percentages from the second-best levels stipulated in the contracts could seriously distort capacity investment decisions for future wells. On the other hand, if future discoveries are expected to be sold in an unregulated environment, the efficiency gain from a one-time reduction in take obligations is not offset by adverse precedential effects on future investment. In this event, a prima facie case can be made for intervention to reduce take obligations to levels consistent with efficiency absent regulation. However, these potential benefits must be weighed against the ability of the government to intervene advantageously. Inasmuch as optimal take percentages depend upon characteristics of individual wells, effective intervention would require well-by-well adjustments. Given the government's previous record on well-specific regulation (see fn. 1), the practicality of this solution is in doubt.

producer, leading to the adoption of take provisions in excess of socially optimal levels. To the extent that the drainage problem is exacerbated by the number of sellers in the field, the results in Table 5.2 suggest that take percentages are raised by less than one-half of 1 percent above the socially optimal level for each additional producer in a given field. This implies that, on average, take percentages exceed their socially optimal levels by less than two percentage points due to the externalities associated with competitive extraction from a common pool.

[22] While such renegotiation is certainly not costless, it is likely to be less expensive and more precise than either judicial or legislative intervention.

Chapter 6

CONTRACT DURATION AND RELATIONSHIP-SPECIFIC INVESTMENTS: EMPIRICAL EVIDENCE FROM COAL MARKETS

Paul L. Joskow

This paper seeks to test empirically the importance of relationship-specific investments in determining the duration of coal contracts negotiated between coal suppliers and electric utilities.[1] The analysis makes use of information for a large sample of coal contracts that were in force in 1979. It takes as a starting point Oliver Williamson's 1983 definitions and categorization of relationship-specific investments and applies them to the characteristics of coal market transactions. It also follows Williamson and Benjamin Klein, Robert Crawford, and Armen Alchian (1978) and assumes that risk aversion is not an important factor determining the structure of vertical relationships between coal suppliers and electric utilities.[2]

Coal market transactions are interesting to focus on because there is

Reprinted with permission from the American Economic Review vol. 77, no. 1 (March 1987) © by the American Economic Association.

Paul L. Joskow is Professor of Economics, Massachusetts Institute of Technology. The preliminary version of this paper was written when I was a Fellow at the Center for Advanced Study in the Behavioral Sciences. Leslie Sundt and Rafe Leeman provided valuable research assistance. Keith Crocker, Henry Farber, Oliver Hart, Scott Masten, Jean Tirole, and Oliver Williamson read preliminary versions and made useful suggestions. Three anonymous referees provided helpful suggestions. I benefited from seminar presentations at UCLA, Stanford, and MIT. Support from MIT and the Center for Advanced Study in the Behavioral Sciences is gratefully acknowledged. The views expressed here and any remaining errors are my sole responsibility.

[1] Electric utilities account for over 80 percent of domestic coal consumption.

[2] Other empirical work in this tradition includes Monteverde and Teece (1982) and Masten (1984), which focus on vertical integration: Crocker and Masten (1986), Mulherin (1986),

considerable variation in the duration and structure of vertical relationships between buyers and sellers. I observe spot market transactions, vertical integration, and a wide variety of longer-term contractual relationships with durations ranging from one year to fifty years.[3] My related work (1985) suggests that asset-specificity considerations may be an important factor affecting the structure of vertical relationships in coal markets. The empirical results reported below provide strong support for the hypothesis that buyers and sellers make longer ex ante commitments to the terms of future trade and rely less on repeated negotiations over time, when relationship-specific investments are more important.

1. CONTRACT DURATION AND TRANSACTION-SPECIFIC INVESTMENTS

The reliance on relationship-specific investments to support cost-minimizing exchange is frequently advanced as an important factor explaining why we observe the use of long-term contracts that establish the terms and conditions of repeated transactions between two parties ex ante.[4] According to transactions cost theory,[5] when exchange involves significant investments in relationship-specific capital, an exchange relationship that relies on repeated bargaining is unattractive. Once the investments are sunk in anticipation of performance, "hold-up" or "opportunism" incentives are created ex post, which, if mechanisms cannot be designed to mitigate the parties' ability to act on these incentives, could make a socially cost-minimizing transaction privately unattractive at the contract execution stage.[6] A long-term contract that specifies the terms and conditions for some set of future transactions ex ante provides a vehicle for guarding against *ex post* performance problems.[7]

A coal contract generally specifies in advance a method for determining

and Goldberg and Erickson (1982), which focus on long-term contracts; and my paper (1985), which examines both vertical integration and long-term contracts.

[3] About 15 percent of electric utility coal consumption is accounted for by transactions with integrated suppliers, 15 percent is accounted for by spot market purchases, and about 70 percent is accounted for by contracts with durations of one to fifty years. See my paper (1985: 50–54).

[4] Williamson (1979a, 1983), Klein et al., Oliver Hart and Bengt Holmstrom (1986: 1–2; 86–101). Other reasons for the use of long-term contracts have also been suggested. These include information lags, income effects and risk aversion, and improved monitoring of performance.

[5] I use the term "transactions cost theory" to refer generally to the work of Williamson (1979a, 1983, 1985) and Klein et al.

[6] As Klein et al. discuss, the sunk investments create a stream of quasi rents that gives one party or the other (or both) some ex post bargaining power.

The presence of these contracting hazards and imperfections in the ability of the transacting parties to protect against them does not mean that a deal will not be made. It simply means that the costs of making the transactions—the cost of the coal in this paper—will be higher than it would be if these hazards could be fully mitigated. Both parties have an interest in trying to structure the relationship so that a cost-minimizing deal can be struck.

[7] As discussed in my earlier paper (1985), reputational considerations may provide a natural market constraint on "bad behavior" ex post. Reputational constraints reduce the need to write inflexible long-term contracts to support cost-minimizing exchange in the presence of asset

(*continued*)

the price that the buyer is obligated to pay for each delivery (generally a formula for determining prices for deliveries at each point in time,[8] quantities that the seller is obligated to deliver and the buyer is obligated to purchase at each point in time (usually monthly),[9] the quality of the coal (Btu, sulfur, ash, and chemical composition), the source of the coal, and the period of time over which the contractual provisions are to govern the terms and conditions of trade.[10] The primary readily quantifiable characteristics of coal contracts that appear to vary widely from contract to contract are the quantity and characteristics of the coal contracted for and the length of time that the parties agree ex ante to commit themselves to the terms and conditions specified in the contract. It is this length of time to which the parties agree ex ante to abide by the terms of a contract that I refer to as the "duration" of the contract.[11]

My hypothesis is that the more important are relationship-specific investments, the longer will be the period of time (or number of discrete transactions) over which the parties will establish the terms of trade ex ante by contract. I therefore expect to observe that the variation in the agreed upon duration of contractual commitments is directly related to variations in the importance of relationship-specific investments.[12]

2. ASSET SPECIFICITY AND THE CONTRACTUAL DURATION OF COAL SUPPLY RELATIONSHIPS

Williamson (1983: 526) identifies four distinct types of transaction-specific investments, three of which appear to be relevant to different types of

specificity. Reputational constraints are likely to be imperfect in coal markets, however. At the other extreme, vertical integration may be chosen to deal with ex post performance problems if satisfactory contractual solutions cannot be found.

[8] See my earlier paper (1986).

[9] The typical contract specifies a monthly and annual delivery schedule subject to minimum and maximum production and take obligations. The allowed variations from the contracted quantities in actual contracts that I have reviewed are fairly small.

[10] There are many other provisions as well, including arbitration provisions, force majeur provisions, resale provisions, etc. These provisions are fairly standard in long-term coal contracts, however.

[11] The actual duration of a contract could be longer or shorter than this. Buyers and sellers frequently voluntarily negotiate an extension of an existing contract. Contracts may also be broken through breach or mutual agreement. As far as I can tell from the data that I have reviewed, however, coal contracts are rarely terminated prematurely. See my paper (1986: 2).

[12] To the extent that there are trade-offs between contract duration and the incidence and structure of other contractual "protective" provisions, such as the method for determining price adjustment and quantities, these other provisions should be included in the analysis as well. As indicated above, however, there appears to be relatively little variation in these provisions in my data base, especially relative to the very large variation in contract duration. I therefore feel that it is safe to assume for purposes of this analysis that we have a sample of contracts that essentially holds these other provisions constant. In any event, we can measure the utilization of these other provisions only for a small fraction of the contracts in the data base and therefore cannot examine such trade-offs directly. Note that the coal market is not subject to the kinds of price regulation discussed in Masten and Crocker and Crocker and Masten regarding natural gas contracts.

coal supply relationships. The three types of relevance to coal market transactions are:[13]

(a) Site Specificity: The buyer and seller are in a "cheek-by-jowl" relationship with one another, reflecting ex ante decisions to minimize inventory and transportation expenses. Once sited, the assets in question are highly immobile.

(b) Physical Asset Specificity: When one or both parties to the transaction make investments in equipment and machinery that involve design characteristics specific to the transaction and which have lower values in alternative uses.

(c) Dedicated Assets: General investment by a supplier that would not otherwise be made but for the prospect of selling a significant amount of product to a particular customer. If the contract is terminated prematurely, it would leave the supplier with significant excess capacity. Although Williamson does not discuss it, I think that there is probably a "buyer"-side analogy to the dedicated asset story as well. A buyer that relies on a single supplier for a large volume of an input *may* find it difficult and costly to quickly replace these supplies if they are terminated suddenly and effectively withdrawn from the market and, as a result, a large unanticipated demand is suddenly thrown on the market.

As discussed in more detail in the appendix, I have put together a data base that includes information for nearly 300 contracts between electric utilities and coal suppliers that were in force in 1979. The data base includes information of various kinds regarding the characteristics of the individual coal contracts, the suppliers, the buyers, and the quality and quantity of the coal contracted for. The strategy was to use the information about the individual contracts in the data base and to attempt to measure, at least ordinally, differences in the importance of transaction-specific investments of one or more of the types identified by Williamson for each contract.

Williamson's notion of "site specificity" is the easiest to capture explicitly for coal supply relationships. For most electric generating plants, coal is purchased in one of three major coal-producing regions and then transported by rail, barge, and/or truck (often at least two of these transport modes are involved) to the power plant where it is burned. However, there are a relatively small number of plants that have been sited next to specific mines in anticipation of taking all or most of their requirements from that mine. These "mine-mouth" plants are generally developed simultaneously with the mines themselves. This appears to be a classic case of the cheek-by-jowl relationship that Williamson has in mind when he discusses site specificity.[14] The potential for ex post opportunism problems arising if the parties

---

[13] The fourth is what Williamson calls "human asset specificity" (1983: 526). Jean Tirole has suggested to me that Williamson's four types of relationship- or transaction-, specific investment are simply different instances of the same phenomenon. I believe that this is correct. However, I find the distinctions to be quite useful for empirical applications.

[14] This is discussed in much more detail in my 1985 paper.

were to rely on repeated bargaining appears to be especially great in this case.[15] I therefore expect that contracts for supplies for mine-mouth plants will be much longer than the average contract involving supplies to other types of plants, other things equal.[16]

Let us turn next to physical asset specificity. When coal-burning plants are built, they are designed to burn a specific type of coal (see my 1985 paper; Richard Schmalensee and myself, 1986; my paper with Schmalensee, 1985). By "type" of coal, I mean coal with a specific Btu, sulfur, moisture, and chemical content. The type of coal that a generating unit is designed to burn affects its construction cost and its design thermal efficiency. Deviations from expected coal quality can lead to a deterioration in performance or require costly retrofit investments. Thus, when a plant is designed, the operator becomes "locked in" to a particular type of coal.[17]

The fact that a plant is locked in to a particular type of coal does not necessarily imply that the buyer is locked in to a specific supplier, however. Whether or not the plant design/coal characteristic lock in also leads to a lock in with the current supplier depends on other characteristics of the transaction. In particular, it is likely that the relationship between this type of asset-specificity and ex post hold up or opportunism problems is related to inter- and intraregional variations in coal quality, least cost supply technology, and transportation alternatives.[18]

The characteristics of coal produced in the United States vary systematically among the three major coal-producing regions. The eastern coal-producing districts produce high-Btu coal of reasonably uniform quality. The midwestern coal-producing districts produce lower Btu coal that generally has a very high sulfur content. Coal quality is also more variable than that in the East. Finally, the western coal-producing districts generally produce coal with a much lower Btu content and a very low sulfur

[15] Williamson (1983) states that common ownership is the predominant response to site specificity. My work with coal supply arrangements indicates that common ownership (vertical integration) is much more likely to emerge for mine-mouth plants than other types of plants, but that contracts are also used to govern exchange for about half of the mine-mouth plants constructed since 1960. We would probably see more vertical integration for mine-mouth plants if state and federal regulation of electric utilities did not discourage it. I have argued elsewhere (1985) that to the extent that electric utility regulation biases coal supply arrangements at all, it is probably to make short-term purchases more desirable than they might otherwise be. While utilities might also like to integrate backwards into coal production to shift profits from a regulated to an unregulated activity, the regulatory process has discouraged this.

[16] I have included two plants in this category that are not technically mine-mouth plants but have economic characteristics that are identical to those of mine-mouth plants. For example, if a mine and a plant are connected by a transportation facility (a slurry pipeline or a rail line) built and owned by the supplier or buyer specifically to transport coal from a specific mine to a specific plant, the associated coal contract was grouped with the mine-mouth plants.

[17] Exactly how locked in is a variable of choice, however.

[18] Transportation costs are on average a large fraction of delivered costs and lining up efficient transportation arrangements for large quantities of coal can be a time-consuming process.

content. The quality of the coal varies quite widely throughout the western region.[19]

In addition to variations in coal quality among the regions, there are also systematic variations in the least-cost technology for producing coal and in the transportation alternatives available. In the East, relatively small underground mines are economical and the supply of eastern coal can be expanded fairly quickly. Relatively abundant transportation alternatives, combined with relatively short average transport distances, mean that transportation is not likely to be a significant barrier to a buyer's obtaining alternative supplies. In the West, large surface mines that can be most economically expanded in large "lumps" are the least-cost production technology. Transportation alternatives are poor, the average transport distance quite long, large unit train shipments are the most economical transport method,[20] and utilities often must rely on one or two railroads to move the coal. The situation in the Midwest lies somewhere between these two extremes.[21]

There are also systematic differences in the relative and absolute importance of spot markets in the three supply regions.[22] On average, from 1974 through 1982 spot market transactions accounted for roughly 15 percent of total domestic coal purchases by electric utilities. In 1982, spot market sales accounted for about 10 percent of coal supplies or about 60 million tons. However, in the western region, less than 2 percent of the coal delivered to electric utilities was purchased on the spot market, or less than 5 million tons.[23] The spot market is more active in the Midwest, accounting for about 8 percent of deliveries in 1982 or about 10 million tons per year. The spot market is most active in the East where about 18 percent of deliveries went through the spot market in 1982 or about 45 million tons.[24]

These considerations imply the following: Coal suppliers are likely to be less able to exploit the lock-in effect associated with boilers designed to burn

---

[19] The midwestern region is sometimes broken up into two subregions (eastern and western interior) in discussions of coal supply. The western region is sometimes broken up into three or more subregions. Texas, where lignite coal is produced, is often considered a separate producing region. My data base has no contracts for Texas coal and I do not discuss that area here.

[20] Unit train cars are often owned or leased by the utility rather than by the railroad.

[21] See Zimmerman (1981: 17–36).

[22] Spot market sales also vary from year to year. Spot market transactions tend to be higher when coal miner strikes are anticipated as utilities seek to build up stockpiles or after coal mining strikes are over and stockpiles are replenished. The volume of spot market transactions also varies in response to unanticipated changes in coal supply and demand.

[23] The aggregate volume of spot market transactions for western coal is quite small compared to the annual quantity of western coal contracted for in a typical contract. The contracts for western coal in my data base have a mean quantity of about 1.8 million tons per year and a maximum quantity of over 8 million tons per year.

[24] I believe that the wide variation in the importance of the spot market in different regions is largely related to the same economic considerations that lead me to conclude that the importance of asset specificity also varies from region to region.

coal with specific characteristics in the East than in the West.[25] Thus the protection of a long-term contract is likely to be more desirable from the buyers' (and the sellers'—see below) perspective, for transactions involving western coal relative to transactions involving eastern coal, with midwestern coal falling somewhere in between.

Finally, let us turn to "dedicated asset" considerations. The available information in the data base does not make it possible for us to know specifically whether the supplier made general investments that would not have been made but for the prospect of selling a *significant amount of product* to a particular customer and if the contract is terminated prematurely it would leave the supplier with excess capacity (see Williamson, 1983: 526).[26] Williamson's conceptualization of dedicated assets implies that the importance of this factor in structuring coal supply relationships should vary with the quantity of coal that is initially contracted for, other things equal. The larger the annual quantity of coal that is contracted for, the more difficult it is likely to be for the seller to quickly dispose of unanticipated supplies (if the buyer breaches) at a compensatory price, and the more difficult will it be for a buyer to replace supplies at a comparable price if the seller withdraws them from the market. Thus, I expect that the greater the annual quantity of coal contracted for the longer will be the specified duration of the contract.

Because of systematic variations in the optimal scale and capital intensity of coal production across regions, dedicated asset considerations are also likely to be more important for western coal than for eastern coal. The greater hererogeneity in coal supplies and the difficulties of obtaining suitable transportation for it in the West suggest that dedicated asset problems are likely to be more severe in the western than the eastern region. The very thin spot market in the western region should be especially problematical for both sellers and buyers when large contractual commitments are breached because of the heterogeneity of the coal, the characteristics of least-cost production and the limited transportation alternatives. This all implies again that contracts for western coal should have longer contractual durations than contracts for eastern coal.

To summarize, if variations in the importance of relationship-specific investments do in fact lead to variations in the extent to which the parties precommit to the terms of future trade ex ante, I expect to find that the duration of contractual relationships specified at the contract execution stage

[25] Generating plants located along the eastern seaboard that use coal essentially always use eastern coal. These plants are also more likely to have units that have multifuel capabilities than plants located elsewhere and can switch back and forth between coal and oil or gas (often with some performance penalty). See my paper with Frederick Mishkin (1977). Purchasers of eastern coal with multifuel capabilities will be less susceptible to opportunism problems when coal and oil prices are close together.

[26] Indeed, as a practical matter, it is unclear to me how one could ever go about determining this directly given the data that are likely to be available for analysis. The coal contracts that I have reviewed to sometimes have language that appears to recognize the dedicated asset notion directly, but the absence of an explicit statement cannot be assumed to imply that dedicated asset considerations are not important.

will vary systematically with three primary observable characteristics of coal supply transactions. First, whether the plant taking the coal is a mine-mouth plant or not. I expect to observe longer-term contracts negotiated for mine-mouth plants. Second, with the region of the country in which the coal is produced. I expect the western region to have the longest contracts and the eastern region the shortest with the midwestern region having contracts with prespecified durations that lie in between. Third, with the annual quantity of coal contracted for, I expect that coal supply arrangements involving large annual quantity commitments will be supported by longer contracts than supply arrangements involving smaller quantities of coal.

3. MODEL SPECIFICATION AND ESTIMATION

I am primarily interested in estimating a set of simple relationships between the duration of contractual commitments (*DURATION*) specified by the parties at the contract execution stage and (*a*) the *annual* quantity (*QUANTITY*)[27] of coal contracted for, (*b*) a dummy variable (*MINE-MOUTH*) that takes on a value of 1 for a mine-mouth plant and zero otherwise, and (*c*) dummy variables that indicate the coal supply region in which the supplier is located (*MIDWEST* and *WEST*, so that regional effects are measured relative to contracts for eastern coal). Additional variables are considered in the next section.

The data base that I use includes information for approximately 300 coal supply contracts between domestic coal suppliers and investor-owned electric utilities. The contracts included in the data base were negotiated in various years up through 1979 and were in force at least for part of 1979. The data are discussed in more detail in the appendix. Information on all variables of primary interest for this study is available for 277 of the contracts in the data base. I present estimates using both the full 277 observation sample as well as a subsample consisting of 169 contracts that involve deliveries dedicated to a single power plant.[28] Table 6.1 provides the mean, standard deviation, minimum and maximum values, and a brief description for all of the variables used in this section and subsequent sections for both the primary sample and the single-plant subsample. Table 6.2 is a correlation matrix for all of the variables in the two samples with the correlations for the 277 observation sample below the diagonal and those for the 169 observation subsample above the diagonal.

[27] Quantities are expressed in terms of the thermal (Btu) content of the coal. The basic results are not affected when quantities are expressed in tons. For the extensions reported in the next section, normalizing quantities for Btu content makes it possible to more accurately examine the effects, if any, of contract quantities relative to total plant and untility utilization of coal.

[28] Several people suggested to me that relationship specific investment effects are most likely to be revealed for contracts that dedicate all supplies to a single plant. I also focus on this subsample to obtain the data necessary to explore issues discussed in the next section.

TABLE 6.1
Sample Statistics

Variable	Observations	Description	Mean	Minimum	Maximum	Standard Deviation
DURATION	277	Contract duration (years)	12.75	1.00	50	10.43
	169		14.18	1.00	43	10.77
QUANTITY	277	Annual contract quantity (trillion Btu's)	20.45	0.3696	183.00	24.62
	169		22.83	0.3696	183.00	27.05
PLANT PROPORTION	169	Fraction of total plant use from contract	0.44	0.03	1.00	0.35
UTILITY PROPORTION	169	Fraction of total utility coal use from contract	0.19	0.003	1.00	0.23
PLANT QUANTITY	169	Plant utilization of coal (trillion Btu's)	51.47	2.95	172.42	41.69
UTILITY QUANTITY	169	Utility utilization of coal (trillion Btu's)	221.54	2.95	919.80	270.56
PLANT/UTILITY	169	Plant use as fraction of total utility use	0.455	0.007	1.00	0.323
MINE-MOUTH	277	Mine-mouth plant dummy variable		(D = 1; 14 Observations)		
	169			(D = 1; 14 Observations)		
WEST	277	Western region supply dummy		(D = 1; 54 Observations)		
	169			(D = 1; 44 Observations)		
MIDWEST	277	Midwestern region supply dummy		(D = 1; 68 Observations)		
	169			(D = 1; 47 Observations)		
DATE-71	277	Contracts signed 1971–3; dummy		(D = 1; 43 Observations)		
	169			(D = 1; 29 Observations)		
DATE-74	277	Contracts signed 1974–7; dummy		(D = 1; 116 Observations)		
	169			(D = 1; 71 Observations)		
DATE-78	277	Contracts signed 1978–9; dummy		(D = 1; 71 Observations)		
	169			(D = 1; 38 Observations)		
YEAR	277	Year contract executed	1974	1955	1979	4.49
	169		1974	1955	1979	4.64

[a] Data sources and variable definitions can be found in the appendix.
[b] The 169 observation subsample includes contracts dedicated to a single plant.

TABLE 6.2
Correlation Matrix

						169 Observation Sample						
277 Observation Sample	DURATION	QUANTITY	LOG-QUANTITY	MINE-MOUTH	MIDWEST	WEST	YEAR	PLANT PROP.	UTILITY PROP.	PLANT/UTILITY	PLANT QUANTITY	UTILITY QUANTITY
DURATION	—	0.60	0.68	0.64	0.004	0.51	−0.57	0.58	0.43	0.05	0.29	0.02
QUANTITY	0.60	—	0.78	0.42	−0.04	0.28	−0.35	0.48	0.43	0.05	0.41	0.11
LOG-QUANTITY	0.64	0.80	—	0.30	0.02	0.32	−0.44	0.57	0.42	0.02	0.45	0.17
MINE-MOUTH	0.54	0.38	0.27	—	−0.09	0.41	−0.37	0.46	0.41	0.05	0.10	−0.05
MIDWEST	0.14	0.08	0.11	−0.06	—	−0.37	−0.20	0.04	−0.04	−0.06	−0.03	−0.15
WEST	0.41	0.25	0.26	0.39	−0.28	—	−0.10	0.46	0.40	0.16	−0.06	0.16
YEAR	−0.63	−0.39	−0.44	−0.31	−0.27	−0.08	—	−0.28	−0.11	0.13	−0.16	−0.11
PLANT PROP.	—	—	—	—	—	—	—	—	0.61	−0.11	−0.24	−0.14
UTILITY PROP.	—	—	—	—	—	—	—	—	—	0.66	−0.08	−0.36
PLANT/UTILITY	—	—	—	—	—	—	—	—	—	—	0.15	−0.57
PLANT QUANTITY	—	—	—	—	—	—	—	—	—	—	—	0.34
UTILITY QUANTITY	—	—	—	—	—	—	—	—	—	—	—	—

Note: Figures below the diagonal are for the 277 observation sample, those above the diagonal are for the 169 observation subsample.

I work first with three simple specifications of the contract duration equation:

$$DURATION_i = a_0 + b_1 QUANTITY_i$$
$$+ b_2 QUANTITY_i^2 + b_3 MINE\text{-}MOUTH_i$$
$$+ b_4 MIDWEST_i + b_5 WEST_i + u_i \tag{1}$$

$$DURATION_i = a_0 + b_1 LOG\text{-}QUANTITY_i$$
$$+ b_3 MINE\text{-}MOUTH_i + b_4 MIDWEST_i$$
$$+ b_5 WEST_i + u_i \tag{2}$$

$$\log(DURATION_i) = a_0 + b_1 LOG\text{-}QUANTITY_i$$
$$+ b_3 MINE\text{-}MOUTH_i + b_4 MIDWEST_i$$
$$+ b_5 WEST_i + \log(u_i) \tag{3}$$

where i indexes contracts and u_i is an error term whose characteristics will be discussed further below.

I have allowed $(QUANTITY)$ to enter these relationships nonlinearly by introducing a quandratic in quantity $(QUANTITY\text{-}SQUARED)$ in (1) and using the natural logarithm of quantity $(LOG\text{-}QUANTITY)$ in equations (2) and (3). Since power plants have useful lives of roughly forty years and the costs of breach are likely to decline over time as plants and mines age, I expect that the impact of quantity on contractual duration will diminish as quantity increases. The following pattern of coefficient estimates for the three equations is implied by the hypothesized relationship between asset specificity and contract duration:

1. All of the b_i's should be positive, except for b_2, which could be positive, negative, or zero (no nonlinearity), although I expect that it will be negative.
2. b_4 should be smaller than b_5.

Equations (1), (2), and (3) are estimated in three different ways. First, I present ordinary least squares (OLS) estimates of each equation for both samples. Next, I present OLS estimates that introduce dummy variables which indicate the date that the contracts were executed. Finally, I present maximum likelihood estimates based on the assumption that we have a truncated sample drawn from a population with either a normal or a log-normal density function. I discuss the rationale and results for each estimation approach and also present OLS results for contracts with suppliers in each of the three regions.

3.1. OLS Estimates

If we assume that the u_i in (1), (2), and (3) are independently distributed and drawn from a normal distribution with mean zero, then OLS will yield an unbiased estimator of the coefficients of interest. I proceed first with this assumption and provide estimates for alternative assumptions about the error structure below. The OLS results are presented in Table 6.3. The first three columns are estimates for the three equations using the 277 observation sample. Columns 4, 5, and 6 contain estimates for the 169 observation subsample.

The OLS estimates are, in all cases, consistent with the hypothesized relationship between asset specificity and contract duration. The effects of annual contract quantity, region, and mine-mouth plants have the predicted signs and are estimated quite precisely. A mine-mouth plant is predicted to have a contract that is about 16 years longer than those of other plants. Contracts with eastern producers are 3 to 5 years shorter than those for western and midwestern producers. Contracts with western producers are 2 to 3 years longer than those with midwestern producers. The difference in duration between the *WEST* and the *MIDWEST* is generally not significant at the 5 percent level for the 277 observation sample, but is significant for the single-plant subsample. An increase in annual contract quantity of 22 trillion Btu's (roughly 1 million tons) yields about a 13-year increase in contract duration. As a general matter, the estimates are more precise for the sample of contracts dedicated to a single plant.

3.2. OLS Estimates with Contract Date Dummies

The desirable properties of the OLS estimates depend on the strong assumptions made about the error structure. Since the contracts in the data base were signed at many different times, it is natural to consider the possibility that contracting practices changed over time. Not only might the duration of a typical contract have changed over time, but such changes may have been correlated with changes in contract quantities, supply location, and the development of mine-mouth plants over time. Failing to include variables indicating contract dates could then lead to a correlation between the independent variables and the error term. The OLS estimates would then be biased. To check to see if the estimates are sensitive to the presence of a left-out variable reflecting the contracting date, in Table 6.4 I report estimates of equations (1), (2), and (3) that have contract date dummies included. These contract date dummy variables are *DATE*-71, which is equal to 1 for all contracts signed between 1971 and 1973 inclusive, *DATE*-74, which equals 1 for contracts signed between 1974 and 1977, and *DATE*-78, which equals 1 for contracts signed in 1978 and 1979. Since a separate variable for contracts signed prior to 1971 is not included, the coefficient estimates are all relative to pre-1971 contracts (i.e., the constant

TABLE 6.3
Contract Duration[a]

Independent Variables	277 Sample			169 Sample					2SLS Estimate Duration
	DURATION (1)	DURATION (2)	LOG-DURATION (3)	DURATION (4)	DURATION (5)	LOG-DURATION (6)	DURATION (7)	DURATION (8)	Duration (9)
QUANTITY	0.4289 (0.0373)	—	—	0.4091 (0.0040)	—	—	—	—	—
QUANTITY-SQUARED	-0.0024 (0.00030)	—	—	-0.0020 (0.00003)	—	—	—	—	—
LOG-QUANTITY	—	4.4206 (0.3742)	0.5057 (0.0425)	—	4.2080 (0.4069)	0.4942 (0.0453)	4.2022 (0.4617)	4.2057 (0.4084)	5.1066 (0.812)
MINE-MOUTH	16.3300 (2.0496)	16.4317 (2.0045)	0.5104 (0.2279)	15.9583 (1.9106)	16.2300 (1.8421)	0.4616 (0.2050)	16.3432 (1.9426)	16.2284 (1.8477)	15.4391 (1.968)
MIDWEST	3.4267 (0.9682)	3.8795 (0.9821)	0.5154 (0.1116)	2.7832 (1.0928)	2.7843 (1.1032)	0.5785 (0.1228)	2.7317 (1.1295)	2.7848 (1.1065)	2.4268 (1.153)
WEST	5.3550 (1.357)	5.2033 (1.1641)	0.6142 (0.1323)	5.9856 (1.2346)	5.6108 (1.2586)	0.6844 (0.1401)	5.6456 (1.3406)	5.6391 (1.2751)	4.8916 (1.394)
PLANT PROPORTION	—	—	—	—	—	—	0.9729 (1.9806)	—	—
UTILITY PROPORTION	—	—	—	—	—	—	-2.0570 (2.5832)	—	—
PLANT/ UTILITY	—	—	—	—	—	—	—	-0.2246 (1.4265)	—
Constant	3.6770 (0.6586)	-0.7902 (0.9579)	0.6014 (0.1089)	3.9334 (0.8109)	0.0155 (1.0917)	0.6242 (0.1215)	-0.0146 (1.0978)	0.1157 (1.2665)	-1.8922 (1.852)
Corrected R^2	0.61	0.60	0.51	0.71	0.70	0.61	0.70	0.70	
Observations	277	277	277	169	169	169	169	169	169

[a] OLS estimates. Standard errors of coefficient estimates are shown in parentheses.

TABLE 6.4
Contract Duration[a]

Independent Variables	DURATION (1)	DURATION (2)	LOG-DURATION (3)	DURATION (4)	DURATION (5)	LOG-DURATION (6)	DURATION (7)	DURATION (8)
QUANTITY	0.3120 (0.03547)	—	—	0.3355 (0.0406)	—	—	—	—
QUANTITY-SQUARED	-0.0018 (0.00027)	—	—	-0.0018 (0.00029)	—	—	—	—
LOG-QUANTITY	—	3.0482 (0.3655)	0.3245 (0.0380)	—	3.3485 (0.4330)	0.3631 (0.0446)	3.2847 (0.4923)	3.3461 (0.4344)
MINE-MOUTH	13.9437 (1.8482)	13.6701 (1.8260)	0.3140 (0.1899)	14.6494 (1.8495)	14.6907 (1.8347)	0.3792 (0.1891)	14.5742 (1.9423)	14.6800 (1.8403)
MIDWEST	1.6814 (0.8785)	1.9761 (0.8952)	0.3029 (0.0931)	1.4906 (1.0544)	1.6405 (1.0786)	0.4083 (0.1112)	1.5543 (1.1083)	1.6323 (1.0821)
WEST	4.8429 (1.0301)	4.8662 (1.0549)	0.4831 (0.1097)	5.1054 (1.2183)	5.1731 (1.2524)	0.5137 (0.1291)	5.0697 (1.3338)	5.1258 (1.2676)
PLANT PROPORTION	—	—	—	—	—	—	0.9930 (1.8907)	—
UTILITY PROPORTION	—	—	—	—	—	—	-0.9138 (2.4975)	—
PLANT/UTILITY	—	—	—	—	—	—	—	0.3785 (1.3660)
CONSTANT	12.0145 (1.2526)	9.4184 (1.5307)	1.7205 (0.1592)	9.2341 (1.5185)	6.1982 (1.8612)	1.4220 (0.1918)	6.1583 (1.8853)	6.0806 (1.9142)
DATE-71	-2.3734 (1.2715)	-2.4564 (1.2876)	-0.0988 (0.1339)	-0.7282 (1.4890)	-0.9103 (1.5057)	-0.0311 (0.1552)	-0.9389 (1.5290)	-0.9455 (1.5154)
DATE-74	-6.6815 (1.2647)	-7.3044 (1.1446)	-0.5098 (0.1190)	-3.9714 (1.3483)	-4.3786 (1.3685)	-0.3149 (0.1410)	-4.3848 (1.3789)	-4.4134 (1.3781)
DATE-78	-10.5052 (1.2647)	-10.6151 (1.2976)	-1.3926 (0.1349)	-7.0789 (1.5540)	-6.5193 (1.6324)	-1.0317 (0.1682)	-6.4995 (1.6702)	-6.5749 (1.6493)
Corrected R^2	0.70	0.69	0.67	0.74	0.73	0.69	0.73	0.73
Observations	277	277	277	169	169	169	169	169

[a] OLS/Contract date dummies. Standard errors of coefficient estimates are shown in parentheses.

term). This aggregation of signing dates was made to reflect major shocks to coal supply and/or demand.[29]

While the introduction of these contract date dummy variables may help to control for contract date related correlations between the error term and the independent variables, the estimated coefficients of these variables themselves have no obvious economic meaning. This is because of the nature of the sample. Recall that I observe contracts *in force* in 1979. If we think of the population as consisting of contracts written for particular plants (i) in a particular year (t), we can observe a contract only if

$$DURATION_{it} \geq (1979 - \text{Contract } YEAR) \qquad (4)$$

This means that of those contracts signed in 1970, I can observe, in 1979, only those that had durations of at least 9 years, while I will observe shorter contracts that were signed in later years. Even if there were no changes in contracting behavior over time, we would inevitably find that the coefficients of the contract-date dummies indicate that the average length of a contract in the sample is negatively correlated with the date of the contract.[30] The coefficients of the contract date variables can therefore tell us nothing directly about the changes in contracting behavior over time.

With these considerations in mind, we can turn to the results reported in Table 6.4, columns 1 through 6. The results obtained are again consistent with the hypothesized relationship between asset specificity and contract duration. The coefficients of the quantity, mine-mouth, and regional variables continue to be of the predicted signs and relative magnitudes. The only interesting difference between these results and those reported in Table 6.3 is that the difference between the durations of contracts signed with western and midwestern producers is now generally statistically significant at the 5 percent level for both samples.

3.3. Maximum Likelihood Estimates

A third alternative for estimating these equations is to follow Keith Crocker and Scott Masten (1986), who work with a sample of natural gas contracts with similar sampling properties, and assume that the sampling procedure which chooses contracts in force in a single year (1981 in their paper) represents a classical sample truncation problem as discussed by G. S. Maddala (1983: 165–70). The population of contracts then implicitly consists

---

[29] The 1971–73 period is just after the Clean Air Act Amendments of 1970 were passed; the 1974–77 period is the period after the Arab oil embargo and includes the subsequent increases in fossil fuel prices. The 1978–79 period coincides with the beginning of a slowdown in utility capacity additions. These periods are discussed in more detail in my paper (1986). The aggregation chosen is the same used to analyze pricing behavior in that paper. The results reported here are not sensitive to this aggregation, however. The same qualitative results are obtained if separate dummy variables are used for each year during the 1970s plus a separate dummy variable for pre-1965 and 1966–70 contracts.

[30] In the sample, the simple correlation between contract date ($YEAR$) and $DURATION$ is about -0.60. See Table 6.2.

of all contracts written since the earliest contract in the data base. We obtain a truncated sample because we observe contracts only if the duration of the contract is greater than or equal to L_i, where L_i is equal to 1979 minus the contract date. In this case, OLS estimates of (1), (2), and (3) would be biased, because the sampling process is likely to induce a correlation between the independent variables and the error term.

We can obtain estimates with desirable asymptotic properties by specifying the likelihood function of the sample, given the nature of the sampling truncation, and then solve for the maximum likelihood estimates (MLE) of the coefficients of interest. Following Maddala (166), I assume that the population relationship between contract duration and the independent variables has a normally distributed error and that each observation is truncated at L_i. This leads to a standard maximum likelihood estimator.

The maximum likelihood estimates are reported in Table 6.5, columns 1 through 6.[31] The results are again quite consistent with the hypothesized relationship between asset specificity and contract duration. The signs and magnitudes of the coefficients of $QUANTITY$, $MINE\text{-}MOUTH$, $WEST$, and $MIDWEST$ are again as predicted. With the exception of the mine-mouth dummy in equation (3), the coefficients are estimated quite precisely. The magnitudes of the estimated coefficients in this table are difficult to compare directly with those in Tables 6.3 and 6.4 because of the need to incorporate the truncation effects into estimates of contract duration.[32] Correcting for the sample truncation, the estimates reported in Table 6.5, column 5, for example, yield the following expected durations: The expected duration evaluated at the means of the independent variables is 10.5 years (compared to a mean of 14.2 years for the truncated 169 observation sample). Mine-mouth plants have contracts with an expected duration that is about 12 years longer than the average non-mine-mouth plant. Midwestern contracts are about 3.5 years longer than eastern contracts. Western contracts are about 11 years longer than eastern contracts and 6 years longer than midwestern contracts. The difference between western and midwestern contracts is generally significant at the 5 percent level.[33]

---

[31] The estimates were obtained using the MLE routine in the *Statistical Software Tools* package (Version 1.0 as of October 1986) developed by Jeffrey Dubin and R. Douglas Rivers running on an IBM XT. The estimates in cols. 3 and 6 assume that the density function is log-normal. Contracts executed in 1979 have been dropped since the likelihood function includes terms that require taking the logarithm of $L_i = (1979 - YEAR)$, which is zero for contracts written in 1979. Since the shortest contract in the data base has a duration of one year, we can impose a lower bound between zero and 1 on L_i to include all observations. Estimates obtained using different lower bounds does not change the results, so I simply report results for the sample excluding the small number of contracts in the data base executed in 1979.

[32] See Maddala (167).

[33] I have also produced maximum likelihood estimates of equation (2) for subsamples consisting of pre-1974 contracts and those signed between 1974 and 1979. The hypothesized relationship between contract duration and the variables representing variations in asset specificity persists for both subsamples.

TABLE 6.5
Contract Duration[a]

Independent Variables	DURATION (1)	DURATION (2)	LOG-DURATION (3)	DURATION (4)	DURATION (5)	LOG-DURATION (6)	DURATION (7)	DURATION (8)	2SLS ESTIMATE DURATION (9)
QUANTITY	0.7948 (0.1046)	—	—	0.5807 (0.0717)	—	—	—	—	—
QUANTITY-SQUARED	-0.0043 (0.00061)	—	—	-0.0030 (0.0004)	—	—	—	—	—
LOG-QUANTITY	—	11.8527 (1.5663)	0.6733 (0.0897)	—	8.4367 (1.0816)	0.6340 (0.0816)	8.2709 (1.0854)	8.4505 (1.0815)	8.5737 (3.5777)
MINE-MOUTH	16.5557 (4.2407)	13.8763 (3.8955)	0.2407 (0.5714)	15.5484 (2.9435)	14.4004 (2.7764)	0.2736 (0.4614)	14.1237 (3.0120)	14.3841 (2.7650)	15.4508 (2.1083)
MIDWEST	8.3650 (2.8188)	8.1377 (2.5461)	0.4493 (0.2281)	5.0050 (2.5018)	4.7042 (2.4511)	0.5376 (0.2763)	4.4397 (2.5221)	4.7468 (2.4820)	2.4404 (2.1797)
WEST	15.4864 (4.1940)	13.8045 (3.4244)	1.0500 (0.0500)	11.7771 (3.4220)	10.5506 (2.4220)	1.0522 (0.2416)	10.1238 (2.6136)	10.4730 (2.4095)	6.9477 (1.8329)
PLANT PROPORTION	—	—	—	—	—	—	2.4401 (3.7927)	—	—
UTILITY PROPORTION	—	—	—	—	—	—	-2.0043 (3.1937)	—	—
PLANT/UTILITY	—	—	—	—	—	—	—	1.4626 (2.1945)	—
Constant	-18.4532 (5.7203)	-35.6427 (7.2690)	-0.4699 (0.26709)	-6.9510 (3.4094)	-19.0118 (4.6758)	-0.2789 (0.2448)	-19.0377 (4.8545)	-19.7755 (4.8645)	-36.1521 (6.9717)
Log-likelihood	-781.08	-769.29	-174.29	-475.17	-466.99	-101.60	-466.68	-466.83	-451.38
Observations	277	277	255	169	169	169	169	169	169

[a] Maximum likelihood estimates. Standard errors of coefficient estimates are shown in parentheses.

TABLE 6.6
Contract Duration[a]

Dependent Variable: *DURATION*

Independent Variables	WEST (1)	MIDWEST (2)	EAST (3)	EAST (4)	WEST (5)	MIDWEST (6)	EAST (7)	EAST (8)
LOG-QUANTITY	3.4825	5.1249	4.2362	4.2968	3.5878	4.0269	4.408	4.4992
	(1.0714)	(0.7646)	(0.4668)	(0.4661)	(1.0992)	(0.6538)	(0.5798)	(0.5786)
MINE-MOUTH	18.4179	11.8107	—	17.6804	17.616	12.8372	—	17.0887
	(2.5064)	(5.1695)		(3.7348)	(2.3183)	(3.6363)		(3.8111)
Constant	6.819	1.365	−0.3975	−0.5265	7.2101	3.4074	0.4106	−0.6028
	(3.1610)	(5.1695)	(1.1159)	(1.1151)	(3.3441)	(1.8264)	(1.4256)	(1.4246)
Corrected R^2	0.68	0.42	0.35	0.43	0.73	0.52	0.42	0.54
Observations	54	68	155	158	44	47	78	81

[a] OLS by region. Standard errors of coefficient estimates are shown in parentheses.

3.4. Estimates for Individual Coal Supply Regions

Finally, in Table 6.6, I report estimates of the relationship between *DURATION, LOG-QUANTITY*, and *MINE-MOUTH* for each coal supply region.[34] The samples do not include any mine-mouth plants using eastern coal, so columns 3 and 7 simply report the estimated relationship between *DURATION* and *LOG-QUANTITY*. There are in fact a few mine-mouth plants in the East and I have some information for three of them. These were not included in the sample because the data base did not have information on annual contract quantities for them. However, I was able to obtain information for delivered quantities for three eastern mine-mouth plants and have augmented the sample to include these plants, using delivered quantities rather than contract quantities as the values for the *QUANTITY* variable. These results are reported in columns 4 and 8 of Table 6.6.[35]

The effects of contract quantity and the mine-mouth dummy on contract duration are clearly not simply associated with the contracting behavior for coal from a particular region. The expected effects are found in each of the three regions. The coefficients of *QUANTITY* and *MINE-MOUTH* are of the expected signs and are estimated precisely in all cases. While there are differences in the magnitudes of the coefficients of these variables between the three regions, they are not very large numerically and equality of the coefficients of *QUANTITY* and *MINE-MOUTH* across regions cannot be rejected at standard significance levels. Contracts basically simply get longer as we move from east to west, other things equal.

4. ALTERNATIVE MEASURE OF ASSET SPECIFICITY

Clearly, the hypothesized relationship between contract duration and the variables that I have chosen to capture variations in asset specificity is quite robust to alternative specifications, samples, and estimating technique. Nevertheless, it is natural to ask whether there are alternative or additional factors that might explain the observed variations in contract duration. One argument that has been suggested to me is that it is not only the size of the contractual commitment that is likely to be important, but also the fraction of a plant's, and perhaps the utility's, requirements obtained from a specific contract. The argument is that as a larger fraction of a plant's requirements is associated with a specific supplier, "physical asset specificity" attributes are likely to be more important and lead to longer contracts. It has also been suggested to me that opportunism problems are likely to be less severe if the utility as a whole is not heavily dependent on supplies provided

---

[34] I report only this variant of equation (2) to conserve space. It should be clear by now that the alternative specifications of (1), (2), and (3) do not yield any important differences in results.

[35] The inclusion of these three additional observations does not change the aggregate results.

pursuant to a specific contract. These arguments imply that variables measuring plant and/or utility "dependence" on a specific contract should be introduced into the contract duration relationship.

To examine this possibility, I have included variables in (2)[36] that measure the fraction of a plant's requirements (*PLANT PROPORTION*) and the fraction of the total coal requirements of the utility (*UTILITY PRO-PORTION*) that operates the plant which are accounted for by a particular contract. As an alternative, I also estimate (2) introducing a variable that is equal to total plant utilization of coal divided by total utility utilization of coal (*PLANT/UTILITY*). I can estimate these relationships only for the contracts that are for delivery to a single plant because it is only for these contracts that I can construct a meaningful measure of plant-specific dependence (i.e., the 169 observation subsample must be used).

The results are reported in columns 7 and 8 of Tables 6.3, 6.4, and 6.5. The coefficient estimates for *PLANT PROPORTION* and *UTILITY PROPORTION* are very imprecise. They are of opposite signs and are neither individually nor jointly significant at conventional significance levels. The coefficient of *PLANT/UTILITY* is also very imprecise and varies in sign depending on estimating technique. Introducing these variables has no effect on the estimates for the primary variables of interest. These results imply that a plant or utility that relies on a single supplier for a large fraction of its requirements, or that depends heavily on a specific plant, does not encounter significant hold-up problems per se. The lock-in effect associated with designing plants to burn a particular type of coal becomes a potential contractual problem only to the extent that the other asset specificity characteristics are active.

5. CONTRACT QUANTITY

Before concluding, it is useful to explore the role of asset specificity in determining annual contract quantities since this variable plays such an important role in the contract duration equation. A relationship between contract quantity and asset specificity potentially emerges because of the presence of all three types of asset specificity. First, other things equal, physical asset specificity considerations suggest that a plant operator would like to relay on a specific supplier producing a particular type of coal at a particular location to the greatest extent possible.[37] This implies that contract quantity should vary directly with the coal requirements of the

---

[36] Including these variables in (1) and (3) does not change the results and I report the results for (2) in order to conserve space.

[37] One might also argue that, other things equal, a buyer would rather rely on a single supplier to conserve on more traditional types of transaction costs associated with negotiating, monitoring, and enforcing contracts with multiple suppliers.

individual plant (*PLANT QUANTITY*).[38] On the other hand, the more a utility comes to rely on a single supplier, the more costly a breach of contract may be. This suggests that a utility may be willing to rely more on a single supplier for an individual plant the larger is total utility utilization of coal (*UTILITY QUANTITY*) given the utilization of a specific plant.

Second, in the case of mine-mouth plants, the nature of the ex ante location/investment decision involves the mutual expectation that all or most of a plant's requirements will be taken from the proximate supplier. This implies that the quantity per contract will be larger for mine-mouth plants, other things equal.

Finally, as discussed above, when utilities design plants to closely match specific coal quality attributes they will have an interest in relying more heavily on a specific supplier who contracts to supply coal from a seam with these characteristics. This is likely to be an especially important consideration for coal supplies from the western region.

I estimate the following relationship using the single-plant (169 observation) subsample to determine empirically whether and how these considerations affect annual contract quantities.

$$
\begin{aligned}
QUANTITY_i = {} & c_0 + d_1 PLANT\text{-}QUANTITY_i \\
& + d_2 PLANT\text{-}QUANTITY_i^2 + d_3 UTILITY\text{-}QUANTITY_i \\
& + d_4 UTILITY\text{-}QUANTITY_i^2 + d_5 MINE\text{-}MOUTH_i \\
& + d_6 MIDWEST_i + d_7 WEST_i + v_i
\end{aligned} \tag{5}
$$

I expect d_1, d_3, d_5, d_6, and d_7 to be greater than zero, and d_7 should be larger than d_6.

Equation (5) is estimated in two different ways. First, OLS estimates are presented. Second, OLS estimates with a correction to reflect the possibility that I have a censored sample are also presented. The OLS estimates of the coefficients of (5) may be biased as a result of the sampling procedure discussed earlier. We observe contract quantity only if contract duration is greater than or equal to (1979—contract *YEAR*), so we have a censored sample. This implies that the random error (v) in the contract quantity equation (5) may be correlated with the random error (u) in the contract duration equation. If this is the case, the random error (v) in the contract quantity equation will be a function of the independent variables in the contract duration equation. The OLS estimates of the coefficients of the independent variables in the quantity equation (5) would then be biased if they are correlated with the independent variables in the duration equation. In particular, independent variables that appear in the contract duration equation may appear to be significant when introduced as independent

---

[38] Ideally, we would like to look at specific generating *units* rather than specific generating *plants* where plants have multiple units with different design characteristics. Unfortunately, coal supply information is not available at the generating unit level.

TABLE 6.7
Contract Quantity[a]

Independent Variables	Dependent variable: $QUANTITY$			
	OLS		OLS/H	
	(1)	(2)	(3)	(4)
PLANT QUANTITY	0.2501	0.3133	0.2128	0.2827
	(0.0441)	(0.1573)	0.0489	(0.1578)
PLANT QUANTITY-SQUARED	—	−0.00066	—	−0.00067
		(0.0010)		(0.00099)
UTILITY QUANTITY	0.00349	0.0672	0.00393	0.06376
	(0.00689)	(0.0311)	(0.00685)	(0.03104)
UTILITY QUANTITY-SQUARED	—	−0.00007	—	−0.000063
		(0.00003)		(0.000032)
MINE-MOUTH	29.7932	27.1594	30.3261	27.775
	(6.8591)	(6.8997)	(6.8251)	(6.879)
WEST	13.5416	13.5865	8.4955	8.9738
	(4.6437)	(4.6259)	(5.4680)	(5.4597)
MIDWEST	5.2469	4.856	2.5832	2.4749
	(4.1841)	(4.1708)	(4.4371)	(4.4193)
H	—	—	−66.7618	−60.6647
			(38.7474)	(38.5749)
Constant	1.7329	−4.2283	10.6708	4.0997
	(3.5879)	(5.0515)	(6.2951)	(7.3027)
Corrected R^2	0.33	0.34	0.34	0.35
Observations	169	169	169	169

[a] Standard errors of coefficient estimates are shown in parentheses.

variables in equation (8) when in fact they are not.[39] Since three variables that appear in the quantity equation (5) also appear in the duration equation, this is a potential problem here.

We can obtain consistent estimates of the coefficients of (5) by obtaining maximum likelihood estimates of a reduced-form contract duration equation[40] to generate a sample selection correction H for each observation, adding the estimated values of H to (5) and then estimating the augmented equation (5) using OLS. The coefficient of H is then a consistent estimate of the covariance of u and v.

The results are reported in Table 6.7.[41] The OLS results appear in columns 1 and 2, and the OLS results with H introduced appear in columns 3 and 4. In both cases, estimates with and without quadratic terms in plant

[39] See Judge et al. (1985: 610–13); and Heckman (1976, 1979).
[40] $QUANTITY$ and LOG-$QUANTITY$ are treated as being endogenous.
[41] The mean value for H is 0.076.

and utility quantities are reported. The results are generally consistent with my expectations. Larger plants tend to place larger orders and utilities with larger aggregate requirements do so as well, although the utility effect is generally small. The quadratic in plant quantity is not significantly different from zero. The coefficient of the mine-mouth dummy has the predicted sign and is estimated fairly precisely. Mine-mouth plants have contracts that are nearly 1.5 million tons larger (30 trillion Btu's) than other plants ceteris paribus. Regional differences in supply characteristics lead to larger contracts with western suppliers than with suppliers elsewhere. The coefficient of the correction variable H is negative, although not quite significant at the 5 percent level (two-tailed test), implying that the errors in the duration and quantity equation are negatively correlated. Including this correction does not have dramatic effects on the results for the coefficients of interest, however. The primary effect is to reduce the magnitude and significance of the coefficient of *WEST*.

Finally, for the record, I report two-stage least square (*2SLS*) estimates of equation (2) in Table 6.3, column 9, and the equivalent of two-stage least squares for the maximum likelihood estimates of equation (2) in Table 6.5, column 9.[42] The estimates do not change in any important way from those obtained using the other estimating techniques in either case.

6. CONCLUSIONS

The purpose of this paper has been to examine empirically hypotheses about the relationship between the duration of coal contracts and the presence of the three types of relationship-specific investments discussed by Williamson (1983).[43] I argue that as relationship-specific investments become more important, the parties will find it advantageous to rely on longer-term

[42] I assumed that *LOG-QUANTITY* is endogenous, and use the right-hand side variables in (5) as instruments for the *2SLS* results reported in Table 6.3, col. 9. Obtaining the equivalent of *2SLS* estimates for the case in which I treat the sample as being truncated and use maximum likelihood techniques is more complicated. Following Maddala (234–40) and Lee, Maddala, and Trost (1979), I proceeded in the following way. First, I estimate a reduced-form duration equation using maximum likelihood techniques. This allows me to obtain consistent estimates of H_i which can in turn be used to obtain consistent estimates of a contract quantity equation as discussed above. I use these estimates of the quantity equation to obtain predicted values of *QUANTITY* or *LOG-QUANTITY*, which are then used in place of *QUANTITY* and *LOG-QUANTITY* to estimate equations (1) and (2) using maximum likelihood techniques. The results reported in Table 6.5, col. 9, assume that log(*PLANT QUANTITY*), log(*UTILITY QUANTITY*), *MIDWEST*, *WEST*, and *MINE-MOUTH* are exogenous variables. These variables are used to estimate a reduced-form duration equation using the maximum likelihood technique described earlier. An equation for log(*QUANTITY*) is then estimated using log(*PLANT QUANTITY*), log(*UTILITY QUANTITY*), *MIDWEST*, *WEST*, *MINE-MOUTH*, and H (generated from the reduced-form duration estimates) using OLS. The predicted values from this equation are then used instead of *LOG-QUANTITY* in (2) to obtain the maximum likelihood estimates reported. Specification (1) has also been estimated using this approach. The results appear to be robust.

[43] As well as similar considerations of transaction-specific investments identified by Klein, Craword, and Alchian (1978).

contracts that specify the terms and conditions of repeated transactions ex ante, rather than relying on repeated bargaining. I make use of a large sample of coal contracts to examine this hypothesis. The empirical results obtained provide fairly strong support for this hypothesis. They are quite robust to alternative model specifications, samples, and estimating techniques. The results therefore provide additional empirical support for the view that the structure of vertical relationships between buyers and sellers is strongly affected by variations in the importance of relationship-specific investments.

APPENDIX

Here I discuss the sources of the data and the construction of the variables. The data base that I rely on was constructed from a variety of sources for use in a research project focusing on vertical relationships between electric utilities and coal suppliers. This is one of three papers that have been produced so far from this project.

The construction of the data base began with the choice of contracts to use in the analysis. Contracts were chosen if they appeared in *both* the 1981 and 1983 editions of *The Guide to Coal Contracts* (Pasha Publications) and for which information necessary for the project was reported. Contracts had to appear in both publications because some information that was desired appeared in one or the other publication, but not both. This also made it possible to check for errors and inconsistencies in the contract characteristics reported. To appear in both publications, contracts had to be in force in 1979. In five cases, actual contracts were used to supplement the data available from the primary sources.

This collection procedure resulted in a sample of 296 contracts (of which 277 had enough information to be used here), which generally had the following information, some of which is used in this paper and some of which I am using in related work:

1. Information required to calculate the agreed-upon duration of the contract (see discussion below).
2. Contract quantities for 1979, 1980, and/or 1981 in tons.
3. The contract specifications for the Btu content and the sulfur content of the coal.
4. The identity of the seller and the location of the mine.
5. The identity of the buyer and the destination of the coal.
6. The base price for the coal at the time the contract was signed.
7. The actual price for the coal in 1979, 1980, and/or 1981.
8. Delivered quantities in 1979, 1980, and/or 1981.
9. Actual Btu and sulfur content of the coal.

Once the contract sample was selected, individual contracts were matched with specific utilities and power plants (where possible). Two publications were utilized to obtain coal quantity and quality (Btu content) information by plant and utility: *Cost and Quality of Fuels for the Electric Utility Industry* (U.S. Department of Energy, various years) and *Steam Electric Plant Factors* (National Coal Association, various years). For public utility holding companies, coal utilization for subsidiaries was aggregated. Jointly owned plants were assigned to the operating company.

The three coal supply regions represent aggregations of smaller U.S. Bureau of Mines (BOM) districts. The West was defined as including BOM districts 16 through 23. The Midwest included BOM districts 5, 9, 10, 11, 12, 14, and 15. BOM district 15 includes Texas, but we have no contracts for coal produced in Texas. The East includes coal from the remaining BOM districts, primarily in Appalachia. The differences between regions are discussed in more detail in my 1985 paper. The *Keystone Coal Industry Manual* (Mining Information Services) and an atlas were used to help locate mines in specific BOM districts.

The variable definitions and construction are as follows:

DURATION: Contract Duration: The contract data base generally provides information for the date the contract was executed, the termination date, and (less frequently) the date of first delivery of coal. A specific month and year is often provided, but sometimes the source specifies only years. Because the contract execution date was available more often than the date of first delivery and because the two are generally quite close together, contract duration was measured as contract termination year minus execution year. Initial experimentation with duration measured using the date of first delivery or using month and year indicated that the results were unaffected, so the definition that preserved the largest number of contracts was used.

QUANTITY: Annual contract quantity in trillion Btu's The contracted tonnage reported for 1980 (if that was not available, or obviously not representative, 1979 or, alternatively, 1981 was used instead) was multiplied by the contracted Btu content of the coal to arrive at the contract quantity variable.

MINE-MOUTH: Mine-mouth dummy variable that is equal to 1 if the plant is a mine-mouth plant and zero otherwise. The information in my 1985 paper combined with the coal destination information in the *Guide To Coal Contracts* was used to construct this variable. The Navajo and Mohave plants were included in this category as well since they have economic characteristics very much like a mine-mouth plant.

MIDWEST: A regional dummy variable that equals 1 if the coal is from a midwestern mine (as defined above) and zero otherwise. The contract data base provides information on mine location.

WEST: A regional dummy variable that equals 1 if coal is from a western mine (as defined above) and zero otherwise.

PLANT QUANTITY: Annual plant utilization of coal. Coal utilization by a plant to which a specific contract is dedicated (at least 90 percent of the coal delivered to a single plant) for 1980 (1979 or 1981 if necessary to match *QUANTITY*) in trillion Btu's Obtained from the Department of Energy and National Coal Association publications identified above.

UTILITY QUANTITY: Annual utility utilization of coal. Coal utilization in 1980 (or 1979 or 1981 if necessary to match other data) by the utility operating a plant to which a contract is dedicated. Obtained from the Department of Energy and National Coal Association publications identified above.

PLANT PROPORTION: Delivered contract quantity in Btu's divided by plant utilization in Btu's. Delivered contract quantity in tons was pulled from the contract information for 1980 (or 1979 if 1980 was not available) and multiplied by the delivered Btu content of the coal to obtain quantities delivered to a specific plant under a contract dedicated to that plant. This figure was then divided by *PLANT QUANTITY*.

UTILITY PROPORTION: Delivered contract quantity in Btu's (as defined above in definition of *PLANT PROPORTION*) divided by utility utilization of coal in Btu's for 1980 (1979 or 1981 otherwise).

PLANT/UTILITY: *PLANT QUANTITY* divided by *UTILITY QUANTITY*.

YEAR: The year specified as the execution date of the contract.

DATE-71: A dummy variable that equals 1 for contracts signed in 1971, 1972, and 1973.

DATE-74: A dummy variable that equals 1 for contracts signed in 1974, 1975, 1976, and 1977.

DATE-78: A dummy variable that equals 1 for contracts signed in 1978 and 1979.

The mean, standard deviation, minimum, and maximum values of these variables for the 277 observation sample and the 169 observation (single delivery point) subsample are contained in Tables 6.1 and 6.2. The data for the variables used in this paper are available upon request.

Chapter 7

CONTRACTING PRACTICES IN BULK SHIPPING MARKETS: A TRANSACTIONS COST EXPLANATION

Stephen Craig Pirrong

1. INTRODUCTION

Contracting in the ocean bulk shipping industry is remarkable for two reasons. First, the entire continuum of contracting practices is represented there. Spot contracts, forward contracts, medium- and long-term contracts, and even vertical integration are common in bulk shipping markets. Second, complex long-term contracts and vertical integration exist despite the fact that the characteristics identified by transactions cost economists as making spot or simple forward contracting uneconomic (site, physical asset, and human asset specificities) are conspicuously absent in these markets.[1] Contracting practices in bulk shipping markets therefore present a challenge to transactions costs theory.

In this article I argue that transactions costs are indeed important in these markets but that the considerations that influence bulk shipping contracting practices are somewhat different than those usually emphasized. Specifically, time and space factors in shipping markets may create "temporal specificities"[2] that encourage costly haggling between shippers and carriers

Reprinted from the Journal of Law and Economics, vol. XXXVI (October 1993) by permission of the University of Chicago Press. © 1993 by The University of Chicago. All rights reserved.

Stephen Craig Pirrong is Assistant Professor of Business Economics and Public Policy, the University of Michigan. This paper benefited greatly from the comments of my colleagues Scott Masten and Ted Snyder, and an anonymous referee. I am the residual claimant for any remaining errors.

[1] See Williamson (1985), and Joskow (1988), for analyses of how transactions costs affect contracting choices.

[2] Masten, Meehan and Snyder (1991) introduce this term.

over quasi rents if they rely on spot contracts. They can avoid this problem by extending the contracting horizon through the use of forward contracts or term contracts of moderate duration. Such contracts may not eliminate all bilateral monopoly problems and the associated quasi rents, however, because with decentralized bargaining the expiration dates of modest term contracts between different pairs of shippers and carriers frequently will not match. When mismatches in the expiration of contracts of modest length are likely, parties will rely on very long-term contracts or vertical integration.

Several factors affect the severity of these contracting problems. These include the contracting practices in the market for the commodity shipped in bulk, the thickness of the shipping market, and whether the commodity is most efficiently shipped aboard specialized tonnage or general purpose tonnage. I examine the incidence of these characteristics in the markets for the shipment of fourteen separate bulk commodities and find that ship contracting practices in the major markets do indeed largely align with these transaction attributes. Spot contracting prevails, for example, for commodities such as grain and crude oil (since the late 1970s), where shipping markets are thick, there are several alternative supply sources of the commodity shipped, and general purpose tonnage is efficiently employed. Forward contracts, term contracts, and vertical integration dominate where one or more of these attributes is absent. Long-term contracts and vertical integration prevail for commodities that are shipped most efficiently aboard special purpose vessels that are not suitable for carrying other cargoes, even though that can service several shippers of the same commodity.

These results are important because asset specificities in ocean shipping are considerable less acute than in other industries that transactions cost economists have studied previously, such as mine-mouth coal plants and auto-body manufacturing. The persistence of long-term agreements and vertical integration in bulk shipping suggests that specificities far less severe that are found in these industries can pose contracting hazards. Thus, even if the costs of physically redeploying assets are low (as is the case in bulk shipping), spot trading may be less efficient than exchanges governed either by more formal, enduring bilateral relationships or by direct ownership, unless there is a relatively large number of buyers and sellers of the assets.

2. SHIPPING CONTRACTS: A TAXONOMY

Shipping contracts—generally called "charters"—are negotiated between the "shipper" of a commodity, the individual or firm desiring to transport it by ship between two ports, and the "carrier," usually the owner of a ship. There are three basic forms of shipping contract: the voyage charter, the time-charter, and the contract of affreightment.[3]

---

[3] There are many good descriptions of common ship-chartering practices. One of the more recent and comprehensive is Branch (1981).

The voyage charter is the most basic type of shipping contract. Voyage charters typically specify the carriage of a particular cargo (for example, 20,000 metric tons of wheat) aboard a named ship (for example, the *Altai Maru*) between two points (for example, New Orleans to Rotterdam), the loading and discharge dates, and the payment due the carrier. Brokers frequently negotiate voyage charters in a centralized exchange, the Baltic Exchange in London. Others are negotiated by phone directly by the parties or through ship brokers who operate away from the exchange floor. Under a voyage charter the shipowner is usually responsible for all costs incurred on the voyage. Since voyage contracts are usually negotiated shortly (between a few days to two weeks) before the loading of the cargo, they are "spot" contracts, although carriers and shippers sometimes negotiate forward-voyage contracts a month or more in advance of the agreed-on loading date.

Another common form of shipping contract is the time charter, under which the shipper obtains the services of a ship for a specified period of time. Whereas the voyage charter specifies all important characteristics of a particular ship's trip, the time charter allows the charterer to choose its operating pattern to suit his particular needs. He pays the variable expenses arising from his use, including fuel and port charges. The shipowner provides a crew to serve the vessel, except under the relatively rare "bare boat" charter, where the shipper does. Time charter prices are usually quoted on a per diem basis. Parties usually negotiate time charters immediately prior to the transfer of control of the ship, although some are forward contracts. They range in duration from a month to several years; most expire in less than three years, but some extend for fifteen years. Thus, some time charters are short-term, spot agreements, but as their durations are usually long enough to allow the charterer to make several voyages most are essentially a bundle of forward-voyage contracts, or a bundle of options on future voyage contracts.

The last major type of shipping contract is the contract of affreightment (COA).[4] These contracts are usually relatively long-term contracts, typically at least three years and frequently longer than fifteen years in duration. They specify the cargo, minimum and maximum volumes carried over specified time periods, the ports or origin and destination, and the frequency of service. They also frequently set out various performance requirements that the shipper and carrier must satisfy, as well as pricing mechanisms. The most common pricing mechanism is variable cost (usually defined as fuel plus crew) plus a fixed payment.[5] In some instances prices are indexed by the spot charter rates for similar ships or cargoes that prevail at various points throughout the duration of the COA. All of these terms indicate that COAs

---

[4] There are other, similar contract types such as long-term cargo guarantees. Since COAs and cargo guarantees are so similar I do not attempt to distinguish between them.

[5] For longer-term contracts, rates paid carriers sometimes depend on port and canal fees in addition to fuel and crew charges.

are much more than simple rate tarifs between a shipper and carrier. Under a COA the shipper guarantees cargo volumes and the carrier guarantees service frequency in return. Thus, the contract specifies input and output as well as price.

This taxonomy reveals that contractual arrangements in shipping markets are extremely varied. Both spot and forward markets exists. Term contracts are common, and some are quite complex, long-lasting agreements. In addition to these arm's-length transactions, vertical integration is relatively common in some bulk markets. In the next section I attempt to apply a transactions cost analysis to explain this wide range of practices.

3. TRANSACTIONS COSTS AND CONTRACTING IN BULK SHIPPING MARKETS

3.1. Traditional Transactions Cost Theory and Contracting in Bulk Shipping Markets

The foregoing taxonomy raises two questions. First, what explains why some shippers and carriers rely on spot contracts, and others do not? Second, what explains the contract durations and vertical integration decisions of shippers and carriers that do not contract spot? Although some existing theory (applied in some detail in section 3.2 below) helps answer the first question, the second is more difficult. In particular, the prevalence of long-term COAs and vertical integration in shipping markets is somewhat paradoxical from a transactions cost perspective.

Transactions cost theory argues that long-term contracts and integration are likely to be efficient forms of vertical relationships when asset specificities tie a buyer and a seller over long periods of time. These conditions create relationship-specific quasi rents. Given bounded rationality, the costs of negotiating complete contracts, opportunism, and the inability to enforce contracts costlessly, these quasi rents create incentives for wasteful strategic behavior.

Transactions cost theorists have identified three primary sources of specificities: site specificity, physical asset specificity, and human asset specificity (Williamson, 1985; Joskow, 1988). Site specificities are obviously irrelevant in this context, as ships can move. Physical asset specificities are also of little relevance in bulk shipping markets. Some ships are commodity specific, but since there are several shippers of each commodity they are not shipper specific.[6] Therefore, a particular shipper and particular carrier need not face a repeated bilateral monopoly problem. Finally, human asset specificities cannot explain long-term contracts or vertical integration in bulk shipping markets because the skills of a mariner—navigation, engineering,

---

[6] Certain ships, such as iron ore carriers or supertankers, cannot serve *all* shippers of ore or oil because of various physical constraints, but this does not necessarily lead to an enduring match between a particular ship and a particular shipper.

seamanship, and cargo stowage and handling—are quite general and are not specific to any particular firm or ship.

This analysis suggests that the traditional sources of holdup problems are unimportant in bulk shipping because there are few technological or physical barriers to the redeployment of vessels among shippers.[7] The characteristics of certain routes, markets, cargoes, and ships, however, may create time and space factors that make the transactions costs of spot contracting high relative to the transactions costs of forward or term contracting. Participants in these markets will therefore rely on either forward or time chartering or on COAs. Moreover, carriers and shippers will economize on the costs of transacting in the services of ships designed to carry a specific commodity through long-term contracts or through vertical integration. One therefore expects to observe a relation between observable characteristics of a shipping trade and the predominant contracting practice used there. The empirical analysis in section 4 demonstates that such a relation indeed exists.

3.2. Time and Space Factors, Transactions Costs, and the Viability of Spot Contracting in Bulk Shipping Markets

Temporal Specificities and the Efficiency of Spot Contracting

Although contracting problems typically emphasized in transactions cost analyses are not present in bulk shipping markets, shippers and carriers face other difficulties. In particular, time and space considerations may create what Masten, Meehan, and Snyder (1991) call "temporal specificities" that sometimes make spot contracting prohibitively costly. These time and space considerations may create significant quasi rents in the very short term, but these rents dissipate as the time between contracting and exchange increases. Since buyers and sellers competing for quasi rents may waste resources in costly bargaining, forward contracting should dominate spot contracting when these considerations are important.

To see how time and space considerations can affect contracting in an ocean-shipping market, consider a shipper located at port A. Like virtually all bulk shippers, he owns a processing or refinery plant and needs to transport a bulky input from an overseas location to his facility. The n ships (that is, the carriers) available to transport this input are located at a variety of points some distance from A. For simplicity and without loss of generality, assume that ship i, $i = 1, \ldots, n$, requires t_i days to transit from its current location to A, with $t_i < t_j$ for $i < j$ and $t_1 = 0$. If the costs of reaching port A rise with the time required to travel there, or if the shipper is impatient, or both, it is optimal for the shipper at A to patronize carrier 1.

---

[7] Williamson (1985: 89) argues "that contractual problems between independent buyer and supplier are . . . limited" where investments in "durable, general purpose equipment . . . can be costlessly relocated" because "neither buyer nor supplier operates at the sufferance of the other." Although movement of a ship is not costless, it is clear that shipping closely approximates these conditions.

Consider the contracting environment for this shipper-carrier pair. They could negotiate a spot contract to load and carry the cargo immediately. While they may realize gains from doing so, there may be quasi rents at stake as well. These rents may be large if delays in shipment impose great harm on the shipper, or if the carrier's next best cargo-shipping opportunity is sufficiently distant. The shipper and carrier may expend resources in an attempt to capture these quasi rents. Indeed, they may fail to consummate the efficient transaction.

Sometimes quasi rents are substantial. When, for example, a U.S. oil refiner imports crude oil, the refinery is a very specialized asset. Even if he receives some oil, but less than he needs to operate his plant to satisfy demand for the product, the refiner incurs a significant opportunity cost. If the failure to receive oil forces him to shut down his facility altogether, costs may increase even further, given that it is expensive to resume refinery activities. A failure to receive timely oil shipments therefore could impose a significant loss on the refiner.[8]

The carrier might also contribute to the quasi rent at stake. It is quite possible that if he does not carry the cargo from port A, he will have to transit some distance in ballast to find another. Failing to obtain a contract to transport the shipment from A therefore can force the carrier to incur the direct costs of a transit (including fuel and additional crew and wear-and-tear expenses) as well as some indirect costs (the opportunity cost of an idle vessel).

The cost to the refiner equals the benefits he forgoes when operating his plant below capacity for t_2 days; call this amount e. Given the specificity of the facility and the resulting large margin between the price of the output and the price of the raw material, this could be a very large sum, far larger than the cost of shipping the oil from A to the refinery. Similarly, if the carrier's next best alternative cargo is some distance from A, he must incur appreciable costs, f, to avail himself of this opportunity.

With such large quasi rents, the carrier and the shipper face well-known

---

[8] Shippers can protect themselves from such situations by holding larger inventories of the input. (The refiner requires some inventories simply because he uses oil continuously, but he receives shipments at discrete intervals because of the indivisibility of ships.) It is costly to hold inventories, however, of bulky, valuable, or perishable inputs. Inventories may not be, moreover, a credible means of protecting the refiner from a bilateral monopoly position if there are other bottlenecks in the production, transport, or handling of the input. If the firm chooses to contract with carrier $i = 2, 3, 4$, and so forth, rather than bend to carrier 1's demand by drawing down on inventory, it must replace this inventory in order to provide a buffer against future holdups. Thus, an acceleration of shipments must follow a temporary shortfall. If the marginal costs of producing, storing, or handling the input rise rapidly as quantities rise above the levels of production, storage, and handling undertaken in normal operations, this replacement is very expensive; carrier 1 can exploit this added handling expense in negotiations. If the firm's port facilities are limited, for instance, it may pay a large cost penalty to dramatically increase handling rates to receive the replacement of the buffer. This suggests that the refiner must invest in redundant physical facilities in order to rely on excess inventory to avoid bilateral monopoly problems in ocean transport. The refiner may find the contractual means of avoiding these problems (discussed in the following text) far cheaper than the construction and maintenance of buffer facilities that would never be used if they successfully performed their task.

problems. The carrier could refuse to contract with the shipper unless he receives a large part of e. Similarly, the shipper could bid any amount between c and $c - f$ for the carrier's services. This implies a bargaining range of $[c - f, e]$. If there are valuable specific assets at stake, this range could be very wide, particularly if the shipper adds considerable value to the shipped input.

Such a wide range could induce the parties to engage in costly strategic behavior. Contracting "on the spot" therefore may be inefficient in these circumstances because temporal specificities pervade the negotiating environment when ships cannot move instantaneously and costlessly from point to point, thereby optimally matching a particular shipper and a particular carrier. This optimal match creates quasi rents that the transactors may try to capture through the wasteful expenditure of resources.[9]

This analysis implies that spatial/temporal proximity is a form of relationship-specific capital. Relationship-specific capital exists when certain factors create a strong tie between a particular pair of transactors; that is, the value of a transaction between buyer B_1 and seller S_1 is more valuable than a transaction between B_1 and any other seller or S_1 and any other buyer. This tempts traders to engage in wasteful behaviors in order to capture rents.[10]

In the shipping market case, it is readily seen that the relationship-specific capital depreciates quickly, and thus forward contracts and short-term time contracts can substantially narrow the bargaining range.[11] In other words, the severity of temporal specificities diminishes rapidly if the carrier and the

---

[9] It is important to note that these transactions costs are distinct from transportation costs per se. Transportation cost minimization, and the resulting optimal shipper-carrier matches, may create quasi rents and transactions costs.

[10] A commentator on a previous draft of this paper questioned whether the holdup problem analyzed here is a legitimate instance of ex post opportunism. It is certainly the case that it is not contractually ex post, as by assumption no contract has been signed. It is the case, however, that when the parties are negotiating each has resources (for example, the refinery and the ship) *in place* that would be far less valuable if they failed to consummate the efficient transaction. Thus, there are valuable resources vulnerable to holdup; that is, contract negotiations take place *after* resources are in place. It is thus a legitimate instance of ex post opportunism.

Limiting the definition of ex post opportunism to situations where a contract has already been signed and remains in effect precludes application of the concept to the analysis of contract durations. That is, under the limited definition ex post opportunism may be used to explain the choice between arm's-length contracting and vertical integration (the analysis of Klein, Crawford, and Alchian (1978) is a classic example) but has little to say about the choice between different types of arm's-length contracts, including contracts that differ in duration. The important work of Joskow (1985, 1988) provides strong evidence. however, that opportunism problems may arise when contracts expire and that the potential for holdup at expiration motivates contracting parties to choose longer contract durations in order to limit or perhaps eliminate the need for future negotiations. That they do so (rather than vertically integrate) implies that they have some means of controlling opportunism during the contract's life. This strongly suggests that the narrow definition of ex post opportunism is far too limiting.

[11] One can view spatial/temporal matching examined here as a form of site-specific capital. The traditional interpretation of site specificity is that geographic proximity creates quasi rents. The same is true of temporal specificities. Traditional discussions of temporal specificity have assumed that the juxtaposed facilities are very durable, however, so it is useful to distinguish the traditional case from the one examined here where the spatial linkage is fleeting.

shipper can negotiate contracts calling for future, rather than immediate, loading and shipment. Temporal specificity-created quasi rents are therefore reduced when shippers and carriers negotiate forward contracts rather than spot contracts. By contracting sufficiently far ahead, the shipper protects himself from expropriation of his specialized assets. In the context of the foregoing model, by contracting t_j days ahead the shipper can access j ships, rather than just one. The resulting competition between the carriers renders incredible the threat of carrier 1 to refuse transport unless he receives a large premium above his cost; this carrier cannot unilaterally threaten to impose a cost of e on the shipper in this case. Similarly, forward contracting allows carriers to expand their competitive alternatives in order to protect themselves against the unilateral threats of any shipper. These factors make the forward contracting bargaining range smaller than the spot contracting bargaining range, which reduces the scope for inefficient bargaining and strategic behavior. Forward contracting consequently economizes on transactions costs if temporal specificities are acute. Forward agreements may thus represent a discriminating match between contracting problems and contracting solutions.

Although forward contracting is more competitive, it does not necessarily dominate spot contracting. Forward contracting requires the parties to enter into agreements prior to the revelation of all relevant information about the value and costs of the services for which they have contracted. Incomplete forward contracts restrict the ability of shippers and carriers to respond in a value-maximizing way to unforeseen circumstances. They must weigh the advantages of avoiding exposure to market power by increasing competition against the costs of reduced flexibility.

Factors Affecting the Severity of Temporal Specificities

The foregoing implies that forward contracts (including time charters or COAs) economize on transactions costs in markets where temporal specificities are important, whereas spot contracts do so when they are insubstantial. To determine whether actual contracting practices conform to this pattern, one must identify conditions that affect the magnitude of the temporal specificities. Any factor that reduces the substitutability of ships as carriers of a particular cargo should increase the quasi rents that make spot contracting costly. Three conditions affect substitutability.

First, the availability of geographically dispersed alternative cargo sources for the shipper increases the number of ships available to satisfy his requirements. This reduces a particular carrier's ability to hold up that shipper as the latter's ability to acquire the cargo from several sources reduces his dependence on him. In the context of the oil refiner example, if he can purchase oil to satisfy his refining requirements in Saudi Arabia, Nigeria, or Indonesia, he can access a larger number of carriers in a given amount of time than if he can only purchase oil in Nigeria. Since geographically dispersed supply sources make a shipper (carrier) less vulnerable to expropriation by a spatially advantaged carrier (shipper), forward contracting is less beneficial under these circumstances, and spot contracting may survive.

It should be noted that geographic dispersion of the production of a commodity alone may not be sufficient to ensure that a shipper can acquire it at several points. There must also be a *liquid spot market for the commodity* at each of these points; otherwise, a given shipper may not be able to acquire suppliers there. Even if production of a commodity transported by sea takes place at a variety of sites, temporal specificities may abound if each shipper can obtain it from only one or two of them because supply sources are firm specific.

Second, competition is more acute (and temporal specificities less severe as a result) on "thick" markets, that is, markets where shippers offer cargoes and carriers make voyages on a virtually continuous basis. Even if carriers operate under spot contracts, on a thick market a large number arrive to carry at any point in time, allowing shippers to choose from many carriers. Similarly, a continuous stream of shippers arrives on a thick route. Carriers therefore have many competing contracting opportunities available and consequently need not transit to distant locations to find alternative cargoes.[12]

The thickness of the shipping market at a particular port depends on the characteristics of the cargo flows originating there. Ports from which shippers dispatch large numbers of moderately sized lots of cargo on a continuous basis, for instance, are thick shipping markets. As a result of the moderate size of the lots here, many ships are required to handle the traffic. (Shippers may dispatch large numbers of relatively small cargoes from a particular port because it is near a major source of the cargo but serves a large number of spatially separate destinations.) As a result of the constant stream of cargoes originating at the port, carriers that go there have many shippers to contract with. This attracts vessels, which ensures that shippers there find many ships capable of carrying their cargo. Shippers and carriers find spot contracting viable under these circumstances.

Other conditions make a market relatively thin. In particular, because of the nature of shipping costs, even if the volume of traffic shipped from port B is very large, the shipping market may be thin if most of this cargo is shipped to a single destination, say, port C. The average variable and fixed costs of shipping a ton of cargo fall with the size of the ship over a wide

---

[12] An example may illustrate the concept of thickness more clearly. Many travelers arrive at O'Hare Airport in Chicago needing to travel downtown, Knowing this, many cabs congregate there. As a result, cabdrivers know that they will get a fare with high probability, and travelers know that they will get a cab after a very short wait (if they have to wait at all). Under these circumstances, a traveler need not contract ahead with a cabbie in order to assure a prompt pickup; decentralized spot contracting is feasible here. If, however, a rider needs a cab on an isolated side street in an exclusive suburb where few people use cabs, it is highly unlikely that he would readily find one by just standing in front of his house. Since the traffic here is thin, few cabs go there without having prearranged a fare. Thus, the suburban traveler will call a cab company—that is, contract forward—to obtain a ride.

range.[13] If shippers consistently dispatch large volumes of cargo between a particular pair of ports, it is optimal to use very large ships to carry it. For a given volume of cargo the use of larger ships implies that fewer are needed to satisfy port B's traffic. In this circumstance, shipments are lumpier and the number of voyages smaller. The market is therefore thinner. The larger the ship employed, moreover, the larger the quasi rents at stake for the shipper: a single holdup hurts a shipper less if to ship 10,000 tons he uses ten 10,000 deadweight (dwt) carriers than if he ships the entire 100,000 tons in a single load.[14]

Third, temporal specificity problems are mitigated if the shipper can efficiently utilize general purpose vessels. A shipper of a commodity transportable in a such a bottom has more contracting opportunities than the shipper of a commodity that is most efficiently carried in a ship designed specifically for it.[15] Similarly, the owner of a general purpose carrier has access to a wider variety of cargoes than the owner of a commodity-specific ship. A multipurpose carrier can often "tramp" around (hence the term "tramp steamer") from port to port to find a cargo, whereas the shipper of a generic cargo is able to contract with several such ships.

In summary, carriers and shippers should utilize spot contracting for commodities for which temporal specificities are unimportant. They are likely to be so when shippers can acquire the commodity they transport at a variety of spatially separate locations, when multipurpose vessels can carry it, and when many shippers and carriers operate on a single trade. When some or all of these conditions do not hold, forward or term agreements economize on transactions costs.

3.3. Optimal Contract Duration and Vertical Integration in Markets Where Spot Contracting Is Inefficient

Contractual Specificities and Contract Duration

The foregoing analysis identifies factors that make forward and term contracting more efficient than spot contracting, but it does not imply an optimal duration of forward and term contracts. It does not imply whether simple forward contracts pertaining only to a single voyage or time charters

---

[13] Average fixed costs fall because a ship's carrying capacity depends on its volume, but the construction cost varies more closely with its surface area. Average variable costs fall for a similar reason. Drag—and hence fuel cost—depends on surface area, which rises less rapidly than carrying capacity. Moreover, manning requirements usually rise less rapidly than capacity.

[14] The problem of determining optimal ship size is similar to the well-known problem of determining the optimal inventory order quantity. Storage costs and constraints on ship size resulting from technological and port limitations place upper bounds on shipment size. Optimal ship size also increases with shipping distance, as on such routes ships spend a larger fraction of time at sea, and the operating cost advantages described in the preceding footnote become more pronounced.

[15] An example of the latter case is wood-chip shipping. Special chip carriers can transport this commodity far more efficiently than a general purpose carrier.

of moderate length reduce transactions costs significantly, or whether shippers and carriers must negotiate long-term contracts governing many voyages.

Since simple one-voyage forward contracts or time charters of relatively modest duration should eliminate the bargaining problems arising from temporal specificities while affording shippers and carriers considerable flexibility, temporal specificities alone cannot explain the existence of long-term charters, COAs, or vertical integration. When shippers and carriers negotiate forward contracts or term contracts of modest duration to avoid temporal specificity problems, however, they may create another difficulty; "contractual specificities" may arise when an agreement expires.

Contractual specificities exist when a contract between a shipper and carrier expires, but all other vessels the shipper can utilize and all the other shippers the carrier can service are under contract for a considerable time thereafter. This shipper and carrier are in a bilateral monopoly situation during the interval between the end of their contract and the termination of the next expiring agreement. Unless the contracts of several shippers and carriers expire nearly simultaneously the transactions costs of negotiating a new agreement are high if shippers and carriers have significant quasi rents at stake. The incentives for strategic behavior at contract expiration are acute in these circumstances. This situation is likely to be repeated, moreover, at each expiration date.

Contractual specificities may create larger quasi rents than temporal specificities alone; it may be physically possible for another ship to reach a certain port to serve a shipper whose firm-specific assets require an input shipment to operate efficiently, but this is of little solace if it is already engaged to another. Similarly, even if a ship can transit to another port for cargo, it is uneconomic to do so if other ships already have a contract to carry that cargo. Forward contracting prior to the expiry of the existing contract does not allow the parties to circumvent this problem since by assumption the other ships capable of carrying the cargo and the other shippers with cargo to transport will not be freed from their obligations until sometime after its expiration date. Forward contracting therefore does not eliminate all incentives for costly opportunistic behavior unless a significant number of these forward contracts expire approximately contemporaneously.

This suggests that a considerable degree of coordination among contracting parties is sometimes required to eliminate the conditions in which costly strategic behavior thrives because the transactions costs of forward/medium-term contracting between a shipper and a carrier depend on the contracts binding other shippers and carriers. The dependence of this pair's transactions costs on the chartering choices of others may make forward contracting inefficient because the minimization of these costs requires coordination of expiration dates between many shippers and carriers. Such coordination may not arise from decentralized interactions among shippers and carriers and is likely to be extraordinarily expensive to achieve through explicit cooperation.[16]

If all parties negotiate contracts with durations equal to the expected economic life of the ship they employ, or if shippers purchase their own vessels, they eliminate their dependence on others, avoid the need for cooperation, and thereby reduce transactions costs. This is true because under these circumstances it is optimal to construct a new ship at contract expiration rather than find employment for the old one. If the shipbuilding and ship-operating markets are competitive, the shipper can contract at low cost with a carrier to provide a new vessel, and the carrier can then contract (again at low cost as a result of competition) with a yard to build the ship. Alternatively, the shipper can purchase a ship directly. The parties have little incentive to haggle over the services of an obsolete ship when its contract expires because the appropriable quasi rents at stake are trivial. They avoid contractual specificity-related transactions costs, therefore, when they contract for a long period or when a shipper integrates. Long-term contracting therefore makes a shipper and carrier largely independent of other shippers and carriers. Similarly, a shipper who vertically integrates avoids contractual specificity problems and the related transactions costs.

Long-term contracting or vertical integration involves costs, of course, particularly when future demand and supply conditions are uncertain and state contingent contracting is prohibitively expensive. These costs (arising from lower flexibility and increased probability of contractually ex post opportunism) serve to limit contract durations, and thus one may observe contracts of duration less than a ship's life as shippers and carriers trade off these costs against the costs of contractual specificity. Nonetheless, contractual specificities provide a strong inducement to extend the contracting horizon, and long-term agreements or vertical integration efficiently match

---

[16] Forward contracting is thus a game of coordination. Such games usually have many equilibria, but the mechanism by which the parties arrive at a particular equilibrium is usually unspecified. It would be miraculous if agents acting independently and in ignorance of the actions of others were to choose identical expiration dates, particularly inasmuch as many shipping contracts are proprietary. A coordination game equilibrium is best viewed, therefore, as a self-enforcing contract arrived at by negotiations among the affected parties. The negotiations required to reach this equilibrium are likely, however, to be extremely costly.

Decentralized negotiation might work if each shipper-carrier pair was aware of the expiration date of many other charters. They could then negotiate an agreement with an expiration date matching those of other charterers. Contractual specificities could still be a problem, however, if the other parties can extend existing agreements, thereby unexpectedly reducing the competition at the original expiration date.

Explicit forward or futures markets where shippers and carriers trade claims on future shipping services for very distant dates could facilitate coordination. Given the numerous time-space state of the world combinations in such a market, however, many prices would be necessary to do so. The costs of supporting such a complex market could make it infeasible. See Rosen (1988) for a discussion of similar issues. Moreover, since the optimal allocation of ships will typically require some to ballast between ports, the relevant assignment problem is quadratic in terms of the analysis of Koopmans and Beckmann (1957). They demonstrate that no equilibrium price vector exists for quadratic assignment problems. Finally, it may be very costly to enforce forward contracts of this sort. For these reasons, a complete forward market may be costlier than long-term contracting.

the attributes of shipping transactions and those of the contracts that govern them.

Factors Affecting the Severity of Contractual Specificities

Contractual specificities are likely to be important in the contracting for the shipment of a commodity most efficiently transported aboard a relatively small number of ships designed specifically to handle that particular good. Given the thousands of general purpose carriers in existence, even decentralized and uncoordinated contracting for their services should result in a continuum of contract expiration dates. Under these circumstances, shippers and carriers have competitive contracting opportunities available when their contract expires and are invulnerable to holdup. If temporal specificities exist for a particular commodity, therefore, contractual specificities are not important if a large number of ships can carry it economically. One-voyage forward contracts or COAs and time charters of moderate duration prevent temporal specificity related holdups without creating contractual specificities.

If there are significant economies in carrying a particular commodity in a ship tailored to its peculiar handling and stowage characteristics, however, it is improbable that several independently negotiated short- or medium-term contracts between the owners of these vessels and shippers of the commodity will always expire contemporaneously. Since there are few such ships (relative to the number of general purpose carriers), long gaps between expiration dates of forward/term contracts might occur frequently if transactors were to choose the expiration dates of these contracts independently. As a result, shippers and carriers of certain cargoes would be repeatedly vulnerable to contractual specificities if they were to rely on contracts of modest length even if there are several of each. They therefore find long-term contracting or vertical integration efficient. Even if the technological and physical barriers to the redeployment of vessels among shippers are minimal, therefore, a significant potential for holdup exists at contract expiration unless either the agents enter long-term contracts for the services of commodity-specific ships or shippers own these vessels directly.

3.4. Summary and Implications

The severity of temporal and contractual specificities determines bulk shipping contracting choices. Where temporal specificities are unimportant, shippers and carriers contract spot. When various factors—including market thinness, the unavailability of supplies of the shipped commodity from non-firm-specific sources, or efficiencies arising from the use of specialized tonnage—create significant temporal specificities, the parties will contract forward, using time charters or COAs of modest duration. Shippers and carriers in a specialized ship market who utilize long-term contracts or shipper ownership avoid the costs of contractual specificities even when several shippers can employ these vessels efficiently. The type of contract observed in a trade should therefore depend of the following: the characteristics if the cargo flows, the nature of the markets for the transported commodity, the geographic dispersion of supply sources, and the characteristics of the ships employed in that trade.

4. EVIDENCE ON CONTRACTING PRACTICES IN BULK SHIPPING MARKETS

4.1. Introduction and Data Sources

In this section I examine contracting practices in fourteen bulk markets. Volume in these markets accounts for well over 95 percent of all shipments of commodities in bulk; the remaining 5 percent is divided among myriad commodities, each of which is shipped in relatively trivial quantities.[17] I have obtained information from a variety of sources. For general information about contracting practices in shipping and commodity markets I have used a variety of reports issued by H. P. Drewry Shipping Consultants Ltd. These are the best (and in some cases the only) public sources concerning prevailing contracting practices as many of the longer-term deals are proprietary. I have conversed with Drewry consultants and shipping industry participants to confirm certain points and answer questions not addressed specifically in public sources. I have also found considerable information concerning the terms of commodity and shipping contracts reported in trade publications including the *Journal of Commerce* and *Drewry's Shipping Statistics and Economics.*[18]

I obtained the data reported below concerning the number of charter fixings on various trades, the types and duration of such fixings, and the time elapsed between fixing and loading dates from public reports of charter fixings contained in these two publications. According to industry sources, the majority of, but not all, voyage and time charter agreements are included in such public reports. I acquired data on the number of ships of various types through correspondence with Lloyd's of London's Maritime Information Service. This service monitors the construction, deployment, and ownership of virtually every operational or laid-up oceangoing ship.

Observed shipping contracting practices are strongly associated with the factors identified above. Shippers on all spot chartering markets employ general purpose tonnage to carry commodities traded on liquid spot markets

---

[17] The limited information that I have been able to gather on several minor trades also strongly suggests that temporal and contractual specificities determine shipping contracting practices. This information states that shippers employ commodity-specific vessels to transport salt, gypsum, liquified sulfur, liquified propane, methanol, tapioca, and specialty chemicals and obtain these vessels under either long-term contract or direct purchase.

[18] Joskow (1985) was able to rely on a comprehensive compendium of coal contracts for his data source. There is no such systematic description of international commodity or shipping contracts, so I have necessarily relied on public announcements and analyses of such contracts to characterize them.

on relatively thick trade routes, whereas commodities not commonly transported under spot agreements fail to meet one or more of these criteria. Moreover, contract durations appear to be strongly related to factors that influence the importance of contractual specificities. Long-term contracts of affreightment, cargo guaranties, time charters, and vertical integration are common in all trades employing commodity-specific shipping tonnage.

4.2. Spot Shipping Contract Markets

Participants in the grain, ferrous scrap, and fertilizer trades use spot shipping contracts extensively.[19] Long-term contracts are rare in these markets. The flowing descriptions show that shippers can readily obtain supplies of each of these commodities at geographically dispersed, liquid spot markets. Moreover, many of the routes are very thick. Finally, general purpose vessels can carry each of these commodities efficiently. These factors blunt temporal specificities.

Grain

Large trading companies such as Cargill, Continental Grain, Louis Dreyfus, and Bunge dominate the international grain market. These companies buy and sell grain from a myriad of geographically dispersed sources to consumers and processors worldwide. There are also many smaller traders active in this market. Wheat is exported by sea from New Orleans and other ports in Louisiana and Texas, the Great Lakes, the Pacific Northwest, Australia, and Argentina. Corn is exported from the U.S. Great Lakes and the Gulf of Mexico. Soybeans are exported in large quantities from U.S. ports, Europe, and Brazil. The destinations of these cargoes are disparate and include a myriad of ports in Asia, Europe, Africa, South and Central America, and the Middle East, and the spatial pattern of grain flows varies considerably as a result of fluctuations in supply and demand conditions in exporting and importing countries (46 H. P. Drewry Shipping Studies 57, 1976).

As a result of the standardization of grades and the fungibility of grain, buyers can purchase large quantities at each of these export locations on liquid spot markets. There is a very liquid cost, insurance, and freight market (c.i.f.) for grain in barges and a free on board (f.o.b.) market for boatloads of grain at the Gulf of Mexico. By contracting a grain merchant, c.i.f. broker, or f.o.b. broker, a buyer can readily obtain thousands of tons of grain in barges, boats, or railcars for immediate or forward delivery at the Gulf. Merchants can also obtain grain at inland points (for example, central Iowa) through an extensive dealer/country elevator network and arrange transport to a major export point via barge, rail, of truck on a spot basis. Furthermore, since the title to a single lot of grain frequently changes hand in transit in what are called "strings" in the lexicon of the trade, shippers can actually

---

[19] Crude oil shippers have relied on spot contracting since the early 1970s, whereas thermal-coal shippers did so prior to the early 1980s. These markets are described in section 4.4.

acquire grain already bound for consumption points. The existence of futures markets in grains and the widespread quotation of spot prices is further evidence of the existence of liquid and accessible markets for these commodities. Grain supplies are not, therefore, firm specific.

The extreme thickness of the major grain export routes also mitigates temporal specificities. Ships leave the ports of New Orleans or the Parana River in Argentina with high frequency. During 1989 (the last full year for which data are available), for instance, vessels made approximately 3,500 calls to load grain on the lower Mississippi River.[20] As a result, a shipper in these markets can be fairly confident that a vessel will be in close proximity when needed, and a carrier knows that there is a high likelihood that several cargoes will be available if he travels to a major grain port.

Finally, general purpose vessels are the main carriers of grain. The physical characteristics of grain do not require specialized tonnage (as is the case for liquefied natural gas or wood chips) or handling equipment. Indeed, virtually any ship that can fit through the Panama Canal (that is, "Panamax" carriers of approximately 80,000 dwt and smaller ships) can carry grain economically on any major trade route, whereas many ports in major importing countries cannot service large ships. Thus, many grain shippers utilize "handy-sized" vessels in the 20,000–50,000 dwt range; ships below 30,000 dwt carry 75 percent of the world's grain cargoes, whereas ships above 100,000 dwt carry only 8 percent.[21] There are literally thousands of small ships currently trading: in 1990 there were 2,131 dry (that is, nonpetroleum) bulk carriers of between 10,000 and 30,000 dwt, and there were 1,425 ships between 30,000 and 50,000 dwt. This abundance of ships facilitates spot contracting for grain shipping.

Each of these factors mitigates temporal specificites, and, as one would expect, spot chartering dominates grain-shipping contracting arrangements: vertical integration, long-term COAs, and extended time charters are relatively rare (95 H. P. Drewry Shipping Studies 44 1981). Drewry estimates that 60 percent of ocean grain shipments are transported under voyage and trip charters, and an appreciable fraction of the remainder is shipped on relatively short-term time charters.[22] Parties fix these charters quite close to the loading date. An examination of fixings reported in the *Journal of Commerce* and *Drewry's Shipping Statistics and Economics* reveals that the time lag between fixing and loading on grain shipments from the United States is very short. During 1989, the time between fixing and loading dates ranged between zero days (for "prompt" loading) and fifteen days. The

---

[20] Correspondence with officials from the South Louisiana Port Commission and the Port of New Orleans.

[21] 46 H. P. Drewry Shipping Studies 59 (1977), 91; H. P. Drewry Shipping Studies 5 (1981).

[22] A considerable fraction of the residual is shipped by the national shipping lines of the importing countries, rather than on ships obtained under arm's length contracting. For example, the Soviets (and now the Russians) operated a vast national fleet and shipped a considerable fraction of their grain imports aboard these vessels.

median difference between the fixing date and the earliest lay date was seven days.[23] Given the nature of grain markets, ports, and flows, the shortness of the interval between fixing and loading is consistent with the notion that these factors mitigate temporal specificities and make spot contracting feasible.

There is some limited vertical integration and long-term time chartering in the grain market. Cargill's subsidiary, Tradax, for instance, owns eight ocean carriers, whereas Bunge owns several ships and has secured more under long-term time charters. These ships tend to be large; the trade vessels average over 100,000 tons, whereas the Bunge carriers are in the 120,000–140,000 ton range. Since there are far fewer of these larger vessels than Panamax and handy-sized ships, temporal and contractual specificities are likely to be more important for them.[24] Thus, it is not surprising that vertical integration and long-term contracting in the grain market are limited to the larger bulk and combined carriers.

Fertilizer

Trading houses are active in the trading and shipping of fertilizer and related products. Fertilizer is traded on primarily a spot basis, and long-term contracts are not important in this market. There are now futures markets for fertilizers, and spot quotations for important fertilizer products (such as diammunium phosphate) are widely available. General purpose ships can carry this commodity. Moreover, the lower Mississippi River—a very thick market for general purpose tonnage—is a major source of fertilizer. Unsurprisingly, shippers of fertilizer rely mainly on single voyage charters to ship it (112 H. P. Drewry Shipping Studies 37, 1983).

Ferrous Scrap

Trading houses and metals brokers are also active in the market for ferrous scrap. Supplies of this material are ubiquitous. All developed nations generate large amounts of scrap. It is widely traded on a spot basis, as the widespread quotation of spot scrap prices attests; industry publications such as *Iron Age* and the *Scrap Price Bulletin* carry extensive lists of spot scrap prices and advertisements from scrap metal brokers. Scrap does not require specialized tonnage. These factors mitigate temporal-specificity problems, and as one would expect shippers to rely primarily on spot charters to ship ferrous scrap.

---

[23] I determined these figures from the charter fixings reported in *Shipping Statistics and Economics*. The difference given equals the amount of days elapsing from the reporting date (which is usually the same as the fixing date, although some reports are delayed) and the first lay date. Where no specific first lay day was reported (as when a whole month like August 1989 is reported as the lay date instead of a specific day such as August 5, 1989) I used the earliest date in the lay period.

[24] 95 H. P. Drewry Shipping Studies 47 (1981). The subsequent discussion of contracting practices in the iron ore market provides considerable detail about the numbers of larger ships currently trading.

4.3. Forward and Long-Term Contract Markets

Shippers and carriers in the oceanborne iron ore, Great Lakes iron ore, wood chip, Japanese automobile, bauxite and alumina, liquefied natural gas, coking coal, and cement shipping markets do not rely on spot contracting to any significant degree. Instead, term contracts of various forms and durations govern the relation between shippers and carriers. The following descriptions demonstrate that temporal specificities are likely to be important in each market. Since these goods are frequently shipped in commodity-specific bottoms, moreover, contractual specificities are of potential significance. Unsurprisingly, long-term arrangements predominate in these markets.

Oceanborne Iron Ore

Iron ore is the highest tonnage dry-bulk cargo. There are several major exporters of ore, including (in descending order of 1987 shipments) Brazil, Australia, India, Canada, and Liberia. Despite the size of the trade, and the relatively large number of geographic sources, there is no well-developed spot market for ore. Steelmakers obtain it from firm-specific mines, most of which operate under long-term contracts with steel mills, although some are integrated facilities. This firm specificity reflects the need to tailor refining processes to the characteristics of the ore and the efficiencies of very large-scale operation.[25] Shippers transport the ore to firm-specific port facilities near their mills. These producers have specialized productive assets at stake and cannot obtain ore from alternative sources on short notice.

Iron ore has always been a "big ship" trade. Large ships are preferred because ore flows in large, relatively stable quantities between a relatively small number of ports separated by vast distances (a large proportion of the ore travels more than 5,000 miles, whereas shipments from Brazil to Japan move 11,500 miles). Steel firms have always employed the largest dry bulk vessels in operation at any time to haul ore, and the size of these vessels has increased significantly over time. During the early 1970s a 100,000-tonner was a big ship, and almost all carriers of this size were in the ore trades. Currently a 150,000-tonner or larger is considered big, and again a large fraction of these are employed carrying ore.

Three types of ships commonly find employment in the ore trade: specialized ore carriers, strengthened bulkers, and combined carriers (ore/bulk/oil [O/B/O] and ore/oil [O/O] ships). Ore carriers and strengthened bulkers are preferred in the Australia-Japan and Peru/Chile-Japan trades, as there are no backhaul cargoes, and consequently specialized carriers are more efficient. Combination ships were very popular in the 1970s and early 1980s on the Brazil-Japan and Brazil-Europe trades, as after discharging ore they can make a short ballast voyage to lift oil in the Mideast for backhaul to the Caribbean or South America. Although steelmakers still

---

[25] H. P. Drewry Shipping Studies 31 (July 1986); H. P. Drewry Shipping Studies 35 (July 1987). Japan Iron and Steel Federation, The Steel Industry of Japan (1989). Correspondence with the International Iron and Steel Institute.

use combination carriers, they are being supplanted even on the trades they once dominated that emanate from Brazil.

The use of very large ships makes iron ore routes very thin. The most recently negotiated seven-year contract between a major Australian supplier of ore and its primary Japanese consumers, for instance, calls for the shipment of between 17.5 million and 23.5 million tons of ore per annum over the contract period. Given that ships hauling this ore handle approximately 150,000 tons per trip, between 120 and 160 vessel calls per year are required to satisfy the lifting requirements at this port. In total, approximately 420 large bulkers call on the five major Australian ore ports. Approximately 350 large bulkers call at the three Brazilian ports per year. These numbers of calls are far smaller than was observed for the world's major grain port.

Because steelmakers rely on the very largest ships to carry ore, they can utilize a relatively small number of them. As of 1990 there were only 215 bulkers, ore carriers, and combination carriers of 125,000 dwt or better in service. Most carriers have relatively few contracting alternatives outside the iron ore trade as well.

The firm specificity of ore sources and the small number of carriers and shippers suggest that temporal specificities are important in this market. It is probable, moreover, that decentralized short-term forward contracting would lead to contractual specificity problems for specialized ore carriers and very large bulkers and combined carriers as a result of the relatively small number of ships suitable to the trade, as these vessels have few uses outside the ore trades and shippers require them to move ore efficiently.[26] Thus, spot contracting should be relatively rare; shippers and carriers should utilize long-term contracts or vertical integration for the ore carriers and the largest bulkers and combined carriers, whereas shorter-term contracts are feasible for the more modest-sized combination carriers and bulkers.

Observed practices generally follow the expected pattern. A very large fraction of iron ore—at least 90 percent—is shipped under time charters, contracts of affreightment, or cargo guarantees of various maturities, with the residual transported under spot contracts.[27] The durations of the time charters and COAs depend on the type of ship involved. Japanese steelmakers generally secure ore carriers and very large bulk carriers (VLBCs, that is, ships larger than 125,000 dwt) under COAs and cargo guarantees

---

[26] Ore shippers that routinely employ large ships cannot readily substitute smaller ships in their place. Steelmakers expand port facilities to accommodate the big ships, and although these facilities can handle smaller ships they operate at significantly lower throughput rates when doing so. As a result, the costs of handling ore rise when shippers use small ships, and the reduction in the handling rate may prevent a steelmaker from receiving the amount of ore required to operate at capacity. Small ships are consequently poor substitutes for large ones.

[27] 112 H. P. Drewry Shipping Studies 37 (1983) and correspondence with H. P. Drewry consultants. According to H. P. Drewry figures, reported single voyage charters account for only 5 percent of all ore shipped by sea. Since some single voyage charters are not reported publicly, this represents a lower bound on the amount of single voyage ore chartering. Industry analysts argue that at least half (and probably far more) of all ore charters are reported.

extending for eight to fifteen years. *Shipping Statistics and Economics'* monthly review of bulk shipping developments (including ship orders and deliveries) attempts to provide information on the future employment of a new ship. I examined these reviews over the 1984–89 (inclusive) period. They report that 65 percent of bulk carriers of 140,000 tons and greater ordered or delivered during this period secured long-term cargo guarantees from steelmakers or electric utilities, whereas others were purchased by shipping firms with well-known long-term relations and contracts with steelmakers (for example, Bocimar). They reported no such commitments for Panamax and smaller vessels (except for specialized carriers) despite the fact that many more of the smaller ships were built in this period. Although this disparity could arise if buyers of smaller ships simply fail to divulge contracts with the regularity of the buyers of the large ships, industry experts claim that this is not the case; smaller vessels seldom operate under long-term commitments, while the larger vessels are seldom built without them.

It is of considerable interest to note that ore carrier COAs are almost always negotiated prior to the construction of the ship it governs. Indeed, the banks financing construction of a ship to be employed in the ore trade often will not provide funds unless a carrier has a bona fide, long-term COA or other cargo guarantee in hand.[28] The behavior of the banks suggests that holdup costs are a potential concern. Requiring the carrier to obtain a long-term contract that specifies a minimum stream of payments protects the bank against losses arising from default that could occur because of holdups at the expiration dates of short-term time chargers.

Steelmakers secure general bulk carriers and combination vessels under contracts of varying durations. As one would expect, combination carriers operate under long-term charters or COAs less frequently than specialized ore carriers, but steelmakers often secure the very largest combination ships on a long-term basis immediately after their construction. In 1981 all eighteen combination carriers larger than 165,000 dwt were on long-term (at least eight years from construction date) cargo guarantees from major steel firms, as were half of those of between 125,000 and 165,000 dwt. Few large combination ships have been constructed since 1981, but those few (including two 300,000 dwt ships contracted to Krupp for ten years) have received long-term commitments from steel firms. Moderately large bulk carriers and combined carriers (100,000 dwt and smaller) usually operate under time charters and cargo guarantees of generally modest (six months to two years), through variable, durations. There are some modest-sized bulk carriers and smaller combination vessels, however, that either operate under longer-term time charters and cargo guarantees or are owned by steelmakers. The British Steel Corportion owns bulk carriers, some of which are of modest size, and leases others under ten-year bare-boat charters. Similarly, the Italian steelmaker Sidermar owns a fleet of bulk carriers, while the American steel

---

[28] 63 H. P. Drewry Shipping Studies 26 (1978), *Shipping Statistics and Economics*, various issues.

companies U.S. Steel, Republic Steel, and Bethlehem also own relatively small bulk carriers (under 80,000 dwt) through wholly owned shipping subsidiaries.

Although contractual specificities should be less important for these smaller vessels, the prevalence of vertical integration and long-term contracting for them may still reflect transactions cost economizing. They were built or contracted for in the early 1970s, they were considered large, and then these ships were originally built contractual specificities were likely more important for them than is currently the case. The long-term contracts and steelmaker ownership of the smaller tonnage could be artifacts, therefore, of specificities that were important at the time of contracting.

Great Lakes Iron Ore

In its major features the Great Lakes iron ore market is quite similar to the international ore markets described above. Specialized self-unloading ships carry ore from captive mines to captive handling facilities. According to industry participants, steel firms obtain 90 percent of this ore from mines in which they have an ownership stake (which can vary in size) or with which they have a ten- to twenty-year contract. Other ore is obtained under shorter contracts that still typically exceed one year in duration. There is little if any spot cargo trading analogous to the grain or crude oil markets. Only about seventy ships are currently in operation serving four major steel producers.

Ship contracting practices are also similar in the two ore markets: spot contracts are virtually unknown, and very long-term relationships between shippers and carriers are universal. Indeed, major U.S. steelmakers have owned and operated tonnage since the development of the domestic ore industry in Minnesota and the Michigan Upper Peninsula in the early twentieth century. Of late several steelmakers have sold their owned tonnage to independent operating companies, but leased it back under long-term arrangements.

Wood Chips

Several Japanese papermakers (including Toyo Pulp, Oji, Jujo, Mitsubishi, Taio, Tohuku, and Daishowa) ship wood chips from the Pacific Northwest, Oceania, and Chile to Asia. Extremely specialized ships dominate this trade because conventional bulk carriers can load only two-thirds of their rated tonnage in chips as a result of the commodity's high volume to weight ratio (that is, its stowage factor). The high stowage factor also prevents special chip vessels from carrying any other type of cargo economically because (a) the ships would swamp if they were to carry even a modest cubic volume of a conventional cargo since these are far heavier per unit of volume than chips, and (b) as a result of the extreme beam of wood chip carriers, cargo handling equipment designed for conventional cargoes cannot reach the far side of their holds.[29] Because of the size of the trade and this specialization, there are now ninety-four wood chip carriers operating worldwide. At most, forty ships operate on any particular route, and consequently each market is relatively thin.[30] Compared to markets like grain or crude oil shipping, there are very few carriers and shippers in this market.[31]

These factors suggest that neither spot contracts nor forward contracts with durations significantly shorter than the life of the ship should exist in this market. This is indeed the case. Long-term (ten years or more) COAs specifying minimum volume and service requirements prevail. *Shipping Statistics and Economics* reported the existence of long-term carriage agreements for 90 percent of the wood chip carriers ordered or delivered in 1984–89; this is a lower bound since some agreements go unreported. As in the iron ore market, ship financiers usually require the wood chip carrier to obtain a bona fide COA with a duration approximating the life of a ship prior to lending money for construction.[32]

Cement

Cement manufacturers are the primary marketers of their product; spot trading is relatively unimportant. Cement manufacturers own loading terminals and discharging terminals in importing countries. These considerations imply that cement manufacturers have specific assets at stake and cannot readily obtain the product from other sellers on short notice. These factors contribute to temporal specificities.

Although a wide variety of ships can carry bagged cement, cement shipped in bulk (the primary means of shipment today) requires special handling and places some constraints on ship design. Special shaping of the holds of ships allows them to carry larger quantities of cement because this cargo reposes in the hull differently than other dry commodities. Cement is dusty, and ships must be cleaned prior to loading another cargo that the dust would contaminate. Thus, although generalized bulk carriers can transport cement, there are advantages to shipping it in specialized ships or using a general purpose ship repeatedly to avoid frequent cleanings and adjustments to holds.

Most cement transported on "short-sea" (that is, short-distance) routes is carried in small (under 10,000 dwt) specialized cement carriers. A large fraction of the cement shipped long distances travels aboard specialized

---

[29] 63 H. P. Drewry Shipping Studies 22 (1978). Again, since several paper companies ship chips, the vessels are commodity rather than shipper specific.

[30] These ships commonly make nine voyages per year. 99 H. P. Drewry Shipping Studies 34 (1981). Thus, the number of ship calls per year on any major wood chip route is approximately only 300.

[31] During downturns in the chip market some carriers have converted their chip carriers to conventional carriers or PCCs. Conversion entails considerable expense.

[32] *Shipping Statistics and Economics*, various issues. 99 H. P. Drewry Shipping Studies 34. 59 H. P. Drewry Shipping Studies 59. Mitsui O.S.K. Lines and Nippon Yusen Kaisha Annual Reports, 1981–90.

oceangoing cement carriers. There is a relatively small number of these specialized ships (208 under 10,000 dwt and 46 above 10,000 in 1983) in existence. Generalized bulkers also carry cement.

Given the nature of cement markets and shipping technology, one should not observe spot contracting for cement shipping. Indeed, COAs and vertical integration are the dominant forms of ship contracting in the cement trades. Vertical integration is quite common, particularly in the short-sea trades, and major cement shippers own the larger, long-distance trade cement ships. Each of the five cement carriers delivered or ordered (as reported in *Shipping Statistics and Economics*) in 1984–89 was purchased by cement companies. Cement shippers usually charter in general purpose ships under moderate term COAs, cargo guarantees, and time charters. Thus, contracting practices in this market align with transactions cost attributes.

Bauxite and Alumina

The market for bauxite is similar to that for iron ore and coking coal. The major aluminum producers (ALCOA, ALCAN, Reynolds, Alusuisse, Pechiney, and Kaiser) own bauxite mines. Stuckey estimates that in the post-World War II period firms received between 80 and 90 percent of their bauxite from vertically integrated sources in the Caribbean, Guinea, and Australia (Stackey, 1983: 43–64). They acquired the remainder in arm's-length transactions governed by contracts of very long duration. For instance, contracts between some Japanese manufacturers and Australian mines are greater than twenty-five years in duration (Stackey, 1983: 118–121). Firms rely on firm-specific sources of bauxite because of the necessity of matching refining technology to the specific ore refined, and the disparity of ore characteristics. Since refiners cannot use just any bauxite, the supply sources pertinent to any refiner are fairly limited, firm specific, and usually geographically concentrated. Bauxite is smelted into alumina before it is refined into aluminum. Alumina smelters are sometimes located tooth-and-jowl with bauxite mines. There is no well-developed spot market for this intermediate product. Manufacturers almost always ship alumina from vertically integrated facilities to owned processing plants. As a result, temporal specificity problems should preclude spot contracting for the shipment of both of these aluminum raw materials.

Both specialized and generalized ships are employed in this trade. Most of the North American shippers employ specialized self-unloading bauxite and alumina carriers (although they also employ more generalized bulkers), and some Japanese refiners also utilize specialized carriers. European shippers tend to use generalized bulkers. Contracting specificities should be important for the specialized vessels but not particularly important for the common bulkers.

Given these conditions, it is unsurprising that spot chartering is not an important contracting practice for bauxite and alumina. The major North American aluminum producers own specialized ships either directly or through wholly owned shipping subsidiaries, whereas Japanese shippers obtain specialized ships under long-term cargo guarantees with domestic shipping companies. They also obtain some generalized bulkers under cargo guarantees of moderate duration. European refiners usually employ more generalized bulk tonnage and obtain shipping tonnage under COAs of varying but typically moderate durations.

Liquefied Natural Gas (LNG)

Some sellers and distributors of natural gas (such as pipeline utility companies) buy this commodity from producers in Indonesia, Malaysia, and Algeria under long-term contracts. These contracts are typically twenty to twenty-five years in duration and require the buyer to lift minimum quantities of gas.[33] The contracts are a direct consequence of the specificities inherent in the processing and use of LNG.

In order to transport gas from producing to consuming regions (nine utilities in Japan import 60 percent of the world's LNG production with the balance going to several utilities in Western Europe and the United States) by ship, it must be cooled to −162 degrees centigrade. To maintain these low temperatures, ships carrying LNG are very specialized. These vessels utilize several large, strengthened stainless steel spheres to contain the liquefied gas, as well as shipboard refrigeration equipment. Moreover, their crews require extensive training to transport this volatile cargo safely. The ships are extremely costly to build (about eight times as expensive per ton deadweight as a crude oil tanker) and cannot carry other commodities. There are only about eighty-five such ships in existence, of which about seventy have capacities greater than 50,000 cubic meters.

These conditions, and the prevalence of long-term contracts in the LNG market, create the potential for acute temporal and contractual specificity problems in LNG shipping. As a result, there is no spot market for LNG carriers. Shippers of this commodity obtain tonnage either through long-term contracts (with durations approximating the life of the ship) or vertical integration. Japanese utilities obtain LNG carriers under long-term charters with a consortium of Japanese shipping companies. At least two American pipeline companies—Panhandle Eastern and El Paso—purchased several LNG carriers to carry gas from Algeria to the United States.

A recent development further illustrates the importance of contractual specificities in the LNG market. The developers of the proposed Trans-Alaska Gas System, which (if built) will transport natural gas from Prudhoe Bay to a terminal located to the southwest for transport via ship to the Far East, have stated that they will not begin construction of the pipeline until they secure long-term contracts from Asian and Australasian utilities. Moreover, the American shipping company Sea Land has announced that it will build the world's largest LNG carriers to transport this gas, but only if it also secures long-term shipping contracts. Sea Land intends to include

---

[33] 82 H. P. Drewry *Shipping Studies* 61–63 (1980) provides a list of LNG contracts and their terms.

the utilities buying the LNG in a syndicate to finance the vessels. Therefore, although Sea Land will operate the vessels, the shippers will have a substantial financial stake in them, which sharply circumscribes their incentives to behave opportunistically. This is strongly consistent with the view that contractual specificities are acute in the market for these LNG ships.

Japanese Automobiles

There is obviously no spot market for Toyotas or Hondas exported from Japan. Honda cannot buy Toyotas to sell in the United States if a ship fails to arrive to transport Accords. Auto manufacturers have, moreover, specialized assets at stake; dealerships and advertising are worthless with no cars to sell. There are considerable cost advantages, furthermore, to using specialized pure car carriers (PCCs) to ship automobiles. Cars can be driven on and off the ship (thereby eliminating the need for special handling equipment), and they can be stowed efficiently to prevent damage during transit. These factors create temporal specificities.

The number of carriers in use is relatively small (compared to generalized grain carriers, for instance), and consequently the markets are relatively thin. There are currently 413 car carriers in existence, many of which are obsolete car bulkers or ships specialized for "short-sea" (for example, intra-European or intra-Asian) shipments. Market participants estimate that approximately 150 PCCs service the main American, European, and Australian import markets. These usually carry between 3,000 and 6,000 cars per voyage.

The absence of spot markets for automobilies and the thinness of PCC routes make spot contracting intractable. The small number of vessels also creates contractual specificities. One expects to observe, therefore, long-term contracts between automobile companies and automobile carriers.

This is indeed the case. Particular shipper-carrier pairs have cooperated closely with one another over long periods of time. These informal long-term relations are supported by formal long-term contracting. Japanese automobile makers secure PCCs under COAs with Japanese shipping firms including Nippon Yusen Kaisha (NYK) and Mitsui O.S.K. Lines (MOL).[34] Car carriers frequently secure COAs from the shippers prior to construction in order to facilitate financing. According to industry participants, these contracts are typically five to ten years in duration, less than the (roughly) fifteen-year expected life of a PCC. These participants assert that the difficulties of pricing a vessel's services over its full life make it very costly to contract over a fifteen-year period. Shippers and carriers have few alternatives available to them at contract expiration, so bilateral monopoly characterizes negotiations at this time. Negotiations tend to be long and

---

[34] In the mid-1970s Mazda and Nissan owned shares of PCCs in conjunction with NYK and MOL. Toyota has not vertically integrated into shipping at any time, and Mazda and Nissan no longer have interests in PPCs. Japanese shipping firms carry approximately 80 percent of all automobiles exported from their country. Volvo is a part owner of Atlantic Container Lines, which ships Volvos from Sweden to North America.

costly as a result, often lasting a year or longer. Thus, shippers and carriers explicitly trade off the costs of flexibility and ex post opportunism against the costs of contractual specificity when negotiating contract durations.

Coking Coal

Because of the necessity of adapting steelmaking capital to the characteristics of coking coal, steelmakers obtain this product from captive suppliers that they either own or buy from under long-term contracts. There is no coking coal spot market to speak of. Shippers therefore are vulnerable to temporal specificites as they cannot obtain alternative supplies on short notice. Coal is now usually shipped in moderately large general purpose bulkers in the 80,000–100,000 dwt range, although larger ships (150,000 dwt and better) are becoming increasingly common. The markets are relatively thin, with large bulk carriers making less than 200 port calls per year in the major South African, Australian, and Canadian ports.

These factors suggest that the transactions costs of spot chartering for coal shipping are high relative to the costs of forward contracting but that the problems here are not as acute as for wood chips or LNG. As a result, forward and term contracts of moderate duration should prevail while very long-term contracts are unnecessary. Indeed, shippers and carriers seldom contract spot to transport coking coal. Most coal—at least 90 percent—is shipped under contracts of affreightment that guarantee minimum cargo volumes and specify service frequency. These COAs typically extend for less than three years, although fifteen-year contracts are not unusual, particularly in the Japanese import trades where shippers now employ VLBCs. There is, moreover, some vertical integration in this market. Several major coal sellers, including Utah International, Kaiser, Shell Coal, and D. K. Ludwig, own very large bulk vessels, and the steelmakers named earlier who have integrated into shipping use their ships to transport coke as well as ore.

4.4. Markets Where Contracting Practices Have Changed

Crude Oil

Changes in contracting practices that have occurred since 1973 for the shipment of crude oil provide a remarkable illustration of the importance of temporal specificities in determining contracting practices. Prior to 1973, the seven major oil refiners—British Petroleum, Exxon, Gulf, Mobil, Royal Dutch Shell, Socal, and Texaco—dominated the distribution (as well as the refining) of crude oil. The majors obtained the bulk of the supplies transported by sea from Middle Eastern, West African, and Indonesian producers under equity contracts or preference agreements; in 1973, 90 percent of the 30 million barrels traded internationally were purchased under equity agreements. These contracts gave the majors rights to lift crude from particular sources. These sources were consequently "tied" to the majors. The majors were, moreover, tied to these oil suppliers as they could not readily obtain large quantities of oil from others on short notice. This created a potential for temporal specificities in the shipping market. Since there were numerous tankers afloat at the time, however, the scope for contractual specificities was limited; there were 3,198 tankers averaging 55,000 dwt trading in 1972.[35] There was some potential for contractual specificity in the market for "supertankers," very large crude carriers (VLCCs), and ultralarge crude carriers (ULCCs), given the relatively small number of these ships.

Given these market conditions, it is unsurprising that although there was some spot contracting, most oil was carried in ships secured under forward contracts or time charters of modest duration, or in refiner-owned vessels. In 1973, about half of the time charters lasted less than one year, while about 44 percent extended for two years or more, with some extending longer than five years. These relatively modest durations (and their variability) are unsurprising; one would not expect contractual specificities to be important for any but the largest crude carriers as the large number of tankers plying the trade led to a continuous expiration of contracts without any explicit coordination of expiration dates.

There is some evidence that tanker time charter durations depended on the importance of contractual specificities. Tankers under time charters with more than five years to expiration averaged 91,000 dwt. Tankers under time charters with durations of five years or less averaged 73,200 dwt. The average size of tankers with forward commitments for time charters with durations in excess of five years equaled 210,000 dwt, whereas the average size of ships with forward commitments for time charters with durations of five years or less equaled 150,000 dwt. Larger tankers (for which contractual specificities were more acute) were more likely, therefore, to be on long-term charters. Since many large tankers traded on the spot market or operated on time charters of six months to two years, however, contractual specificities do not explain completely chartering practices in crude oil markets prior to 1973.

The existence of vertical integration and some longer-term charters in these markets is, however, somewhat difficult to understand. Refiner-owned tonnage accounted for between 30 and 40 percent of the total throughout the 1960s and early 1970s. Although contractual specificities should have been most acute for the very largest tankers, the VLCCs and ULCCs (as there were only eighty such ships in existence), in 1972 refiners owned a smaller fraction of supertanker tonnage—31.39 percent—than they did of tankers overall—32.39 percent. Refiners owned, moreover, a larger share (52.7 percent) of the tonnage in the 10,000–19,999 dwt tanker category than they did in any other category, even though there were more ships in this category (453) than in any other. Although ownership at a point in time reflects past decisions, and may in turn reflect past rather than current

---

[35] During the early 1970s *Shipping Statistics and Economics* published statistics on the distribution of charter expiration dates in the major trades measured in the number and tonnage of tankers that would be available in each month. According to these figures, contracts lapsed almost continuously. For each month and each major trade at least thirty to forty charters expired.

contracting conditions, only contemporary conditions affect contracts for new buildings. New buildings in 1972 exhibited a pattern similar to that described for existing tonnage. Refiners had committed to purchase 85 percent of tankers on order of 29,999 dwt or less but only 33 percent of those on order of 175,000 dwt or greater. Contractual specificities do not appear, therefore, to have been crucial determinants of refiner ownership decisions.

Crude oil shipping contracting practices changed dramatically in the 1970s. Importantly, this change in ship contracting coincided with a decline in the firm specificity of crude oil supplies. As a result of actions that culminated in 1979–80 by producers in the Organization of Petroleum Exporting Countries (OPEC), the spot market for crude oil grew dramatically in importance, while the amount of oil lifted under longstanding long-term equity contracts declined considerably. Spot chartering of oil shipping tonnage consequently grew in importance while the extent of vertical integration and time chartering diminished.

In 1973, the OPEC nations began to curtail the equity rights that tied oil supplies to the majors. This process accelerated with Iran's abrogation of all such contracts following the revolution in 1979. The cumulative effect of this process was to reduce dramatically the proportion of oil obtained under long-term contracts. As noted earlier, prior to 1973 the majors obtained virtually all of their Middle Eastern oil under such contracts. This proportion fell to 50 percent by 1978, and 42 percent by 1980.[36]

This process was accompanied by the development of the spot oil markets in Rotterdam and futures trading in crude oil and refined products in the United States and Great Britain.[37] Moreover, oil traders proliferated during this period and to a large extent supplanted the majors as primary marketers of crude oil. One industry observer noted that "oil markets increasingly are characterized by short term arrangements" and "the importance of arms length trading in oil products [as opposed to obtaining supplies from captive sources] is generally increasing (Roeber, 1979: 181–83). Another noted that refiners could take advantage of the newfound worldwide availability of crude sources to rapidly adjust their crude oil sources (Mering, 1982: 13). Put another way, refiner oil supply sources became far less firm specific as a result of the decline in importance in equity agreements and the rise of the spot oil market.

The market for oil shipping responded to this change in the market for crude oil. The importance of short-term spot chartering grew dramatically, while long-term time charters declined in importance. Moreover, oil majors scrapped owned tonnage at a more rapid rate than the market as a whole. The average length of time charters also fell. Finally, the length of deferment in forward-shipping contracts declined dramatically.

Oceanborne oil shipments in the period 1973–80 were very stable, varying within a range of roughly 1,500–1,700 million tons during this interval.

[36] Mohnfeld (1982); 98 H. P. Drewry *Shipping Studies* 36.
[37] Roeber (1979): Mering (1982).

The geographic pattern of trade, moreover, remained virtually unchanged. Single voyage spot chartering activity by oil refiners exploded, however, from 176.4 million dwt in 1973 to 390.3 million dwt in 1978 to 455.9 million dwt in 1980. Spot chartering by oil traders (middlemen, brokers, and speculators) rose from 39.5 million dwt in 1973 to 105.2 million dwt in 1980. Most of the seventy-three charterers that entered the market between 1973 and 1980 were traders.[38]

Most of the single voyage charters were (and are) true spot contracts. During 1980 the difference between the fixing and loading dates ranged between zero and ninety days. The mean and median differences were far closer to the lower end of this range and equaled approximately ten days.[39]

The duration of time charters (which accounted for the lion's share of the oil not shipped under voyage contracts) also fell during the 1973–80 period. In 1973, 54 percent of all time charters were for one year or longer, with 44 percent for two years or longer. In 1980, only 20.2 percent of all time charters were of a duration greater than one year, with only 12 percent greater than two years. The figures for 1984 and 1990 are comparable to those for 1980.

The distribution of tanker ownership changed too as the crude spot market developed. Specifically, vertical integration became less important. Total tanker tonnage grew negligibly (0.4 percent) from 1976 to 1981, before declining 5 percent between 1981 and 1985. The seven majors, moreover, reduced their fleets by 13.8 percent between 1976 to 1981, and a further 12.4 percent from 1981 to 1985. As a result, refiner-owned tonnage has declined from approximately 35 percent of the total in 1972 to 15 percent today.

The forward market for oil transport changed dramatically as well. In 1973, only 33 percent of forward fixings required delivery less than four months after the signing of the contract, whereas deferment exceeded twenty-four months for 15 percent of all forward fixings. By 1980, the period of deferment was less than one month for 72 percent of all fixings, whereas deferments of twenty-four months or more represented only 0.5 percent of all forward-tanker contracts. Forward chartering also became less prevalent during this period.

In sum, this evidence strongly suggests that the firm specificity of supply sources can create temporal specificities that induce firms to avoid spot shipping transactions. During the 1973–80 period the crude oil market was radically transformed. Spot market transactions supplanted the procurement of significant quantities of crude oil from refiner-specific supply sources during this period. This evolution of a spot oil market gave shippers much more flexibility to obtain crude from a variety of sources on short notice and therefore made them far less vulnerable to temporal specificities. This

---

[38] The dramatic increase in the number of oil brokers also illustrates the evolution of petroleum trading toward spot trading arrangements.

[39] The median difference between shipping and loading dates was still about ten days in 1989.

reduced the transactions costs of spot contracting for tankers, and as a result such tanker transactions supplanted to a considerable degree the time charters, forward fixings, and vertical integration that had prevailed in the pre-1973 era.

Thermal Coal

Thermal coal (also called "steam coal") is used to fuel electrical power generation plants and cement kilns. Prior to the dramatic rise in the price of oil, most coal shipped in bulk vessels was coking coal. The oil shock ushered in a boom in the oceanborne trade of thermal coal in the late 1970s. At the initiation of this boom, long-term thermal coal contracts were relatively rare, and utilities and trading companies traded large quantities on a spot basis. The sources of thermal coal were, moreover, geographically dispersed with extensive production in the United States, South Africa, and Australia. Coal traders consequently were not strongly tied to any particular cargo source.

Some thermal coal shipping trades were relatively thick at the peak of the boom. During peak seasons several ships laden with thermal coal sail weekly, for instance, on the routes between Hampton Roads (in the United States) to Japan. Ships make calls on an almost daily basis at the South African Richard's Bay facility as well. This thickness also insulates shippers and carriers from bilateral monopoly problems.

Prior to the mid-1980s shippers typically employed carriers in the 50,000–100,000 dwt range to haul steam coal. As a result of capacity constraints at many of the more important thermal coal ports, moreover, vessels in the lower end of this range predominated. In 1980 there were at least 745 bulk ships of between 50,000 and 80,000 dwt, and 350 bulk carriers of between 80,000 and 150,000 dwt. Certain combination carriers—ore/bulk/oil ships—also carried significant quantities of coal. In 1980, 230 combination carriers of at least 80,000 dwt were active, many of which traded in coal. Thus, coal shippers had access to over 1,000 vessels to handle their cargo.

These three market characteristics reduced the transactions costs of spot contracting for thermal coal shipping. Unsurprisingly, such contracting was common in this market. At the beginning of the coal boom large amounts of coal were shipped on a spot basis. As with the grains, these contracts were usually fixed one or two weeks prior to the time of loading.

As the thermal coal market has matured, suppliers and utilities have entered into long-term contracts. Moreover, thermal coal ports have expanded capacity to serve larger vessels, so shippers are now employing VLBCs with some frequency, although some coal is still transported aboard smaller general purpose vessels in the 50,000 dwt–90,000 dwt range. As noted earlier, there are far fewer VLBCs trading than moderately sized generalized carriers.

Shipers secure these hulls under COAs of varying durations. Those for the midsized vessels typically extend for less than three years. Fifteen-year contracts are not unusual in the Japanese import trades where shippers now employ VLBCs.

The evolution of contracting for coal shipping again suggests that contractual and temporal specificities are important. Spot contracting was common when the industry was relatively new, firm-specific supply arrangements for coal had not developed, and shippers employed relatively small carriers. As long-term contracts for thermal coal and very large ships have become more common, contract durations have increased, and spot contracting has become less pervasive. Moreover, shippers and carriers employ very long-term contracts for the very large vessels for which contractual specificities are most likely to be important, and they use contracts of modest duration for smaller ships less likely to be plagued by these specificities.

Lumber and Logs

Lumber and logs are sold by major lumber companies. These firms obtain timber from their own lands and market it themselves in foreign countries. They also operate specialized handling terminals. Given this extensive integration there is no spot market in logs and lumber. Lumber companies have specialized marketing and production investments at stake at home and abroad and cannot readily access supplies of timber from other sellers.

Prior to the containerization revolution in liner shipping, lumber and logs typically were shipped aboard conventional 'tween-deckers or Liberty ships. These vessels were unspecialized, and lumber shippers relied on relatively short-term contracting for their services.

In the 1960s and 1970s the international traffic in lumber increased dramatically. This increase in oceangoing timber traffic made it economic to ship timber in specialized vessels with wide hatches, boxy holds, and specialized handling gear since conventional bulkers cannot handle or stow this commodity efficiently. There are 87 log carriers and 278 lumber carriers in operation with several shippers. As a result of the relatively slow handling times and multiple port calls, these vessels make few voyages per year. This suggests that the markets served are thin.

Given the conditions in the market for logs and lumber, and the nature of the shipping technology, transactions cost considerations suggest that neither spot contracts nor moderate-duration term contracts are efficient in this market for shippers that use the services of entire vessels and the carriers that supply them. In fact, long-term time charters and vertical integration are the predominant forms of organization for specialized carriers. Major timber companies including Weyerhauser and the Swedish concern SCA own shipping subsidiaries. Others, such as Seaboard and Japanese shippers, obtain specialized tonnage under long-term time charters. Lumber companies purchased or extended long-term cargo guarantees for each of the four lumber carriers reported as delivered in *Shipping Statistics and Economics* in the 1984–89 period.

4.5. SUMMARY

The foregoing analysis of bulk shipping market contracting practices reveals that shippers and carriers spot contract for the shipment of commodities transported on thick markets aboard general purpose tonnage and identifies which firms obtain from nonspecific sources. When one of these conditions fails to hold, shippers and carriers use either time charters or COAs in place of spot contracts. Table 7.1 summarizes these results. It lists each of the commodity trades studied and specifies whether each trade is characterized by firm-specific supplies, the use of specialized ships, and thin markets. If so, there is a "yes" in the relevant column, and if not, there is a "no" instead.

The table reveals that spot contracting is common only for those markets where there are not firm-specific supply sources, specialized vessels, or thin markets. A "yes" in any category is associated with the use of some longer-term contracting arrangement. A "yes" answer to all three questions is uniformly associated with long-term contracting and/or shipper ownership. These results are therefore broadly consistent with the theory outlined earlier.

Unfortunately, the high degree of collinearity in the data (that is, for each commodity there tend to be all "yeses" or all "noes") precludes the determination of the marginal contribution of each of these factors to

TABLE 7.1
Bulk Shipping Market Characteristics and Contracting Practices

Commodity	Firm-specific Supplies	Specialized Vessels	Thin Market	Typical Contract
Grain	No	No	No	SPOT
Oil (post-1973)	No	No	No	SPOT
Oil (pre-1973)	Yes	No	No	MTC or VI
Thermal coal (pre-1980)	No	No	No	SPOT
Thermal coal (post-1980)	Yes	Yes/No	No	LTCOA for large ships, MTC for others
Coking coal	Yes	Yes/No		LTCOA for large ships, MTC for others
Fertilizer	No	No	No	SPOT
Scrap	No	No	No	SPOT
Iron ore	Yes	Yes	Yes	LTCOA or VI
Great Lakes ore	Yes	Yes	Yes	LTCOA or VI
Wood chips	Yes	Yes	Yes	LTCOA or VI
Lumber	Yes	Yes	Yes	LTCOA or VI
Cement	Yes	Yes	Yes	LTCOA or VI
Bauxite	Yes	Yes	Yes	LTCOA or VI
Liquefied natural gas	Yes	Yes	Yes	LTCOA or VI
Autos	Yes	Yes	Yes	LTCOA or VI

Note. LTCOA = long-term contracting: VI = vertical integration: SPOT = spot chartering: MTC = medium-term chartering.

contracting practices.[40] Despite this, however, the results demonstrate decisively that the physical redepolyability of an asset may be a necessary, but is certainly not a sufficient, condition for spot contracting to prevail. The results suggest that assets must be rapidly and continuously redepolyable among many potential users in order to avoid opportunism problems.

5. CONCLUSIONS

This article has examined theoretically and empirically how transactions costs affect bulk shipping contracting practices. Time and space factors and market characteristics determine whether spot contracting is feasible. Spot contracting should prevail on thick markets; for commodities available on geographically dispersed, liquid spot markets; and for commodities transportable aboard general purpose ships. Shippers and carriers should contract forward when some or all of these conditions do not obtain. If spot contracting is impractical, the duration of contracting horizons should depend on the type of tonnage employed to carry a commodity. Shippers and carriers should use relatively long-term contracts (or vertical integration) for commodities shipped on thin markets aboard a relatively small number of special purpose ships. Observed contracting practices in the fourteen most important bulk shipping markets align closely with these attributes.

This review of bulk shipping contracting has some important implications for transactions cost analysis. First, and most important, it suggests that an asset must be physically redeployable on short notice among a large number of users if buyers and sellers are to avoid contractual hazards when transacting on a spot or short-term basis. At least four or five shippers can employ even the most specialized ships included in this sample of trades, but long-term arrangements prevail in these markets, nonetheless. Second, the survival of long-term contracts in many shipping markets implies that reputation can be an efficient means of deterring contractually ex post holdups (as argued by Coase, 1988) Third, the fact that shippers and carriers enter into formal contracts of (sometimes) extended duration implies that reputation and repeat transactions are not sufficient to deter strategic behavior in the absence of a formal agreement.

---

[40] The crude-oil experience suggests that the existence of firm-specific supply sources is an important determinant of temporal specificity. The bauxite and cement trades, where there is a mixture of ship types, also suggests that the use of commodity-specific ships is an important determinant of contractual specificities. While general purpose vessels utilized to carry these commodities typically operate under short-term charters, the ships designed specifically to carry them invariably operate under long-term contracts or are shipper owned.

PART

II

VERTICAL INTEGRATION

VERTICAL INTEGRATION AS ORGANIZATIONAL OWNERSHIP: THE FISHER BODY–GENERAL MOTORS RELATIONSHIP REVISITED

Benjamin Klein

I have always considered my work with Armen Alchian and Robert Crawford (1978) on vertical integration to represent an extension of Coase's classic article on "The Nature of the Firm." By focusing on the "hold-up" potential that is created when firm-specific investments are made by transactors, or what we called the appropriation of quasi-rents, I believed we had elucidated one aspect of the Coasian concept of transaction costs associated with market exchange. We hypothesized that an increase in firm-specific investments, by increasing the market transaction costs associated with a hold-up, increased the likelihood of vertical integration. This relationship between firm-specific investments, market transaction costs, and vertical integration was illustrated by examining the contractual difficulties that existed when General Motors purchased automobile bodies from Fisher Body and the corresponding benefits that were created when the parties vertically integrated.

It is clear from Coase's lectures that he considers our analysis not to represent an extension of his earlier work, but rather to be an alternative, incorrect explanation for vertical integration (1988: lecture 3). Coase recognizes that an increase in the quasi-rents yielded by firm-specific investments creates a hold-up potential. However, he argues that there is no

Reprinted from the Journal of Law Economics, and Organization vol. 4, no. 1 (Spring 1988). © 1988 by Yale University. All rights reserved. ISSN 8756-6222. Reprinted with the permission of Oxford University Press.

Benjamin Klein is Professor of Economics, the University of California, Los Angeles. I am grateful to Harold Demsetz, Kevin James, Timothy Opler, and Oliver Williamson for useful comments.

reason to believe that this situation is more likely to lead to vertical integration than to a long-term contract. Although long-term contracts are imperfect, opportunistic behavior is usually effectively handled in the marketplace, according to Coase, by a firm's need to take account of the effect of its actions on future business. Coase claims that before writing his classic paper he explicitly considered opportunistic behavior as a motive for vertical integration, in particular as it applied to the General Motors–Fisher Body case, and explicitly rejected it.

Unfortunately Coase's rejection of the opportunism analysis is based upon too simplified a view of the market contracting process and too narrow a view of the transaction costs associated with that process. A more complete analysis of how vertical integration solved the opportunistic behavior problem in the Fisher Body–General Motors case provides insight into the nature of the transaction costs that are associated with the market contracting process and how vertical integration reduces these costs. The primary transaction costs saved by vertical integration are not the "ink costs" associated with the number of contracts written and executed but, rather, are the costs associated with contractually induced hold-ups. The analysis indicates that hold-up potentials are created not solely from the existence of firm-specific investments, but also from the existence of the rigidly set long-term contract terms that are used in the presence of specific investments. Vertical integration, by shifting ownership of the firm's organizational asset, creates a degree of flexibility and avoids this contractually created hold-up potential, thereby resulting in significant transaction cost savings.

1. LONG-TERM CONTRACTS AS SOLUTIONS TO AND CAUSES OF HOLD-UP PROBLEMS

Coase is correct in believing that in many cases contractual arrangements, rather than vertical integration, can be and are used to solve hold-up problems. For example, consider the case of building a house on a piece of land. It is obvious that you would not build the house on land you had only rented for a short term. After the land lease expired the landowner could hold you up for the quasi-rents on your house investment. However, this does not mean that you need necessarily own the land, that is, vertically integrate, to solve this problem. The hold-up problem potentially could be solved by the use of a long-term rental contract on the land negotiated before the house was constructed. Since land is the type of input where anticipated quality variations are very small or nonexistent, a long-term rental contract is certainly a feasible way to minimize the hold-up potential without vertical integration.

The long-term exclusive dealing contract adopted by Fisher Body and General Motors in 1919 can be explained as an analogous contractual means to avoid a hold-up potential without vertical integration.[1] Since Fisher Body had to make an investment highly specific to General Motors in the stamping machines and dies necessary to produce the automobile bodies demanded by General Motors, a significant hold-up potential was created. After Fisher made the investment, General Motors could have attempted to appropriate the quasi-rents from the investment by threatening to reduce their demand for Fisher-produced bodies, or even to terminate Fisher completely if price were not adjusted downward. The exclusive dealing clause, which required General Motors over a ten-year period to buy all their closed metal bodies from Fisher Body, limited the ability of General Motors to opportunistically threaten Fisher Body in this manner. The contractual arrangement thereby reduced Fisher Body's reliance on General Motors' reputation and encouraged Fisher Body to make the specific investment.

Although the ten-year exclusive dealing contractual arrangement protected Fisher against a General Motors hold-up, it created a potential for Fisher to hold up General Motors. Fisher could take advantage of the requirement that General Motors could not purchase elsewhere by increasing price or decreasing quality. The contract attempted to protect General Motors against this reverse hold-up potential by specifying a formula by which price would be set over the ten-year period at a competitive level. In addition, in a further attempt to minimize the potential Fisher hold-up of General Motors, the contract also included most-favored nation provisions so that the price could not be greater than what Fisher Body charged other automobile manufacturers for "similar" bodies. Such a "price protection" clause prevents a hold-up because a price increase or decrease to any buyer is guaranteed to be given to all buyers. Hence, established buyers that are "locked-in" by a specific investment or a contractual commitment are protected by the seller's desire to make profitable new sales.

In spite of the existence of a long-term contractual arrangement with explicitly set price and price protection clauses, there is still some probability that a hold-up may occur. This is because not all elements of future performance are specified in the contract. Due to uncertainty and the difficulty of specifying all elements of performance in a contractually enforceable way, contracts will necessarily be incomplete to one degree or another. This creates the possibility for transactors to take advantage of the contract to hold-up their transacting partner. For example, the long-term land rental contract in the house construction example may permit the landowner to hold-up the house owner by opportunistically controlling the water supply to the house, or by failing to build a wall to prevent erosion of the land under the house, or by closing a road on the land for claimed repairs and thereby threatening to restrict access to the house.

---

[1] The contractual agreement between Fisher Body and General Motors can be found in the minutes of the Board of Directors of Fisher Body Corporation for November 7, 1919. Analysis of this case is taken in part from Klein, Crawford, and Alchian (1978: 308–10).

Even though contracts are incomplete, the reputations of the transacting parties limit the economic feasibility of hold-up threats. It is the magnitude of these reputations and the corresponding costs that can be imposed on a transactor that attempts a hold-up that define what can be called the "self-enforcing range" of the contractual relationship. Transacting parties enter contractual arrangements by making specific investments and setting contract terms in such a way so that they are likely to be within this self-enforcing range where a hold-up will not occur. However, there is some probability that market conditions may change (for example, the value of the quasi-rents accruing to one of the parties unexpectedly increases) so that it pays for one transactor to hold-up the other in spite of the loss of reputation.[2]

For example, in the General Motors–Fisher Body case demand for the closed metal bodies manufactured by Fisher increased dramatically. When the contract was entered into in 1919 the dominant production process for automobiles consisted of individually constructed, largely wooden, open bodies; closed metal bodies were essentially a novelty. Demand for closed metal bodies grew extremely rapidly and by 1924 accounted for more than 65 percent of General Motors' automobile production.[3] This shift in demand moved the contractual arrangement outside of the self-enforcing range and made it profitable for Fisher to hold up General Motors.

Although Fisher could have taken advantage of many imperfectly specified terms of the contractual arrangement, such as delivery times or quality characteristics, Fisher effectively held up General Motors by adopting a relatively inefficient, highly labor-intensive technology and by refusing to locate the body-producing plants adjacent to General Motors' assembly plant.[4] This hold-up mechanism had the advantage, from Fisher's viewpoint, of increasing profitability since the contractually specified price formula set price equal to Fisher's "variable cost" plus 17.6 percent, placing a 17.6 percent profit upcharge on Fisher's labor and transportation costs. The profit upcharge presumably was designed to cover Fisher's anticipated capital costs, which may have been difficult to isolate and measure for General Motors shipments and, therefore, were unreimbursable under the contract formula. The contract may appear to be imperfect, but it was only deficient ex post. If demand had not grown so rapidly, Fisher's reputation (that is, loss of future business with General Motors and possibly other automobile manufacturers) combined with the most favored nation clause may have been an effective constraint on Fisher Body behavior. However, the large increase in demand placed Fisher's short-run hold-up potential of General

[2] This probabilistic equilibrium differs from the analysis in Klein, Crawford, and Alchian, where hold-ups were assumed not to be present in long-run equilibrium and existed solely because of transactor myopia or ignorance. Kenney and Klein present a discussion of the "self-enforcing range" and this equilibrium, together with the implications of the analysis for contract law.

[3] *Sixteenth Annual Report*, General Motors Corporation, year ended December 31, 1924.

[4] See deposition testimony of Alfred P. Sloan, Jr. in *United States*, v *Dupont & Co.*, 366 U.S. 316 (1961), 186–90 (April 28, 1952) and 2908–14 (March 14, 1953).

Motors, even with Fisher being forced to give up new and future sales, outside the self-enforcing range.

The Fisher Body–General Motors case illustrates that while long-term contract terms and transactor reputations may prevent hold-ups and encourage specific investments by tying the hands of the transacting parties. long-term contract terms may also create hold-up problems. Therefore, it is misleading to assert, as Coase does, that "opportunistic behavior is usually effectively checked" in the market by long-term contracts and the existence of transactor reputations. Although the assertion is true, a more complete analysis must recognize that transactor reputations are limited and that contracts may actually create, rather than solve, hold-up problems. It was the long-term, fixed price formula, exclusive dealing contract adopted by the transactors in response to the potential General Motors hold-up of Fisher that created the enormous Fisher hold-up potential of General Motors. The magnitude of this contractually caused hold-up was likely much greater than the quasi-rents on the General Motors–specific investments made by Fisher which the contract was attempting to protect in the first place. Although writing down binding contract terms may economize on limited brand name capital and reduce the probability of being outside the self-enforcing range, the rigidity of long-term contract terms may create a much larger hold-up potential if events actually place the parties outside the self-enforcing range. To avoid this rigidity transactors may intentionally leave their contracts incomplete and thereby give themselves "an out" if market conditions get "out of line."

It is this contractually induced hold-up potential and the costs associated with rigid ex-post incorrect contract terms, illustrated so forcefully in the Fisher–General Motors case, that represent the major transaction costs of using the market mechanism to solve the hold-up problem. These transaction costs include the real resources transactors dissipate in the contractual negotiation and renegotiation process in the attempt to create and execute a hold-up. Transactors will search for an informational advantage over their transacting partners and attempt to negotiate ex-ante contract terms that create hold-up potentials, that is, that are more likely to imply ex-post situations where contract terms are favorably incorrect. Once such a favorably incorrect situation arises, transactors will dissipate real resources during the renegotiation process in the attempt to convince their transacting partner that a hold-up potential does exist. In the Fisher–General Motors case these renegotiation transaction costs consisted of the costs associated with improper plant placement and low capital intensity of production before vertical integration occurred.[5]

---

[5] In addition to the transaction costs associated with negotiating contractual arrangements and the transitional transaction costs associated with the renegotiating process when these arrangements do not work out in practice, there are the social costs associated with transactors not making specific investments and entering contractual arrangements to begin with. Transactors anticipate the rent-dissipating transaction costs associated with contractual negotiation

(*continued*)

These transaction costs associated with the use of a long-term contract represent the theoretical reason why the presence of firm-specific investments is more likely to lead to vertical integration. Specific investments create the necessity for long-term contractual terms which, in turn, imply the rent-dissipating transaction costs associated with the possibility of contractually created hold-ups, In the absence of specific investments, long-term contract terms are unnecessary and spot contracts can be used. Since the costs associated with vertical integration are generally incentive-type costs that are unrelated to the level of specific investments, vertical integration will be more likely the greater the level of specific investments. The greater the level of specific investments and hence the greater the potential costs of using the market (as more explicit and rigid contractual mechanisms must be devised to protect the specific investment), the greater the likelihood that vertical integration will be the solution.

2. PHYSICAL CAPITAL VS. HUMAN CAPITAL

Vertical integration is the form in which the hold-up of General Motors by Fisher Body eventually took place, with General Motors acquiring the Fisher Body stock owned by Fisher at terms that were highly favorable to Fisher. Why did not General Motors merely make a lump sum cash payment to Fisher and renegotiate the contract, fixing ambiguous terms and hoping that another large unanticipated event would not occur in the future to shock the relationship out of the self-enforcing range? One reason is that the change in demand to closed metal bodies made Fisher a much more important specialized input supplier to General Motors, with the Fisher hold-up potential reaching essentially the entire General Motors industry-specific investment. In principle, with an ex-post incorrect contract, Fisher could potentially hold up General Motors for their entire automobile manu-facturing and distribution organization. This enormous hold-up potential would imply extremely large rent-dissipating transaction costs during the contractual negotiation and renegotiation process as General Motors at-tempted to protect against and Fisher attempted to take advantage of the hold-up possibilities.

Vertical integration appears to avoid these transaction costs by eliminating the second transactor. This is obvious for cases of physical capital, such as the house construction–land ownership example, where a hold-up, by

and renegotiation because they recognize the limits to their reputation capital, the uncertainty of the world, and the necessary imperfections of contracts. Therefore, independent of an risk aversion, transactors will avoid entering contractual arrangements where there is a significant probability that the arrangement will not work out. The equilibrium contractual arrangements that transactors voluntarily adopt in the marketplace may appear, consistent with Coase's assertion, to handle opportunistic behavior—in the sense that we are unlikely to observe opportunism occurring very frequently. However, we do not see all the specific investments not made and the contractual arrangements not adopted when transactors anticipate a significant probability of being outside the self-enforcing range.

definition, becomes impossible with vertical integration. It is cases like these that lead to the obvious conclusion that vertical integration will more likely, be used when the hold-up potential, that is, the quasi-rents from firm-specific investments, are large. As Joskow (1988) convincingly demonstrates, this insight regarding the economic motivation for ownership of firm-specific physical capital has significant empirical relevance.

However, many real-world examples involve human capital and not merely physical capital as the important firm-specific asset.[6] Since the specific human capital is embodied in individuals who by law cannot be owned and who have the potential to behave opportunistically under any alternative organizational arrangement, vertical integration does not eliminate the other transactor and the hold-up problem. In such cases it is unclear exactly what gains are entailed by vertical integration.

To understand the gains from vertical integration in the context of human capital, the economic question should be phrased not (as we have done in the house construction–land ownership case) as whether to own or rent an asset, but, as Coase essentially phrased it, as whether to make or buy an input. The former question applies only to physical capital while the latter question applies to human capital. When a firm buys an input in the marketplace, it generally does not own the physical capital associated with its production. A firm that produces an input itself also may not own the physical capital associated with its production (for example, the building where the firm has its offices). However, as we shall see, a firm that makes rather than buys an input generally has a particular relationship with the firm-specific human capital.

These issues can be focused by considering the Fisher Body–General Motors case again. If the hold-up problem were based solely on the General Motors–specific physical capital investments made by Fisher Body and had nothing to do with Fisher Body human capital, General Motors could have solved the problem by owning the physical capital. General Motors could have owned their own dies and stamping machines and let Fisher use this capital to make auto bodies for them, avoiding the hold-up problem while taking advantage of whatever cost advantage Fisher possessed in producing bodies.[7]

---

[6] See, for example, the discussion in Klein, Crawford, and Alchian (313–19) and Williamson (1979a: 240–45).

[7] Coase discusses this as a particular contractual solution to the hold-up problem (1988; lecture 1). See also Monteverde and Teece (1982b). Fisher's cost advantage was unlikely due to economies of scale in the production process. Evidence for this is the fact that, after demand growth and integration, Fisher supplied bodies solely to General Motors. This is one difference between the Fisher Body case and the A. O. Smith case discussed by Coase (1988: lecture 3). There appear to be significantly greater economies of scale in producing automobile frames than producing automobile bodies, with Smith supplying frames then and now to multiple automobile manufacturers, thereby raising the cost of vertical integration as a solution to the hold-up problem (see Stigler, 1951). It is also important to note that the investment in automobile frame production is, apparently, less buyer-specific than the investment in automobile body production.

One problem with this solution is that the extent of the General Motors–specific physical capital investments is likely to be much greater than merely the dies and stamping equipment. There are, for example, complementary physical capital investments that must be made by Fisher in plant, with the associated questions of plant location and the assurance to Fisher of continued General Motors demand for the facility. These questions presumably would have to be handled by contract. To avoid contractual rigidity and the induced hold-up problems associated with ex post incorrect contract terms, General Motors could own all the physical capital and merely contract with Fisher to run the operation. While such an arrangement would create marginal distortions regarding the use of the General Motors capital equipment by Fisher, it would appear to solve the hold-up problem if the problem were based solely on specific physical capital investments.

However, much of the specific investment necessary to produce automobile bodies consists of Fisher human capital investments that, by definition, cannot be owned by General Motors. General Motors can finance Fisher's human capital investments but would require some long-term fixed price contractual commitment to prevent Fisher from threatening to terminate the relationship if General Motors did not make a lump sum payment to them equal to the quasi-rents from the human capital investment. Vertical integration, in the sense of making Fisher an employee, rather than an independent contractor, does not eliminate the potential hold-up. As opposed to physical capital, the specialized human capital would presumably still be owned by Fisher even after General Motors' vertical integration. Rather than ownership, a long-term contractual arrangement, with its associated rigidities and potential hold-up problems, must be used by the transactors.[8]

Since, by definition, one cannot own human capital, how did the vertical integration of General Motors with Fisher reduce the hold-up problem? As opposed to the case of physical capital, vertical integration did not eliminate the Fisher brothers. After vertical integration General Motors no longer bought bodies from Fisher Body Corporation. After vertical integration General Motors "made" bodies with the assistance of Fisher. However, did making the Fisher brothers employees compared to being independent contractors change things in any essential way? Although General Motors would now own the plants and presumably be able to tell the Fisher brothers where to locate them, the Fisher brothers became employee managers with the ability to hold up General Motors for their human capital-specific investments by threatening modification on some other dimension.

---

[8] For example, one contract term that is used in employment arrangements in the entertainment industry, where the employer may make a substantial transactor-specific investment, is a right of first refusal clause. This clause reduces the credibility of hold-up threats since it requires the employee attempting to increase his wage by the amount of the quasi-rents from the employer's investment to threaten to quit working completely, rather than merely to threaten to quit the firm and work elsewhere.

3. VERTICAL INTEGRATION AS ORGANIZATIONAL OWNERSHIP

Although the use of an employee rather than an independent contractor arrangement may imply important legal differences and hence different constraints on the contracting process, such as the ease of termination by the employer and the required loyalty of the employee, I agree with Coase that the employer-employee contract does not represent the essence of a firm.[9] The transition of the Fisher brothers from independent contractors to employees does not explain what General Motors gained through vertical integration.

Vertical integration not only made the Fisher brothers employees of General Motors, but also converted all the employees of Fisher Body Corporation into employees of General Motors. General Motors moved from "buying" automobile bodies to "making" automobile bodies by obtaining ownership of the Fisher Body organization, including all the labor contracts of the cooperating workers in that organization and all the knowledge of how to make automobiles contained in that organization. It is in this sense of owning a firm's set of interdependent labor contracts and the firm-specific knowledge embodied in the organization's team of employees that an owner of a firm can own the firm's human capital.[10]

Vertical integration may solve a hold-up potential even when it hinges on human capital, and, hence, the number of transactors are not reduced by the integration because it involves transferring ownership of a productive team. For example, if we consider the Fisher Body–General Motors case it is unlikely that it was the Fisher brothers themselves who possessed all the relevant firm-specific human capital information. It was much more likely that this information was possessed by the entire group of Fisher employees and was embedded in the Fisher organizational structure. Vertical integration did not merely transfer the Fisher brothers from independent contractor to employee status, but also transferred ownership of the Fisher organization and the set of interdependent labor contracts to General Motors.

The primary reason a hold-up cannot occur after such a transfer of rights is because collusion is difficult with a large number of entities. If there were only one employee or a few key employees, they could threaten to leave and

---

[9] See Coase (1988; lecture 3) where he identifies this as the main weakness of his 1937 article.

[10] The concept of specific knowledge which affects a firm's production technology and which is vested in and transferable with the firm has been discussed by numerous authors. Rosen notes that such a firm-specific information asset may be created over time by the discovery of trade connections and the assembly of an efficient "production team" and presents a model where specific knowledge is acquired through (or as a by-product of) a firm's production experience. A similar concept is developed in Prescott and Visscher (1980) and is related to the evolutionary theory of the firm presented by Nelson and Winter (1982). The importance of information accumulation within the firm as a kind of progress function was originally discussed by Alchian (1959) and Arrow (1962). This concept may explain why bankruptcy law provisions, which are designed to prevent the production team from disbanding, make economic sense. While physical assets generally may be salvageable, bankruptcy, accompanied by the discontinuance of a firm's operations, may destroy the organizational assets of the firm. The analysis also provides an economic justification for the "failing firm" defense in merger law.

(subject to legal constraints on trade secret or goodwill theft) take the organization with them. However, with many key individuals involved, the organization will generally be secure. A threat that all the individuals will simultaneously shirk or leave if their wages were not increased to reflect the quasi-rents on the organizational capital generally will not be credible. After vertical integration the Fisher brothers will not be able to hold up General Motors by telling all the employees to leave General Motors and show up on Monday morning at a new address. This is, in general, not economically feasible or, more important, legally possible. It is in this sense of large team organizations that vertical integration can imply ownership of human capital assets in a manner quite similar to ownership of physical capital assets.

Our analysis implies that the General Motors integration with Fisher Body is analytically quite similar to the land–house example. By integrating with Fisher, General Motors acquired the Fisher Body organizational capital. This organization is embedded in the human capital of the employees at Fisher but is in some sense greater than the sum of its parts. The employees come and go but the organization maintains the memory of past trials and the knowledge of how to best do something (that is, how to make automobile bodies). This organizational asset can be thought of as a big machine called the Fisher Corporation. When this machine was owned by the Fisher brothers, it was necessary to write an explicit automobile body supply contract, which ex post turned out to create significant hold-up problems. With vertical integration General Motors avoided these contractual difficulties by buying the machine (the Fisher Corporation) and, in the sense of eliminating the need for an automobile body supply contract, eliminating the second transactor (the Fisher brothers).[11]

4. ORGANIZATIONAL OWNERSHIP VS. INPUT COORDINATION

Coase would likely agree that it is useful to consider the firm as an organization. He recognizes that it is the existence of cooperating labor inputs, and not merely a single employee, that represents a firm relationship. "The employer-employee contract approaches the firm relationship but . . . the full firm relationship will not come about unless several such contracts are made with people and for things that cooperate with one another"

---

[11] In contrast, the Grossman and Hart (1986) model of vertical integration consists of single person firms where, by definition, ownership of organizational assets cannot be transferred or consolidated. Grossman and Hart concentrate solely on physical assets and the question of which particular physical assets firms own. However, the essential question of vertical integration is not asset ownership but the make-or-buy decisions of firms. General Motors may own all the physical capital in the Fisher plant yet buy the bodies from an independent Fisher Body Corporation. The Grossman and Hart answer to the question of the distribution of physical asset ownership, which relies on employee incentive effects, cannot explain the incidence of vertical integration. Although vertical integration of Fisher and General Motors may lead to increased monitoring of the Fisher brothers because they no longer bear the full value consequences of their behavior, most of the managers at Fisher Body, both before and after integration with General Motors, are employees and not owners of Fisher physical capital.

(1988: lecture 3). However, Coase emphasizes the role of the firm not as an owner of organizational assets, but as a coordinator and controller of cooperating inputs. One must consider the firm, Coase says, as "running a business." And the economic question regarding institutional form involves a "comparison of the costs of coordinating the activities of factors of production within the firm with the costs of bringing about the same result by market transactions or by means of operations undertaken within some other firm" (1988: lecture 3). It is this concept of coordination of a team of inputs that Coase attributes as the essence of a firm.

The concept of a central contracting agent that serves as a hub of a group of interdependent contracts and by coordination eliminates the necessity of contracts between those individuals assumed to be at the end of each of the spokes may appear to provide some insight into the nature of the firm. It is in the sense of coordinating control of a team that the number of market relationships is reduced and substituted for administrative decisions. This concept corresponds to Coase's notion of a reduction in the number of market transactions when vertical integration occurs (1988: lecture 3). However, every transactor in the marketplace purchasing inputs that are assembled into a final product can be considered as a hub of a series of contractual arrangements. The suppliers of the separate inputs need not have any contractual arrangement with one another. Although vertical integration may appear to eliminate the necessity for contractual arrangements between cooperating inputs, it does not.

Unfortunately, in considering whether transactors will adopt a firm or market arrangement, Coase in 1937 and again now has incorrectly identified the costs of using the market mechanism with the narrow transaction costs of discovering prices and executing contracts (1937: 390–91; 1988: lecture 3). However, vertical integration implies small, if any, savings in terms of these shopping and contract execution costs. Ownership of an organization essentially reduces the number of contracts that must be executed by, at most, one. General Motors must still have separate contracts with all the employees of Fisher Body. If the Fisher brothers remain, two new employee contracts must now be written to replace the old independent contractor body supply contract. If the Fisher brothers leave, there will be one less contract.

Rather than a decrease in the number of contracts, what vertical integration alters is the nature of the contractual arrangement. The one contract that is eliminated creates a new relationship between the transacting parties. It is no longer necessary for General Motors to prespecify production conditions (such as body plant locations, capital intensity, delivery times, and so forth) or prices. Although General Motors may actually write many of these conditions down in their internal interdivisional communications and, therefore, not save any "ink costs," these documents no longer have the force of contract law.

The absence of a legal constraint creates increased flexibility and a decreased possibility of a contractual hold-up. General Motors and Fisher no longer need to expend real resources in the attempt to determine all of the many events that might occur during the life of the production relationship and write a prespecified response to each event. Most of these events are highly unlikely and, by integrating, General Motors can wait until future conditions emerge before determining what should be done. As discussed above, not only do General Motors and Fisher save the allocatively wasteful transaction costs involved in searching for informational advantages in negotiating prespecified contractual responses, but they also avoid the real resource costs during the renegotiation process once ex-post market conditions turn out to be substantially different from the pre-specified contract terms. Instead of contractual rigidity and the associated hold-up potential, the relationship becomes flexible to unanticipated market conditions.

While some commentators, including Coase, may identify this increased flexibility associated with vertical integration with the ability to coordinate or "direct" inputs, I do not believe that it is useful to focus on this ability as the central characteristic of a firm. Direction of inputs is neither a necessary nor a sufficient condition for defining a firm. For example, a conglomerate firm may merely own another firm (the organizational asset of another firm) without directing the firm's team of inputs. Alternatively, I may direct my gardener every weekend regarding what I want him to do for me, but I do not own a gardening firm. If the gardener has a group of workers that he uses to carry out my instructions, it is he who owns a gardening firm in the sense of an organization. By my direction I am specifying the particular services I desire. However, I am merely buying the particular services in the marketplace; it is the gardener who is "making" the particular services.

Direction of inputs can be accomplished in the marketplace as long as there are no specific investments made by the transacting parties and, therefore, no need for long-term contracts. Spot contracts in a competitive market can provide, in principle, a mechanism for perfect coordination and direction of cooperating inputs. A miller of flour, for example, may be able to contract in the spot market for supplies of wheat and have complete flexibility to alter in quantities and qualities as required by shifts in his demand. The miller may demand in the market (that is, "direct" producers to supply) increased quantities or different qualities of wheat, without any fear of a hold-up.

However, most market relationships entail transaction-specific invest-ments and, therefore, the possibility of a hold-up. A magazine publisher, for example, may want to shift production of an issue (say, delay and increase the quantity of a press run to take account of a late-breaking story). Because of transaction-specific investments magazine printing services cannot be purchased in a perfectly competitive spot market. If the publisher purchased printing services from an independent printing firm, the printer may refuse to be "directed" in this manner without some side payment. Because of this hold-up potential, long-term contractual arrangements specifying particular contingencies and payment arrangements will be used. But these contract terms are necessarily imperfect and, as we have seen in the General Motors–Fisher Body case, may lead to the possibility of an even greater hold-up potential.

Transaction-specific investments are pervasive and exist in cases where there are no obvious specific physical capital investments. Even with regard to, say, wheat it may be costly to switch suppliers. It takes time to find new suppliers and to check product qualities and services (delivery times, reliability and the like). Similarly wheat suppliers must learn about particular millers' payment practices, delivery requirements, working schedules, and so on. It is because transactors make these specific investments in particular suppliers that real-world demand curves are never perfectly elastic. However, it is important to recognize that if transactor-specific investments were unimportant, spot contracts could be used and transactors would have the full ability to "direct" cooperating inputs in the marketplace. From an analytical point of view, vertical integration is not necessary in order to coordinate or "direct" cooperating inputs in the production process.

5. CONCLUSION

Given the presence of specific investments in an exchange relationship, transactors will have to decide whether to use a long-term contract or vertical integration to solve the hold-up problem. Vertical integration entails the widely recognized possibility of increased costs associated with somewhat reduced incentives and increased bureaucracy. I have discussed here the other side of the equation—the transaction costs associated with long-term contracts. The important element of these transaction costs are not the "ink costs" of writing contract terms emphasized by Coase, but the significant rent-dissipating costs borne during the negotiation and renegotiation contracting process as transactors attempt to create, avoid, and execute the hold-ups implied by necessarily imperfect long-term contractual arrangements.

While vertical integration may imply an increased ability to direct cooperating inputs compared to a long-term contractual arrangement, one must not confuse what an integrated firm may do with the basic economic motivation for the integration. Vertical integration, by shifting ownership of an organizational asset, permits transactors to avoid the transaction costs associated with a hold-up potential in the presence of specific investments. Whether transactors adopt vertical integration as a solution to a particular hold-up potential depends upon the magnitude of these specific investments, combined with the ability to write long-term contracts that flexibly track market conditions without creating an alternative hold-up potential, Since the ability to write and use long-term contracts depends, in part, upon the underlying market uncertainty and on the level of transactor reputations, these factors will also influence the likelihood of vertical integration.

This analysis of the motivation for vertical integration is consistent with the fundamental point recognized by Coase fifty years ago—that a transaction within the firm is something that is inherently different from a transaction in the marketplace. The view of the firm as merely a "nexus of contracts" that has developed in reaction to Coase's fundamental distinction between the firm and the market[12] is incomplete and misleading, I now agree with Coase that there is a useful analytical and not merely legal distinction to make between interfirm and intrafirm transactions. Firms are more than particular groups of explicit and implicit contracts. They consist of valuable team assets and developed mechanisms of handling information and control. By consolidating ownership of these organizational assets in the hands of one firm, vertical integration eliminates the need for one fundamental contract and creates an increased ability to flexibly direct production. As a consequence, a significant hold-up potential is reduced, along with an important range of transaction costs.

[12] See, for example, Alchian and Demsetz, and Klein (1983).

Chapter
9

SUPPLIER SWITCHING COSTS AND VERTICAL INTEGRATION IN THE AUTOMOBILE INDUSTRY

Kirk Monteverde and David J. Teece

1. INTRODUCTION

In recent years, economists have begun the systematic exploration of transactions cost issues, for example, see Williamson (1975, 1979a). Research has also been initiated on know-how and its relationship to the nature of the firm. Although commonly ignored in economic theory, specialized know-how has important ramifications for organizational design. In particular, vertical integration issues arise when industrial know-how, including skills, becomes deepened and specialized to a particular firm. This article attempts to draw together the literatures on transactions cost and industrial know-how, and it brings them to bear on the analysis of efficiency incentives for backward vertical integration in the U.S. automobile industry.

2. VERTICAL INTEGRATION BY U.S. AUTOMAKERS

In the context of the U.S. automobile industry, we are interested in explaining why firms take parts production in-house. We hypothesize that assemblers will vertically integrate when the production process, broadly defined,

Reprinted from the Bell Journal of Economics, vol. 13, no. 1 (Spring 1982). © 1982. Reprinted with permission of RAND.

Kirk Monteverde is Associate Professor, St. Joseph's University; David J. Teece is Mitsubishi Bank Professor and Director of the Institute of Management, Innovation, and Organization, the University of California at Berkeley. We would like to thank Charles Holloway, Paul Kleindorfer, and the referees and editors for many useful comments.

generates specialized, nonpatentable know-how. When production processes are of this kind, both assembler and supplier are exposed to the possibility of opportunistic recontracting. Even if the title to specialized equipment used by the supplier is held by the assembler, this need not provide protection against rent appropriation if transaction-specific know-how has been generated. The existence of transaction-specific know-how and skills and the difficulties of skill transfer mean that it will be costly to switch to an alternative supplier (Teece, 1977, 1980). An assembler will tend to choose vertically integrated component production when high switching costs would otherwise lock the assembler into dependence upon a supplier and thereby expose that assembler to opportunistic recontracting or to the loss of transaction-specific know-how.

Within the vehicle manufacturing industry, supplier switching costs appear to be associated principally with development activities for new automotive parts. The design of a new vehicle model is a complex, five-year-long undertaking. Some components cannot be procured by simply announcing to suppliers performance and design requirements. The "specs" are often unknown ex ante. Consequently, preproduction heuristic development is critically important to the evolution of many vehicle parts. This process generates production as well as design knowledge. A supplier working in cooperation with the assembler on preproduction development gains a first-mover advantage because of knowledge acquired during development. This suggests the following testable hypothesis:

> The greater is the applications engineering effort associated with the development of any given automobile component, the higher are the expected appropriable quasi rents and, therefore, the greater is the likelihood of vertical integration of production for that component.

We shall test this hypothesis. The dependent variable we construct is dichotomous: each sample component is coded as being predominantly manufactured either in-house or by an external supplier. We next define a set of independent variables that may be expected to influence the choice between in-house production and external purchase, with our primary interest centering upon the influence of applications engineering. We then employ probit analysis to estimate the relationship between the independent variables and our measure of vertical integration.

To form the dependent variable, a list of 133 automotive components was obtained from an assembler. For each of the components, we ascertained the extent of vertical integration by General Motors and Ford for U.S. production in 1976. Each of the 133 components was recorded as either produced internally or sourced externally. For proprietary reasons, data about the exact percentage of each item in our sample that was manufactured in-house were not divulged. Hence, we took internal production of 80 percent or more of a component as an operational definition of integrated production. Taken together, the 133 component groupings include most of the major items that go into a complete vehicle.[1] Thus, the sample provides a representative picture of vertically integrated production for Ford and General Motors in 1976. The data are presented in Table 9.1.

Consider the independent variables. An excellent operational measure of applications engineering effort is the cost of developing a given component. Firms in the industry have these data on a component-by-component basis, but because of the data's proprietary nature, we were not able to gain direct access to them. However, a source within the industry who is privy to the data provided an engineering cost rating for our sample of automotive components.[2] This yielded a surrogate measure of relative engineering effort. The rating was done on a 10-point scale with each component considered to require from "none" to "a lot" of engineering investment. We assume that such a rating scale provides a reasonable enough approximation to interval scaled data to allow use of parametric procedures.

To avoid misspecifications of the model, three sets of control variables are introduced. The first control variable distinguishes components that are specific to a company from those that are generic. Some of the components included in the sample (e.g., fasteners) are not designed specifically for any single automaker. These are items for which traditional spot market contracting may be expected to operate quite well; and for these components there would appear to be no incentive to integrate. However, components that are not specific to a single assembler's product may be expected to be among those rated as requiring the least applications engineering. To ensure that the engineering variable does not indicate a statistical relationship with integration that actually arises because nonspecific components will not be attractive integration candidates, a "component specificity" variable is introduced into the model.

The determination as to which sample components represent assembler-specific parts and which do not was accomplished with the cooperation of a replacement parts wholesaler. Company officials were asked to isolate those components for which identification of the manufacturer, make, and model of the automobile was not necessary to procure a replacement

---

[1] One conspicuous absence, however, is that of tires, none of which are produced by either Ford or General Motors. It should also be noted that two items, steel and vinyl, which are included in the sample, might better be classed as "basic materials" rather than components, as both are further upstream in the production process than most of the other items in the sample. However, the list submitted by our sources was accepted without alteration, except for the elimination of "miscellaneous" categories and unidentifiable part names.

[2] The source was the design engineer for one of the major U.S. automakers who had responsibility for supervising development of a new generation of small, fuel-efficient vehicles to be manufactured in the United States. The reliability of his ratings was tested by obtaining a separate set of ratings from another automotive engineer. The two sets of ratings shared a correlation coefficient of 0.8, adding confidence that our ratings were a meaningful surrogate for the underlying construct.

TABLE 9.1
The Backward Vertical Integration of Ford and General Motors

Part category	Ford	GM	Part category	Ford	GM
Body			Valves (intake and exhaust)	1	N/A
Body sheet metal	1	1	Radiator	1	1
Exterior ornamentation			Fan		
Paint (topcoat)			Air cleaner	1	1
Primer			Air cleaner element		1
Bumpers	1	1	Carburetor		1
Body lamps	1	1	Fuel pump		1
Sealed beam bulbs		1	Starter	1	1
Weatherstrip			Distributor	1	1
Mirrors—outside			Spark plug		1
Mirrors—inside		1	Ignition coil	1	1
Interior trim	1	1	Oil filter	1	1
Interior ornamentation		1			
Carpeting and mats			Emission components		
Headlining	1	1	Catalytic converter		1
Safety belts			Air pump		1
Inertia locks			Carbon cannister	1	1
Lock—cylinders			Substrate and coating		
Door handles		1	PCV, EGR, etc. valves		
Hinges (door, hood, decklid)	1	1	Chassis		
Window regulator (power)		1	W.C., H.C. (optional)		
Window regulator (manual)	1	1	Wheel covers and hub caps (std.)		1
Glass	1		Coil springs	1	1
Windshield wiper motor	1	1	Leaf springs		1
Windshield washer system	1	1	Shock absorbers	1	1
Crash pad		1	Upper and lower arms	1	1
Seat frame and springs			Spindle assembly	1	1
Seat pad		1	Driveshaft assembly	1	1
Seat tracks (man. and elec.)		1	Wheels	1	
Lamp bulbs		1	Wires		
Head restraints	1	1	Rear axle	1	1
Headlamp assembly	1	1	Drums		
Sealers and insulation			Master brake cylinder		
Armrests		1	Power brake booster		1
Grill			Parking brake		
Frame			Muffler		
Jack and wrench			Tailpipe/inletpipe		
Engine mounts			Brakes		
Engine			Disc caliper and rotor		1
Engine stampings	1	1	Front suspension	1	1
Cylinder head	1	1	Rear suspension	1	1
Block	1	1	Transmission		
Manifold (intake and exhaust)	1	1	Auto. transmission assy.	1	1
Crankshaft	1	1	Auto. transmission cases	1	1
Camshaft	1	1	Manual trans. assembly		1
Piston	1	N/A	Steering		
Piston ring			Manual steering gear	1	1

"1" denotes 80 per cent or more of component requirements produced in-house as of 1976.

TABLE 9.1 (*continued*)

Part category	Ford	GM	Part category	Ford	GM
Steering (*continued*)			Electrical		
Power steering gear	1	1	Instrument cluster and panel	1	1
Steering linkage		1	Speedometer cable assembly		1
Steering column	1	1	Fuel sender	1	1
Steering wheel		1	Alternator	1	1
Power steering pump		1	Regulator	1	1
Steering assembly	1	1	Battery		1
Fuel			Horn	1	1
Fuel tank	1	1	Battery cables		1
Gas cap			Wiring harness		1
			Radio	1	1
Ventilation			Tape player		1
A/C assembly	1	1	Speakers		1
Evaporator	1	1	Antenna		1
Expansion valve		1	Speed control system	1	1
Vacuum motors		1	Clock		
Blower wheels			Switches		
Blower motors	1	1	Other		
Heater assembly	1	1	Tubing (brake/fuel lines)		
Heater core	1	1	Antifreeze		
Compressor		1	Oils and grease		
Clutch		1	Steel		
ATC components		1	Standard parts, fasteners		
Condensor	1	1	Vinyl	1	
Dehydrator/receiver		N/A	Water pump assembly	1	1
Hose assemblies		N/A	Oil pump	1	

unit.[3] We assume that those components for which make and model information is not critical are not company-specific in original assembly. Using this procedure, a group of 30 items was identified as non-company-specific.

The second control variable relates to the identity of the sample firms. Because we developed a combined cross-sectional model aggregating both Ford and General Motor's data, we include a dummy variable to control for systematic differences between these two firms with regard to vertical integration.

The third set of control variables relates to systems effects. The automobile represents not simply an assemblage of parts, but a "system"—a set of objects with relationships between the objects and their attributes (Hall, 1973: 103). In the vehicle "system," the "objects" are the individual components, and the

---

[3] The actual question was: "Please examine the following list of 133 automotive components and indicate which of the noncaptive items on the list could be procured as replacement units without necessarily having to know the manufacturer, make, and model of the vehicle for which the replacement is sought. That is, which of the following categories of parts may be expected to be largely common across several manufacturers' vehicles."

relationships between components consist principally of their mechanical or electrical interrelations and their "packaging"—the latter being the industry's term for physically fitting all components within the dimensions of the body. Clearly, design and implementation for any system as complex as an automobile must be tightly coordinated.[4] Because of the superior coordinating properties of vertical integration,[5] the degree to which any given component's design affects the performance or packaging of other components is a potentially important consideration in explaining the likelihood of vertically integrated production of the given component (Armour and Teece, 1980).

As shown in Table 9.1, the components were first grouped into nine categories (body, engine, emission components, chassis, transmission, steering, fuel, ventilation, electrical) and a tenth miscellaneous category. These categories were subsequently collapsed into six subsystems by merging emissions with engine, transmission and steering with chassis, and fuel tank and cap with body. The aggregation was based on expert evaluation of the degree of technical interrelatedness among the components. Vertical integration is predicted for components with large systems effects. Since we are unable to rank the subsystems according to the degree of interrelatedness, we simply posit that different subsystems will display different levels of vertical integration. Thus, a set of dummy variables was introduced into the model to represent each component's membership in a subsystem.

The predictor variables were combined into a single model estimated by probit techniques. A vector of parameter estimates for β was derived to maximize the log likelihood function:

$$L = \sum_{i=1}^{n} y_i \ln F(x_i'\beta) + \sum_{i=1}^{n} (1 - y_i) \ln [1 - F(x_i'\beta)]$$

where y_i is 1 if the ith component is integrated in production and zero otherwise; x_i is the vector of values of the independent variables for the ith observation; and $F(x_i'\beta)$ takes the specific form:

$$F(x_i'\beta) = \frac{1}{\sqrt{2\pi}} \int_{-\infty}^{x_i\beta} e^{-u^2/2} \, du$$

[4] White observes that: "The complex process of designing, producing, testing, and modifying an automobile requires a high degree of coordination. Engine, transmission, frame, body, brakes, windshield, and other components all have to perform well with each other and have to be in the right place at the right time in the right quantities" (White, 1971: 78).

[5] Vertical integration permits executive fiat to be used to achieve the requisite coordination in a timely fashion (Williamson, 1975). Scherer also notes the coordination benefits of integration and offers an example from the auto industry: "The benefits from integration also increase with the complexity of product component interrelationships. It is easier to make the various parts of an automobile fit together when all parties to the coordination effort work for the same boss than when design changes must be processed through a purchasing office" (Scherer, 1980: 90).

The x_i vector contains, for each sample point i, the values of the eight independent variables defined below:

$$ENGINEERING_i = \begin{cases} \text{rating of the } i\text{th observation on the amount of} \\ \quad \text{engineering effort required in designing the part} \end{cases}$$

$$SPECIFIC_i = \begin{cases} 1 & \text{if the } i\text{th observation corresponds to a part} \\ & \quad \text{specific to a single assembler} \\ 0 & \text{otherwise} \end{cases}$$

$$COMPANY_i = \begin{cases} 1 & \text{if the } i\text{th observation was from General Motors} \\ 0 & \text{if the } i\text{th observation was from Ford} \end{cases}$$

$$ENGINE_i = \begin{cases} 1 & \text{if the } i\text{th observation corresponds to an engine} \\ & \quad \text{and emissions subsystem part} \\ 0 & \text{otherwise} \end{cases}$$

$$CHASSIS_i = \begin{cases} 1 & \text{if the } i\text{th observation corresponds to a chassis,} \\ & \quad \text{transmission, and steering subsystem part} \\ 0 & \text{otherwise} \end{cases}$$

$$VENTILATION_i = \begin{cases} 1 & \text{if the } i\text{th observation corresponds to a} \\ & \quad \text{ventilation subsystem part} \\ 0 & \text{otherwise} \end{cases}$$

$$ELECTRICAL_i = \begin{cases} 1 & \text{if the } i\text{th observation corresponds to an} \\ & \quad \text{electrical subsystem part} \\ 0 & \text{otherwise} \end{cases}$$

$$BODY_i = \begin{cases} 1 & \text{if the } i\text{th observation corresponds to a body,} \\ & \quad \text{fuel tank and cap subsystem part} \\ 0 & \text{otherwise} \end{cases}$$

The parameter estimates for β_1 through β_8, the asymptotic t-statistics corresponding to these eight predictor variables, and the model summary statistic are given in Table 9-2.

Recall that in-house production of 80% or more of a component's output was selected as the operational definition of vertical integration. To establish the robustness of the results, we also obtained a listing of those items which would be considered integrated were the cutoff changed to 70% and then to 90%.

The principal point to note about the results in Table 9.2 is that regardless of the threshold chosen, the variable used as a proxy for transaction-specific skills ("engineering") is highly significant. The development effort associated

TABLE 9.2
Probit Coefficients, Asymptotic *t*-Statistics (in parentheses), and χ^2-Statistic in Equation to Explain Vertical Integration (defined upon three thresholds for percentage of in-house parts production.)

Coefficient estimated	Related variable	Vertical integration defined as in-house production of:		
		$\geq 70\%$	$\geq 80\%$	$\geq 90\%$
β_1	ENGINEERING	0.1319	0.1461	0.1453
		(3.24)[a]	(3.57)[a]	(3.54)[a]
β_2	SPECIFIC	0.8773	0.8186	0.7902
		(3.64)[a]	(3.33)[a]	(3.15)[a]
β_3	COMPANY	0.7388	0.7125	0.9010
		(4.22)[a]	(4.05)[a]	(5.08)[a]
β_4	ENGINE	0.5521	0.5348	0.7168
		(1.21)	(1.17)	(1.47)
β_5	CHASSIS	0.0615	0.0003	0.03051
		(0.138)	(0.001)	(0.637)
β_6	VENTILATION	0.3620	0.4903	0.6552
		(0.733)	(0.983)	(1.25)
β_7	ELECTRICAL	0.6861	0.6905	1.085
		(1.48)	(1.49)	(2.18)[b]
β_8	BODY	0.0857	−0.2293	0.1152
		(0.201)	(−0.532)	(0.248)
χ^2 Value		110.064[a]	111.291[a]	126.676[a]

[a] Indicates significance beyond the .001 level.
[b] Indicates significance beyond the .05 level.

with the design of any given automotive component is shown to be positively related to the likelihood of vertically integrated production of that component, thereby confirming the central hypothesis of this article.

Second, the coefficient on the "*SPECIFIC*" variable is also positive and statistically significant, which lends support to the hypothesis that only components specific to a single assembler will be candidates for vertical integration. It can also be seen that the coefficient for the "*COMPANY*" variable is positive and statistically significant, thereby indicating that General Motors is more integrated into component production than is Ford.

Finally, the systems-effects hypothesis is only mildly supported by the probit analysis. With the exception of the "*ELECTRICAL*" variable in the $\geq 90\%$ integration threshold case, none of the coefficients on the five dummy variables taken alone indicates a significant relationship with backward integration. Nevertheless, the set of five systems effect dummies, taken together, significantly contributed to the explanatory power of the model.

In general, the change in magnitude of the coefficients was minor as the definition of vertical integration was altered. The variation was the greatest among the individual subsystem variables that, with the one exception of the electrical subsystem variable, were not found to be significantly different from zero.

3. CONCLUSION

Transactions cost considerations surrounding the development and deepening of human skills appear to have important ramifications for vertical integration in the automobile industry, thereby supporting the transactions cost paradigm advanced by Williamson. GM and Ford are more likely to bring component design and manufacturing in-house if relying on suppliers for preproduction development service will provide suppliers with an exploitable first-mover advantage. We posit that this is a result of the high switching costs entailed if the supplier acquires transaction specific know-how at the assembler's expense. Since know-how cannot simply be transferred from supplier to supplier like a book of blueprints (Winter, 1980), backward integration is the more prudent course of action. General Motors and Ford also have a preference for backward vertical integration when the components are firm-specific and their design must be highly coordinated with other parts of the automobile system.

Hence, the vertical structure of GM and Ford appears to be based at least in part on efficiency considerations. Specifically, the structure appears to be designed to take advantage of the coordinating properties of hierarchies as well as the ability of internal organization to reduce the exposure of the automakers to opportunism from suppliers—a hazard which is apparently absent in the less integrated Japanese industry[6] where "the relationship between the major auto firm and its satellite suppliers is one of total cooperation" (Ouchi, 1981: 19).

---

[6] We posit that cooperation between the auto companies and remaining suppliers will also characterize the U.S. industry because the integrated and "quasi-integrated" (Monteverde and Teece, 1982) structure of the industry has eliminated most occasions for opportunistic rent appropriation.

C h a p t e r
10

THE ORGANIZATION OF PRODUCTION: EVIDENCE FROM THE AEROSPACE INDUSTRY

Scott E. Masten

The interface between successive stages of production is frequently governed by contractual agreements, and the efficiency of such arrangements has been the subject of considerable attention in the economic literature. But production is organized administratively within firms as well as contractually between them, and given the practical limitations of bureaucratic organization, the relevant question can be seen to be not merely whether contractual deficiencies exist but how severe such deficiencies may be relative to the alternative costs of organizing production internally. The important issue from an institutional choice perspective thus becomes how the particular details of a transaction affect the *differential* efficiency of alternative organizational forms.

Recent theoretical work has sought to identify such relationships.[1] In particular, the choice between internal and external organization and, in the event of the latter, the choice of contract terms have been related to several

Reprinted from the Journal of Law and Economics, vol. XXVII (October 1984) by permission of The University of Chicago Press. © 1984 by The University of Chicago. All rights reserved.

Scott E. Masten is Professor of Business Economics and Public Policy, the University of Michigan. I would like to thank Oliver Williamson and Roger Sherman for helpful comments. The cooperation of the General Electric Company is also gratefully acknowledged. Support for this research was received from the Center for the Study of Organizational Innovation and from Sloan and National Science Foundation grants for the study of Transaction Cost Economics at the University of Pennsylvania. The paper was completed while I was at the University of Virginia.

[1] See, in particular, Klein, Crawford, and Alchian (1978); and Williamson (1979a). A formal model treating the make-or-buy decision as part of a producer's overall optimization problem may be found in Masten (1982).

critical parameters of the transaction. This paper presents some evidence of the practical import of those relationships, based on a study of input procurement practices in the aerospace industry.

The administration of procurement in this industry is two tiered. On the first level, the government chooses a prime contractor who is assigned overall responsibility for a particular program; and on the second, the contractor manages the production of the system itself, including what is of particular interest here—the administration of subcontracts. This paper considers pro-curement practices at both levels. To begin, the essential elements of the theory will be briefly reviewed in Section 1. Section 2 then presents the results of an examination of input procurement for an aerospace system containing nearly two thousand component specifications. Tests are based on a probit model of the dichotomous choice between internal and external procurement of supplies. The estimated coefficients provide indirect measures of the relative costs of internal and external procurement with respect to several qualitative variables. Following this, the procurement policies of the federal government are reviewed and interpreted in light of the theory, with particular emphasis on the form of the relationship between the government and the prime contractor. Conclusion and additional comments appear in the final section.

1. THE MAKE-OR-BUY DECISION

Having selected an end-product line, a producer must decide which in the stream of intermediate products and processes successively combining to form his eventual output he will administer within the organization and which he will delegate to outside suppliers, along with the terms under which any external procurements would take place. In practice, this series of procurement decisions—sometimes referred to as a producer's make-or-buy program—involves a large number of considerations including design requirements; inventory needs; quality control; production, overhead, and transportation costs; and the capabilities, capacities, and negotiating strength of potential suppliers relative to those of the producer himself.[2]

Transaction cost economics has sought to place these concerns within an economic context and relate the outcome of individual make-or-buy decisions to details of the transaction. According to that view, the choice among alternative organizational arrangements is part of an agent's overall optimization problem, and the net value of a transaction organized in a particular manner depends not only on the losses due to potential mis-allocations of resources but also on the costs of conducting the transaction itself. Hence, a manager choosing a procurement mode will consider, in addition to the value of the goods and services actually procured, both the opportunity costs of the additional demands that would be placed on

---

[2] These concerns and many others are evident in Corey (1978) and were also present in internal memoranda and discussions with company representatives.

his time and attention by internalizing a transaction and the various "organizational" expenses that would be involved in dealing with outside suppliers. The latter include the costs of negotiating the terms under which exchange is to take place and, oftentimes, the various expenses associated with adopting and upholding formal contractual agreements.

In general, the organizational costs associated with market exchange increase, the more specialized, profitable, and durable are the investments associated with a given transaction. Idiosyncratic assets, because of their specialized and durable nature, imply that parties to a transaction face only imperfect exchange alternatives for an extended period. The more specialized those assets, the larger will be the quasi-rents at stake over that period, and hence the greater the incentive for agents to attempt to influence the terms of trade through bargaining or other rent-seeking activities once the investments are in place.

The role of contracts is to prevent such activities from dissipating too large a portion of the gains from trade by stipulating acceptable behavior at the outset of a transaction-specific relationship. But contracts incur expenses in both specification and enforcement that limit their usefulness. First, because contingent performance is costly to stipulate and even more difficult for courts to administer, contracts typically contain few provisions and, as a result, tend to be inflexible mechanisms for governing exchange. The greater the complexity of the transaction and the level of uncertainty associated with it, the greater the likelihood of being bound to an inappropriate action, and hence the greater the implicit costs of contractual organization. This inflexibility, in turn, tends to constrict the time span of contractual agreements. Because confidence that any given state of the world will obtain decreases the more distant the relevant horizon, committing yourself to a particular activity becomes less desirable the more remote the specified date of performance. A trade-off therefore exists between the opportunity costs of being bound to an inflexible agreement and the hazards of negotiating follow-on procurements in a condition of bilateral monopoly. In sum, the more idiosyncratic are the investments associated with a particular transaction, the greater are the incentives to incur the costs of writing more detailed and longer term contracts. Greater uncertainty or complexity of a transaction, however, implies, on the one hand, an incentive to write more detailed agreements and, on the other, a disincentive to commit to long term contractual relationships.[3]

Greater complexity would also, of course, put additional strain on decision makers under internal organization, which is intended to eliminate rent seeking by internalizing the quasi-rents that are the object of that behavior.[4]

---

[3] The trade-offs involved here are discussed at greater length in Masten (1982).

[4] In the case of specialized human capital, quasi-rents cannot be eliminated by internalization in the same way that they can with physical capital. Rather, hierarchical organization seeks to substitute internal for third-party adjudication of conflicting interests. Thus, from this perspective, the firm becomes a quasi-judicial body entrusted by its members to resolve disputes and enforce cooperative behavior.

But the possibility of rendering decisions in an adaptive, sequential fashion under internal organization reduces the need relative to contracting of exploring and enumerating the full contingency tree ex ante (Williamson, 1975). Nevertheless, the expediency of internalizing successive transactions is limited by the bureaucratic inefficiencies that inevitably develop as organizations get large.

2. INPUT PROCUREMENT IN THE AEROSPACE INDUSTRY

There is an abundance of supportive, if informal, evidence illustrating the relationships discussed above. A recent article on the semiconductor industry, for example, revealed the existence of a correlation between design specificity and the internal procurement of supplies in the production of electronic components: "Most major chip buyers, after trying but failing to get the big producers to serve their needs for low volumes of custom circuits, have launched chip-production lines of their own and today turn out almost all of the custom chips made as well as two-thirds of such semi-custom products as gate arrays" (*Business Week*, 1982: 36H).

In addition, the article contended that the reason that downstream producers found it necessary to develop in-house production capabilities for these products, despite the expertise of the established chip manufacturers and "the high cost of maintaining internal production," was to avoid the "frictions between vendors and customers" encountered in a market where specialized designs are highly profitable and increasingly complex (*Business Week*, 1982: 36D–L).

Although accounts of this type can be illuminating, they lack the authority often accorded formal tests of hypotheses. Unfortunately, the level of detail at which the theory operates has made rigorous applications difficult. One way in which the information requirements can be moderated, however, is to restrict attention to a single industry. This reduces the need for absolute measures for such variables as design specificity and complexity and permits qualitative tests based on ordinal rankings of inputs by their characteristics. Recently, this strategy has been employed by Kirk Monteverde and David Teece (1982a) to analyze vertical integration in the automobile industry and by Thomas Palay (1984) in a study of railroads. The present paper examines related issues in the context of defense-related production, an area in which specialized designs are common and the alternative values of investments often limited.

The model I wish to test is the following: Let G_i be the institution chosen by the producer to govern the acquisition of product or process i, and let G_i^* represent internal organization of that activity and $\tilde{G}_i$ external or "market" procurement. Then the outcome of the producer's make-or-buy decision can be summarized as

$$G_i = G_i^* \quad \text{if} \quad L_i^*(\omega_i) < \tilde{L}(\lambda_i, \omega_i)$$

and

$$G_i = \tilde{G}_i \quad \text{if} \quad L_i^*(\omega_i) \geq \tilde{L}(\lambda_i, \omega_i)$$

TABLE 10.1
The Make-or-Buy Program

Category	Quantity	Make	Buy
Top and major subassemblies	17	17	—
Components assembly	185	114	71
Structure machining	11	5	6
Structure forgings	8	—	8
Mechanical detail parts	138	53	85
Connectors	180	—	180
Printed wire board assembly	80	80	—
Flexible/hard printed wire boards	151	147	4
Electrical piece parts	971	11	960
Heat shields	4	—	4
Insulating materials	62	10	52
Harness/coax	80	80	—

where L_i^* is the cost of maintaining production internally and $\tilde{L}_i$ is the cost of market-mediated exchange, depicted as a function of the specificity (λ) and complexity (ω) of the transaction.

The aerospace system studied contained 1,887 component specifications, each of which was identified as either a "make" or "buy" item by a team of company representatives made up of the managers of the material systems and manufacturing engineering departments and members of their staffs. The disposition of the entire make-or-buy program is summarized by generic category in Table 10.1.

The procurement team was asked to complete questionnaires designed to elicit information about the attributes of the items and associated investments. Each of the items within several of the cells in Table 10.1 shared similar characteristics, permitting completion of a single questionnaire for the entire cell. The remaining cells were randomly sampled in approximate proportion to the ratio between the size of the cell and the total number of components in the system. The result was thirty-four individual observations, which can be statistically weighted to reflect their actual distribution in the program.[5]

From this information, two measures of specificity were developed. The first, corresponding to design specificity, was based on whether an item was identified as used exclusively by this company (highly specialized), used or easily adaptable for use by other aerospace firms (somewhat specialized), or used in other industries (relatively standard). "Electrical piece parts" such as transistors and resistors, for example, would be standard items, while

[5] Since the data for this study were generated from a choice based sample, weighted exogenous sampling maximum likelihood estimation was employed. For a discussion of the properties of these estimators see Manski and Lerman (1977).

hybrid circuits designed to individual specifications would be considered highly specialized.[6]

A second variable was created to reflect site specificity based on whether colocation or grouping of facilities or processes was considered to be an important factor in production. Various economies may arise from positioning successive operations side by side. But if associated assets are costly to reposition, their alternative use value may be low. Such was the case in this system with the computerized lathes and other machinery used to bore and mill nose cones. The machinery itself has a number of uses. However, because of transfer and control costs between operations, the configuration and geographical location of the equipment is important. Meanwhile, installation and removal costs make relocation impractical. Consequently, once the assets have been positioned, they are more or less committed to a particular use.

Since this study focused on a single system, it was not possible to test the effects of demand uncertainty on the internalization decision using these data alone. Complexity, however, may be used as a proxy for the degree of uncertainty on the production side; the more complex a component, the more details to be accounted for and the more dimensions in which something can go wrong. To determine the relative complexity of the components, a ranking system used internally by the company was adopted. In that three-way classification scheme, "A-items" were the most and "C-items" the least complex.

For estimation purposes, the following specification of the model was employed:

$$L_i^* = \bar{B} + b \cdot \omega_i + u_i$$

and

$$\tilde{L}_i = a \cdot \lambda_i + c \cdot \omega_i + v_i$$

where u_i and v_i are random errors assumed to have independent normal distributions, and a, b, and c are coefficients. $\bar{B}$ represents the "administrative burden" of internalizing a transaction and would be expected to be positive. Since complexity increases the costs associated with organizing production both administratively within firms and contractually between them, both b and c should be positive. But because flexibility in contracting demands prior anticipation of potential problems, while internal organization permits adaptation to changing circumstances in a sequential fashion, the differential effect of complexity on the costs of alternative organizational arrangements favors internal organization over contractual exchange (Williamson, 1975). Hence, we would expect $c - b > 0$. Finally, the coefficient on item specificity,

---

[6] Although *asset* design would be preferable to *input* design as a measure of specificity, it is difficult, even at this level of disaggregation, to separate the specialized from standard assets used in the manufacture of a given input. The fact that specialized inputs may at times be produced using standardized assets, however, merely implies that input design measures will have lower *t*-statistics than would asset design; hence, information on the latter would only improve the explanatory power of the model. See below.

a, is also expected to be positive, reflecting the greater potential for opportunistic behavior in idiosyncratic transactions.

Since L^* and $\bar{L}$ are not actually observed, the estimation is based on the disposition of the dichotomous make-or-buy choice. The probability that input j will be produced inside the firm is

$$\mathrm{pr}(L_j^* < \tilde{L}_j) = \mathrm{pr}[u_j - v_j < a\lambda_j + (c - b)\omega_j - \bar{B}]$$
$$= F[a\lambda_j + (c - b)\omega_j - \bar{B}]$$

where $F(\cdot)$ is the normal distribution. The likelihood function of the model is

$$\Lambda = \prod_{i=1}^{n} F[a\lambda_i + (c - b)\omega_i - \bar{B}]^{y_i}\{1 - F[a\lambda_i + (c - b)\omega_i - \bar{B}]\}^{(1 - y_i)}$$

where $y_i = 1$ if item i is produced internally and zero if acquired outside the firm. The actual explanatory variables used in the estimations were

$$\mathrm{COMPLEX}_i = \begin{cases} 1 & \text{if the item is rated as complex (A- and B-items)[7]} \\ 0 & \text{otherwise (C-items)} \end{cases}$$

$$\mathrm{SPECI}_i = \begin{cases} 1 & \text{if the item is highly specialized} \\ 0 & \text{otherwise} \end{cases}$$

$$\mathrm{STANDARD}_i = \begin{cases} 1 & \text{if the item is relatively standard} \\ 0 & \text{otherwise[8]} \end{cases}$$

$$\mathrm{COLOC}_i = \begin{cases} 1 & \text{if colocation of assets or processes is considered} \\ & \quad \text{important} \\ 0 & \text{otherwise} \end{cases}$$

Maximum likelihood estimates for the weighted observations and corresponding statistics are presented in Table 10.2. The column on the far right-hand side of the table, "mean of variable," indicates the proportion of inputs possessing that characteristic.

The coefficients on both COMPLEX and SPECI are highly significant and positive as expected, indicating that the probability of internalization is higher for complex and highly specialized inputs. But although the coefficients for COLOC and STANDARD have the expected signs, statistical confidence in these estimates is low.[9]

---

[7] No significant difference was found in the coefficients on A- and B-items in any of the various specifications of the model experimented with.

[8] The variables SPECI_i and $\mathrm{STANDARD}_i$ were derived from the same ordinally measured construct. "Somewhat specialized" items are the omitted category.

[9] The insignificant coefficient on STANDARD implies that there is not significant difference between the effects of "standard" items and the omitted category, "somewhat specialized" items, on the internalization decision. In other words, "standard" items are at least as likely to be procured externally as are "somewhat specialized" components.

TABLE 10.2
Estimated Coefficients for the Make-or-Buy Decision

Variable	Coefficient	t-Ratio	Mean of variable
CONSTANT	−3.8657	−6.8064	1.00000
COMPLEX	1.8865	5.4444	0.84208
SPECI	3.3696	6.5486	0.34605
STANDARD	−2.7775	−0.1724	0.50874
COLOC	5.1120	0.1269	0.09433

χ^2: 32.0788, 4 df[a]
Pseudo R^2: 0.610734[b]
Proportion of observations for which $y = 1$: .2729.

[a] Indicates that the equation is significant beyond the .001 level.
[b] This measure is analogous to standard R^2s. Its properties are discussed in Amemiya (1981).

Note also that the constant term in this equation has a large effect on the probability of internalization. This coefficient reflects the predisposition of management toward external procurement and, given the specification of the model, can be interpreted as an indirect measure of the administrative burden incurred by internalizing an additional transaction. Each of the remaining coefficients provides an estimate of the implicit costs of contracting *relative* to this burden for transactions possessing the corresponding characteristic.

The matrix in Figure 10.1 presents the estimated probabilities that components possessing the corresponding characteristics will be produced internally.[10] As is apparent from these estimates, the degree of specialization is by far the most important determinant of organizational form in this system. The lack of alternative uses for a component increases the probability that it will be procured internally from less than 1 percent to 31 percent for relatively uncomplex items and from 2 percent to 92 percent for more complex components. Since the omitted category includes those inputs used only in

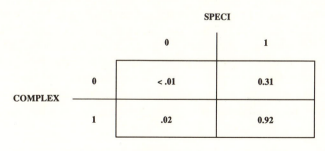

Figure 10.1

[10] Specifically, the probability that component i will be procured internally is $F(-3.8657 + 1.8865\text{COMPLEX}_i + 3.3696\text{SPECI}_i)$ where F is the cumulative normal distribution.

other aerospace applications, these estimates suggest that the existence of alternative uses for a component, even in a fairly highly concentrated industry such as this, warrants reliance on external procurement.

The complexity of an item also increases the probability that it will be "sourced in-house." Moreover, as expected, the hazards of incomplete contracts in complex environments appear to be much greater when specialized designs are involved, increasing the likelihood of internalization from 31 percent to 92 percent (as compared with less than 1 percent to only about 2 percent for items which are only "somewhat specialized"). Thus, as predicted by the theory, the need to employ specialized designs appears to be a necessary condition for the breakdown of market-mediated exchange and the subsequent internalization of production, especially where fairly complex products are involved.

Additional detail missed in the surveys but obtainable case by case further supports the hypothesized relationships. For instance, the system design called for both rigid and flexible printed wire boards. Although both types involved specialized designs, the flexible boards could be produced using standard equipment and were procured externally. The hard boards, on the other hand, were unique items that could not be produced using existing facilities. Not having an expertise in this area, the company sought to establish outside sources but found that manufacturers were "unwilling" to take on the business. The fact that the company was obliged to develop its own production capability suggests that the "organizational savings" from sourcing outside the company were not adequate to compensate potential suppliers for the hazards to which they would be exposed by incurring such specialized costs. However, the components that, although specially designed, could be produced with standard assets were not subject to those hazards. Such evidence supports the contention that asset design is a more powerful predictor of organization form than is input design.

The survey also indicated other factors of concern to procurement managers in deciding whether to internalize production. Among the more important were the existence of preexisting production capability or capacity and the perception of a need for "control" over the production process. But each of these concerns is itself explained in large part by the degree of complexity and specificity of the item: the company was more likely to have previously developed a capability or capacity for the production of more specialized and complex components, and the perception of a need for control arose primarily in those cases in which the market or the courts were least likely to regulate transactions effectively, again when production was highly specialized and complex.

3. GOVERNMENT PROCUREMENT POLICIES

Although data sufficiently detailed to permit evaluation of all the hypotheses of the transaction-cost paradigm are not yet available, it is possible at least to compare the concerns identified in these theories with the procedures adopted by procurement managers. This section selectively examines several of the federal government's procurement policies to see how well they conform to the theory presented in section 1.

3.1. Make-or-Buy Policies

Although in defense-related production the basic responsibility for procurement decisions, as with all management functions, remains with the firm, the government reserves the right to review a prospective contractor's make-or-buy program.[11] Of particular interest from the standpoint of the present analysis is that proposed make-or-buy programs need only be submitted for review "where the work is complex, the dollar value substantial, and there is not adequate price competition" (¶ 32, 887). More specifically, information on a prospective contractor's make-or-buy program is *not* required by the government (¶ 32, 888):

(i) when a proposed contract has total estimated value of less than $1,000,000 . . .;

(ii) in research and development contracts, unless the contract is for prototypes or hardware and it can reasonably be anticipated that significant follow-up quantities of the product will be procured;

(iii) when the contracting officer determines that the price is based on adequate price competition, or established catalog or market prices of commercial items sold in substantial quantities to the general public . . .; or

(iv) when the contracting officer determines that the work is not complex.

What is notable about this passage is that each of the stipulations contained in it has a direct correlate in transaction-cost theory: special attention or precautions are unnecessary for transactions which (i) are low in value, (ii) are not likely to generate first-mover advantages in follow-on production, (iii) are accompanied by price competition or involve standard products, or (iv) are not complex. If the value of the contract is small, the potential losses to an inappropriate make-or-buy program will also be small and therefore will not generally justify the cost of review. Where large amounts are at stake, however, an improper make-or-buy decision can have more serious consequences. Review is also desirable where research and development activities will bestow extended advantages on the agent; a contractor's decision to subcontract some part of this work to another firm may leave both the prime contractor and the government open to extortion in subsequent dealings. In contrast, items which are generally available pose

---

[11] The government defines a contractor's make-or-buy program as "that part of a contractors's written plan which identifies the major subsystems, assemblies, subassemblies, and components to be manufactured, developed, or assembled in his own facilities, and those which will be obtained elsewhere by subcontract." Defense Acquisition Regulations, Gov't Cont. Rep. (CCH) ¶ 32, 888. The objective of such reviews is to assure that the contractor has applied "sound business and technical judgement" and that his decisions will not "adversely affect the government's interests," ¶ 32, 888.15.

relatively few such hazards. Finally, when work is not complex, an agent has fewer opportunities to deceive the government about his costs and is therefore less likely to be successful in obtaining unwarranted price adjustments.

3.2. Procurement Hazards and Remedies

The government's policies for administering its own acquisitions further reveal its awareness of the potential for opportunistic behavior on the part of contractors and of the conditions under which such behavior is most likely to emerge. "Buying in" is one manifestation explicitly recognized as a potential hazard. "'Buying in' refers to the practice of attempting to obtain a contract award by knowingly offering a price or cost estimate less than anticipated costs with the exception of either (i) increasing contract price or estimated cost during the period of performance through change orders or other means, or (ii) receiving future 'follow-on' contracts at prices high enough to recover any losses on the original 'buy-in' contract" (¶ 32, 069).

Contracting officers are advised to be particularly alert to this possibility when performance of the contract involves substantial "preproduction engineering, special tooling, special plant rearrangement, training programs and such nonrecurring costs as initial rework, initial spoilage, and pilot runs," (¶ 32, 866) all of which represent specialized investments in the transaction. Where such investments are at stake, the government provides several policy options directed at preventing the incidence of buying in at the outset of the relationship.

Acquisition of Special Tooling

One option, applicable at least in cases where first-mover advantages are embedded in specialized physical capital, is for the government to take title to specialized assets.[12] Opportunism by the original contractor can then be countered by transferring the assets to more cooperative suppliers. The government's policies covering the acquisition of special tooling and special test equipment address this alternative in detail, clearly indicating a sensitivity to the trade-offs between the hazards of leaving title to specialized tooling with contractors and the costs of internal administration.

> *Policy.* It is the policy of the Department of Defense that contractors provide and retain title to special tooling required for the performance of defense contracts to the maximum extent consistent with sound procurement objectives. Government acquisition of title or the right to title in special tooling creates substantial administrative burden, encumbers the competitive procurement process and frequently results in the retention of special tooling without advantage commensurate with such burden. In certain instances, however, the acquisition of special tooling or rights thereto may help the Government obtain fair prices, recover the residual value of special tooling paid for by the Government, and increase

---

[12] This alternative is referred to as quasi-vertical integration by Monteverde and Teece (1982b).

competition in subsequent procurements by increasing the number of sources, where tooling is susceptible of use by more than one contractor, considering its adaptability and all costs of movement.[13]

The instances in which acquisition is likely to be beneficial are precisely those in which buying in is apt to be a problem, namely, where because of "start-up costs or other nonrecurring costs, . . . the successful offeror is likely to become, in effect, a sole source for follow-on procurements" (¶ 32, 866).

The data accumulated on the aerospace system discussed in the preceding section indicate that the government frequently employs the option to acquire special tooling. Of the fifty-four investments in special tooling or test equipment covered by the surveys, the government retained title in all but seven instances. Moreover, with one exception involving proprietary technology, each of the latter either was ranked as having a high alternative use value or had a shorter use life than the average for the forty-seven to which the government acquired title.

The expediency of this policy toward special tooling depends heavily on the mobility and adaptability of the assets in question; rents will still accrue to equipment unless it can be removed and reassigned to other uses or users at low cost. In addition, the policy cannot eliminate advantages that arise from specialized know-how acquired through performance of the contract.

Extended Contracting

Because the latter policy option applies only where specialized investments are easily transferable, the government provides other methods to attempt to forestall buying in. In particular, where specialized investments cannot be internalized for adaptability or administrative reasons, government policy calls for the use of more extensive contracting: "To avoid or minimize the opportunity for 'buying in' on a procurement which is likely to be succeeded by one or more 'follow-on' procurements, the Government should obtain from the contractor a binding price commitment covering as much of the entire program as is practicable. Such a commitment may be secured through employment of one of the following procurement techniques: (i) multi-year procurement . . .; or (ii) price options for additional quantities. . . ." (¶ 32, 069).

Quantity options are intended for use in contracts where "additional requirements are foreseeable but not known and . . . realistic competition for the option is impracticable once the initial contract is awarded" (¶ 32, 423; also see Use of Options, ¶ 32, 081). Similarly, multiyear contracting and subcontracting are encouraged where "the item is expected to be obtained only from a sole source during the entire multi-year period" (¶ 32, 082). But because of the rigidity of contracting in general, multiyear agreements

[13] Defense Acquisition Regulations (¶ 34, 705). See also the criteria in ¶ 34, 705.10. "*Special tooling* means all jigs, dies, fixtures, molds, patterns, taps, gauges, other equipment and manufacturing aids . . . which are of such a specialized nature that, without substantial modification, their use is limited to the development or production of particular supplies or parts thereof, or the performance of particular services" (¶ 34, 657). A similar definition applies to special test equipment (¶ 34, 657.35).

should only be adopted if "(i) the contract or service is of stable design and specification [and] (ii) the quantity required is reasonably firm and continuing" (¶ 32, 081), that is, where the degree of uncertainty is moderate. Thus, the terms and conditions under which extended contracting is to be employed indicate a perception of the benefits and hazards of the institution that coincides with the arguments outlined in section 1.

4. CONCLUSIONS

Evidence from both stages of the defense procurement process indicates a general reluctance on the part of administrators to internalize transactions: government procurement policies refer explicitly to the "substantial administrative burden" incurred in acquiring and managing equipment and facilities, and estimations of actual contractor procurement practices indicate a strong "predisposition" toward external sourcing. But it is a reluctance that can be overcome by exposure to the hazards of market exchange when components are specialized and complex, as the evidence also attests.

Overall, the data on the aerospace system support the contention that design specificity and complexity are necessary, if not sufficient, conditions for the breakdown of cooperation in market-mediated exchanges and the subsequent integration of production within the firm. In addition, the procurement policies professed by the government provide supportive detail not yet available in the formal analysis, such as the effects of uncertainty on the scope of contractual agreements and the relevance of the absolute value of investments on the need for specialized governance structures. How one views this evidence depends on one's prior assumptions. In a descriptive sense, these excerpts suggest that agents engaged in procurement activities are concerned with the sorts of issues addressed in the transaction-cost paradigm. From a prescriptive standpoint, the model indicates that the government's policies in this regard are appropriate and sensible. Whether or not these policies are actually carried out is, of course, another matter (see, for example, Williamson, 1976b).

Finally, the estimations reported here provide an indication of the relative efficiency of contractual and hierarchical organizational forms. While at a rudimentary level at present, this sort of analysis may eventually permit economists to assess the value of particular contractual arrangements to the parties involved and, subsequently, to evaluate the desirability of adopting alternative legal conventions or of government interference in contractual relationships.

P A R T

III

HYBRIDS

C h a p t e r
11

EXCLUSIVE DEALING AND VERTICAL INTEGRATION: THE EFFICIENCY OF CONTRACTS IN THE TUNA INDUSTRY

Edward C. Gallick

1. OVERVIEW

The procurement of tuna by U.S. processors relies on a complex set of formal and informal contractual arrangements between tuna processors and captains. Domestic processors make investments in modern tuna vessels in return for exclusive supply contracts and a share of the net earnings of the vessel. Each captain generally co-owns his vessel with a processor and is largely responsible for the fishing operations of the vessel. In return, the captain earns a share of the net earnings of the vessel, a wage for being a crew member, and a bonus for exceptionally large annual catches.

What initially motivated this inquiry was the observation that the price processors paid for domestic tuna was typically below the (delivered) price paid for comparable foreign tuna. Although this price differential suggested the possibility of monopsony power among processors in the procurement of domestic tuna, an FTC investigation found that the price difference reflected, in part, the nonprice payments that processors extended to captains. Consequently, there was insufficient evidence to support a case against the major processors. Its structural characteristics notwithstanding, the industry appeared to behave competitively.

Excerpted from chapters 1 and 2 of Exclusive Dealing and Vertical Integration: The Efficiency of Contracts in the Tuna Industry. Federal Trade Commission, Bureau of Economics, Staff Report (August 1984).

Edward Gallick is a Senior Economist at the Federal Communications Commission. When this report was prepared, the author was a member of the professional staff of the FTC Bureau of Economics. It reflects solely the views of the author, and is not intended to represent the position of the Federal Trade Commission, or necessarily the views of any individual Commissioner.

The FTC finding that a significant portion of the observed price differential is explained by the nonprice payments on U.S. landed tuna raises two questions: (1) what explains the remaining portion of the price differential and (2) why do processors make nonprice payments for domestic tuna? At issue is whether the remaining price differential and the nonprice payments are consistent with competition in the U.S. tuna industry.

The first objective of this study is to show how contracting for U . S. tuna promotes efficiency and therefore competition despite structural and behavioral characteristics which may suggest the contrary. One possible explanation of the remaining differential between the U.S. price and the relatively higher foreign price is that the foreign price reflects the higher costs of marketing tuna through competitive auctions. The theory is quite simple: The U.S. market differs from foreign markets in that most consumption in the U.S. is of canned tuna rather than raw tuna. As a result, the inspection, sorting, and grading required for the fresh fish market (in foreign ports) represents an unnecessary cost in the U.S. market. To reduce these costs to efficient levels, it would be preferable for processors to simply buy the boatowner's entire unsorted catch at a price reflecting average quality. However, if processors tried to do this without restricting the boatowner's ability to sell part of his catch elsewhere, boatowners would have an incentive to sell the higher quality tuna to competing processors (at higher prices) and thus increase the sorting and inspection costs of marketing tuna. Exclusive dealing contracts between boatowners and processors that require that a boat's entire catch be sold to a particular processor prevent the duplicative inspection and sorting costs that would otherwise result.

The second objective of explaining the emergence of nonprice payments is achieved by noting that nonprice payments emerged with the introduction of a major technological change in the method of domestic harvesting. The fishing technology changed from a pole-and-line method to a mechanized net retrieval system. Joint ownership of modern tuna vessels by U.S. captains and processors also increased due to this change. Both nonprice payments and vessel co-ownership became necessary because the technological change in fishing increased the costs of using exclusive dealing arrangements to procure domestic tuna. The principal hypothesis is that the change in technology increased the expected contract costs of exclusive dealing to such an extent that vessel co-ownership emerged as an additional efficient form of organization. In turn, nonprice payments by processors are an efficient response by processors to correct the malincentives of the captain that result from co-ownership of a technologically improved vessel. Thus, an understanding of nonprice payments requires an understanding of vessel co-ownership.

Since vessel co-ownership is only one of several institutions which simultaneously emerged in the modern period, however, it cannot be analyzed independently of the other new institutions. Additional new institutions are (1) the provision of vessel financing by processors, (2) a change in the method of determining tuna prices, and (3) the levying of demurrage fees on processors for delays in vessel unloadings. Accordingly, another objective of the study became the explanation of the emergence of all these institutions. Although the analysis is necessarily more complex, its implications are richer and more easily tested.

The study is therefore broader than the initial questions that motivated it. In brief, this is a study of contracting for the supply of U.S. landed tuna. The study demonstrates that the efficiency of such contractual arrangements justifies a differential between U.S. and foreign tuna prices. The emergence of vessel co-ownership and other institutions are methods of minimizing the costs of maintaining the exclusive dealing arrangements between captains and processors. But the use of vessel co-ownership or any other institution is not costless. One cost of vessel co-ownership, for example, is that it provides the captain with an incentive to over-use the vessel. Nonprice payments are a means of reducing this cost of vessel co-ownership. The ultimate effect of exclusive dealing and its ancillary institutions is to increase the supply of U.S. landed tuna and to increase the quantity of canned tuna available for U.S. consumption.

2. THE SPECIALIZED ASSETS HYPOTHESIS

2.1. Introduction

Since at least the early 1950s, the procurement of domestic tuna by U.S. processors has relied on exclusive dealing contracts with U.S. harvesters. In the mid-1960s, however, a major technological change in the method of harvesting stimulated the construction of modern tuna vessels. The introduction of these new vessels was associated with a number of institutional changes in the industry. For example, some processors became joint owners in the new vessels while others provided second mortgages and guarantees on the vessel mortgages issued by banks. The method of determining the tuna price was changed from the time of delivery to the time of departure (to the fishing grounds). Demurrage fees (or fines) were also levied on processors who failed to off-load a vessel within ten days.

One major purpose of this inquiry is to provide an explanation of these new institutions. The hypothesis is that the institutional changes are a response to the increase in costs of exclusive dealing produced by the new fishing technology. The general theory is that exclusive dealing is necessary if certain costs in the procurement of U.S. tuna are to be avoided. The technological change increased the costs of using exclusive delivery contracts and thereby threatened to increase tuna procurement costs. In response, several institutions emerged to reduce these contract costs and to maintain the efficiency of the U.S. tuna marketing scheme. The lower costs of marketing domestic tuna relative to foreign tuna may explain why the domestic tuna price is typically below the foreign price.

2.2. Contracting in the Bait-Boat Period

Until the early 1960s, the domestic tuna fleet was comprised of a large number of "bait boats."[1] Tuna was caught with live bait fish using hooks and line. Captains wholly owned their boats and contracted with processors[2] for delivery of the catch. Why processors contracted for the delivery of tuna is not obvious. In fact, it may seem that a competitive auction could efficiently allocate each incoming tuna delivery among the several competing processors. An understanding of this contracting incentive is fundamental to our understanding of the competitive nature of the industry. Thus, we first consider the major provisions of the contract and attempt to identify the principal motivation for contracting.

The fishing contract generally provided for the following:

1. the method of determining the tuna price,
2. the limits, if any, on the quantity delivered,
3. the services to be provided by the processor such as financial, accounting, and legal, and
4. the exclusive delivery of the catch to the processor.[3]

The tuna contract price was typically a daily posted price offered by each processor to U.S. captains (under contract) upon their return to port with a harvest available for immediate processing[4] Although the price often remained relatively stable over several months, there was never an ex ante commitment by processors to guarantee a price on future tuna deliveries. Throughout the bait-boat period, the price of domestic tuna was always determined at the time of delivery. This method of pricing reflects the processor's requirement for a continuous supply of tuna. If the rate of incoming boats was less than expected by the processor, his posted price would rise until some captains found it profitable to stop fishing and return to port with their current harvests. Conversely, if processors anticipated an abnormally long queue of boats ready for off-loading, the posted price would fall until the rate of incoming boats declined to the rate consistent with the processing requirements of the tuna plant.

If processors were concerned only with procuring a steady inflow of tuna to maintain desired rates of canned tuna production, competitive contracting

---

[1] Marasco (1970: 12–17, hereinafter referred to as the Marasco Study).

[2] Throughout this discussion, the term *processors* will always refer to U.S. processors. For emphasis, the term *domestic* or *U.S. processors* is sometimes used. All other processors will be referred to explicitly (e.g., foreign, European, or Japanese processors).

[3] Adams and Hamlisch (1952: 19–26, hereinafter referred to as the FTC Report); Forbes, Stevenson and Co. (1968: 4–5, hereinafter referred to as the Forbes-Stevenson Study); and the Marasco Study (30).

[4] Tuna processors had no in-plant freezer capability and therefore could not accept frozen tuna. Thus, the processing technology required that tuna deliveries be thawed so that the tuna could be directly off-loaded into the plant for immediate processing. See Forbes-Stevenson Study (IV-5).

for tuna deliveries appears to be inefficient relative to a competitive auction. That is, it is unclear why processors would prefer to contract with a subset of the tuna fleet, given the option to bid for each catch of the entire fleet. The decision of the captain to return to port would depend on the expected daily price determined by all processors (and incoming deliveries), in contrast to a daily posted price offered by a single processor to his contracted boats. The processor with the highest opportunity cost of running short of tuna (and reducing his rate of canned tuna production) would be able to outbid all other processors for the next incoming tuna delivery. The auction would therefore seem to allocate each tuna delivery to its highest valued user. From an efficiency point of view, such an open competitive auction appears to be preferred. Consequently, the motivation for competitive contracting is unlikely to be found in the pricing provision.

Throughout the 1950s, U.S. boatowners attempted to obtain minimum volume guarantees (Forbes-Stevenson Study (Chapter IV, 1–2); and Marasco Study (chapter II, 13–15)). Processors sometimes opposed such quantity guarantees since they tended to reduce the ability of the processor to procure tuna from foreign suppliers. During times of abnormally low foreign tuna prices, U.S. processors sought to acquire the right to "tie-up" its domestic contract boats. That is, deliveries of imported tuna could be substituted for the expected future deliveries of domestic tuna by requiring U.S. contract boats to remain in port (or tie-up) and not resume fishing for a specified number of days. Thus, tie-up orders represented an attempt by processors to limit the (maximum) annual harvest of U.S. contract boats and to substitute cheaper imported tuna. More recently, however, contracts in this period generally omit an explicit quantity provision, with the apparent understanding that the processor will accept the entire harvest of each U.S. boat under contract.

The fishing contract also recognizes that the processor may provide advance money for each fishing trip (and/or accounting and legal services to the boatowner). The term of the contract is a stated number of years or as long as the boatowner or boat remains in debt to the processor, whichever is longer. Generally, if the processor extended a trip advance (loan) to the captain, the expected harvest on that trip would be taken as collateral, and the principal and interest would be deducted from the gross revenues of the harvest upon delivery to the processor (Marasco: 47). Thus, the provision of trip advances by the processor would not extend the length of the contract unless the size of harvest was unusually small. Such changes in the term of the contract could often be avoided by obtaining short term (operating capital) loans from commercial banks.

Exclusive Dealing

The principal motivation for U.S. fishing contracts appears to be reflected in the exclusive-dealing provision. The U.S. tuna marketing arrangement, which relies on exclusive-dealing contracts by captains, is a means of eliminating some of the marketing costs inherent in competitive auctions.

Competitive bidding among tuna processors in the U.S. market is likely to result in excessive sorting of tuna into "blocks" and duplicative inspections of each "block" of tuna offered for sale. A block of tuna refers to the number of tons of a given tuna category. For example, a 100-ton block of skipjack tuna may refer to 100 tons of frozen, whole skipjack weighing between 10 and 13 pounds each. One initial cost of a competitive auction is to sort tuna into blocks. Although sorting costs would be minimized by offering each harvest as a single block, prepurchase inspection costs would be substantial since the units within the block would be extremely heterogeneous. Further, the harvest may be so large and diverse that the winning bidder may sort out units he cannot use and resell them in one or more blocks. Consequently, each harvest is likely to be sorted into a number of blocks. Whether the competitive auction is socially desirable will depend, in part, on whether sorting costs are socially desirable.

Another cost of a competitive auction is prepurchase inspection costs incurred by the bidders. In a competitive auction, it is quite possible for several potential buyers to bid on the same block. Each bidder therefore inspects the same block to determine its value. Yet only one bidder will purchase the block. The costs of such duplicative inspections may be justified if the bidders possess different tastes. For example, if fresh tuna is not sufficiently categorized by number of days after harvest (e.g., $\frac{1}{2}$ day, 1 day, or 2 days), some bidders my search among otherwise similar blocks until a particular degree of freshness is found. Buyers my disagree on the value or alternative uses of fresh tuna as its degree of freshness diminishes. In this instance, competitive search would be socially desirable.

On the other hand, if some average amount of search by all bidders would result in each bidder placing the same value on each block, duplicative inspections would be socially wasteful. There would be no social gain from the aggregate inspections performed by all potential bidders relative to the one inspection by the bidder who ultimately acquires the block. In a canned-tuna market such as the U.S., duplicative inspections of tuna are socially undesirable. There is no social value of such competitive bidding oversearch by tuna processors because they would all agree on the value of each block, given some minimum amount of prepurchase inspection. U.S. canners (potential buyers) are unlikely to disagree on the quality attributes of tuna (such as its freshness, yield, taste, and use) or on the value of any given set of attributes. Under these conditions, there is a strong incentive to eliminate competitive bidding oversearch and to reduce other marketing costs of procuring domestic tuna. If sellers or buyers could prevent such wasteful activity, they could potentially gain an amount equal to the real resources expended in competitive bidding oversearch. To the extent that the alternative marketing scheme can also reduce the sorting of tuna into blocks, an additional savings in marketing costs may be realized.

Although prices preset by the captain (seller) or the processor (buyer) may eliminate the potential for competitive bidding oversearch, each pricing scheme introduces the potential for another type of oversearch. If the captain attempted to set some average price over a tuna catch of varying quality, processors would tend to search out the higher quality and to reject the lower quality units.[5] As long as the captain had less than perfect information about the market value of each unit, processors would attempt to obtain an information advantage over the captain in order to search out the under-priced units.[6] In response, the captain may sort the catch into more homogeneous blocks, each with an average price closer to the average market value of the units within each block. However, as long as the preset price differs from the market clearing price for each quality within a block, processors will continue to search out the higher-quality units. Consequently, such buyer oversearch results in duplicative inspection and excessive sorting costs. Perhaps more importantly, since the captain is not the final user of the tuna, he would never be able to fully communicate the quality of the catch to the processor. Regardless of the amount of search performed by the captain to determine average quality and price, the processor would have to fully reinspect the catch to determine, for himself, the true average quality of the harvest.

If, on the other hand, a processor inspected a captain's entire catch and made a one-time offer of a single price reflecting the average quality or value of all units in the catch, sorting and inspection costs might be dramatically reduced. Such a pricing scheme, however, provides the captain with an incentive to supply only the below-average quality units and to offer the remaining higher-quality units to another processor. As a result, sorting costs are not significantly reduced, and duplicative inspections are not eliminated. As long as the harvest is not homogeneous, a single price (based on the average value of all units in the harvest) will always create this form of adverse selection.

This adverse selection, however, can be constrained by an exclusive-dealing contract. The purpose of the exclusive-dealing provision of the fishing contract is to reduce oversearching and its associated costs. Throughout the term of the exclusive supply contract, the captain must deliver all catches to the contracting processor. The price of each catch is determined at the time of delivery after the processor makes a prepurchase inspection. Although the price still reflects the average value of all units in the catch, the exclusive delivery requirement prevents the captain from sorting out the above-average quality units and offering them to another processor. In this way, exclusive dealing minimizes sorting costs and eliminates duplicative inspections

---

[5] The quality of tuna varies with its size, condition, and species. For canning purposes, one major quality attribute is size: larger tuna can be processed more quickly and cheaply and in this production sense are of higher quality. Similarly, tuna delivered in a semiprocessed condition (e.g., gilled and gutted) represent a higher quality since the remaining processing time and cost is reduced relative to round (or whole) tuna. In the consumption sense, white-meat or albacore tuna is considered higher in quality because it possesses a less "fishy" taste than the lightmeat species, such as yellowfin and skipjack.

[6] The tuna example is analogous to the example of the wholesale marketing of rough uncut diamonds in Kenney and Klein (1983). Kenney and Klein refer to such buyer behavior as Gresham's Law oversearching; see Kenney and Klein (502–5).

initiated by domestic tuna harvesters. The incentive for processors to accept the captain's entire catch, to minimize prepurchase search, and to eliminate duplicative inspections is provided by an exclusive dealing contract that enables processors on average to earn rents (see Kenney and Klein: 505–9). In effect, the domestic tuna price is discounted below its (costly search) market price to processors who require exclusive delivery contracts. This discounted price is necessary to encourage processors to accept all tuna contract deliveries, including occasional deliveries of below-average quality. In this way, prepurchase search costs are minimized by keeping the inspection sample small, and duplicative inspections are avoided by eliminating sales to noncontracting processors.

This tuna price discount is reflected in the processor's share of the cost savings under the U.S. marketing scheme. In essence, the price discount is "paid" or offset by the avoidance of excessive inspection and sorting costs.[7] As long as the present value of these expected price discounts (over the term of the contract) exceeds the present value of sorting and competitively bidding for substitute blocks of tuna (that are undervalued by other bidders), exclusive dealing arrangements will be required by processors, ceteris paribus.

U.S. captains agree to exclusive delivery contracts because such contracts reduce sorting costs and, in turn, the marginal cost of harvesting. Since skipjack and yellowfin often share the same fishing grounds, and since each species can vary substantially in size (quality), harvesting costs could be saved if the catch could be marketed with minimal sorting.[8] Each harvest, for example, might be delivered as "run of the catch" (i.e., without sorting by size or species). As the harvest is off-loaded for sale to processors, sorting limited to species and damage (e.g., crushed, bruised, or broken fish) could be performed. Thus, for any given tuna price, a reduction in sorting costs would be expected to lead to larger and more profitable annual harvests. Competition among captains to supply processors, however, will result in the passing of this cost saving on to processors in the form of lower prices and larger deliveries of domestic tuna. Ultimately, such reductions in processing costs benefit consumers in the form of lower prices and higher quantities of canned tuna.

---

[7] In a perfectly efficient marketing arrangement, the "rents" merely reflect the distribution of the cost savings (per unit of output) to the buyer (processor). Such payments should not be interpreted as a bribe or side payment offered by the seller (captain) that, in turn, increase his costs of production. Rather, the improved efficiency of the marketing scheme relative to a competitive auction, for example, is expected to result in lower production costs to the seller and lower input prices to the buyer. The ultimate effect is greater output of the final product to consumers.

[8] It appears that U.S. captains perform a minimal amount of sorting. The major types of sorting are (1) to remove all nontuna species from the catch and (2) to remove tuna that are under the legal size limit. The remaining tuna are believed to be further sorted only to minimize damage in the storage wells until delivery to the cannery. The larger tuna, for example, are generally placed in the bottom of the wells to avoid crushing the smaller tuna. Based on Orbach (1977), and McNeely (1961).

In short, exclusive dealing contracts are efficient in the marketing of U.S. landed tuna because they avoid unnecessary marketing costs. Some of the marketing cost saving will be retained by captains and processors to offset the costs of exclusive dealing, and the remainder of the cost saving will passed on to consumers.

The Potential Appropriation of Quasi Rents by Tuna Processors

The quasi rent of an asset is any payment in excess of that necessary to keep the asset in its current use (or market). Since the highest-valued alternative use of an asset is its salvage value, the quasi rent of an asset is simply any payment over its salvage value.[9] For example, if a newly restored "classic" automobile can be used as a taxi at a daily rental value of $180 or as an exhibit in a museum at a daily rental of $100, the quasi-rent earned by the automobile is $180 − $100 = $80 per day.

Whether the quasi rent is appropriable depends on the alternative *users*, if any, of the asset in the same *use*. Thus, if I bid $180 to use the car as a taxi and you bid $150/day, the potentially appropriable quasi rent is $180 − $150 = $30 per day. That is, I can contract with the owner to rent the automobile as a taxi for $180/day and then impose costs on (or "hold up") the owner up to $30/day. Since the next highest-valued user of the automobile is only willing to pay $150/day, the owner is no worse off renting the car to me. If I was the only user of the automobile in the taxi market, I could potentially appropriate $180 − $100 = $80, or the entire quasi rent earned by the automobile in its current use (Klein, Crawford, and Akchian, 1978). On the other hand, if there were several taxi drivers who valued the automobile at $180/day, the quasi rents would not be appropriable.

One consequence of the exclusive delivery provision of the fishing contract is that it makes each delivery of tuna a specialized asset. A U.S. captain who agrees to an exclusive delivery contract must deliver his tuna catches to a specific U.S. processor. Exclusive dealing therefore eliminates all alternative *users* (processors) of tuna harvested under contract. In addition, the principal alternative *uses* of tuna are pet food and industrial products such as fish meal and body oil. These products are dramatically lower in value relative to canned tuna and, equally important, they are typically produced as by-products by the tuna processors. Hence, freshly caught tuna under contract to a processor represents an extremely specialized asset, the quasi rent value of which is potentially appropriable.

Under these conditions, U.S. processors have an ability to hold up U.S. harvesters in the sense of opportunistically taking advantage of some unenforceable provision of the contract (see Klein, 1980; and Williamson, 1975). Processors were in a position to renege on their contracts in at least two ways: (1) by imposing costs on captains in the form of unnecessary

---

[9] Thus, the size of the potential holdup may be overestimated if we ignore the possibility that the asset may switch to another use (market). This is why it is necessary to distinguish between alternative users and uses.

off-loading delays and (2) by refusing to accept the catch unless the (implicit) contract price was lowered. Let us consider each in turn.

Throughout the bait-boat period, processors were able to impose unloading delays on boats under contract despite the captains' beliefs that such delays were often abitrary and/or unnecessary. The legitimate reasons for delaying vessel off-loadings are so numerous and varied that the processor could always claim a "legitimate" reason, when in fact he was acting opportunistically. The degree of bargaining power held by domestic captains varied inversely with the arrival of imported tuna at domestic ports. That is, the greater the number of foreign deliveries arriving at a processor's dock, the weaker the ability of U.S. captains to avoid off-loading delays and lengthy price negotiations.[10] Consequently, the order in which a domestic vessel arrived into port was no indication of the order in which it would be off-loaded. Between 1964 and 1966, for example, the monthly average unloading time for U.S. vessels ranged from a low of 3 days to a high of 33 days.[11]

Perhaps more important, the typical fishing contract has always provided the processor with an escape clause allowing him to refuse delivery. The FTC report finds that in 1952, the typical contract contained the following escape clause (FTC Report: 22):

> In the event the canner is unable to accept delivery of fish by reason of strikes, fire, labor difficulties, breakdowns or any cause beyond the control of the canner, the canner has the privilege of refusing to accept such deliveries provided the canner shall immediately use due diligence in finding another canner or canners who will accept immediate delivery; otherwise the fishermen, at their option, may make delivery of fish to such other canner or canners as they may desire until such time as the canner notifies the fishermen that he is ready and able to accept further deliveries.

The fishing contracts in the mid-1960s contained a similar provision:

> If, as a result of any condition or cause beyond the reasonable control of canner, canner is unable at any time to accept or pack fish caught by boat owner, canner shall have the right to refuse to accept fish hereunder and shall not be required to pay for any fish not accepted or canned. Without in any way limiting the generality of the foregoing, plant breakdown, shortage of labor or materials, fire, government regulations, force majeure, strikes, boycotts and other union activity preventing prompt delivery and processing of fish, shall be deemed to excuse canner from accepting or packing fish hereunder.[12]

---

[10] FTC Report (22–30); interviews with industry sources during the FTC industry-wide tuna investigation; Forbes-Stevenson Study, chapter III; deGraeve and Forbes (1954: 8), (hereinafter referred to as the Tuna Imports Study); and the Marasco Study (chapter II, 14).

Between 1950 and 1965, the percentage of imported to total U.S. tuna deliveries increased fivefold and represented 50 percent of the processors' tuna requirements by the early 1960s.

[11] FTC Report (22–23); and data provided by the American Tunaboat Association (ATA), cited in the Forbes-Stevenson Study, Table 11 (III-18).

[12] Tuna fishing agreements subpoenaed in FTC industry-wide tuna investigation, document numbers BE3-l and BE3-2.

In one respect, the escape clause seems reasonable because processing plants throughout the bait-boat and early purse-seiner periods had no freezer storage capability and therefore processed tuna as it was off-loaded from incoming boats. At the same time, however, such an escape clause provides the processor with a means of refusing delivery unless the price is lowered (i.e., to behave opportunistically).

It seems clear that with exclusive contracts tuna processors had the potential to hold up U.S. captains. The high contract costs to specify the necessary contingencies to prevent the processor from behaving opportunistically, to police and detect a contract violation, and to prove the violation in the courts made it unlikely that an explicit contract could eliminate the holdup potential of processors. Even if an explicit contract could eliminate opportunistic behavior, the costs of doing so were likely to make this form of organization prohibitively costly.

Since the *potential* holdup is created by the exclusive delivery provision of the fishing contract, it may seem irrational on the part of the captain to agree to such a provision. If there is no *incentive* to behave opportunistically, however, it would be quite rational for captains to enter into exclusive deals with processors. Recall that the motivation for exclusive dealing is to eliminate excessive sorting and inspection costs. Thus, both captain and processor should expect to share in the net benefits of a lower-cost marketing scheme for domestic tuna. The costs of eliminating the holdup incentive can be simply viewed as a cost of exclusive dealing. If the savings in marketing costs exceed the cost of preventing the holdup, exclusive dealing remains efficient. What is required, then, is a viable alternative to explicit contracting.

One alternative to explicit contracting that may eliminate the holdup incentive of the processor is implicit contracting.[13] Implicit contracts or guarantees are market-enforced by the threat of termination of future business if opportunistic behavior occurs.[14] The captain, for example, could offer the processor a future premium (or extra payment) sufficient to assure contractual performance. If the processor violates the contract, all future business is immediately withdrawn and all expected future premiums are lost by the processor.[15] As long as the captain and processor both agree that the present value of the future premiums exceeds the present value of

---

[13] The distinction between explicit and implicit contracts is more fully described in Klein, Crawford, and Alchian (303–7).

[14] A model of how a market enforcement mechanism can assure contract performance is provided in Klein and Leffler (1981).

[15] If both parties are assumed to know the length of the current contract, then it is also assumed that neither party can determine with certainty the last transaction in the contract period. Alternatively, if both parties can identify the last transaction within the current contract, then there must exist some positive probability that the contract will be renewed. Under these assumptions, a finite uncertain horizon is assured, and implicit contracting becomes a rational alternative mode of organization. See, for example, Telser (1980).

the short-run gain from reneging on the implicit contract, the opportunistic incentive of the processor will be eliminated.[16]

A possible alternative or partial substitute to the pure price-premium method of assuring contract performance is the use of nonsalvageable production assets (Klein and Leffler: 627–33). The normal return (quasi rents) to such an asset also acts to assure contract performance. One competitive equilibrium would be defined where the present value of the nonsalvageable production assets owned by the processor equaled the present value of his reneging on the implicit contract. Given this condition, if the processor were to behave opportunistically, all U.S. captains would refuse to deal with him, and he would be forced to procure tuna from more costly sources. The increase in production costs would result in losses and eventually drive the processor out of the industry. Although capital inputs (e.g., buying a tuna-canning machine rather than buying cans from an independent supplier) increase standard production costs, such expenditures may reduce the price premium paid by captains (and the corresponding brand-name assets acquired by processors) to assure contractual performance. Competition among processors to contract with captains may therefore substitution of nonsalvageable production assets for brand-name assets.

Since the carrying capacity of bait boats is small relative to modern tuna vessels,[17] and since the smaller boats make numerous deliveries (or "repeat sales") to the same processor each year,[18] the expected short-run profit from holding up the captain is not substantial.[19] Assuming that U.S. captains costlessly communicate among one another, a holdup of any U.S. tuna boat will result in a termination of business by all captains delivering to the opportunistic processor. The costs of being branded an opportunistic

[16] The premium stream does not create excess profits in the long run. One condition for a zero-profit equilibrium is that the present value of the premiums offered by the captain equal the present value of the nonsalvageable brand-name assets (or collateral) acquired by the processor to guarantee his contractual performance. The premiums include a normal rate of return to the brand-name assets. See Klein and Leffler (626–27).

A second condition for a no holdup equilibrium is that the present value of the premiums not exceed the present value of the savings in marketing costs, net of the present value of price discounts necessary to encourage processors to accept *all* tuna deliveries under the exclusive-dealing contract, including occasional deliveries of below-average quality.

[17] The weighted average carrying capacity of bait boats over the 1946–66 period is approximately 200 tons. Based on data reported in Broderick (1973, Appendix Table 7: 343, hereinafter referred to as the Broderick Study).

[18] The largest bait boats (commonly referred to as clippers) average four to five trips a year. In contrast, smaller bait boats have been reported to make over 30 trips in a 90-day period. See FTC Report (13–15); U.S. Department of Commerce, NOAA, NMFS, *Tuna 1947–72: Basic Economic Indicators*, Current Fishery Statistics No. 6130, (Washington, D.C.: June 1973: 3); and U.S. Department of Commerce, NOAA, NMFS, *Analysis of the Operations of Seven Hawaiian Skipjack Tuna Fishing Vessels, June–August 1967*, by Richard N. Uchida and Ray F. Sumida, Special Scientific Report, Fisheries No. 692 (March 1971: 6).

[19] Further, the bait boats built before 1945 were of wooden construction and therefore relatively short-lived. Dry rot, sea life, and tropical storms tended to damage the wooden hulls. See, for example, Roesti (1960: 82; sometimes referred to as the Roesti Study).

processor by the industry would therefore include (1) the loss of all expected future premiums paid by captains delivering to the processor under implicit contracts at the time of the holdup, (2) the loss of all nonsalvageable assets employed to produce brand-name capital and tuna at the harvesting stage, and (3) the additional costs of procuring greater proportions of annual tuna requirements from the foreign export market (due to the reluctance of U.S. captains to renew or negotiate supply contracts with the processor).[20] The present value of these costs is likely to be substantially greater than the present value of a one-time holdup on a single delivery of tuna harvested by a bait boat. A processor who reneged on such a contract would therefore be worse off. Consequently, the incentive to behave opportunistically is not likely to be strong. In this case, exclusive dealing is not only rational, it is also socially efficient.

Thus, in the bait-boat period, exclusive-dealing arrangements appear to be efficient. What remains unexplained, however, is why U.S. processors began to commit assets to the harvesting sector in the late 1960s. Beginning in 1967, processors began to hold equity interests in vessels, to extend second mortgages to harvesters, and to guarantee vessel loans. Other major institutional changes included the pricing of tuna before the vessel departed for the fishing grounds (instead of upon its return with the catch) and the imposition of demurrage fees on processors who failed to unload vessels within a specified number of days. Although exclusive dealing contracts continued to prevail throughout the 1960s and 1970s, the increasing involvement of the processors in the harvesting operation was unquestionable. Since these new institutions appear at the same time as a technological change in the method of fishing, we consider how the change in technology might have affected the costs of exclusive dealing in the modern (purse-seine) period.

2.3. The Technological Change in Fishing

The first major impact of the new technology was observable between 1958 and 1963: the larger bait boats were modified to permit fishing with a technologically improved, mechanized net retrieval system. It was not until 1967, however, that newly constructed purse-seine vessels were added to the U.S. fleet on a significant scale. (See Table 11.1.) For this reason, 1967 marks the beginning of the modern purse-seiner period. The technological change in fishing provided captains with the opportunity to transform labor-intensive, hook-and-line vessels into more capital-intensive purse-seine (net) vessels.

One major effect of the technological change was to dramatically increase the tuna-carrying capacity of the new purse-seine vessels. Throughout the last 20 years of the bait-boat period (1946–66), the average carrying capacity

---

[20] If this cost becomes prohibitive, any nonsalvageable assets in the processing stage will also be lost.

TABLE 11.1

Gross Additions to Carrying Capacity of U.S. Purse-Seine Fleet
(measured in tons and number of vessels)

Year	Conversions		New Seiners		Total Additions	Total Additions divided by Fleet Capacity
	Tons	Vessels	Tons	Vessels	Tons	Percent
			Transition Period			
1958	0		0		0	0
1959	3,979	(13)	0		3,979	59.9
1960[a]	14,684	(52)	0		14,684	141.1
1961	8,324	(20)	460	(1)	8,784	36.5
1962	4,319	(10)	779	(1)	5,098	15.9
1963	4,659	(6)	779	(1)	5,438	15.5
1964	0		779	(1)	779	1.9
1965	0		550	(1)	550	1.4
1966	0		550	(1)	550	1.4
			Modern Period			
1967	0		4,030	(5)	4,030	10.5
1968	0		6,214	(9)	6,214	15.5
1969	1,860	(3)	6,810	(10)	8,670	19.9
1970	0		7,700	(7)	7,700	15.4
1971[a]	0		18,950	(17)	18,950	34.0
1972	900	(1)	16,850	(14)	17,750	25.2
1973	0		13,300	(12)	13,300	15.4
1974	0		9,605	(9)	9,605	10.0
1975	0		11,650	(11)	11,650	11.3
1976	0		6,900	(5)	6,900	5.9

Source: "Description of the United States Tuna Fleet: December 31, 1976," by the American Tunaboat Association, 1976 Summary of Newly Constructed Tuna Purse Seiners: Chronological Listing.

[a] Peak year within period.

of a bait boat was 200 tons. During the first 10 years of the modern purse-seine era (1967–76), 105 newly constructed seiners entered the U.S. tuna fleet. The carrying capacities of these vessels ranged from a remarkable high of 2,175 tons to a low of 150 tons. On average, the technologically superior purse seiner possessed a carrying capacity of 1,000 tons—five times the capacity of a bait boat.

The increase in the carrying capacity of purse-seine vessels contributed to a substantial increase in total fleet capacity, despite the reduction in the number of vessels in the fleet.[21] The average fleet capacity of 42,809 tons during the bait-boat period increased to 73,560 tons by 1971 (or by 72

---

[21] Fleet capacity is defined as the maximum tonnage that can be harvested if every vessel in the fleet makes one fishing trip and returns to port with a full load of fish.

percent) with purse seiners accounting for 95 percent of total fleet capacity.[22] At the same time, the average number of boats in the fleet declined from 215 to 158, or by approximately 25 percent.

In short, the major effects of the new fishing technology on the size and composition of the U.S. tuna fleet were as follows:

1. to increase the carrying capacity of the new vessels entering the fleet,
2. to increase total fleet capacity and,
3. to almost eliminate bait boats from the fleet.

2.4. Contracting in the Purse-Seiner Period

The Potential Holdup of Purse-Seine Tuna Deliveries and the Emergence of Countervailing Institutions

One effect of the technological change was to disturb the no holdup equilibrium in the bait-boat period. The dramatically larger carrying capacities of the modern purse seiners increased the potentially appropriable quasi rents on each tuna delivery. The maximum delivery by an average seiner was 1,000 tons. This represented five times the maximum delivery of a typical bait boat. From the viewpoint of the contracting processor, the potential short-run gain from postcontractual reneging was five times greater in the purse-seine period than in the bait-boat period. The change in fishing technology therefore increased the expected gain and, at the same time, reduced the expected costs of opportunistic behavior. Consequently, there was much less incentive for the processor to honor the implicit contract. Under these conditions, captains would be unlikely to agree to the same exclusive delivery contracts as in the bait-boat period. Moreover, without some form of exclusive dealing, the marketing costs saved under the U.S. tuna-marketing arrangement could be lost.

In addition, the introduction of modern purse seiners to, and the displacement of numerous small bait boats from, the tuna fleet resulted in less frequent deliveries or "repeat sales" to each contracting processor. A reduction in the frequency of deliveries, ceteris paribus, reduces the present value of the expected future premiums under the implicit contract. The present value of $12 received at the end of one year, for example, is less than the present value of $1 received at the end of each month for twelve months, assuming a positive rate of interest. Similarly, if a processor receives a single 1,000 ton delivery from a purse seiner at the end of 60 days, the present value of a $1/ton premium on the seiner delivery will be less than the present value of the same $1/ton premium on 10 bait-boat deliveries, each for 100 tons and

---

[22] Compiled from data reported in the Broderick Study, Appendix Table 7: 343. By 1978, total fleet capacity reached a high of 115,546 tons and represented a 170 percent increase over the average fleet capacity in the bait-boat period. *Annual Report of the Inter-American Tropical Tuna Commision: 1978* (La Jolla, Calif.: 1979, Appendix II, Table 4: 158).

arriving every 6 days over the 60-day period. The cost of behaving opportunistically therefore decreases.

In response to the adverse effects of the technological change on exclusive dealing, countervailing institutions[23] emerged in the purse-seiner period to reduce the processor's incentive to behave opportunistically. Let us consider the effects of four new institutions: (1) joint ownership in the vessel, (2) guarantees on vessel mortgage loans, (3) price determination prior to each fishing trip, and (4) demurrage fees for delays in vessel off-loadings.

In sharp contrast to the bait-boat period, processors generally held an equity interest in the new purse seiners entering the U.S. fleet. Most processors typically held at least a 20 percent minority interest in the vessel. Under joint ownership, any costs that the processor may impose on the harvesting operation will also reduce the return to his vessel equity. More specifically, the (dollar) return on the processor's equity will fall in direct proportion to his ownership interest. If the processor owns 40 percent of the vessel, for example, a $100,000 reduction in vessel earnings imposes a $40,000 reduction on the return to his equity. Co-ownership in the new seiners therefore reduces the processor's incentive to behave opportunistically.

Unless the processor wholly owns the vessel, however, joint ownership may be insufficient to fully offset the increased holdup potential of the modern purse seiner. From the perspective of the processor, joint ownership represents a partial integration backwards into harvesting. If the processor is only a minority owner in harvesting but a majority owner in processing, he may still have an incentive to hold up the captain under an exclusive delivery contract. This is because the loss on his vessel equity will be more than offset by the gain in equity on his processing operation. Consider, for example, a processor who holds a 40 percent ownership interest in a purse seiner and wholly owns a tuna processing plant. A $100,000 reduction in the cost of tuna due to an unexpected price concession by the captain reduces the processor's earnings in harvesting by $40,000 but increases his earnings in processing by $100,000. The net gain to the processor is $60,000. Without the co-ownership interest in the vessel, the processor would have realized a net gain of $100,000. Thus, the joint ownership requirement does reduce the likelihood of postcontractual reneging.

The additional provision of mortgage guarantees, however, further reduces the likelihood of the holdup. One effect of the mortgage guarantee is to limit the ability of the processor to shift earnings from the harvesting to the processing operation. That is, the earnings of the vessel must always be sufficient to cover the loan payments to the bank. If the loan goes into default, the assets pledged by the processor under the loan guarantee are subject to sale by the bank to the extent necessary to retire any outstanding debt under

---

[23] Fundamentally, an institution is any means of decreasing a transaction cost. Harold Demsetz, for example, treats an institution as a means of internalizing transaction costs. The nonexistence of an institution in the bait-boat period implies that it had no relative advantage. See Demsetz (1964; 1967).

the loan agreement. Thus, the effects of joint ownership and mortgage guarantees are reinforcing and, to some extent, substitutable.

From the perspective of the captain, the joint provision of a guarantee and a second mortgage may represent a stronger substitute for equity held by the processor. The provision of guarantees on first mortgages is most important when the processor does not hold an equity interest in the vessel. Whereas the guarantee limits the ability of the processor to shift earnings from the harvesting to the canning stage, the expected payments of interest on the second mortgage limit the processor's ability to reduce earnings at the harvesting stage. Second mortgages without guarantees, however, represent a weaker substitute for equity. The reason is that the default provision of the second mortgage agreement is likely to give the processor (lender) the right to repossess and sell the vessel and to keep the sale proceeds net of the principal on the first mortgage. As a result, the processor may not lose his principal on a second mortgage. On the other hand, if the processor held equity instead of a second, a reduction in vessel earnings resulting in default on either the first or second mortgage could impose an equity loss on the processor (and the captain). Thus, the guarantee is able to limit the greater potential to shift earnings to the canning stage when the processor holds little, or no, vessel equity. By requiring the processor to guarantee the first mortgage and to also hold the second, any opportunistic behavior by the processor that reduces vessel earnings also increases the probability of bankruptcy and the possible loss of his assets pledged under the guarantee plus the interest income and principal on the second. The following empirical observation is thereby suggested: the provision of equity is expected to be inversely related to the joint provision of guarantees and second mortgages by the processor.

Another major institutional change was to determine the domestic price of tuna *prior* to the vessel's departure to the fishing grounds. In the bait-boat period, processors offered prices on delivered tuna ready for immediate processing. This apparently put the harvesters at a great disadvantage, since their catch was subject to deterioration in the holds of their vessels while they were negotiating prices or waiting to be off-loaded. In 1967, the American Tuna Sales Association (ATSA), a marketing cooperative, was established to assume the sales responsibilities for the domestic tuna fleet, with the exception of those vessels wholly owned by processors. Since 1968, the price of domestic tuna received by each ATSA member is determined prior to its departure on a new fishing trip. As a result, the ability of the processor to renege on the (implicit) contract price for tuna is substantially limited.

In addition, the potential for unnecessary delays in vessel off-loadings appears to be restrained by a fourth major institutional change. Off-loading delays had been a principal source of dissatisfaction among captains in the bait-boat period. Beginning in 1968, however, the ATSA was permitted to charge the processor a demurrage fee of $1 per ton for each day that tuna remained on board eleven or more days after returning to port. On a

1,000-ton purse seiner, for example, the fee could be as high as $1,000/day. Thus, the ability of the processor to hold up the captain by threatening to delay off-loading his vessel was reduced in the purse-seiner period.

The Malincentives of the Countervailing Institutions and Their Nonemergence in the Bait-Boat Period

Malincentives associated with vessel co-ownership and mortgage guarantees discouraged adoption of these institutions during the earlier bait-boat period. The malincentives of vessel co-ownership are analogous to those of share-cropping in which the agent has an incentive to undersupply his labor and overuse the principal's assets, in this case, the jointly owned boat (Cheung, 1968).[24] Mortgage guarantees, meanwhile, increase the captain's ability to obtain loans, which, like debt, distort an agent's investment incentives. In the tuna industry, a captain with a majority equity interest in the vessel may promise lenders that he will operate his vessel in a particular manner. Once the loans are approved, however, the captain may undertake much riskier operations in an attempt to substantially increase the return on his equity despite the increased risks (costs) imposed on the lenders. Consequently, lenders may attempt to specify in the loan agreement how the vessel will be operated. Such provisions are unlikely to cover all contingencies and may seriously limit the ability of the captain to operate the vessel efficiently (Macaulay, 1963). To the extent that lenders anticipate these incentives, the terms of the loan will be modified. A higher rate of interest, additional collateral, and a larger guarantee may be required. As long as these costs are less than the opportunity loss of not fishing for tuna, the captain will accept the loans, despite their higher cost.

The (malincentive) costs of providing guarantees in the bait-boat period appear to be high. Captains generally invested their entire personal savings to own their own boat. Their personal savings, however, rarely exceeded the minimum loan requirements set by commercial banks. Thus, the mortgage on the boat was large relative to the captain's equity. As a result, additional loans secured by processor guarantees were likely to create the incentive for the captain to take greater risks with his boat. Given that the modern bait boats had a cruising range of 10,000 miles and that a single trip could take up to 100 days,[25] the costs of monitoring the activities of the captain were quite high. In addition, the refrigeration, navigation, communication, and foreign repair capabilities throughout most of the period were significantly

---

[24] More generally, co-ownership creates agency costs (which include monitoring costs) between the principal (processor) and the agent (captain) (see Jensen and Meckling, 1976). To offset the underfishing incentives of captains under vessel co-ownership, processors began to offer bonuses for exceptionally large seasonal catches. In addition, processors assumed some of the responsibility of the harvesting operation as a way to restrain or counter vessel overuse, including paying for (and sometimes arranging for) repairs and maintenance of the vessel, unloading crews at dockside, and insurance on the vessel. The additional costs incurred by the processor were deducted from the tuna price.

[25] U.S. Department of the Interior, Fish and Wildlife Service (1953: 31; hereinafter referred to as the DOI Survey); and Orbach (3).

inferior to those available in the modern period. Consequently, the possibility of (1) the boat sinking, (2) delays in foreign ports due to unavailability of repair parts, (3) the catch spoiling, or (4) problems with the availability or condition of the live bait (DOI Survey: 220–22) was much higher in the bait-boat than in the purse-seiner period. A captain who attempted to increase his catch by fishing more distant waters or by extending the length of the trip was therefore increasing the riskiness of the harvesting operation.

The high transaction costs of establishing a tuna price for each bait boat before it departed for the fishing grounds rendered the "empty boat auction" method of pricing too costly relative to the (ex post) posted price system used throughout the bait-boat period. For any given annual harvest, the smaller carrying capacity of the boats in the bait-boat fleet required that they complete more trips.[26] As a result, the number of ex ante price determinations would be substantially greater in the bait-boat period than in the modern purse-seiner era. Since the costs of estimating the ex ante prices vary directly with the number of trips (and are independent of the size of the harvests by individual boats or the entire fleet), the empty boat auction would be more costly to operate in the bait-boat period.[27]

There are a number of transaction costs associated with an empty boat auction. One significant transaction cost is precontract search costs.[28] By fixing an ex ante price for each fishing trip, the captain and the processor are, in effect, agreeing on how to distribute the expected gain from each trip. Consequently, both the captain and the processor have a stronger incentive to search for information about future costs and prices than under an ex post pricing scheme. Thus, the ex post pricing arrangements utilized throughout the bait-boat period can be viewed as a means of reducing pre-contract search costs. In addition, contract enforcement and renegotiation costs are likely to be higher under ex ante pricing. As the expected contract price rises above the market price at time of delivery, the processor has a greater incentive to renege on the price agreement. Similarly, as the contract price falls below the market price, the captain has a greater incentive to renegotiate a higher price. The ex post pricing provision together with the relatively short length of the contracts used in the bait-boat period served to lower such costs.[29] A third possible cost of the empty boat auction relates to the

---

[26] Although the carrying capacity of tuna fleets operating during the 1948 to 1959 period was larger than the capacity of the modern purse-seiner fleets, the average capacity of a bait boat was substantially below that of a modern purse seiner.

[27] Since the empty boat auction permits the captain and the processor to *individually* determine the price for each fishing trip, such an ex ante pricing scheme may also enable the processor to price discriminate among the incoming deliveries. In contrast, the (ex post) posted price system makes it more difficult to price discriminate since the processor would have to change his posted price for all deliveries rather than for the deliveries of an *individual* captain.

[28] In the market for petroleum coke, this cost is explained by Goldberg and Erickson (1982).

[29] The shorter the length of the contract, the less likely is a substantial divergence between contract and market prices and the incentive for postcontractual reneging. This positive relationship between contract length and enforcement costs is suggested in Cheung (1969).

processor's inability to inspect the catch prior to agreement on its price. Such "blind" selling arrangements way provide the captain with an incentive to lower the quality of the catch (below the average quality expected by the processor), in an attempt to increase the size of the catch.[30] The captain, for example, may harvest tuna that are smaller than the average size implicit in the ex ante price. From the processor's viewpoint, this represents a reduction in quality because smaller tuna require more processing than larger tuna.[31] Under ex post pricing arrangements, however, the costs of blind selling can be reduced substantially.

The institution of demurrage fees clearly recognizes the ability of the processor to arbitrarily delay vessel unloadings. The malincentive (cost) introduced by such a levy is to encourage captains to return to port prematurely in order to "earn" the demurrage fee. Since the demurrage fee is a substitute for net income, the captain will stop fishing before catching a full load if the opportunity loss (of a larger catch) is at least offset by the gain in demurrage fees. Thus, boats approaching full capacity and fishing along the coastlines of California and Mexico could easily increase their earnings by returning to port during times of unusually long unloading queues. In the bait-boat period, a demurrage fee would have been extremely costly because of the small capacities of many of the boats, the numerous deliveries made by the smaller boats, and the local nature of the fishing operation for many of the boats in the fleet.

The malincentive cost of the demurrage fee explains why the fee was set below the exact level of the true damages necessary to compensate the captain. The fee was introduced in 1967 and was set at $1 per ton for tuna that was not unloaded after 10 days in port. This closely approximates the cost of additional refrigeration and rejects (spoilage) due to unloading delays.[32] The setting of the demurrage charge equal to the refrigeration and reject costs of a delay is therefore a means of compensating the captain for additional operating costs attributable to the delay without also providing the captain with the incentive to return to port prematurely.

3. SUMMARY AND IMPLICATIONS

The principal motivation for exclusive delivery contracts in the bait-boat period is to avoid duplicative inspection and sorting costs in the marketing of U.S. tuna. Exclusive dealing, however, transforms the domestic tuna harvests into a specialized asset. The return to a specialized asset, by definition, is a quasi rent. Consequently, the contracting processor has an incentive to renege on the contract and attempt to appropriate the quasi rents

---

[30] For a discussion of "blind" selling and seller brand names, see Kenney and Klein (515–16).

[31] In the modern purse-seiner period, processors did, in fact, complain about the problem (cost) of correctly anticipating average size of the catch; see Forbes-Stevenson Study (IV-4).

[32] In 1956, the layover costs of the larger bait boats were estimated at 75 cents per ton; see *California Fisheries Trends and Review for 1956* (4).

of the tuna catch. The processor could, for example, threaten not to accept the entire delivery unless the captain conceded to some nominal price for his tuna. Alternatively, the processor could threaten to prolong price negotiations and/or vessel off-loading unless the captain agreed to a lower price. Under these conditions, captains would not likely agree to exclusive deliveries.

The possible loss in marketing cost savings yielded by the U.S. tuna-marketing arrangement, however, provides the processor and captain with the incentive to reduce the size of the potential holdup. Since explicit contracting appeared to be too costly an alternative, implicit contracting was considered. The two necessary conditions for a no holdup equilibrium are: (1) that the captain and processor both agree that the present value of the future premiums (or quasi rents on nonsalvageable production assets) exceeds the present value of the short-run gain from reneging on the implicit contract, and (2) that the present value of the future premiums not exceed the present value of the savings in marketing costs. Both conditions appeared to be met because bait boats tended to make numerous small deliveries throughout the year. Consequently, the potential gain from a one-time holdup of a bait-boat delivery was likely to be small. Hence, the implicit premiums were likely to be small and the net savings in marketing costs were likely to be substantial.

The technological change in the method of harvesting disturbed the no holdup equilibrium in the bait-boat period. By reducing the frequency of tuna deliveries and by increasing the carrying capacity of the new vessels, the processor's incentive to behave opportunistically increased. Under these conditions, captains would be unwilling to accept exclusive delivery contracts.

As in the bait-boat period, the possible loss in marketing cost savings provided processors and captains with the incentive to reduce the increased holdup potential. Within the first year of the purse-seiner period, four new institutions emerged. Possible contractual disputes regarding price and unloading delays were specifically recognized by instituting an "empty boat" pricing scheme for tuna, and demurrage fees for unloading delays. Joint ownership more generally discouraged postcontractual reneging by imposing a cost on the processor for any reduction in vessel earnings. Lastly, mortgage guarantees limited the incentive of the processor to hold up the captain by shifting earnings from the harvesting to the canning stage of production or by reducing vessel revenues below the value of the next scheduled mortgage payment. As long as all contract costs (including the costs of institutional changes) do not exceed the savings due to the avoidance of excessive inspection and sorting costs (under the U.S. tuna-marketing arrangement), exclusive delivery contracts remain efficient in the purse-seiner period.

C h a p t e r

12

UNITED STATES v. UNITED SHOE MACHINERY CORPORATION: ON THE MERITS

Scott E. Masten and Edward A. Snyder

1. INTRODUCTION

Although *United States* v. *United Shoe Machinery Corporation* ranks among the most famous of antitrust cases, the economic principles involved in the

Reprinted from the Journal of Law and Economics, vol. XXXVI (April 1993) by permission of the University of Chicago Press. © 1993 by The University of Chicago. All rights reserved.

Scott E. Masten is Professor of Business Economics and Public Policy, the University of Michigan; Edward Snyder is Professor of Business Economics and Public Policy and Director of the William H. Davidson Institute, the University of Michigan. We would like to extend our thanks for helpful comments to Ian Ayers, Patrick DeGraba, Victor Goldberg, D. Bruce Johnsen, James Meehan, Michael Meurer, Eric Rasmusen, Alan Schwartz, Richard Zerbe, participants at seminars at the Department of Justice, Antitrust Division and at Boston University, the University of Chicago, Columbia University, the University of Connecticut, Cornell University, George Mason University, the University of Michigan, Massachusetts Institute of Technology, North Carolina State University, the University of California, Los Angeles, the University of Southern California, Washington University, Yale University, and at the National Bureau of Economic Research's "Program in Industrial Organization" conference. We gratefully acknowledge the financial support of the Lynde and Harry Bradley Foundation, the RGK Foundation, and the Office for the Study of Public and Private Institutions. We would also like to express our gratitude to the United Shoe Machinery Corp. and especially John Meuse, Nick Gelsomini, and George Armstead for providing access to their files and records, to Edward McCarthy for additional data and consultations, and to Justice Department officials for their help in obtaining records from the case. James Bohn provided excellent research assistance. Parts of this research were completed while Masten was a John M. Olin Faculty Research Fellow at Yale Law School.

dispute have remained obscure.[1] The most prominent economic issues have been (i) the role of leasing as a solution to the durable-goods-monopoly problem and (ii) the exclusionary potential of specific lease provisions. Of these, the durable-goods-monopoly rationale appears to have gained the greater acceptance among economists—an occurrence due in no small part to Chicago School arguments that challenged the logic of anticompetitive exclusion.[2]

Two developments, however, have stimulated renewed interest in United's motives and the overall merits of the case. The first was the realization that the duration of United's leases was inconsistent with the durable-goods-monopoly argument. Whereas short-term leasing facilitates monopoly pricing of durable goods by curbing the monopolist's temptation to cut prices to successive customers, United's leases were originally seventeen years in duration and were subsequently shortened (first to ten and later to five years) only at court direction.[3] Second, new theoretical models have overcome the logical hurdle to exclusionary claims by demonstrating that exclusion may indeed be profitable despite the need to compensate customers or suppliers for the resulting loss of competition.[4] If claims of anticompetitive exclusion cannot be rejected a priori, then lease terms and other contractual provisions that limit rivals' access to markets must be evaluated on their merits.

In this article, we offer what we believe to be a tenable efficiency defense of United's practices against the charge of anticompetitive exclusion. Specifically, we argue that leasing served as an alternative to contractual

---

[1] *United States* v. *United Shoe Machinery Corporation*, 110 F. Supp. 295 (D. Mass. 1953). aff'd; 347 U.S. 521 (1954) (hereafter cited as District Court Opinion).

[2] The Chicago views were developed by Aaron Director and Edward Levi, Ward Bowman, Richard Posner, and Robert Bork. Director and Levi (1956) argued that exclusionary practices tended to be unprofitable because it is costly "to impose additional coercive restrictions on . . . suppliers" (292). Bowman argued in the same year that Kaysen's analysis of *United* was flawed because, if customers preferred leases of shorter duration and with less restrictive elements, they would have been willing to pay a premium. Posner (1976) cited *United Shoe* to illustrate his claim that suppliers must compensate customers for exclusionary contract provisions: "[C]ustomers of United would be unlikely to participate in a campaign to strengthen United's monopoly position without insisting on being compensated" (203). Bork (1978) criticized the court's reasoning that United's practices could be anticompetitive without being predatory and concluded conversely that, in the absence of predatory behavior, the presumption must favor efficiency. Bork, like the others, did not attempt to provide an affirmative efficiency explanation for the practices, however.

[3] As originally expounded by Ronald Coase (1972), buyers of durable goods will be reluctant to pay monopoly prices initially without a guarantee that prices will not be lowered in the future. Leasing offers such an assurance insofar as the manufacturer, by retaining ownership rights to the existing stock of capital, will bear some of the losses from additional production and distribution. The size of the manufacturer's losses, however, is inversely related to the length of the lease contract. Hence, shorter-term leases offer more effective guarantees to buyers than do longer-term leases. The inconsistency between the theory and the duration of United's leases has been previously noted by Victor P. Goldberg (1990); and Wiley, Rasmusen, and Ramseyer (1990).

[4] Specifically, Phillipe Aghion and Patrick Bolton (1987) show how a firm can profit from exclusionary practices despite the need to compensate customers for agreeing to exclusionary terms if the contract can be structured to extract economic rents from third parties, either potential rivals or future customers.

warranties for assuring the quality of machines and as a way to foster the provision of a range of manufacturer services and information in support of the productive use of that equipment. Shoe machines were remarkably complex and heterogeneous instruments, costly to develop and prone to failure. The efficient operation of a shoe factory required a large number of these complex devices and an assortment of services that included guidance on the selection and configuration of shoe machines, training in their operation, timely and effective repairs, and the dissemination of technical advice on shoes and shoe manufacturing generally. The complexity of shoe machines and of related services would have left conventional contractual arrangements hopelessly incomplete and susceptible to conflicts. By making the proceeds from machinery transactions contingent on the retention and use of machines, leasing promoted the supply of quality machines and the generation and dissemination of nonpatentable innovations and know-how without the need for comprehensive contracting.

The importance of innovation and know-how to sustaining efficient production in the shoe industry also underlay the long-term and exclusionary features of United's leases that were the central component of the government's complaint. Specifically, the government cited three provisions of United's leases for their exclusionary effect: (1) return charges due upon termination of a lease, (2) minimum monthly usage charges on machines subject to per-unit payments, and (3) the "full-capacity" clause that required lessees to "use the machine to its full capacity upon all shoes upon which the machine is capable of being used."[5] Combined with the long term of the leases, these provisions can be justly interpreted as impeding adoption of competitor machines. The relevant question, however, is whether the impediments they created were excessive in relation to organizational problems encountered in the industry. We argue, to the contrary, that the duration and restrictive features of United's leases established appropriate incentives to retain and use machines and, in particular, were necessary to prevent customers from attempting to escape paying for information and services from which they had already benefited and that could be profitably used with competitors' machines. We more broadly contend that the structure of United's leases reflected the desire of transactors generally to economize on the costs associated with governing exchange and resolving disputes.

Our investigation has two advantages over recent studies by Victor Goldberg (1990) and by John Wiley, Eric Rasmusen, and Mark Ramseyer (1990) that also explore efficiency rationales for United's practices. First, although each suggests plausible efficiency justifications for leasing durable goods, neither attempts to reconcile their rationales for leasing with the specific provisions of United's leases. Second, these studies also fail to account for United's selective use of leasing and pricing arrangements. Of the

---

[5] Civil No. 7198 (D. Mass. filed December 15, 1947, at 30) (hereafter cited as Complaint). The government also objected to United's practice of providing repair services without separate charges.

343 machines United offered at the time of the case, only half were available on lease-only terms. Of those, half levied charges on a per-operation basis while the balance relied exclusively on monthly rental fees. A satisfactory theory should generate testable hypotheses regarding United's pricing and leasing policies as well as explain the important elements of the overall structure of its leases.

We begin in section 2 with a description of the nature of the intermediate market for shoe machines. Then, in section 3, we present two efficiency motives for leasing in such circumstances, discuss what form such leases should take, and present testable hypotheses regarding the use and structure of United's leases. Section 4 contains econometric evidence that United systematically selected the terms under which it offered its machines to reflect these incentive considerations. A more thorough examination of the details of United's leases and their implementation shows United's practices to be broadly consistent with the efficiency arguments we present. Sections 5 and 6 offer brief discussions of the practices of United's predecessors and competitors and of the aftermath of the case. We conclude with some observations on the implications of the *United* decision and on public policies toward exclusionary contracts generally.

2. AN INDUSTRY PRIMER

The organizational problems encountered in the market for shoe machines trace ultimately to the nature of shoes and of shoe demand.[6] From a mechanical standpoint, the most distinctive features of shoes are their complex shape and extreme heterogeneity. To accommodate the intricate curves and irregular surfaces of shoes, shoe machines had to perform complex motions in multiple spatial planes—actions that required major advances in machine technologies. At the same time, these machines had to be easily adjustable to the variety of styles, sizes, materials, and constructions in or of which shoes were made. There were at least eighteen principal methods of producing a shoe,[7] each of which entailed between one hundred fifty and two hundred operations.[8] Although wood, fabrics, and, later, rubber were also employed, the principal raw material remained leather, which varied almost continuously in its thickness, strength, and flexibility. To provide an

---

[6] The court record provides considerable detail on the nature of shoe production and the services provided by shoe machinery manufacturers. Following an extensive review of these facts, Judge Charles Wyzanski questioned "not the accuracy, but the relevance of the generalizations" (District Court Opinion: 300–302, 329–32). See also Kaysen (1956).

[7] Request for Findings of Fact of the United Shoe Machinery Corporation in the District Court of the United States for the District of Massachusetts, 24 (January 1952) (hereafter cited as United Facts).

[8] On Their Toes, *Baron's*, September 28, 1959, at 3; Footwear's Desperate Drive for Productivity, *Bus. Week*, June 10, 1972, at 68. Approximately half of the operations to produce a shoe were performed by hand.

approximate fit to feet of varying dimensions, shoe manufacturers normally produced over one hundred and often over two hundred size-width combinations for each shoe design, the attributes of which varied in turn with both function and fashion. Accordingly, shoe machines, unlike other manufacturing equipment of the period, could not be designed for repetitive operations on large, homogeneous lots. Rather, "[t]he machine-type performing each operation, though a special tool from the point of view of the operation performed, [had to] be a general tool in relation to each shoe in process requiring the operation" (United Facts: 47).

The reliability of these complex devices was a critical concern to shoemakers. Shoe fashions were inherently unpredictable and transient. As a result, retailers intially placed orders for new styles in small volumes. Shoemakers then were expected to deliver repeat orders of successful styles on short order. Delays in delivery implied missed sales opportunities and could lead to cancellations of orders. In addition, the failure of one machine could disrupt operations throughout a plant, idling both labor and other machinery.[9]

Surmounting the technical problems associated with designing machines capable of reliably performing the varied and intricate operations of producing a shoe required "advanced engineering skill, familiarity with the problems of shoe-making, and generally, prolonged expensive research" (District Court Opinion: 302), endeavors to which United devoted considerable resources. At the beginning of 1950, United had 572 employees engaged in research on shoes, materials, machines, and processes and had spent approximately $4.3 million on research during the preceding year. The only machinery manufacturer with a larger research laboratory was General Motors. Over the fifteen years or so leading up to the case, moreover, United had trained all of its own inventive talent. Its research and development efforts made it one of the five largest patent holders in the United States.[10]

The result of those efforts was the development of a large number of complex and interdependent machines, the productive use of which depended heavily on the initial provision and continued flow of a range of supplementary services. In 1948, United offered 343 types of machines, of which a shoe manufacturer would need from thirty-seven to one hundred to perform the operations required to produce a shoe. The efficient combination and arrangement of those machines varied depending on the manufacturing process adopted, the type and quality of shoes being produced, the scale of production, and the skills and experience of employees. Identifying the best techniques and most productive combination and configuration of machines and training the work force in their proper use and maintenance demanded extensive knowledge of both shoe machines and manufacturing.

---

[9] According to United, production interruptions often led to "cancellations of orders, tying up of inventories, and strained labor relations" (United Facts: 48). Also see District Court Opinion (302).

[10] In addition, United devoted much of its research effort to improvements in existing machines, many of which were not patentable (Kaysen: 171–76).

Once in operation, shoemakers were also in frequent need of advice on problems encountered during the course of production. This advice, which often had "little or nothing to do with any individual machine," included "the application of broad know-how along shoe making and manufacturing lines" and involved, in addition to technical advice on machine operations, "the analyzing of problems, whether arising from styles, materials, constructions, labor skills or any one of many factors and the giving of expert advice and assistance to help the manufacturer to make more and better shoes at lower cost."[11]

Finally, despite extensive efforts to improve reliability, the tasks expected of many shoe machines were so complicated that malfunctions were inevitable.[12] When a breakdown did occur—the incidence of which increased during peak demand periods when machines were most intensively used—shoemakers wanted rapid and effective repair services. To meet those demands, a servicer had to have a comprehensive knowledge of both shoe machines and their interactions. Although malfunctions were often the consequence of parts wear or breakage on a particular machine, failures also resulted from defective materials or work performed by a machine or operator earlier in the manufacturing process. Repairs that did not treat the ultimate source of the breakdown would lead to recurrent failures and repeated delays.[13]

The parties best situated to provide the services auxiliary to shoe machinery were the machine manufacturers themselves. Much of the expertise needed to use and repair machines arose as a by-product of their engineering and manufacture.[14] Repair activities, in turn, provided an important source of feedback on machine and manufacturing problems and on developments in shoe styles and constructions that aided in the improvement of existing machines as well as in the development of new machines and shoe production processes.[15] Hence, the production of shoe

---

[11] Brief for Appellant, Appeal from the United States District Court for the District of Massachusetts to the Supreme Court of the United States, 191 (October 1953) (hereafter cited as Appeal). United divided its services into four general categories. In addition to the application of general shoemaking know-how, United listed three types of service "essentially related to specific machines" that consisted of "the installation of new United machines, the instruction of operatives in their use, and their subsequent repair, maintenance, and adjustment" (Appeal: 192). Note that, while installation and repair are specific to individual machines, machine layouts and training in the operation of a machine provide knowledge generalizable to similar equipment of other manufacturers.

[12] "No matter how skillfully designed, these complicated machine types will require frequent service" (District Court Opinion: 302).

[13] United called its ability to trace the source of failures throughout the shoe manufacturing process its "most important service" (United Facts: 49).

[14] United discussed at length the sources of its expertise and the advantages of its breadth of experience relative to shoemakers in developing and maintaining a stock of knowledge on the manufacturing of shoes (Appeal: 204–6).

[15] United kept extensive records of machine breakdowns and problems (District Court Opinion: 323).

machinery and associated services exhibited significant scope economies grounded in the knowledge necessary to design, manufacture, and support machines.[16]

In both the scope of services it offered and its size, United dominated the industry. To satisfy shoemakers' needs for information and service, United developed and maintained, in addition to its machine-engineering personnel, a sizable staff of experts on the problems of shoe production. Its planning department offered assistance "to shoe manufacturers desiring engineering surveys on production methods, on costs, on factory layouts, and other matters" (District Court Opinion: 322), while its "Shoe Ex" department existed solely to tackle difficult shoemaking problems encountered by its customers. To meet repair needs, United kept an inventory of 107,000 types of spare parts and maintained a staff of 1,500 employees in sixteen branch and twenty-nine suboffices in seventeen states, who were responsible for keeping its machines in good working order. Of these, 828 were "roadmen" who, in addition to repairing machines, installed new machines, instructed operators in their use, and, when asked, would "give expert advice on how to improve the quality of shoe production, give help in various technical shoemaking and shoe factory problems, and, in general, [be] available for all sorts of counsel and cooperation" (District Court Opinion: 322).

United was also the only manufacturer offering a full line of shoe machines. Yet, despite an average market share of machines outstanding of approximately 85 percent, potential competition plus a sizable group of active competitors limited United's ability to exercise market power. In 1947, United faced a competitive fringe consisting of more than eighty firms, including twenty-two known competitors for its major machines. Competitor machines, moreover, were available for all essential steps in the shoe-manufacturing process.[17] An indication of the depth of United's concern about competition from rival machinery was its efforts to keep track of that machinery; at the time of the case, United had about 76,000 "Outside Machine Reports" in its files, detailing the installation, use, and removal of non-United machines in its customers' factories. Evidence that this competition prevented United from exercising market power is its apparent failure to capture the substantial value created by shoe machines. Although labor savings from the mechanization of shoe production were enormous, shoe machinery costs represented only about 2 percent of the wholesale price

[16] There also appeared to be economies of convenience for shoemakers in dealing with a single provider of a wide range of related products and services. See District Court Opinion (340). As David Teece (1980) has noted, problems in the transfer of know-how rather than joint-production economies per se determine whether production should occur within a single organization.

[17] District Court Opinion (339). Of the 1,460 shoe firms operating 1,650 factories in the United States, approximately 1,220 were United customers. Hence, at least 240 firms produced shoes in the United States without United equipment. Kaysen (27), District Court Opinion (322).

of a shoe.[18] Consistent with this, the court found "no evidence that United has secured a monopoly profit on its total operations, or on the machinery branch as a whole (District Court Opinion: 325).

In sum, the shoe-machinery industry was one in which research, information, and service were paramount.[19] Despite United's conspicuous dominance of the market, the availability of numerous complex yet dependable machines and the efficient provision of a range of supplier services—rather than United's monopoly power—were shoemakers' foremost concerns.[20] Testifying in court, an officer of Compo, United's main rival, stated, "The shoe machinery manufacturing industry is really a service industry.... When a shoe manufacturer leases a Compo machine, he becomes the beneficiary of a service system which is made up of the skills, 'know-how', knowledge and experience of the whole Compo organization whose primary business is to see to it that he is successful in making cemented shoes" (Appeal: 224). The organizational problem confronting the industry was how best to assure that that know-how and experience would be efficiently applied to the development, manufacture, and support of shoe machinery.

3. A BELATED DEFENSE

As stated in section 1, a satisfactory explanation of United's leasing practices should account for both United's selective use of leasing and the overall structure of its leases. We begin this section with a discussion of leasing's dual roles in fostering the provision of quality machinery and the dissemination of know-how and then consider how these leasing functions interact with the design and restrictiveness of lease agreements.

3.1. A Comparative Analysis of Leasing

Leasing offers two distinct, albeit related, benefits.

---

[18] District Court Opinion (340). To produce a thousand men's welt shoes a day without the aid of shoe machinery would have required roughly a thousand skilled craftsmen. With a full line of shoe machines, the same number of shoes could have been produced with between fifty and sixty workers. Since United's formation in 1899, improvements in shoe machinery alone were estimated to have reduced the number of workers needed to produce a given number of shoes by 35 percent (United Facts: 428). Labor costs, in comparison to shoe machinery costs, accounted for approximately 25 percent of the wholesale price of a shoe at the time of the case (United Facts: 35).

[19] Less than 20 percent of United's machinery expenses reflected manufacturing costs, with research, service, distribution, and administrative activities accounting for approximately equal shares of the remainder (Kaysen: 118).

[20] "As seen by the shoe manufacturer, United's activities are clearly benevolent. The testimony of 15 shoe manufacturers, representing a wide variety of firms in terms of size, location, types and price of shoe manufactured, and general history, leaves no doubt of this. The testimony occupied some 900 pages of the transcript, and nearly the whole of it shows that the shoe manufacturers consider themselves well and cheaply served by United (202). Also, see testimony cited in United Facts (230–41).

Assuring Machine Quality

When the prospective reliability and other performance attributes of complex, durable goods are difficult to discern at the time of purchase, outright sales pose well-known moral-hazard problems. Receiving payment up front, a manufacturer has no interest, beyond its reputation, in the ultimate performance of its product.[21] A common solution to the durable-goods-quality problem is for the manufacturer to warrant the product.[22] But warranties are fundamentally contractual obligations and, as such, face the same obstacles in formation and enforcement as contracts generally.[23] Again aside from reputational considerations, a manufacturer's only incentive to honor its warranty is the legal sanctions a dissatisfied customer can bring to bear. The larger the cost of meeting its contractual obligations, the greater the incentive to evade performance. Where the product and its associated environment are complex, the difficulty of exploring contingencies, allocating responsibilities, adjudicating disputes, and crafting effective remedies is likely to undermine the utility of contractual guarantees.

Leasing offers an alternative to the durable-goods-quality problem that avoids many of the practical limitations associated with contractual warranties. In particular, by affording the customer the threat of terminating the exchange, leasing makes the proceeds from machinery transactions contingent on the realized value of machines. The prospective loss of revenues on current (as well as future) transactions provides manufacturers the incentive to keep machines operational ex post and, knowing this, to develop quality machines ex ante.[24] More important, leasing makes the incentives to develop and support quality machinery largely self-enforcing and thus avoids

[21] On the role of reputation in contracts generally, see Klein and Leffler (1981). As we argue below, fault for shoe machine failures was difficult for third parties to assess. To the extent that other customers had difficulty ascribing blame for a particular customer's misfortunes, the strength of the reputation deterrent to cheating is diminished. Moreover, the combination of machine durability and fallibility may itself combine to undermine the reputation function. While the cost of supporting existing machinery is proportional to the stock of machines in use, the incentive to continue that support is related to the flow of new machine sales. As the stock of machines outstanding rises relative to the level of sales, the cost of supporting existing machines may eventually exceed the loss of the reputation premium on future sales. In 1947, the total number of United machines outstanding was 115,787 (District Court Opinion: 304–5); by comparison, in 1950 United's expected shipments for 1951 were 11,355 machines (Kaysen: 37).

[22] On the theory of warranties, see Priest (1981); and Cooper and Ross (1985).

[23] For a discussion of remedies for breach of warranties, see Chapman and Meurer (1989).

[24] This motive was noted by Kaysen (190): "Since United is paid on performance ... the design of rugged, high-performance machines is stimulated. Every improvement in an existing machine which increases its production rate, or decreases the repair time ... benefits the manufacturer. ... By contrast, in a sales market. United would profit only once and thus would have no stimulus to continue improvements of existing machines." Wiley, Rasmusen, and Ramseyer also include a product-quality motive as one of six potential efficiency rationales for leasing generally. Their brief discussion, however, does not apply this reasoning to the circumstances in *United* in a systematic way and, as the discussion below reveals, is incomplete in several important respects. The warranting function of leasing has also been noted previously by David Flath (1980); and David T. Levy (1988).

the practical limitations of contractual guarantees. As long as nothing in either the contract or the nature of the transaction prevents it, a customer can respond unilaterally to interruptions or decreases in the value of machine services by returning the machine.[25] In effect, leasing transforms the transaction from the discrete sale of durable machines to the continuous sale of instantaneous machine services.[26]

Contracting for Knowledge

Leasing may also serve as a practical means of motivating the development and provision of expert advice where direct contracting for the transfer of information is infeasible. The problems of selling information where the customer does not know the value of the information beforehand are well known (see Arrow, 1971; Williamson, 1975; and Teece 1980). But even where the *potential* value of a supplier's information is understood, the customer may be unable to determine whether the information and advice actually obtained was the best the supplier had to offer and almost surely would be unable to prove the contrary in court. Answers to questions such as, "Was the instruction of operators as conscientious as it should have been?" and "Were engineering surveys thorough and machine layouts the best feasible?" are known ultimately only to the provider of the information. As a result, contractual assurances may do little to guarantee a machine manufacturer's complete and enthusiastic conveyance of its expertise and know-how.

If the value of information received is correlated with some measurable index such as the output of the firm, then compensating suppliers for the provision of information as a function of that index has desirable

---

[25] Leases would have to leave the right to terminate the lease largely unconditional to avoid introducing the prospect of litigation. Generally, the fewer the restrictions on returns and the shorter the lease term, the stronger the incentives to produce quality products. On the length and structure of United's leases, see below.

[26] The advantages of leasing, moreover, could not be replicated by selling machines with service contracts that made payments for service contingent on the performance of machines. Examples are service contracts for copiers and laser printers that charge for service on a per copy rather than per visit basis. Specifically, service calls are made free of charge for the duration of the contract, which is specified in terms of a total number of copies. The contract is more likely to be renewed and will be renewed sooner if the service firm promptly and effectively repairs machines so that machine output is not interrupted.

Sales with service contracts and leasing differ in evasion incentives, however. To replicate fully the incentives of leases, manufacturers would have to provide machines (virtually) free and collect compensation exclusively through cancelable charges for service. Under such terms, however, a customer who discovers that he has received a high-quality machine will wish to cancel the contingent payments to avoid paying for the machine, to which the manufacturer would have no effective recourse. Alternatively, a sale that capitalized a large part of the expected value of a machine in an initial payment (with correspondingly lower contingent payments) would invite the manufacturer to produce poor-quality equipment and either deteriorate service or contrive cancellation of the contract by claiming customer mistreatment of the assets. Whereas the only recourse available to disputants under a service contract is litigation, leasing relies on self-help. Specifically, under leasing, the manufacturer has the unilateral option of retrieving and the customer of returning the machine if the other behaves opportunistically. Attempts to structure installment-contract sales to mimic leases would pose similar problems. It is possible that the existence of sale- and service-contract arrangements are at least partly the byproduct of antitrust challenges to manufacturer leasing of durable goods.

properties.[27] Thus, to the extent information contributes to the success of machinery users, attaching an "information premium" to the rental price of machines would establish an incentive for a manufacturer to supply such information. The more machines employed, the longer each machine is retained, and, if usage-based charges are assessed, the more intensively a machine is used, the larger will be the total implicit payment.

Circumstances in the intermediate market for shoe machines supported leasing for both its warranting and information-transfer purposes. As the record reviewed in section 2 makes clear, shoemakers cared about the supply and quality of a wide range of services and information as well as about the quality of the machines themselves. Shoe machines and the tasks they were designed to perform, meanwhile, were often so complicated that complete specification of their performance attributes would have been infeasible, leaving ambiguity as to the expectations of the parties and abundant scope for opportunistic efforts to shift responsiblility or contrive cancellation of contractual guarantees.[28] Even where blame lay clearly with the manufacturer, problems securing the timely repair of defective or broken equipment would have diminished the value of contractual warranties. Optimal response time to a call for repairs vaired as a function of both when the breakdown occurred (peak versus nonpeak periods, for instance) and the opportunity cost of allocating repair personnel and parts across customers. On the one hand, the complex and variable nature of servicing needs across factories and individual machines would have precluded comprehensive specification of timing requirements and damages for delays. Relying on court interpretations of contract stipulations for "timely" or "prompt" repairs, on the other hand, would have been unpredictable and expensive where legitimate delays were likely to be indistinguishable from strategic ones.[29]

---

[27] See Rogerson (1989). Rogerson applies this argument to awarding prizes for innovation to defense contractors. The discussion below shows that Rogerson's analysis extends beyond regulatory settings to anywhere the quality of information cannot be judicially verified but is correlated with a verifiable index. Parallels also can be drawn to the role of royalty payments in motivating the supply of manufacturer services such as national advertising in franchise arrangements.

[28] With performance expectations imprecisely defined, determining the optimal allocation of responsibility for individual failures would, in a large number of cases, have been virtually impossible. Operator errors and the use of faulty materials, for instance, were common sources of machinery malfunctions. Whether responsibility for a failure rested ultimately on the shoemaker, however, would have been unclear given that machine versatility, particularly its adaptability to varying sizes, styles, and materials, was a valued but largely unspecifiable aspect of machine design.

[29] Legitimate delays might result from temporary shortages of spare parts, employee turnover or illness, or the precedence of customers with greater urgency of demand. The frequency and potentially high cost of machine failures exposed shoe machine users to the threat of holdups on repairs. The ability to provide prompt repairs required a stock of spare parts and a ready, proximate, and knowledgeable repair staff. By threatening to delay repairs, an opportunistic supplier could attempt to extract a premium on repairs. Masten, Meehan, and Snyder (1991) refer to the source of holdups that derive from the need for precise timing of performance as *temporal specificity*.

Lease versus Sale

The features common to the warranting and information-transfer functions of leasing are, first, the limitations of contracting that make explicit stipulation and direct compensation for the desired commodity impractical, and, second, the contingent nature of the payment stream that motivates performance of any activity that increases the demand for the services of the leased good. Against leasing's advantages, however, must be weighed its limitations. First, under leasing, residual rights of control and claims on the residual value of assets do not reside with the party that actually uses the equipment, diminishing the high-powered incentives to maintain and use machines with appropriate care.[30] Although a lessor may discipline a lessee for misuse or abuse of machinery by refusing to renew a lease or, depending on the terms of the lease, by repossessing machines, detecting abuse requires active monitoring by the lessor, which can be accomplished, obviously, only at additional cost. Second, rewarding information supply via machine transactions distorts machine-usage incentives. Because information charges attached to machines must exceed the cost of transferring the information to motivate its supply, paying for information indirectly through lease charges inefficiently discourages use of machines at the margin.[31]

Where information is of a type that can be priced and sold independently and where the attributes of assets are sufficiently simple so that quality can be adequately discerned or described at the outset of the transaction and responsibilities for breakdowns assigned ex post, sales will generally be preferred.[32] As assets become more complex and their quality more important, however, the costs of writing and enforcing contractual warranties are likely to grow relative to the benefits of customer ownership, raising the likelihood that leasing will become the favored organizational arrangement. Similarly, the more important and complex the information to be transferred, the more difficult it will be to sell information directly, and the greater the advantage of charging implicitly for information through machine rentals.[33]

---

[30] Thus, the transfer of ownership under leasing relative to sales raises many of the same issues and trade-offs involved in the analysis of integration decisions. Obviously, if transactors could contract over all possible actions affecting the value of the machine, ownership would be irrelevant. Typically, however, some actions are left unspecified, wherein ownership allocates all residual rights over the asset in question. See Grossman and Hart (1986). In the analogy to integration decisions, sales, which are dependent on contractual assurances of quality, correspond to the contractual or market mode and leasing to integration. On the relationship between ownership and high-powered and low-powered incentives, see Williamson (1985).

[31] Another, more mundane, drawback of leasing is simply the additional bookkeeping costs that must be incurred collecting and recording periodic payments under leases, compared with one-time sales.

[32] Also, a customer is more likely to be able to accomplish repairs of simple machines personally. ("[M]achines ... of simpler construction [are] not likely to develop troubles too complicated to be attended to by the operator or the shoe manufacturer's own mechanics" (United Facts: 229).

[33] An alternative to leasing would have been forward integration into shoe manufacturing. Forward integration would have forfeited the high-powered incentives of the large number of independent shoemakers and would likely have posed antitrust problems of its own.

3.2. Lease Design

Lease Duration, Termination, and Exclusion

The arguments of the preceding subsections suggest that leases should generally allow both customers and manufacturers broad scope to terminate the transaction. For leases to warrant quality, the lessee must be able to curtail payments if quality or service declines. The quicker the response, the greater the discipline customers exercise over manufacturers. Similarly, leasing will only serve its information-transfer function if the lessor's revenue varies with the quality of the information provided. The longer and more restrictive the lease, the more closely leasing resembles sales. Hence, these functions of leasing require that leases should be short-term, readily terminable, or, in the case of usage-based charges, that usage levels should be freely and continuously variable.[34] Finally, leases should also afford manufacturers wide discretion to repossess machines. To the extent leasing reduces customer incentives to operate machines with appropriate levels of care, manufacturers would want to monitor machine use and retrieve abused equipment, thereby terminating the stream of quasi rents accruing to the customer's use of the machine (compare Klein and Murphy, 1988). The power of that threat will be greatest in leases that facilitate detection of abuse and retrieval of equipment.

The advantages of unrestricted, unilateral termination may be reduced, however, where circumstances enable either party to act opportunistically. Generally, transactors enter long-term contracts either to limit costly haggling over appropriable quasi rents or to control free riding on services and information that one of them provides. Thus, if shoe machines were specially designed for particular shoe factories, a lessee or lessor might have been tempted to exploit his termination authority strategically, subverting leasing's critical self-enforcing character.[35] In actuality, however, shoe machines were neither specialized to particular customers nor expensive to relocate.

Free riding, in contrast, was a genuine concern. First, most of United's machinery improvements, though important, were not patentable.[36] As the court acknowledged, elimination of United's ability to exclude would "confer

---

[34] Although Wiley, Rasmusen, and Ramseyer noted the inconsistency between the duration of United's leases and the durable-goods-*monopoly* rationale, they apparently did not recognize the same inconsistency in the durable-goods-*quality* explanation.

[35] If such opportunistic terminations were difficult to distinguish from legitimate ones, the self-enforcement advantages of leasing over warranties would disappear. An untested prediction of our theory is that sale (customer ownership) is likely to be preferred to leasing where durable goods are customer specific.

[36] The court cited "United's practice of continuing improvement of existing machine types and models by so-called blue-bulletin changes, representing both patented and unpatented improvements, the advantages of which are made available to lessees through installation of the parts required by each change" (Appeal: 247). The vast majority of United's machinery improvements were not patentable; on average, machinery research resulted in approximately 8 patentable and 192 nonpatentable (blue-bulletin) improvements over the life of a machine (Kaysen: 171–74).

upon United's competitors the unearned opportunity to copy the unpatented features of United's machines. These competitors get a free ride" (District Court Opinion: 350; see also Kaysen: 76). Second, the implicit pricing of information and services gave shoemakers an incentive to free ride on United's investments in shoemaking know-how. As the description of United's services in Section 2 indicates, much of the information United provided was, in fact, of a type that could be profitably used with competitors' equipment. Although installation and repairs were wholly specific to individual machines, the selection and layout of machines, operator training, and general shoemaking know-how all provided knowledge that was in varying degrees generalizable to similar equipment from other manufacturers. Where the benefits of information accrue over an extended period but are not specific to a particular manufacturer's product, customers may seek to avoid implicit information charges embodied in the price of a full-service supplier by switching to alternative suppliers for some portion of their needs. Having acquired that knowledge, shoemakers had an incentive to return or reduce usage on the machine or machines to which implicit information premia had been attached and substitute similar equipment from a "no-frills" supplier.

To prevent free riding from undermining the supply of free-ridable services, transactors would want to restrict in some way lessees' ability to substitute competitors' equipment.[37] Stipulation of monetary deterrents to switching within long-term agreements would serve this purpose. In addition, transactors would want to attach information premia to machines most crucial to the production process and for which hand labor is a poor substitute to hinder a lessee's ability to escape paying implicit charges by bypassing machines. Finally, offering machines on lease-only terms would prevent the direct substitution of nonlease equipment and the development of a market in secondhand machines that could substitute for leased machines. To preserve the benefits that motivated leasing in the first place, however, deterrents to returning machines should be conditional on machines being abandoned opportunistically to escape paying for information received. Customer returns or usage reductions for other reasons should be afforded far more latitude.

Lease Pricing

Both the warranty and information functions of leasing described above depend on manufacturer revenues correlating with machine performance, a

---

[37] Howard Marvel (1982) has cited free riding on manufacturer promotional efforts to justify the use of exclusive dealing arrangements in the context of retail sales. Prior to 1918, some of United's leases contained a set of "exclusive-use" clauses limiting the ability of customers to use competitor machines on certain operations. See Kaysen (13–16). In that year, the Supreme Court upheld a lower court ruling that these clauses violated § 3 of the recently enacted Clayton Act. The practice of leasing, the then-seventeen-year duration, and other terms (including return charges and the full-capacity clause) were held to be reasonable and lawful at the time (Appeal: 25); (Kaysen: 15).

correlation established whether flat rental rates or usage-based charges are imposed. The greater sensitivity of usage-based charges to variations in demand and machine performance, however, may, under certain conditions, justify the added cost of monitoring machine operations.[38] With flat rental fees, revenue fluctuations occur only if a customer returns or leases an additional machine, whereas receipts from "unit charges" vary continuously with intensity of machine usage. Where the number of machines adopted varies little with the success of a factory, for instance, changes in revenue under monthly-rental leases may be too discrete to motivate machine improvements or the supply of information and services on the margin. Consequently, unit charges would be more desirable where the capacity of a machine dictates the use of only one or a small number of machines of a particular type.

The adoption of unit charges is also likely to be related to the expected cost of machine failures. The higher the expected cost of failures, the greater is the need for prompt repairs and for ongoing improvements to avert breakdowns in the first place. The probability and cost of breakdowns, in turn, are likely to be related to the complexity of a machine and its importance to the production process. More complex machines would tend to be less tolerant of errors and thus more likely to malfunction, have more components subject to wear and breakage, and be more difficult to repair, while the failure of machines central to the production process could impede production throughout the factory.[39] Tying the manufacturer's revenues to the continued operation of these machines through unit charges effectively internalizes to the manufacturer the costs to customers of production interruptions. Indeed, by comparing the reduction of unit-charge revenues from various factories, a machinery manufacturer would have had approximately the correct incentives to allocate repair services and parts across customers.[40]

---

[38] Unit charges would also tend to discourage use of machines on the margin. The costs of metering usage would have been essentially the same on all shoe machines with moving parts. Note that policing usage was not a major problem, given that roadmen made frequent visits to factories and that discrepancies in factory output or in usage rates across machines would have been detectable.

[39] The opportunity for machine improvements was also likely to be greater on more complex machines. Indeed, the number of blue bulletins (which documented improvements; see note 36 above) issued on a machine correlated positively with the measure of machine complexity described below.

[40] In fact, United sometimes "borrowed" parts from underutilized machines in the factory of one shoe firm to use in another firm's equipment when replacement parts were temporarily unavailable (United Facts: 235). The argument with regard to the role of unit charges is not an "as if" one; United explicitly asserted this function in its defense: "It is obviously to United's interest to give the best possible service to its lessees. Its revenue depends on keeping machines in efficient running order" (United Facts: 247). This role of unit charges has also been noted by Wiley, Rasmusen, and Ramseyer, and Goldberg, and by Kaysen (191). The metering of machine output is also consistent with traditional price discrimination explanations for such practices. Price discrimination, however, fails to explain the choice between sale and monthly rental leases as well as many important elements of United's lease structure.

3.3. Summary

The preceding analysis provides several specific predictions about United's practices and the structure of its leases.

1. The merits of leasing relative to sales are likely to be greatest where (i) the need for assurances about the quality and reliability of durable goods and the costs of specifying and enforcing performance of contractual warranties are great or (ii) productive use of machinery requires the development and dissemination of manufacturer-supplied information. The importance of reliability is likely to be greatest on machines critical to the production process, while the difficulty of contracting for machine quality, the need for repairs and technical advice on machine operations, and the opportunity for machine improvements will tend to be higher on more complex machines.

2. For leasing to serve its warranting function, primary responsibility and the expense of repairs must rest with the manufacturer.

3. To motivate the provision of information and repair services, these services should be priced implicitly in the rental price of machines.

4. To discourage free riding on manufacturers' investments on non-patentable innovations and general know-how, (i) information premia should be attached to the most important and widely adopted machines, (ii) such machines should be offered for "lease only," and (iii) those leases should be long-term and penalize inefficient switching. Because customers must be able to return machines to discipline the manufacturer's supply of quality and services, however, return or usage penalties should apply discriminatorily against returns to substitute competitors' machines.

5. To deter lessee misuse of borrowed equipment, lease agreements should authorize the lessor to monitor use and to repossess abused machines.

6. Finally, unit charges should be preferred to flat rental rates (i) where the expected cost of breakdowns and the opportunity for ongoing improvements are greatest (that is, for machines that are most complex and critical to the production process) and (ii) where variation across factories in the number of machines adopted is small.

4. UNITED'S PRACTICES

In this section, we consider United's actual distribution practices in light of the preceding analysis. We begin by examining evidence regarding United's selective use of leasing and pricing arrangements. We then discuss the nature and implementation of United's standard lease provisions.

4.1. Evidence

At the time of the case, United distributed shoe machines under five types of arrangements. Those arrangements and the number of machine types offered under each were: sale only, 42; optional sale or lease, 122; lease with monthly rental charges only (no unit charges), 88; lease with monthly rental plus unit charges, 85; and lease with unit charges only (no monthly rental), 6.[41] Hence, almost half (164 out of 343) of United's machine offerings were available for purchase. Moreover, 35 percent or 9,472 out of the 27,140 optional sale-or-lease machines outstanding in 1947 had been sold, indicating that sale was a real alternative for these machines, contrary to the government's complaint.[42]

Analytically, United faced a two-tiered sequence of decisions consisting of, first, whether to sell or lease machines, and, second, the method by which to price machines if it chose to lease. The analysis of the preceding sections predicts that United should have offered the most complex and important machines for lease only. Simpler, less important machines pose fewer of the incentive problems discussed earlier and therefore should have been more likely to have been offered for sale. Of those machines that United offered for lease, unit charges should have been most common on machines for which adoption rates varied little with the size of the factory and for which the expected cost of breakdowns and opportunity for machine improvements were greatest—again, on the most complex machines and those most critical to the production process.

To test these propositions, we assembled data from the trial record and from information obtained directly from United. Definitions of variables and descriptive statistics for the sample are provided in Table 12.1. To gauge the complexity of machines offered by United, we constructed a variable, PARTS, consisting of the number of parts listed in parts manuals for the original machines. We were able to locate manuals for 193 of the 343 machines United offered at the time of the case.[43]

As a measure of the importance of a machine in the shoe-production process, we employed a classification adopted by the government in the case. Specifically, the government divided machines into two categories: major

[41] Exhibits B, C, D1, D2, and D3, annexed to the Defendant's Answer to the Complaint, May 27, 1948. Each machine type was offered exclusively under one of these five arrangements. Optional-sale-or-lease machines were let under monthly rental but no unit charges. Most optional-sale-or-lease machines and a few lease-only machines also required an initial payment.

[42] Exhibits G-446 and S-59. The sales figure includes only machines sold over the period 1931–47. Since many machines sold prior to 1931 would still have been in operation, these figures understate the true number of sale machines outstanding in 1947.

[43] The distribution of those 193 machines by terms were: sale only, thirteen; optional sale or lease, seventy-four; lease with monthly rental only, forty-eight; lease with monthly rental and unit charges, fifty-four; and lease with unit charges only, four. Hence, data were obtained on more than half of the machines in each category except sale only. Consistent with our hypothesis, United claimed that "those [machines] which are offered for sale only are generally simple machines such as gearless sole cutters, tools and grinders" (United Facts: 182). Manuals for machines of this type were less likely to have been preserved. Another variable of obvious importance to lease-versus-sale decisions generally is the durability of machines. According to United officials, the basic structure of United's machines were made to last indefinitely with the replacement or reconditioning of moving parts. Some machines manufactured in the early part of the century are still in operation today.

TABLE 12.1
Descriptive Statistics

Categorical variables	Description	No. of observations		
LEASE ONLY	= 1, if lease only machine	106		
	= 0, if machine is for sale	87		
UC	= 1, if leased with unit charges	58		
	= 0, otherwise	48		
MAJOR	= 1, if major machine	48		
	= 0, if minor machine	145		

Continuous variables	Description	Mean	SD	Minimum	Maximum
PARTS	= number of machine parts	542	521	28	2,880
MACH/FACT	= (number of machines outstanding within class)/ 1,220	1.07	1.78	0.1	13.40
YEAR	= year machine was introduced ($N = 171$)	1,923	12	1,899	1,944

and minor. Major machines were those that performed "[t]he principal procedures involved in the manufacture of shoes, including upper cutting, upper fitting, stock fitting, lasting, bottoming, and making (Complaint: paragraphs 11, 16). Minor machines, in contrast, were "either auxiliary to major machines in the sense that their functions [were] immediately related to those of major machines, or they perform[ed] work independent of that done by major machines but of somewhat less importance in the shoemaking process."[44] A failure in one of these machines, though still disruptive, could often be mitigated by deferring the task or substituting hand labor.

Finally, the theory predicts that the need for unit charges would be less where the number of machines employed within a given factory would adequately meter the quality of machines and information received. The failure of one among many machines in a given factory may also reduce the urgency of repairs and, hence, the motive for both leasing and unit charges. Although existing records do not contain information on the number of machines of each type employed in each of the 1,220 shoe factories United served (from which a measure of differences in factory adoption rates across machines could be constructed), the record does indicate the total number

---

[44] Complaint (paragraph 16). Although failures of an auxiliary machine were more likely to disrupt operations on associated major machines than were failures of independent minor machines, the resulting interruption in unit-charge flows from the major machine reduced the need for separate unit charges on the auxiliary unit. The government's classification did not distinguish between "related" and "independent" minor machines.

TABLE 12.2
Logit Unit Charge versus Monthly Rental-only Estimations

	(1)	(2)	(3)
CONSTANT	−1.480	−1.504	2,105.3
	(−3.421)	(−3.202)	(0.262)
PARTS	0.0020	0.0025	0.0026
	(2.947)	(3.118)	(3.029)
MAJOR	1.052	1.702	1.644
	(1.989)	(2.756)	(2.644)
MACH/FACT		−0.4213	−0.4323
		(−2.023)	(−2.062)
YEAR			−2.164
			(−0.259)
YEAR^2			0.0006
			(0.255)
N	106	106	100
Log-likelihood	−57.348	−52.151	−47.563

Note: The dependent variable is UC; *t*-statistics are in parentheses.

of machines of each type outstanding, permitting us to calculate the average number of machines per factory (MACH/FACT).[45] Because shoemakers are more likely to need at least one machine within a functional class than a particular model within such a class, we used the average number of machines outstanding within a machine class rather than the number of machines of a particular model.

Table 12.2 presents logit results on the decision of whether or not to employ unit charges on lease-only machines. The coefficients on both PARTS and MAJOR are positive and significant, as expected, while the coefficients on MACH/FACT are negative and significant. Hence, conditional on a machine being offered for lease only, unit charges were more likely to be adopted on major, complex machines and where the number of machines per factory was smaller. We also estimated the model employing a quadratic of the year in which the machine was introduced in order to control for the possibility that the observed correlation between leasing practices and variations in the number of machines outstanding reflected machinery

---

[45] A disadvantage of this measure relative to variations in machine adoption rates is that it is impossible to distinguish whether a high average is the result of a few factories adopting many machines or many factories adopting a small number of machines. Only the former correlates with the success of a specific factory and could form the basis for rewarding the provision of quality machines and information. United's leases restricted the ability of a shoemaker to hold more machines than were necessary to perform the available work (District Court Opinion: 317). To the extent this limits a shoemaker's ability to hold machines as a means of insuring against breakdowns, variations in MACH/FACT would tend to reflect relatively exogenous technological and scale factors. The lack of exogenous variables prevents correcting for potential endogeneity by instrumental methods.

TABLE 12.3
Logit and Nested Logit Lease versus Sale Estimations

	(1)	(2)	(3)	(4)	(5)
CONSTANT	−1.576	7,817.30	−1.344	9,035.8	6,384.1
	(−4.695)	(1.355)	(−3.720)	(1.449)	(1.108)
PARTS	0.0042	0.0033	0.0028	0.0043	0.0018
	(5.143)	(3.824)	(2.708)	(2.557)	(1.844)
MAJOR	1.449	2.622	1.503	3.593	1.161
	(2.495)	(3.103)	(1.656)	(2.238)	(1.460)
MACH/FACT	−2.478	−0.2724	—	−0.4175	—
	(−2.253)	(−2.344)		(−1.805)	
YEAR	—	−8.179	—	−9.438	−6.698
		(−1.362)		(1.505)	(−1.117)
YEAR^2	—	0.0021	—	0.0025	0.0018
		(1.369)		(1.511)	(1.126)
INCLU	—	—	0.3321	−1.029	1.352
			(0.413)	(−0.757)	(1.571)
N	193	171	171	171	171
Log-likelihood	−98.231	−83.887	−88.713	−82.640	−84.098

Note: The dependent variable is LEASEONLY; *t*-statistics are in parentheses.

life-cycle considerations.[46] The results suggest that United's use of unit charges on its leased machines did not vary systemically over time.

Table 12.3 reports the results on the lease-versus-sale decision. Columns 1 and 2 contain results from standard logit estimations. Columns 3–5 present nested logit estimates where the "inclusive value," INCLU, was calculated using the coefficients in column 3 of Table 12.2.[47] The coefficients on PARTS are positive and significant under all five specifications, indicating that more complex machines are less likely to be offered for sale; MAJOR is positive and is significant in all but column 5. In addition, the results indicate that machines adopted in large numbers were more likely to be sold. The results also suggest a modest trend in favor of leasing.

Finally, we regressed the frequency of leasing and sales among the optional term machines on the characteristics of those machines. The mean number of leased machines for the sixty-seven optional term machines for which we

---

[46] Older machines that are becoming obsolete and newer machines that have only recently been introduced are likely to have fewer machines outstanding, other things being the same. United rarely altered its distribution arrangements for particular machine models after their introduction. Hence, the year variables capture trends over time in the decision to lease or employ unit charges on new models.

[47] The nested logit estimation of the lease-versus-sale decision accounts for the option to lease with or without unit charges. Unlike multinomial logit, nested logit avoids the assumption of independence of irrelevant alternatives. See G. S. Maddala (1983: 68–69). For comparison purposes, we estimated the choice of lease, sale, and pricing alternatives using multinomial logit and ordered probit models. The results were consistent with those presented. In particular, the choice categories "ordered" correctly in both models.

had data was 63 percent, with a minimum of 5 percent and maximum of 95 percent. The results indicate that the tendency for more important and complex machines to be leased remained even when customers were given a choice between purchasing and leasing:

$$PCTLEASED = -0.21635 + 1.7868 \cdot MAJOR + 0.00314 \cdot PARTS$$
$$(-0.676) \qquad (2.857) \qquad\qquad (3.749)$$

$$-0.23991 \cdot MACH/FACT, \qquad R^2 = 0.235$$
$$(-1.208)$$

(The dependent variable is defined as $-\log[(100/\text{percent of machines leased}) - 1]$ and t-statistics are in parentheses.)

Thus, overall, United's choice of leasing and pricing arrangements is consistent with the efficiency motives identified above. In particular, minor machines with fewer parts were more likely to be offered for sale, while, among leased machines, complex, major machines were more likely to be offered for lease with unit charges. The average number of machines outstanding also reduced the likelihood of using unit charges and increased the probability of a machine being sold.[48]

4.2. The Structure and Implementation of United's Leases

Although the uniform construction of United's leases precludes formal test of each of our predictions regarding their structure, a more detailed examination of United's lease provisions—and of some significant departures in the way United implemented those provisions—is nevertheless illuminating. Even where United's nominal lease provisions and the hypothesized structure appear to deviate, United's *actual* practices are consistent with the theory. Moreover, the anomalous lease provisions can be fairly interpreted to have supported the interests of the parties in effecting low-cost, efficient adaptations by establishing contractual fallbacks that facilitated "self-help" responses to opportunistic behavior.

Exclusionary Features

As already noted, United's leases at the time of the case were ten years in duration (having been shortened at court direction from seventeen years) and contained three allegedly exclusionary provisions: (1) return charges,

---

[48] We ran the regressions in Tables 12.2 and 12.3 including market share and found that leasing and unit charge adoption were both positively correlated with market share. Other qualitative results were unaffected. Given the endogeneity of market share, correlations between market share and distribution arrangements have no clear interpretation. Regression of market share on PARTS, MAJOR, YEAR, and YEARSQ revealed a positive but weak correlation of market share to PARTS and MAJOR, with all four variables explaining less than 10 percent of the variation in market share.

or "deferred payments," due on return of leased machines;[49] (2) minimum-usage charges for operation of unit-charge machines below a specified level; and (3) a full-capacity clause obligating lessees of unit-charge machines to "use the leased machinery to its full capacity upon all boots, shoes or other footwear or parts thereof made by ... the lessee in the manufacture or preparation of which such machinery is capable of being used."[50] In addition to these express terms, United assessed a commutation charge of 25 percent of monthly rentals or 50 percent of minimum-usage charges on the balance of the lease term for machines returned prior to the expiration of the lease.

Although the application of these terms was nominally uniform, United discriminatorily applied the commutation charges and full-capacity clause in practice. Specifically, United waived the monthly rental and minimum-usage balances due on unexpired leases when machinery returns were made for reasons other than the substitution of a competitor's machine. Similarly, failure to employ a machine at full capacity violated the full-capacity clause only if "the lessee fail[ed] to use the machine on work for which the machine [was] capable of being used, and instead perform[ed] such work by using a competitor's machine" (District Court Opinion: 320). Penalties were not assessed, however, where machine use was attentuated as the result of demand shifts, product abandonment, conversion to manual operations, or replacement with another United machine.[51]

Both the existence and discriminatory application of return and usage restrictions in United's leases are consistent with efficiency motives. Even in the absence of free-rider considerations, efficient lease incentives would justify return charges in proportion to the expenses associated with repossessing and re-leasing returned machines.[52] Where rental prices also include premia

---

[49] With the exception of three minor machine types, all leased machines were subject to this provision (District Court Opinion: 320). Note that return charges were assessed even upon returns at the expiration of the lease and were thus not conditional on premature termination. In effect, return charges were deferred initial payments and, with the exception of interest considerations, were equivalent to lump-sum transfers.

[50] District Court Opinion (316). Violations of the full capacity clause were remedied by billing the customer for use of the machine to its appraised capacity.

[51] The government cited eighty-eight instances between 1932 and 1948 involving twenty companies in which United invoked provisions of its leases to discourage substitution of a non-United for a United machine. Plaintiff's Request for Findings of Fact and Conclusions of Law, January 29, 1953, at 125–65 (hereafter Plaintiff's Request).

[52] In general, optimal return fees or damages for breach of lease may also include the lessor's profits on the unexpired portion of the lease. Ignoring incidental costs associated with the return, it is efficient to return a machine only if the value to the lessee of retaining it falls below the manufacturer's opportunity cost of leaving it with the lessee. Without return fees, however, a lessee would wish to return a machine whenever his valuation fell below the stream of payments required to retain it. To the extent a lessor earned economic rents on the transaction, the alternative value to him of a leased machine is its marginal revenue—equated (in expected terms) to its marginal cost—rather than the rental price. In legal terms, the manufacturer is a "lost-volume" seller and is entitled to the difference between price and cost. U.C.C. § 2-708, comment 2. See also § 2A-528(2) of the proposed U.C.C. article dealing with leases. Awarding lost profits, however, would remove the contingent nature of the seller's profits that was argued earlier to support the provision of quality goods and information. Hence, where leasing has been adopted for these purposes, damages should be limited to incidental costs connected with the return.

for the provision of information that is potentially free-ridable, the need to counter customer incentives to circumvent those premia by substituting competitor machines warrants additional deterrents applied in a discriminatory fashion.

The congruity between United's practices and efficiency concerns does not, however, preclude anticompetitive motives and effects. The profitability of exclusion, for instance, was conceivably greatest on the most complex and important machines. An excluding monopolist, moreover, would want to exclude efficiently.[53] Consequently, the question of whether particular contractual arrangements are anticompetitive turns on the magnitude of the switching costs they create. Specifically, to be anticompetitive, a contract restriction must deter efficient switching. In the absence of free-rider considerations, this means that the incremental price (conditional on retention or use) of a machine must be below the lessor's opportunity cost of leaving the machine with the lessee or, equivalently, that the size of the damage stipulated in the contract exceed the actual damages caused by the termination.[54] Hence, a contract restriction cannot be exclusionary unless it would constitute a penalty under common law.[55]

By this standard, the nondiscriminatory restrictions contained in United's leases do not appear unreasonable. On unit-charge machines, which accounted for over 80 percent of United's lease revenues, return charges amounted to approximately one to two months' rent.[56] Hence, over 98 percent of prospective revenues from United's most complex and important machines were contingent on the use and retention of the equipment. Even on monthly rental machines, where return charges ranged more typically between five and ten months' rentals, over 92 percent of potential lease

---

[53] The optimal barrier to switching in Aghion and Bolton's model of strategic contracting is a function of the efficient level of damages as well as strategic factors. See Masten and Snyder (1989).

[54] Masten and Snyder (1989). The desired incentives can be established in either of two ways: by stipulating a price, p, and damages, d; or through a two-part price schedule with fixed component, F, and incremental price, p'. Using the first form, the buyer pays p if he keeps the machine (or accepts delivery) and d if he returns it, making the cost to the buyer of keeping the machine $p - d$. Under the two-part price contract, the buyer pays $F + p'$ if he keeps the machine and F is he returns it, the cost of retaining the machine being simply p'. The incentives created by the two contracts are equivalent if $p = F + p'$ and $d = F$. Efficiency requires that the cost to the buyer of retaining the machine equal the value or savings to the seller of the buyer's retention, say c. This can be accomplished by setting either $d = p - c$ or $p' = c$. A contract is exclusionary only if $d > p - c$ or $p' < c$.

[55] Specifically, the common law requires that damages stipulated in a contract be "reasonable in light of the anticipated or actual loss caused by the breach"; terms that fix damages in excess of that amount are considered penalties and unenforceable. Restatement (Second) of Contracts § 356 (1979). See also § 2A-504(1) of the proposed U.C.C. article dealing with leases.

[56] These estimates are based on normal machine-usage rates and on predecree price information contained in Report of United Shoe Machinery Corporation under Decree, para. 18, app. D, filed December 15, 1964 (hereafter United Report). Goldberg (1990) arrives at a similar estimate using a smaller sample of lease terms reported in the District Court Opinion (314).

revenue reflected contingent payments.[57] Stated differently, the fixed component of United's lease revenues averaged across leased machines was equivalent to liquidated damages of less than 3 percent of the price of a machine.[58]

The size of the switching deterrent was, of course, larger where a machine was being returned for the purpose of substituting competitors' equipment. As already noted, lessees who replaced a United machine with a competitor's machine were required to pay 25 percent of monthly rentals on monthly-rental-only machines and 50 percent of minimum-usage charges on unit-charge machines due on the unexpired balance of the lease. Since minimum-usage charges represented about 10 percent of revenues expected from unit-charge machines used at full capacity, and unit-charge machines accounted for over 80 percent of lease revenue, these additional charges were compatible with a value of free-ridable information equal to approximately 8 or 9 percent of total lease revenue. Although the record does not permit a precise estimate of the cost of providing those services, United's expenditures on all research and service activities accounted for over 40 percent of its machinery expenses.[59] Hence, if even a quarter of United's research and service efforts reflected expenditures on nonpatentable machinery improvements or free-ridable know-how, its commutation charges would have fallen well within the range of reasonable values for damages caused by the return of machines in order to free ride on those investments. Moreover, note that, because the commutation charge applied to the unexpired portion of the lease, the size of this deterrent declined linearly over the course of the lease. Whereas exclusionary motives provide no basis to expect the strategic component of lease restrictions to decrease over time, a declining schedule of damages is consistent with the desire to adjust deterrents to free riding in proportion to the benefits of information accrued but not paid for.

The minimum-usage provisions implied a similarly small deterrent. Under United's formula, a lessee who used a machine at a level (q) less than the

---

[57] The average was approximately eight months. Optional sale-or-lease machines had somewhat higher return charges and also required initial (or up-front) payments. Hence, optional lease machines had terms that made them closer in nature to sales. Although return charges were larger on monthly rental than on unit-charge machines in percentage terms, the dollar amount averaged approximately $67 on monthly rental equipment compared to $247 on unit-charge machines. The percentage figures reported in the text represent total undiscounted lease revenues minus the fraction of that total represented by the return charges. Since the return charges are deferred to the end of the lease, the appropriately discounted fraction of prospective lease revenue represented by the monthly charges would be even smaller.

[58] The court in this case did not address the reasonableness of United's return fees relative to the common-law standard. An appeals court did address this issue in an earlier case, however, and concluded that deferred fees in United's earlier leases were "not unreasonable compensation for the costs to [United] of replacing the machines in use after the end of a prior lease" and therefore did not constitute penalties. In re Diana Shoe Corporation, 80 F.2d 827, 829 (1936). United's practice was to salvage parts from returned machines for use in the manufacture of new machines (United Facts: 484). Parts accounted for approximately 90 percent and assembly 10 percent of United's manufacturing costs (United Facts: 483).

[59] Kaysen (118). Also see note 36 above.

minimum number of pairs designated in the lease (q_m) was obligated to pay, in addition to unit charges on that output, a proportion of a stipulated minimum monthly payment (M) equal to the ratio of the deficiency to the minimum number of pairs, or $pq + M(q_m - q)/q_m$. The effect was to reduce by M/q_m the marginal cost of producing an additional pair of shoes at output rates below q_m. In practice, the minimum quantity was typically set at approximately 25 percent of machine capacity and the minimum payment at 40 percent of the unit charges for that quantity. As a result, the incremental cost of an additional operation over the first 25 percent of capacity equaled approximately 60 percent of the nominal unit charge. Hence, in contrast to standard minimum bill provisions, United's restriction implied a substantial incremental cost of use below the minimum.[60] Moreover, the implied reduction in unit charges at low production levels established incentives that are consistent with the fact that machines that were being used less intensively needed to be repaired with less haste.

Finally, United's implementation of its lease provisions deviated from their formal terms in ways that increased flexibility. For example, although the formal provisions provided for their uniform application, United waived the minimum-usage charge for four months each year to lessen their burden during periods of slack demand.[61] More significant, United also established what it called a "Right of Deduction Fund," under which 4 percent of all unit and rental charges was credited to an account that lessees in good standing could use to pay return, minimum-usage, and commutation charges.[62] A lessee who had leased a large number of United machines over an extended period gained substantial flexibility to return or reduce usage of United equipment.[63]

In sum, the size, nature, and implementation of United's exclusionary-lease provisions are hard to reconcile with anticompetitive motives. The monetary deterrents to returning or ceasing to use United's machines were small relative to the total value of the lease and appear to have been proportionate to the harm caused United. Even ignoring the moderating effects of the Right of Deduction Fund, the discriminatory charges applied to returns or usage reductions for the purpose of substituting a rival's equipment were modest and declined as the term of the lease progressed, suggesting that United's

[60] For a discussion of minimum-bill provisions, see Masten (1988). For an opinion (written by Judge Richard Posner) interpreting minimum-bill provisions as creating penalties, see *Lake River Corp.* v. *Carborundum Co.*, 769 F.2d 1284 (7th Cir. 1985).

[61] District Court Opinion (321). The application of this waiver was automatic. If the lessee failed to select which four months he wanted waived. United would select those most favorable to him. The waiver also applied to the calculation of commutation charges. In addition, United made available "peak-load" machines and offered thirty-day-trial-period installations on its machines.

[62] District Court Opinion (320). Balances in the Right of Deduction Fund could be applied to any leased machine.

[63] The government acknowledged that the accumulated credits were generally "adequate to take care of current returns of a factory which is in operation, having a large number of United machines" (Plaintiff's Request: 117). See also *Hanover Shoe Inc.* v. *United Shoe Machinery Corp.*, 245 F. Supp. 258 (1965).

objective was not to discourage efficient returns but only large-scale free riding on the advice and technical information it provided.[64]

Lessor Monitoring and Termination

To police against machine abuse and to detect tampering with usage indicators, a shoe manufacturer would want easy access to its machines and the ability to observe their operation. United's leases provided explicitly for such access, reserving to United the right "at all times [to] have free access to the leased machinery for the purpose of inspecting it or watching its use and operation, or of altering, repairing, improving, or adding to it, or determining the nature or extent of its use" (District Court Opinion: 315). United also required lessees to keep records and file reports on the use of its equipment. Where a "breach or default in the performance of any of the conditions contained in the lease" was detected, United reserved the right to terminate the lease "forthwith," whereupon United was authorized to enter the customer's premises and repossess machines.[65] Hence, United's leases sought to lower the costs of detecting and punishing lessee misconduct.

Maintenance and Repairs

Contrary to our prediction (and the representations of many commentators), the responsibility and expense of maintaining and repairing machines under the lease rested with the lessee are not with United. Specifically, United required the lessee "at all times and at his own expense [to] keep the leased machinery in good and efficient working order and condition" (District Court Opinion: 315). Should the lessee fail to maintain machinery in a satisfactory manner, United reserved the right to make any necessary repairs itself and to bill the lessee accordingly. In practice, however, United consistently assumed the burden of repairing its leased machines and charged only for the cost of replacement parts.

This discrepancy between the de jure and de facto responsibility for repairs under United's leases is consistent with a desire to avoid costly legal disputes by reducing the scope for contract evasion. As long as a machine was not abused or its indicator tampered with, United had no incentive to terminate a lease and, moreover, had substantial incentives given the contingent nature of payment under leasing to maintain and repair its machinery. Formal assignment of the obligation to maintain machines to United would have done nothing to augment those incentives and could have provided the lessee with an avenue to contrive cancellation of the lease by claiming unsatisfactory performance on the part of United. Given the difficulty of defining satisfactory performance contractually and the high incidence of breakdowns on even the

---

[64] Returns, in fact, occurred in significant numbers; the district court estimated that between 20 and 25 percent of leased machines were returned within five years (District Court Opinion: 319). Turnover among shoe manufacturers, meanwhile, was 10–12 percent a year (Kaysen: 55). Also see Posner (1976: 203).

[65] District Court Opinion (317–318). Leased machinery remained the property of United, and neither the machinery nor the lease could be transferred to another firm.

highest-quality and best-maintained machines, an opportunistic lessee wishing to return a machine to avoid the implicit charges for information would likely have been able to construct a credible claim of dissatisfaction and thereby evade performance.

Legal assignment of the material and financial burden of caring for machines to the lessee, in contrast, reinforced United's legal authority to punish a customer's tampering and abuse by repossessing machines. Lessees were, in effect, always in gross violation of the lease's maintenance requirements and would thus have found it difficult to challenge a termination by United. Moreover, since United had nothing to gain from prematurely terminating a lease to a productive shoemaker, United could not exploit its termination authority opportunistically. Thus, again, the formal structure of United's leases appears to support desired performance with minimum risk of costly adjudication.

5. COMPETITOR AND PREDECESSOR PRACTICES

The leasing of shoe machines did not originate with United but was a common practice among both United's predecessors and competitors. The practice of leasing shoe machinery had begun as early as the Civil War with the McKay Sewing Machine. Gordon McKay, the industry's most renowned figure, developed a leasing system with royalty charges to overcome resistance to the adoption of his machines (Lindahl and Carter, 1959). In addition, the four companies that merged to form United in 1899 had all offered machines for lease only with lease provisions similar to United's, including return fees, minimum-usage charges, and the full-capacity clause.[66] Like United, these companies provided service and training in the use of machines; "McKay's corps of repairmen kept machines in top condition and taught operators and shoe manufacturers this wholly different system of shoemaking."[67]

Although detailed information on the terms under which United's rivals supplied machines is not available, leasing was clearly the predominant mode of distribution. The record does indicate, moreover, that Compo, a full-service shoe-machinery supplier and United's largest competitor, with roughly 2 percent of the market, also offered its most important machines for lease only and that its leases contained return charges.[58] That shoe machine manufacturers in substantially different market positions responded to the underlying organizational problems in a like manner is additional support for an efficiency interpretation of United's practices.

[66] U.S. v. United Shoe Machinery Co., 222 Fed. Rep. 349, at 385–86 (1915); U.S. v. United Shoe Machinery Co., 247 U.S. 32, at 62 (1911); Brief for United Shoe Machinery Corporation 278 (January 1952).

[67] A Legend and How It Began, 1 United Shoe Machinery Today 4 (1974). The level of services provided by United's predecessors, however, was not as high as United's, nor were repair services as prompt (U.S. v. United Shoe Machinery Co., 1915: 369–72).

[68] Reply of United Shoe Machinery Corporation to Brief of the United States on Relief, (April 11, 1952: 27; United Facts: 201).

6. THE AFTERMATH

In February 1953, Judge Charles Wyzanski ruled that United had illegally monopolized the shoe-machinery market and that United's leasing practices were the means by which it had done so. Rejecting the government's call for dissolution, he issued a decree having three central features. First, he required that United make all of its machines available for sale under terms that "do not make it substantially more advantageous for a shoe factory to lease rather than to buy a machine." Second, he directed that United's leases be shortened to five years and "be purged of their restrictive features." In particular, the full capacity and minimum-usage requirements were completely prohibited, while return fees were sharply restricted and their discriminatory application forbidden. Finally, the decree allowed United to provide instruction and repair services free of charge for thirty days following installation but required that United charge separately for all services, including repairs, rendered thereafter. Thus, the decree circumscribed both United's ability to lease and the structure of its leases.[69]

As a result of the decree, United lost several of the principal instruments through which if fashioned incentives and governed the exchange of machines and services. In particular, the court's restrictions on the size and implementation of switching penalties reduced United's ability to curb free riding and, thereby, its incentive to invest in generating nonpatentable know-how. The requirement that machines be sold on favorable terms (about half of the machines previously leased were purchased between 1953 and 1963)[70] (1) limited the ability of United and its customers to realize leasing's advantages in warranting machines and in safeguarding information transfers and (2) aggravated the free-riding problem by creating a new alternative to United's leased machines in the form of sale and secondhand machines. Finally, segregating repair charges undermined United's incentive to provide prompt repairs and interfered with the warranting function of leasing by weakening the link between machine performance and United's profits.

As might be expected, United sought to mitigate the harm caused by the ruling by adjusting the terms of its leases within the constraints of the decree. Thus, for instance, one effect of the ruling was to alter the relative merits of monthly rental and unit charges. Whereas the court condoned limited return charges on monthly rentals[71] by voiding the minumum-usage and full-capacity provisions, the decree abolished all deterrents to free riding through reductions in machine usage. In response, United eliminated unit charges on eight of the eighty-eight unit-charge machines it offered in 1954 and reduced them on all

---

[69] The decree did not limit the leasing practices of other shoe-machinery manufacturers (District Court Opinion: 349).

[70] Brief for Respondent United Shoe Machinery Corp. (June 3, 1968: 10).

[71] The decree limited the size of return fees to three monthly rental payments. Final Decree, February 18, 1953, para. 6, as modified by orders of the Court, July 12, 1954, and September 17, 1954, as reported in the District Court Opinion (351–54).

TABLE 12.4
Changes in United's Roadmen and Machines Outstanding

Year	Roadmen	Leased machines	Total machines	Ratio of leased to total	Ratio of roadmen to total machines
1920	700[a]	95,595[b]	108,631[b]	0.880	0.00644
1955	846[c]	100,525[d]	113,928[d]	0.882	0.00743
1964	349[c]	28,819[d]	94,355[d]	0.305	0.00370

[a] From *United States* v. *United Shoe Machinery Co.*, 264 Fed. Rep. 138, 143–44 (1920).
[b] Estimate based on Carl Kaysen, *United Shoe* v. *United Shoe Machinery Corporation:* An Economic Analysis of an Antitrust Case 28 (1956); and *United States* v. *United Shoe Machinery Co.*, 264 Fed. Rep. 138, 163 (1920).
[c] From Report of United Shoe Machinery Corporation under Decree Paragraph 18, December 15, 1964, at 41.
[d] From Report of United Shoe Machinery Corporation under Decree Paragraph 18, December 15, 1964, at 8, 10, 18.

but one of the remainder, while increasing the size of both monthly rentals and initial payments on these machines.[72]

But the more important consequence of the decree, and one harder to quantify, was its effect on real variables, such as the quality of United's machinery and services and its research effort to develop new techniques and other shoemaking know-how. One measure of United's service was its employment of roadmen, its principal conduit for machine repairs and day-to-day advice on shoemaking problems. As Table 12.4 reveals, the number of roadmen declined precipitously, both in absolute terms (col. 2) and relative to machines outstanding (col. 6), following the loss of the appeal to the Supreme Court in 1954[73] and implementation of the decree beginning in 1955. To the extent this reduction is indicative of an overall decline in United's support for its machines, it implies a major deterioration in United's performance.

Finally, although attributing the decline of the U.S. shoe industry to the decision in *United Shoe* would be overly heroic, it is nevertheless true that the industry went into a sharp decline in the decades following the decree. The share of imported shoes rose from a tiny fraction prior to 1950 to 25 percent by 1964 and continued to rise thereafter. Furthermore, United's decline definitely preceded that of the domestic shoe industry. Despite the increasing growth of imports, domestic shoe production rose 32 percent during the 1950s and remained at around 725 million pairs during much of the 1960s. By

[72] The decrease in unit charges averaged 30 percent. Kaysen (326) estimated repair costs to average 13.3 percent of total lease costs prior to the decree. Monthly rentals on unit charge machines rose from an average of $5.73 to $29.19 and initial payments from $2.27 to $65.98, compared to average increases from $8.07 to $18.68 in monthly rentals and from $90.36 to $170.08 in initial payments on all leased machinery. Pre- and postdecree lease terms are reported in United Report (81, app. D). Note that the segregation of repair charges might also have led to a reduction in unit charges but would not by itself have dictated increases in other lease charges.

[73] The Supreme Court issued a per curiam opinion on May 17, 1954. 347 U.S. 521 (1954).

contrast, United had lost over a third of its predecision market share by 1963 (United Report: 19).

7. CONCLUDING REMARKS

A reexamination of *United States v. United Shoe Machinery Corp.* is of more than historical interest. First, equipment leasing is an important organizational form, accounting for $36.8 billion worth of transactions in the United States in 1988.[74] Its growing significance is evidenced by the recent creation of a separate Uniform Commercial Code article concerned exclusively with leasing. Understanding the role that leasing plays in commercial transactions is fundamental to assessing the quality of such legal rules and can help inform judges as to their appropriate application in individual cases. Second, judges are repeatedly asked to rule on charges of anticompetitive exclusion, a contemporary example being the litigation over the contract terms governing airline computer-reservation systems.[75] If recently developed theories of strategic exclusion were to stimulate widespread antitrust challenges of contracting practices, *United Shoe* would furnish the legal precedent for courts to dictate the details of commercial dealings. Not only did the case target a variety of specific lease terms, but the court, after ruling against United, entered a judgment that essentially rewrote United's contracts. What limited evidence is available suggests that external interference in the incentive provisions of contracts can seriously diminish the efficiency of contractual exchange (see Crocker and Masten, 1988).

We have argued here that United's leasing practices represented a coherent and measured response to the incentive and governance problems encountered in these transactions. Specifically, leasing performed two distinct but related functions. First, leasing served as an alternative to contractual warranties in motivating the development, production, and servicing of a large number of complex machines. Second, leasing provided a means of indirectly rewarding shoe machine manufacturers for the provision of a wide range of technical advice and shoe-manufacturing know-how and thus offered a partial solution to now-familiar information transfer problems.

[74] *Aviation Daily*, November 7, 1989, at 251. Interestingly, the three largest categories of leased equipment—computers, aircraft, and telecommunications equipment—are, like shoe machinery, complex, durable, and redeployable. IBM lawyers apparently represented a sizable and attentive section of the audience at United's trial. Conversation with John Meuse, chairman of United Shoe Machinery Corp., December 18, 1990. IBM's leasing practices were themselves the subject of private antitrust charges in the 1970s. See Masten and Snyder (1989: 74, 82–83) and cites therein.

[75] See, for instance, *United Airlines, Inc. v. Austin Travel Corporation*, 867 F.2d 737 (1989) (defendant claimed that liquidated damages in computer-reservation-system agreements were unreasonable and violated antitrust statutes). See also the federal carrier-owned computer-reservation-system regulations codified at 14 C.F.R. 255 (1989). The Federal Trade Commission's current investigation of Microsoft's pricing of its software may raise similar issues insofar as the pricing scheme, while discouraging customers from purchasing rivals' products, may encourage the transfer of nonpatentable know-how.

United appears, moreover, to have framed its leases, within the practical limitations on contracting, to promote the efficient provision and use of its machines and services. The long-term and "exclusionary" features of United's leases, for instance, were necessary to prevent customers from reneging on implied promises to pay for United's information and advice through the use of machines. Even United's discriminatory application of return and usage restrictions is consistent with efficiency; to preserve the benefits of leasing while deterring free riding, the magnitude of switching costs should be conditional on machines being returned to substitute competitor equipment. On a broader level, the assignment of powers and responsibilities within United's leases was consistent with a goal of minimizing costly court adjudication in favor of unilateral responses to lease violations.

Finally, data on United's leasing and pricing practices provide evidence that United chose distribution arrangements systematically to reflect the incentive and transaction-cost considerations identified in this article. While it is true, as the prosecution claimed, that United offered its most important machines for lease only, the efficiency advantages of leasing relative to sales were greatest on the most important and complex machines where the limitations of contractual warranties and the hazards of free riding were most acute. The fact that service-oriented shoe-machine manufacturers both preceding and following United's formation leased machines both preceding and following United's formation leased machines under similar terms further supports the view that leasing was a solution to fundamental organizational problems in the industry.

Evidence that contracting practices were sensitive to efficiency concerns does not preclude anticompetitive motives. Doing so requires a showing either that the conditions necessary to sustain anticompetitive behavior are absent or that the restrictions imposed by the contract are insufficient to have an anticompetitive effect. The conditions required for strategic behavior in the few models that explore the exclusionary potential of contracts have not been adequately enumerated and scrutinized. What efforts have been made in that regard suggest either that the circumstances in which contractual exclusion can occur are limited (see Masten and Snyder, 1989; and Rasmusen, 1991) or that distinguishing between strategic and efficiency motives using market screens is difficult (Snyder and Kauper, 1991). As a result, it will often be necessary to assess the reasonableness of specific restrictions on a case-by-case basis. One's willingness to subject widely used contractual terms to antitrust review will depend in part on one's confidence in the ability of judges to recognize the many legitimate purposes served by contract restrictions in diverse and multifaceted business transactions. In our view, the decision in *United Shoe* stands as an illustration of the hazards inherent in such a policy.

C h a p t e r
13

STRATEGY AND TRANSACTION COSTS: THE ORGANIZATION OF DISTRIBUTION IN THE CARBONATED SOFT DRINK INDUSTRY

Timothy J. Muris, David T. Scheffman, Pablo T. Spiller

1. INTRODUCTION

This paper studies the ongoing transformation of the soft drink distribution systems of Coca-Cola and Pepsi-Cola[1] from systems of independent bottlers to captive bottling subsidiaries. In *Strategy and Structure*, Alfred Chandler, Jr. (1962), advanced the hypothesis that successful firms develop strategies to take advantage of new opportunities, and that those strategies then

Reprinted from the Journal of Economics and Management Strategy, Volume 1, Number 1, Spring 1992 by permission of the MIT Press, Cambridge, Massachusetts. © 1992 The Massachusetts Institute of Technology.

Timothy J. Muris is Foundation Professor of Law, George Mason University; David Scheffman is the Justin Potter Professor of American Competitive Enterprise, Vanderbilt University; and Pablo Spiller is Professor of Economics, the University of California at Berkeley. The cooperation and support of PepsiCo, Inc., and support from the Dean's Summer Research Fund at the Owen School and from the University-wide Energy Research Group at the University of California, Berkeley, are gratefully acknowledged. The authors thank Oliver Williamson and a referee for the *Journal of Economics and Management Strategy*, and participants at workshops at Washington University, University of Illinois, University of Southern California, and at the Western Economic Association and Strategic Management Society meetings, for helpful comments. Excellent research assistance was provided by Theresa Burke. The conclusions and opinions expressed here are those of the authors.

[1] We will frequently use Coke or Coca-Cola, and Pepsi or Pepsi-Cola, to denote the soft drink operations of The Coca-Cola Co. and PepsiCo, respectively.

determine the organizational structure required for effective implementation.[2] We find that the changes in the organization of the two leading carbonated soft drink (CSD) firms' distribution systems provide some support for Chandler's hypothesis. The independent bottling system were a unique and effective form of organization for many decades. Changes in the external environment, however, raised the costs of transacting between the parent concentrate manufacturers (CMs) and their independent bottlers. In addition, the new competitive environment required rapidly changing product and marketing strategies, and the implementation of these strategies required the close cooperation of the distribution systems. In essence, Coca-Cola and Pepsi-Cola needed to change the organization of their distribution systems in order to implement effectively the strategies that were stimulated by the new environment, because the relative transaction costs of the independent bottling systems in the environment were too high. Thus, à la Chandler, one might say that structure has followed strategy.[3]

Following the literature inspired by Coase and further developed by Williamson and others,[4] we focus on the role of transaction costs in determining structure, both for the original independent bottling systems and for the change to captive bottling. While we find that relationship-specific investments are an important determinant of the organization of distribution in the CSD industry, the typical "relationship-specific investment leads to vertical integration" story is not sufficient here. Specific investments were present from the beginning of the industry, and, as we will discuss later, were a fundamental determinant of the contracts between the CMs and their independent bottlers. Given the importance of specific investments, however, the question arises as to why distribution was not vertically integrated from the start. A sudden increase in the extent of asset specificity did not trigger the move to captive distribution. Instead, the captive distribution has arisen from changes in the costs of transacting and in the strategies followed by the CMs. Thus, the complexity of real-world transacting requires a theoretical framework that goes beyond the standard treatment of the relationship between asset specificity and vertical integration. Our findings, then, are consistent with arguments put forward by Coase and further elaborated in Williamson,[5] in that we find that even with serious

---

[2] Chandler (1962).

[3] A more formally correct statement would be that strategy and structure were jointly determined by the external environment and relative transaction costs.

[4] See, in particular, Coase (1937), and Williamson (1989), and references therein. See also Klein (1980).

[5] "What decides whether vertical integration or a long-term contract represents the more efficient solution [to problems posed by asset specificity] depends on the absolute relation of the costs of these alternative arrangements" (Coase, 1988). For an initial response to Coase's criticism of the role of specific assets in explaining the internal organization of firms, see Williamson (1988), in particular footnote 5. For a more general treatment of the interaction of specific assets with the governance structure and environmental conditions, see Williamson (1991).

asset specificity problems, relative transaction costs may dictate resolution by contract rather than by vertical integration.

After briefly outlining the history of the independent bottling systems and the nature of the changes in the CSD industry in the last few decades, we then summarize some implications of transaction cost economics for soft drink distribution. With this background, we provide an explanation of why distribution was originally organized as a system of independent bottlers and why Coca-Cola and Pepsi-Cola are now moving to captive distribution. The paper then presents two types of empirical tests of our hypotheses and of the competitive effects of the move toward captive distribution. Our empirical tests shed some light on the antitrust implications of the change in distribution systems.

The first empirical text exploits the difference in the distribution of Coca-Cola and Pepsi-Cola in the fountain channel.[6] Independent bottlers of Pepsi-Cola have, with limited exceptions, the exclusive rights to fountain distribution in their territories. Coca-Cola, on the other hand, had a different distribution system. Coke independent bottlers had exclusive rights to packaged and vended soft drinks in their territories, but, from the outset, Coke kept control of distribution to fountain accounts. The differential performance of the two companies across distribution channels provides some evidence about the determinants and efficiency of independent bottling. A second set of empirical tests consists of statistical analyses of the effects on prices of the move to captive distribution. The effects of company-owned bottling and of a change to company-owned bottling on prices in several cities is estimated from a pooled time series/cross-sectional analysis. Our statistical results indicate that the move to captive bottling has been procompetitive (i.e., results in lower prices). Elsewhere, we have found that unit sales have increased postacquisition, and that the presence of a Coke or Pepsi company-owned bottler or a change to a company-owned bottler leads to a reduction in prices.[7] The analysis of competitive effects, besides providing tests of our hypotheses about the relative costs of distribution systems in different strategic environments, also addresses potential concerns of the antitrust authorities with the move to captive distribution by Coca-Cola and Pepsi-Cola.

---

[6] Fountain soft drinks are those served in unsealed containers, for example, at restaurants. Soft-drink syrup is sold to fountain accounts (e.g., McDonald's), which add carbonated water and serve the mixture to their customers.

[7] In Muris, Scheffman, and Spiller (1993), we estimate the effects of Pepsi's acquisition of a large bottler, MEI, on unit sales of the MEI operation in five cities. We also provide a detailed analysis of the impact of Pepsi's acquisition of MEI on the costs and efficiency of that bottling operation. We find the acquisition resulted in significant cost reductions and increases in efficiency.

2. THE ORIGINS AND DEVELOPMENT OF THE SOFT DRINK INDUSTRY

2.1. The Early Years

From inception, Coca-Cola and other major CMs used networks of independent bottlers to bottle and market their products.[8] Independent bottling began with the Coca-Cola Company and was emulated by other companies, including PepsiCo. Under the Coca-Cola franchise-agreements, the bottlers agreed "to invest in a plant and equipment, and to keep up said plant and equipment in such a condition as will be sufficient to meet satisfactorily the demands of the business in the territory therein referred to, and to increase such investment in said business as the demand for Coca-Cola in bottles in said territory may require."[9]

The bottlers also agreed to purchase syrup from the Coca-Cola Company and not to sell substitutes or imitations.[10] The parent bottling franchisor agreed to "furnish ... sufficient syrup for bottling purposes to meet the [bottler's] requirements ... in the territory ..." at a fixed price of $1.30 per gallon. Moreover, the franchisors gave the bottlers certain exclusive and (in effect)[11] *perpetual* rights within specified territories, i.e., the "sole and exclusive right and license ... to use and vend on Bottled Coca-Cola the trademark name Coca-Cola, and all labels and designs pertaining thereto, in connection with the product 'Bottled Coca-Cola' in the territory ..."[12] The Coca-Cola franchise system grew quickly. By 1910, there were 370 Coca-Cola bottlers; by 1928, there were 1,263.[13]

In 1904, ten years after Coca-Cola was first bottled and one year after Pepsi-Cola was incorporated, Pepsi began the development of its bottling system (Martin, 1962: 22). By 1939, the company's territorial representatives had franchised 341 bottlers (Martin, 1962: 22). The conceptual relationship between Pepsi and its independent bottlers mimicked Coke (exclusive, perpetual territories), with one important difference: Pepsi's franchise agreements also gave its bottlers exclusive, perpetual rights to fountain sales. As we will see, the provision proved to be a significant impediment

---

[8] For a brief history of the major CMs, see "The Seven-Up Division of Philip Morris," Harv. Bus. School Case 9-385-321 (Mar. 1986), "The Dr. Pepper Company," Harv. Bus. School Case 377-146 (July 1982), and "The Seven-Up Company," Harv. Bus. School Case 378-097 (Sept. 1982). See also Martin (1962), Kahn (1960), and Louis and Yazijian (1980).

[9] Coca-Cola bottler's contract.

[10] "[The bottler agrees] not to manufacture, deal in, sell, offer for sale, use or handle, nor attempt to do so, either directly or indirectly, any product that is a substute for or an imitation of Coca-Cola, nor any product that can be used unfairly with Coca-Cola...." (Coca-Cola bottler's contract).

[11] The contract has no fixed term. The term of the contract is, in effect, perpetual, because a bottler could bequeath it to his heirs and, assuming good faith performance, could not be terminated. Termination issues in franchise agreements have been a subject of considerable legal attention. See, for example, Muris (1981).

[12] Parent Coca-Cola kept the rights to distribute to fountain accounts, which for the first few decades of the industry represented most of the sales volume.

[13] See Kahn (1960: 69–78); Louis and Yazijian (1980: 12, 41).

to Pepsi's ability to complete successfully with Coca-Cola in the fountain channel.

2.2. Industry History

To understand the magnitude of the changes in the CSD industry in the last few decades, consider what the industry was like just 30 years ago. At that time, Coca-Cola and Pepsi-Cola, as concentrate manufacturers, played somewhat limited roles relative to their independent bottlers. The CM's duties were essentially threefold: to supply concentrate for a very small number of unchanging products; to decide on the theme of infrequently changing, national advertising campaigns (in consulation with the bottlers); and to try to maintain or increase the selling fervor of the bottlers. The typical bottler operated a simple manufacturing and sales operation in a small territory. It handled a limited number of products and packages, used infrequent promotions, and its customers were generally small. The contracts left to the bottlers the decisions on prices, packages, carrying of new brands of the parent CM or allied brands,[14] and local promotions (with the cooperative advertising programs of the CMs).

In recent decades the CSD industry has become a big business. The Coca-Cola Company and PepsiCo are major corporations. The per capita annual consumption of soft drinks has increased from about 19 gallons in 1966 to over 47 gallons in 1990, and is still growing. Changes in the industry and in the external environment have stimulated new strategies. The "Cola Wars" were declared, and the battle continues. Coca-Cola and Pepsi-Cola have been at the vanguard of ever-changing modern marketing strategies. The two companies have developed successful new products and packages, and manage many more products and package types.[15] Existing products sometimes were changed (because, for example, of the costs of and preferences for sweeteners and caffeine). Coca-Cola even changed the formula for its flagship product. The new marketing strategies required ever more

---

[14] Allied brands are brands of soft drinks not produced by a bottler's CM. For example, many independent Coca-Cola and Pepsi-Cola bottlers also bottle Dr. Pepper, 7Up, and other noncola brands of other CMs.

[15] For example, in 1970 there were only 24 new carbonated nonalcoholic beverages introduced by major CMs into the market. By 1988, this number grew 10-fold to 247. Among these new products, diet and caffeine-free soft drinks have experienced great success. Major new brands that were introduced during the 1980s had captured 17.6% of CSD sales by 1988. Small firms also participated in the trend to develop new products for the market. Between 1987 and 1988, for example, these small companies introduced 482 new drinks. (See Tollison, Kaplan, and Higgins 1991: 71). Growing in step with new products were different types of packages. During the early 1950s, packaging consisted of $6\frac{1}{2}$-ounce or 12-ounce returnable bottles. By the mid-1950s, 10-, 12-, and 26-ounce bottles were introduced. The 1960s ushered in the 12-ounce cans that were later improved with easy-open tops. Packaging continued to adapt to changes in consumer tastes and relative costs of packaging materials. By 1985, containers of 6 ounces to 12 ounces constituted only 50 percent of all packaging compared to 80 percent in 1965. Larger containers, which represented less than 10 percent of volume in 1970, increased to 25 percent by 1985. See National Soft Drink Association Sales Survey of the Soft Drink Industry, 1965–85.

sophisticated use of advertising, particularly television, with a greatly increased pace of change of promotions,[16] A result of all the external and strategic changes in the industry is that the CSD industry is much larger and more complex than it was 30 years ago.

In particular, the world of the CSD bottler is far more complex today. Increased economies of scale in bottling and canning, reduced transportation costs, and the demise of the returnable container have led to a substantial increase in mimimum efficient scale in bottling.[17] Besides being much larger, each bottler now handles many more products, in multiple packages, requiring efficient exploitation of economies of scope. In addition, the bottler's promotional environment is much more complex because of its parent CM's constantly changing national advertising and promotional campaigns—campaigns that work best when coordinated with local promotional activity.

The typical bottler's major customers, supermarkets, mass merchandisers, and leading fast-food franchises, have become larger and more sophisticated over the past 30 years. A significantly larger portion of most bottlers' business is now with customers who are larger than the bottler. Supermarkets, for example, often want to purchase and promote soft drinks over areas larger than the territory of any individual bottler. Under the independent bottling systems, this generally requires cumbersome coordination between the CM and a number (sometimes more than 100) bottlers. Besides the scale of their purchases, the sophistication of large soft-drink retailers has also markedly increased, partly because of the power of modern information technology. For example, scanners now give retailers of food products great control over and knowledge of the movement of individual products on their shelves.[18] Consequently, supermarkets and other sophisticated customers have much more say in the retail promotion of grocery products such as CSDs. Finally, new customers have become prominent, including fast-food franchisors, mass merchandisers, convenience stores, drug stores, gasoline service stores, and large companies that provide CSDs to their employees at work.

Perhaps the most important change in the bottlers' competitive environ-

---

[16] As discussed later, promotional pricing has become a major competitive tactic at the bottling level. See Marketing Fact Book, 1983, 1986, and 1989 editions. Changes in advertising campaigns have also increased competition. For example, Coca-Cola has had nine major national advertising themes since 1970, starting with "It's the Real Thing." See "Coca-Cola's First 100 Years," Beverage World 69 (1986). Pepsi-Cola launched the "Pepsi Challenge" in Dallas in 1975, which increased its sales and market share in many large cities. See "The Pepsi Challenge: Making New Inroads," Beverage World (Sept. 1982). Promotions, however, are not restricted exclusively to pricing. They also involve particular advertising campaigns, as well as special displays.

[17] A Boston Consulting Group study found that each time the output of a plant doubles, the direct labor cost per case for a bottling line declines about 11 percent, while that for a canning line declines about 6 percent, up to about 10 million cases a year. The study also found that unit manufacturing cost declines approximately 30 percent each time volume doubles. See the Boston Consulting Group (1986).

[18] Scanners were introduced in 1974, but were not widely used until 1980. By 1986, 50 percent of the nation's supermarket sales were in stores with scanners. See Harris (1986).

ment has been the dramatic increase in promotional activity. For over a decade, price discounting has been a major weapon in the Cola Wars. CSDs are "on deal" in the grocery store more than any other product, with 75 percent sold at discontinued prices.[19] In some areas, more than 90 percent of the volume is sold at a discount price. Both the amount and intensity of discounting increased through the 1980s, with the percentage of total volume discounted rising from 57 percent in 1982 to 75 percent in 1988, and the average discount increased from 28 percent to 30 percent between those years.

All these changes required bottlers to become larger, more sophisticated, and more efficient, and led to a major consolidation of bottlers during the 1960s and the 1970s. The number of bottling plants in the industry has fallen to under 800 from more than 3,000 in 1970. Individual bottling operations became much larger, bottlers developed cooperative canning and plastic-bottle manufacturing operations, and large independent multifranchise operations (MFOs) were formed.

Beginning in the late 1970s, Coke and Pepsi started creating captive distribution organizations by acquiring some of their larger independent bottlers.[20] Coca-Cola formed Coca-Cola Enterprises ("CCE") as a publicly owned bottling operation, with the parent holding a 49 percent interest. Rather than forming a separate publicly traded corporation for its captive bottling, PepsiCo enlarged and revamped its "bottler of last resort," Pepsi-Cola Bottling Group (PBG),[21] to manage its captive distribution operations. In addition to acquiring many of their independent bottlers, both CMs entered into joint ventures with several other franchisees. Coca-Cola (through CCE) and PepsiCo now each bottle about 50 percent of their total bottled sales and have a minority equity interest of about 15–20 percent in independent bottlers that accounts for about another 20 percent of sales.[22] Thus, Pepsi-Cola and Coca-Cola each own or have an equity interest in bottlers selling about two-thirds of their volume.

The move to captive distribution by Coca-Cola and Pepsi-Cola has stimulated antitrust concern.[23] That the two leading CMs bottle significant amounts of Dr. Pepper and 7UP ("allied brands" in industry terminology)

---

[19] The facts in this paragraph are from *Marketing Fact Book*, 1983, 1986, and 1989 editions.

[20] Some of these transactions were in excess of $1 billion.

[21] Pepsi (and Coke) historically brokered many changes in independent bottling operations, particularly as the size of the average bottler increased markedly because of increases in minimum efficient scale. Prior to a strategic move to captive distribution, PBG had owned and operated bottling operations for a variety of reasons, such as exit of a family-operated operation or buying out a troublesome bottler, generally with the intention of eventually selling off the bottling operation to an independent bottler.

[22] See *Beverage Digest*, "Future Smarts VIII" 14–16 (Dec. 11, 1989) (1989 Winter Soft Drink Seminar). See also *Beverage Digest* (April 20, 1990). The Coca-Cola Company owns a majority interest in Coca-Cola New York, representing about 6 percent of sales.

[23] The soft drink distribution systems have long been of concern to the FTC and private litigants. For more discussion of antitrust concerns with the CSD industry, see Muris, Scheffman, and Spiller (1993).

heightened these concerns. Currently, Pepsi-Cola company-operated bottlers (COBOs) sell about 8 percent of 7UP, while its franchise-operated bottlers (FOBOs) sell another 15–16 percent. Because most of Coca-Cola bottlers sell Sprite, Coca-Cola's own lemon-lime drink, only 7 percent of 7UP is sold through Coca-Cola (COBO and FOBO) bottlers. About 30 percent of Dr. Pepper is sold through CCE or Pepsi-Cola COBOs, while almost 45 percent is sold through Pepsi or Coca-Cola FOBOs (see Muris, Scheffman, and Spiller, 1993).

3. A TRANSACTION COSTS ANALYSIS OF THE INDEPENDENT BOTTLING SYSTEMS

In our economy manufacturers have widely varying degrees of control over their distribution systems. Independent distribution, such as exists in the CSD industry, is unusual among major grocery manufacturers, which distribute mostly through captive sales forces or food brokerage.[24] Transaction cost theory has developed the factors of likely importance in determining the nature of a vertical relationship, one possibility being vertical integration. Next, we describe the prominent factors bearing on soft-drink distribution.

3.1. Specific Investments

Modern transaction cost theory has highlighted the role of asset specificity in the determinants of vertical integration.[25] From the beginning, both the CM and its independent bottlers were required to make substantial relationship-specific investments. The bottler had to invest in CSD-specific equipment and in CM brand-specific capital, mostly through the development of the local market, but also to some extent in physical capital.[26] The CM also made investments in bottler- and brand-specific assets.

---

[24] The typical grocery manufacturer has much more control over its (wholesale) distribution than does Coca-Cola or Pepsi through their independent bottlers. This is clearly the case for most major products that are typically distributed through captive sales forces. A grocery manufacturer also has much more control over a food broker than over an independent bottler. Food brokers are commission sales agents who sell to retailers with the prices, terms of promotion, etc., set by the grocery manufacturer. The typical food brokerage arrangement is a 30-day contract terminable at will. See *Food Broker Facts*, 1989 edition, National Food Brokers Association, Washington, D.C.

[25] For a discussion of the importance of specific investments to the form of distribution, see, for example, Walker and Weber (1984), Anderson (1985), Coughlan (1985), and Anderson and Schmittlein (1984). For a general discussion of the role of asset specificity, see Williamson (1979a).

[26] For example, CM specific bottling and vending equipment.

3.2. Frequency and Complexity of Negotiation

Transactions costs are directly related to the frequency and complexity of negotiations between the manufacturer and distributor. A captive distribution system may greatly economize on those costs relative to independent distribution because the employee-distributor is much more subject to the direction of the manufacturer than an independent distributor, particularly if the independent distributor is protected from termination.[27]

3.3. Scale Economies

As discussed earlier, economies of scale in bottling, at the plant and multiplant levels, have greatly increased in recent years. This development has made it easier to run a captive bottling operation, as the number of separate bottling plants required for national distribution has been decreased dramatically. To the extent that there are economies of scale in management, the relative disadvantage of captive distribution from added managerial resources is reduced. The effect of scale on the incentives of employees, relative to independent business relations, is unclear. A larger-scale operation may find it more difficult to instill the right incentives in its employee-distributors than a smaller-scale one. Alternatively, a larger-scale firm provides more opportunity for advancement than a smaller-scale operation, which may result in enhanced incentive-compatibility between the operation and its employees.

3.4. Monitoring and the Assessment of Separate Contributions

Difficulties in monitoring effort are likely to result in disputes over the division of rewards. How, for example, can a CM determine whether a bottler is devoting sufficient effort? Are the bottler's sales low because it is "shirking" or because the bottler's competitors are especially aggressive? Alternatively, from the bottler's perspective, is the CM's increase in price justified by the costs and efforts of the CM? Even when effort can be adequately monitored, problems can arise in assessing the separate contributions of the manufacturer's and distributor's effort to joint profitability. For example, a dispute might arise over the relative contributions that were made to a distributor's sales by a manufacturer-financed advertising campaign and by the distributor's sales efforts.

---

[27] "A factor of production (or the owner thereof) does not have to make a series of contracts with the factors with whom he is cooperating within the firm, as would be necessary, of course, if this cooperation were as a direct result of the working of the price mechanism. For this series of contracts is substituted one" (Coase, 1937).

3.5. Spillovers

The problems of assessing the contributions made to joint profitability by the CM and independent bottlers are exacerbated when one bottler's actions affect other bottlers. Bottlers, for example, often advertise in media that reach beyond their territory. In addition, many large customers wish to purchase and promote in an area larger then any bottler's territory. Finally, another important source of spillovers is the introduction of new products and packages. Bottlers that cooperate in a successful introduction pave the way for other bottlers.

3.6. Timing and Execution

Independent distribution is a disadvantage when the success of a manufacturer's strategies depends on effective timing and execution requiring the cooperation of distrubutors. A manufacturer with captive distribution need not negotiate with its distributors to introduce a new product, package, or promotional campaign. For a manufacturer with a strategy that requires timing and execution through the distribution system for successful implementation, independent distribution will be a disadvantage, particularly if the manufacturer must negotiate with a large number of independent distributors.

Having identified factors critical to the determination of distrubution arrangements, we now turn to a thorough transaction cost analysis of the organisation of distribution in the CSD industry, beginning with the inception of the independent bottling systems.

4. DISTRIBUTION IN THE FIRST SEVERAL DECADES

The most unusual feature of the early CSD industry is that not only was distribution organized with independent bottlers (instead of captive bottlers or through commission brokerage agents), so was *manufacturing* (bottling)—in essence, Coca-Cola and Pepsi-Cola franchised manufacturing. As we will see, this fact is critical to understanding why the independent bottling systems arose. The CM and bottler were both manufacturers, each of which, by contract, was the only supplier of an essential input to the other.[28] Two central questions arise in considering the original independent bottling system. The first is why bottling was not captive from the beginning, given that bottling involved both manufacturing and distribution and given the large-scale specific investments and interdependence of the CM and bottler; the second is why the particular form of independent distribution (perpetual, exclusive territories) arose. We address each question in turn.

---

[28] The CM provided concentrate to the bottler. The bottler provided distribution to the CM.

4.1. Why Independent Bottlers

Various hypotheses have been advanced for why distribution in the CSD industry was organized with independent bottling. The explanation given the most weight—that the capital requirements for creating a bottling system nationwide were substantial—is unconvincing.[29] The cost of creating a nationwide bottling network was not large in comparison with, for example, the cost of building a major steel mill. Of course, bottled soft drinks were a new product with uncertain demand. But the capital markets usually bear such uncertainty; manufacturing need not be franchised just to raise money in an uncertain world, especially given the risks involved in using independent bottling. Finally, capital requirements would not explain why, once Coca-Cola and Pepsi-Cola became capable of easily raising their capital requirements, they continued to franchise new bottlers.

Because of the value of CSDs relative to shipping costs and the use of returnable (and breakable) containers, soft drink bottling, like dairies,[30] required local manufacturing and a substantial local delivery system. This fact, we believe, provides the basis for the most credible explanation of why distribution was organized as systems of independent bottlers.[31] Already by the 1920s, Coca-Cola's nationwide independent bottling system had over 1,000 bottling plants.[32] Given the state of national communications and transportation systems of the time, management of such a large system of local manufacturing and delivery operations could only be accomplished with an extremely decentralized management structure. Decentralized management with centralized ownership, however, would generate substantial managerial discretion, increasing the risk faced by central ownership. This was particularly true in the early decades of the industry, when modern financial controls and the decentralized, business-unit form of corporate organization that such controls permit were in their infancy—an infancy that did not involve any operation managing hundreds of geographically dispersed manufacturing facilities (see Chandler, 1962). Moreover, the limited communications and transportation systems of the time made decentralization much costlier and riskier that it would be today.[33] Problems that

---

[29] Indeed, economists increasingly reject the theory that the main purpose of franchising is to raise money. See, for example, Williamson (1989) and Rubin (1978).

[30] A dairy faced the additional problem of perishability, which further limited the geographic scope of its market.

[31] As we will see later, if only local distribution, rather than local distribution plus manufacturing plus delivery was required, captive distribution was possible.

[32] See Kahn (1960: 8), and Louis and Yazijian (1980: 9).

[33] A distant company-owned bottling operation could create the same problems as an independent bottler *and* take actions that directly cost the parent money before the parent could discover and solve the problem, given the transporation and communications capabilities of the time. A leading study of business consolidations in the early twentith century found that one of the major reasons for failure was the inability to manage a large number of plants. See Dewing (1914), especially 557–66.

required headquarters involvement could not be resolved quickly, and could produce significant costs until their resolution.

We hypothesize, therefore, that despite the substantial problems posed by asset specificity, independent bottling arose primarily because it was not possible to create an effective organization for operating a vertically integrated company with hundreds of geographically separated manufacturing and local delivery operations, given the primitive transportation and communications systems of the time and the lack of sophisticated financial and management controls. Given the problems posed by the independent bottling systems, companies that learned how to operate through such systems were the ones most likely to be successful.[34] In this sense, although Coca-Cola and Pepsi-Cola are premier marketing companies, the fundamental competitive advantage that allowed them to compete so effectively probably lay in their ability to operate through a very cumbersome distribution system.[35]

4.2. Why Exclusive and Perpetual Territories

The important remaining question is how it was possible for Coca-Cola and Pepsi-Cola and their bottlers to be successful, given the serious asset specificity problems and the infeasibility of vertical integration.[36] As we will see shortly, the answer to that question lies in the fact that the creation of exclusive, perpetual territories resulted in some protection of specific investments and considerable joint dependence of the CM and bottler on the success of the product. In addition, the very simple strategies of the CMs in the early years of the industry resulted in an environment in which CM—bottler disputes were minimized, making independent bottling systems viable. Even then, the complexity of this form of distribution presented significant management problems (see Muris, Scheffman, and Spiller, 1993).

Because the independent Coca-Cola and Pepsi-Cola bottlers had to make long-lived investments that were to a considerable extent specific to CSD distribution (e.g., the bottling plant) and to the parent CM (e.g., investments in market development), bottlers who had to exit the business would not be assured of recoupling their investments.[37] When Coca-Cola and Pepsi-

---

[34] The history and day-to-day business of Coke and Pepsi are filled with major disputes with bottlers that had to be resolved in some manner.

[35] For example, a major reason often advanced for Philip Morris's lack of success with 7UP was that Philip Morris did not have the experience with such a distribution system, and did not comprehend the importance and subtleties of distributing through independent bottlers. Its distribution experience with Miller Brewing Co. apparently was not leverageable into soft drinks. Manufacturing and bottling is centralized in the beer industry, and regulations constrain the flexibility of wholesale distribution.

[36] In fact, Pepsi, although starting shortly after Coke, took several decades (including a number of brushes with bankruptcy) to be successful. One reason may be that Coca-Cola was better able to master the inherent problems posed by its independent bottling system than was Pepsi-Cola.

[37] Because of substantial production and distribution differences, conversion to beverages such as beer would be costly. Because of the limited availability of nationally distributed CSDs, a Coke bottler would not have regarded the possibility of carrying another CSD as a perfect substitute.

Cola were invented, they were viewed as special-occasion beverages. Given the relatively primitive level of national advertising, local "pull" was required to increase demand. Local "pull," however, would not be profitable if the market was not, to some extent, assured. Exclusive territories provided such assurances to the independent bottlers, by protecting them from losing the rewards for their market development efforts to nearby (or new) bottlers who might otherwise ship into their territory, without having to spend the effort to develop the brand.

The bottlers also required assurances regarding the term of their bottling appointments—otherwise they were at risk of the CM expropriating their gains by bringing another bottler (possibly captive) into the territory. The resolution of the problem of specific investments in this case was franchise contracts without a fixed term, which could not be terminated without overwhelming cause. In essence, the contracts are perpetual.[38] The reason for the perpetual term is not clear. Certainly, short-term contracts would be insufficient to protect a bottler's long-lived investment. A fixed term of, say, 25 years might have been sufficient to protect a bottler's investment. This would have required, however, a major renegotiation of the contract in 25 years, an issue to which we turn momentarily.

One reason for having perpetual contracts, we hypothesize, is that it was consistent with a common feature of the other contractual provisions—there was no *requirement* of renegotiation over major issues. Of course, Coca-Cola and the bottler could discuss issues and disagreements, but nothing forced the relationship to begin anew at some point in the future, as would have been the case with finite-term contracts. In particular, neither party had a legal duty to address any concerns of the other party about the basic structure of the agreement. It may be that the contracts were designed to avoid required renegotiation, because an independent bottling system was too fragile to bear the risk of major renegotiations.[39] The contracts and business realities fixed the CM's and bottler's duties and authority fairly clearly. The CM had to produce concentrate and was responsible for national advertising and promotion. The bottler had to sell the CM's product and was responsible for all aspects of the business in its territory. But this sytem provided no mechanism to resolve disputes or to force major modifications of the agreement.

We hypothesize that the simplicity of the CSD business and of the CM's strategies in the early decades of the industry minimized the need for

---

[38] In addition, the original Coca-Cola bottling appointments fixed the price of concentrate in perpetuity. The price provisions of each bottler's contract eventually required modification, which, given the number of independent bottlers, took several years of negotiations—perhaps because the bottlers were reaping a windfall as Coke's costs rose substantially because of large increases in the price of sugar. Coke and Pepsi concentrate prices are now determined by bargaining with their respective bottlers' associations.

[39] Perpetual contracts avoid the end-of-period problem. That is, given that the bottler was expected to be continuously investing in physical and brand name assets, a fixed-term contract could induce the bottler to change its investment strategy prior to the time of renegotiation in an effort to affect the outcome of the negotiation.

coordination between the CM and its bottlers, allowing the inherently risky independent bottling systems to be viable. In the early days of the industry, and for most bottlers thoughout their history, a bottler of Coca-Cola or Pepsi could survive only by successfully selling Coca-Cola or Pepsi in its territory. Similarly, Coca-Cola and Pepsi-Cola could be successful only if they continued to produce a product at a price that their bottlers would sell. Neither concentrate manufacturer introduced new products, and they very infrequently introduced new packages.[40] Modern marketing strategies that require constant change and close coordination of national advertising with local promotion did not exist. A bottler simply had to sell the product in an unchanging package, and its CM simply had to produce syrup and to develop infrequently changing national advertising and promotion. Of course disputes still arose between CMs and their bottlers. But the basic tasks required of the CM and the bottlers were sufficiently separate and compatible with their individual incentives that "fatal" disputes across a large number of bottlers were rare.[41] Major events that would require negotiations that could give rise to disputes (e.g., package and product introductions) were even rarer.

In summary, given the problems arising from the existence of specific assets, the granting of exclusive and perpetual territories was required to balance the relationship between the CM and its bottlers, as well as to minimize sources of significant disputes. Absent exclusive territories with protection against termination, the bottlers were subject to potential opportunistic behavior by the CM, because the bottler's assets were specific to the CM, but the CM's assets were not specific to each individual bottler. Exclusive territories and long-term contracts substantially reduced such risks, thus providing the necessary incentives for bottlers' investments in specific assets.[42] Perpetual, rather than long-fixed-term, contracts may have been used to dispense with the renegotiation required by fixed-term contracts, because renegotiation of the basic contract may have impaired an otherwise fragile system of agreements.

5. DISTRIBUTION IN THE LAST TWO DECADES

We now turn to the last two decades of the industry, in which major changes in the environment and in the strategies of Coca-Cola and Pepsi-Cola

[40] It is of interest to note that lengthy negotiations were required for Coca-Cola to get its bottlers to agree to adopt the now famous "Swirl" bottle, and for Pepsi-Cola to get its bottlers to move to a standardized bottle. In both cases Coke and Pepsi had to subsidize their bottlers in order to obtain their eventual acquiescence. The bottlers were resistant to changing, despite the fact that the Swirl bottle, for example, became one of the most successful packages in marketing history.

[41] The most serious disputes appear to have arisen in situations in which family-owned bottling operations became prosperous enough to engage in profits-leisure trade-offs.

[42] Observe that these specific investments were not introduced primarily to motivate the franchisees to maintain quality, as suggested, for example, by Klein's (1980) discussion of franchise contracts. Rather, the investments were required to develop the local market. The nature of the contractual arrangements, on the other hand, was designed to protect those investments.

stimulated the move to captive distribution. We discuss the major factors of importance behind this move in turn.

5.1. New Environment

The Increase in Size and Complexity of Bottling Operations

As discussed earlier, the increase in economies of scale, the reduction in transportation costs,[43] and the increase in the number of products and packages distributed and introduced in the typical territory are behind the substantial growth in size and complexity of the typical bottler in the past two decades. The increasing importance of promotion via local and regional television, radio, and newspapers, which typically had coverage beyond an individual bottler's territory, also created incentives for bottlers in the same area to consolidate. These factors led to the creation of large regional bottlers—fewer that 15 percent as many bottling plants exist today as in 1950. The larger bottlers control the bulk of all soft drink production, with 192 accounting for two-thirds of all industry sales.[44]

Prior to the recent trend of bottler acquisitions by Coca-Cola and Pepsi, consolidation of independent bottlers resulted in advantages and disadvantages for the parent CMs. A major advantage was that the CM dealt with fewer bottlers, reducing the number of parties with which to negotiate. Consolidation, however, occurred at the same time as a rapid expansion of products, packages, promotions, and an increased sophistication required in marketing. As we will see, the net effects of these changes were a need for much more coordination between the CM and its bottlers, but a reduced ability to implement such coordination. In 1950, when Coca-Cola and Pepsi-Cola had many more bottlers, each CM handled a single product in a few different package types, and advertising and promotions changed infrequently. By 1980, the number of bottlers had dramatically fallen, but far greater coordination was required to implement much more complex strategies for the more than 10-fold increase in products and packages and an even greater increase in the frequency of promotions. A simple measure of the complexity of coordination is the sheer number of separate items that must be coordinated (one measure is the number of bottlers times the number of products times the number of packages times the number of different promotions per period). By this measure, the complexity of Pepsi's and Coca-Cola's distribution systems had dramatically increased from 1950 to 1980 (see Muris, Schieffman, and Spiller, 1993). Besides the dramatic increase in this static measure of complexity, the pace of change also had dramatically increased. Finally, this simple measure of coordination complexity does not take into account the fact that many of the marketing tactics requiring coordination, such as product and package

---

[43] The demise of returnable bottles also reduced effective transportation costs.

[44] Beverage Marketing, *U.S. Soft Drink Market & Packaging Report* (1989: 197).

introductions, etc., were much more complicated than the tactics of only a few decades ago.

Besides the increased complexity of the demands on the distribution system, the now larger bottling operations exacerbated a long-standing problem, namely, that there are always some bottlers who operate according to their own philosophies and strategies, even when this mode of operation conflicts seriously with the operation of a national distribution system. Problems of this kind became more costly with larger bottlers. One substantial bottler who refuses to cooperate in selling to a major fountain customer (e.g., because the bottler does not like the terms) that overlaps several bottler's territories can lose that account for the whole bottling network. Similarly, one substantial bottler who refuses to participate in a particular promotion with a large supermarket chain (or a mass merchandiser such as Kmart or a major fast-food franchisor such as Burger King) may cripple or even kill the whole promotion. And successful implementation of the fast-moving tactics arising from the new strategies of Coca-Cola and Pepsi-Cola required quick, effective execution through their natural distribution systems. But the independent bottler remained contractual king in its now larger territory (or multiterritory operation).

The simplicity of the bottlers' contracts, although having certain advantages to the viability of the independent bottling systems, as discussed earlier, do not provide the CMs with much leverage to bring uncooperative bottlers into line. Historically, the CM has had no direct, contractual means of altering the behavior of independent bottlers, absent buying out the bottlers (which sometimes has been very difficult). The contracts, for example, lack particular provisions dealing with the performance of the bottler or CM. Instead, the bottlers maintain (except in the most egregious cases of poor market performance) de facto perpetual, exclusive property rights in their territories, and they receive assurances about the price of concentrate.[45] In the first decades of the industry, with one product, few packages, and infrequent changes in advertising and promotions campaigns, the lack of CM leverage over its bottlers, although a problem, was not fatal. In the new environment, which requires close cooperation of the CM and the distribution system, the lack of CM leverage over its independent bottlers is a serious impediment to effective distribution.[46]

The increased size of the bottlers made them individually more critical to the operation of the distribution system, greatly raising the costs of uncooperative or opportunistic behavior. One benefit, however, of the increase in economies of scale in bottling is that a CM can now have a captive distribution system without having to manage hundreds of separate bottling facilities. In addition, in comparison with the first few decades of the industry,

[45] In essence, the bottler is assured that all bottlers will be treated similarly and that the CM will not adjust price unilaterally and arbitrarily.

[46] The problems posed by the inability of a CM to control its distribution system are seen most clearly in a comparison of the performance of Coke and Pepsi in the fountain channel, discussed later.

the CM now enjoys the advantages of modern telecommunications and transportation systems and of advanced financial controls that make feasible the management of a number of geographically separated manufacturing operations.

The Importance of Large Accounts

In the past 20 years, the size of large retail and fountain accounts among CSD customers has increased substantially (see Muris, Scheffman, and Spiller, 1993). Even though bottlers and their territories have grown, sales to large customers whose purchases overlap many bottling territories have become increasingly prominent because of the increase in the number of such buyers and their interest in purchasing on a wide geographic basis. Three types of large customers are particularly important: major supermarket chains, other major retail chains such as convenience stores and mass merchandisers (e.g., Wal-Mart), and major fast-food franchisors. As discussed earlier, when a bottler's actions result in spillovers outside its own territory, disputes about the relative contributions of the CM and the involved bottlers to joint profitability will be especially difficult to resolve. The increasing importance of large accounts covering several bottlers' territories is a major source of increased spillovers.

Standardization of terms (delivery, pricing, promotions, etc.) involves cooperation between the CM and all relevant bottlers. Bottlers can (and do) differ significantly in, among other things, their pricing stragegies. Because of the bottlers' contracts and the antitrust law governing resale price maintenance, a CM cannot order its bottlers to adopt a common pricing strategy. As a result, it can be difficult, and sometimes impossible, for the CM to develop a promotion that can be standardized across a major customer's outlets. The intransigence of a few large independent bottlers, or even of one crucial bottler, can cripple the CM's ability to compete with another CM that can offer a standardized promotion through a captive distribution system. As a consequence of these problems, concentrate manufacturers found that they could respond more quickly to the needs of large retailers through their own company bottlers than through independent bottlers. One result has been that company bottlers are often more aggressive and efficient than the independents they replaced, a phenomenon industry observers have noted.[47]

The Growing Sophistication of Customers

The enhanced sophistication of all customers, particularly the larger ones, has increased the inherent disadvantages of independent bottling. For example, checkout line scanners give supermarkets and other mass merchandisers information about CSD sales that was unavailable to them

---

[47] See, for example, *Beverage Marketing U.S. Soft Drink Marketing and Packaging Report* (1989: 203). Our statistical analysis of company versus independent bottlers later in this article provides evidence of this phenomenon.

even 10 years ago—information that they have become quite sophisticated in using. If a chain customer uses such information to demand (or resist) a certain promotion, particularly one that crosses territories, the seller without similar sophistication in sales and promotion analysis is at a disadvantage. While many independent bottlers quickly adapted their operation to this new technology, others have been slow to develop the necessary sophistication. Finally, most bottlers have been traditionally averse to sharing sales information with their CM or with other bottlers, making it difficult to deal with large buyers, because the CM would not have information about sales and promotions at the customer level, information that would be useful for monitoring performance.

5.2. New Strategies

Product and Package Introductions

The new product strategies of Coca-Cola and Pepsi-Cola have resulted in the introduction of many new soft drinks since 1970, with the most successful new product, Diet Coke, introduced in the last decade. Despite these successes, most new products or new packages fail,[48] and this low success rate has important implications for the nature of the relationship between CMs and their bottlers. The success of product introductions hinges, first, on the ability of a manufacturer to convince retailers to take on the product and market it effectively and, ultimately, on consumer acceptance. Concentrate manufacturers face an additional hurdle in introducing a new product or package—they must convince their independent bottlers to handle the new item.[49]

Independent bottlers have conflicting incentives about the introduction of new products or packages. They would generally be willing to handle successful products, but have reduced incentives to bear any of the costs of finding out whether a product will be successful. Ideally, a bottler would like to introduce only successful products; consequently, the bottler has an incentive to wait to see whether the experiences of other bottlers prove that consumers desire the new product.

To gauge consumer reaction at the least possible cost and to minimize losses if the new version fails, most products are test-marketed during their development. A typical large grocery manufacturer will choose particular markets within which to test the supermarket and consumer acceptance of a

---

[48] See "Marketing," *Wall Street Journal*, at B1 (Oct. 9, 1990); see also Kotler (1984: 311). Failure rates for new consumer goods are estimated to be from 40 percent to over 50 percent.

[49] Unlike Pepsi-Cola and Coca-Cola, the typical large manufacturer of nationally branded food products makes all the major decisions regarding the introduction of new products. Such manufacturers determine the extent and nature of advertising and promotion and arrange distribution through captive or controlled distributors. Although a major grocery manufacturer faces the difficult task of convincing supermarkets to handle new products, and convincing consumers to purchase them, it does not have to convince its distribution system to handle the product. See Muris, Scheffman, and Spiller (1993).

new product. Without company-owned bottlers, however, Pepsi-Cola and Coca-Cola have to pick a *bottler*, not a market, because a particular test market is not possible unless the bottler in that area cooperates. Given the bottlers' perpetual, exclusive territories, the ability of CMs to influence recalcitrant bottlers to participate in test marketing or other aspects of product introductions is limited. Thus, complex negotiations often have been required to obtain the cooperation of recalcitrant bottlers, and in some cases, the CM has had to compromise on the desired market or on its strategy.[50]

Investments in product and package introductions (by the CM and the cooperating bottlers) are specific. Unless the parties bearing these specific investments can capture the potential benefits, there is a disincentive to make the necessary expenditures. In theory, a CM might resolve this problem by paying its bottlers for their expenditures in the introduction of new products or packages. In practice, however, such a resolution may be difficult. A major potential problem is that bottler actions have important spillovers, and the CM and affected bottlers may not agree on the value of various bottlers' contributions to the common goal. For this and other reasons,[51] Coca-Cola and Pepsi-Cola have increasingly found it easier to introduce new products and packages in markets in which the company owns the bottlers.

Advertising and Promotion

Another component of the new competitive strategies of the major CMs is their increasingly complex and sophisticated advertising and promotions—a major tactic in the "Cola Wars." Coca-Cola and Pepsi-Cola constantly strive to devise advertising campaigns that best each other. But the ultimate success of these campaigns often depends on the cooperation of the bottlers in implementing the campaign in their territories. Bottlers must cooperate by arranging media spot coverage in their territory and by implementing promotions and pricing for their customers that build on the timing and theme of the national advertising campaign. Bottlers also must provide the CM with information on their sales, efforts, and the reactions of their customers, so that the CM can accurately assess the effectiveness of the campaign. In some cases, individual bottlers will not arrange spot coverage because they disagree with a given campaign.[52] In other cases, some bottlers decline to provide the local "push" (discount pricing) necessary to translate a successful national campaign into sales in their territories. In still other cases, independent bottlers have been reluctant to share sales information with their CM and with each other. Failures in bottler cooperation can significantly impair the success of a major advertising campaign, especially when the bottler involved has a media market that spills over into adjoining

---

[50] Pepsi felt, for example, that the success of its Slice brand of fruit-juice-added soft drinks was undermined by bottler reluctance to carry the brand or, at least, some particular flavors.

[51] For example, the time of the bottler's top management is limited. Introduction of a new product will require use of time that the bottler may feel is better spent elsewhere.

[52] This has been a problem for the celebrity advertising campaigns of the major CMs.

bottlers' territories, or when the bottler's full effort is necessary to create a targeted promotion for a major supermarket chain or fast-food franchisor.

One of the most successful promotions of an established product in history, "The Pepsi Challenge," provides striking confirmation of the importance of bottler coordination and of the difficulty of attaining such coordination.[53] The success of the Challenge depended crucially on bottler execution as well as on the strength of the advertisments. For bottlers to meet new consumer demand from the Challenge and Coca-Cola's expected response, they had to be prepared to place spots effectively, supply retailers with adequate product and displays, develop and execute effective local price promotions, and discuss their results in detail with Pepsi-Cola to help fine-tune the campaign. But the Challenge was a declaration of war on Coca-Cola—a war that some bottlers were not interested in declaring or waging vigorously. Because many independent bottlers resisted participating in the Challenge initially, Pepsi-Cola introduced the campaign through its "bottler-of-the-last-resort," the Pepsi-Cola Bottling Group. Even when the Challenge was demonstrated to be extraordinarily successful, Pepsi still found significant resistance to the Challenge by some of its independent bottlers. Indeed, some independent bottlers, not wanting the participate in the campaign, ran local advertising that did not mention the Challenge at all.

Another problem with promotions is that effective coordination is typically required over large (multiterritory) accounts.[54] The growth of large super-market chains and other large mass merchandisers (Kmart, etc.) has increased the need for negotiations between the CM and the chains to arrange chain-wide promotions. Because bottler territories are frequently smaller than the areas served by large suppermarket chains and other large mass merchandisers, the CM typically must negotiate with multiple bottlers to obtain their mutual participation in a chain-wide promotion. Again, the bottler has the freedom to resist, or to refuse to participate. On some occasions, manufacturers have been forced to make special concessions to recalcitrant bottlers to obtain participation. (Of course, the manufacturer attempts to restrict information about such concessions, because making them to all bottlers could make a promotion unprofitable for the CM.)

5.3. The Role of Allied Brands

There is one other important feature of the CSD industry that we have thus far not discussed—bottlers often handle "allied brands," that is brands of

[53] The "Pepsi Challenge" was launched in 1974 in Dallas, Texas, a predominantly Coca-Cola market. The Challenge presented results of comparative tests that showed a significant preference for the taste of Pepsi. This advertising campaign was perhaps the single most important Pepsi tactic in the Cola Wars in helping Pepsi close the gap with Coke.

[54] See, for example, *Beverage Industry Annual Manual* (1989: 78 (quoting a Pepsi official that several "customers want one Pepsi contact").

competing CMs (but not directly competing products).[55] Although it may appear unusual for a distribution system to carry the products of competitors, such an arrangement is common in food brokerage (and in other industries served by brokers and jobbers). The same broker does not, however, handle close, direct competitors.[56] A broker of frozen food products, for example, might carry the packaged ice cream of one manufacturer and the ice cream bars of another. No manufacturer, other things equal, wants its distribution system to handle a competitor's products. Even handling products that are not directly in competition is a disadvantage because all products, particularly new products, are competing for scarce shelf space. Economies of scale in distribution, however, often require joint distribution to keep costs manageable.[57]

In the CSD industry, scale economies in both manufacturing and distribution are important. Multiple brands can be bottled at less cost in larger plants. Major-brand soft drinks, like many grocery products, are delivered directly to the store. A CM that sells only a small amount to an individual store may find it impossible to have an otherwise desirable captive distribution system. Thus, many allied brands with small sales have found it profitable to seek distribution through the bottlers of other CMs rather than developing their own independent or captive distribution systems.

The only restriction on allied brands in the contracts of independent Coke and Pepsi bottlers is on carrying directly competitive soft drinks, particularly other colas. The lack of restrictions on other soft drink products allowed the independent bottling systems to evolve in a manner somewhat like food brokerage in that the independent bottlers took on allied brands that were not in as direct competition with the "parent" CMs, as were other colas. Thus, the bottlers, the cola CMs, and the CMs of allied brands could take advantage of economies of scale in bottling and distribution. Of course, the more allied brands handled by the independent bottlers, the more difficult for the CMs to introduce products directly competing with those brands. Unlike grocery manufacturers who use food brokers and can simply change brokers if a conflict arises because of a product introduction, Coca-Cola and Pepsi-Cola were stuck with their distribution system.

Antitrust authorities have expressed some concern that the shift to captive distribution could, in theory, harm the allied brands. The evidence suggests, however, that the allied brands have prospered under captive distribution.[58] The captive bottlers benefit from the same efficiencies of handling allied brands as do independent bottlers. Moreover, the allied brands benefit from

---

[55] For the two leading CMs these are noncola brands of soft drinks they do not own, such as 7UP, Dr. Pepper, Orange Crush, etc.

[56] The nature and duties of food brokers are discussed in detail in Muris Scheffman, and Spiller (1993). See also *Food Broker Facts*.

[57] This is also true, of course, of captive distribution systems.

[58] Other studies indicate that captive bottling increases sales of allied brands. See Muris, Scheffman, and Spiller (1993).

the increased efficiency of a captive bottling system. Of course, either the cola or allied brand CM could attempt to exploit the joint dependence between the captive bottlers and the allied brands. The parties, however, have avoided the rigidities of perpetual, exclusive relationships; instead, they have recognized their joint dependence and acted to the mutual benefit of their partner.

5.4. Summary

The new environment and the new strategies of Coke and Pepsi increasingly presented problems for the independent bottling systems, problems that can be summarized as "increased transaction costs." Major factors reducing the efficiency of the independent bottling systems include the following: the growing size and complexity of the CSD industry and of the typical bottling operation, the increased importance of large customers, the greater sophistication of the customers, the increased importance of spillovers, the need to introduce new products and packaging, and the nature of modern product promotion. The CM's strategies have been undermined because bottler cooperation in the implementation of the strategies has become critical for success; yet the increased complexity of the industry wrought by changes in the external environment has reduced the CM's ability to achieve such cooperation.

These problems are perhaps seen most starkly in the price-fixing cases brought against independent bottlers in the late 1980s (see Muris, Scheffman, and Spiller, 1993). None of these cases involved company bottlers. Both Coca-Cola and Pepsi-Cola, with a national and long-run view of the CSD industry, declared and have continued to wage the "Cola Wars," using discounting as a major tactic. Although real prices of soft drinks fell throughout the 1980s, the Cola Wars have been profitable (for Coca-Cola and Pepsi, and efficient bottlers) because they helped fuel an explosive growth in per capita soft drink consumption. Nevertheless, executives of several independent bottlers have tried to opt out of the increased competitive climate through attempting to fix prices.

Captive distribution is a better organization (i.e., lower transaction costs) for dealing with the new competitive environment and strategies of the leading CMs. The increase in economies of scale in bottling in recent years means that a captive bottling system is now viable. The difficulty of managing the more than 1,000 bottling plants of past decades thus has been ameliorated—Pepsi-Cola, for example, now has 63 company-owned plants, which account for about half of its sales. Further, modern communications, transportation, and financial controls greatly reduce the costs and risks of operating geographically dispersed bottling operations. The net effect of the increased mismatch of the independent bottling systems with the new strategies and environment and the reduced costs of captive bottling has been the move to captive bottling by the two leading CMs.

Thus, the move to captive bottling is an example of structure following strategy.[59]

6. EMPIRICAL TESTS

We have hypothesized that the organization of distribution through independent bottlers arose and survived, despite inherent disadvantages, because the costs of operating a captive bottling network with hundreds of geographically separated bottling and delivery operations were prohibitive. We further hypothesized that the costs of distribution through a system of independent bottlers with exclusive perpetual territories became much larger in recent decades because of the new competitive environment and the new strategies of the leading CMs, while the costs of operating a captive national bottling system have declined. One test of these hypotheses arises from a comparison of the organization and performance of fountain and bottled soft drink distribution.

6.1. Fountain Distribution

Although in recent years Pepsi-Cola has drawn even with Coca-Cola in sales of bottled (and canned) soft drinks in supermarkets, where both companies, until recently, distributed through their independent bottling systems, Coke still has a huge lead in fountain sales.[60] Coca-Cola has always had a captive distribution system in fountain, while Pepsi-Cola's bottlers began with exclusive, perpetual rights to fountain distribution in their territories. Although, after many years of negotiation, Pepsi has reached some accommodation (discussed later) with its bottlers on dealing with some major fountain customers, Pepsi remains at a significant disadvantage to its major competitor.[61] From the start, Coca-Cola's fountain distribution system was similar to that of many other grocery manufacturers of the time: It employed company or independent salesmen who operated under the direction of Coca-Cola. Unlike bottling, this system was possible because of economies of scale in syrup production. The much higher value to weight and volume ratios of fountain syrup permitted the centralization of manufacturing into a relatively few plants. Moreover, compared to bottled soft drinks, there is a much more modest scale and frequency of deliveries required in fountain.

---

[59] More precisely, the interaction between the costs of transacting and the efficacy of the new marketing strategies under the different forms of organizing distribution has led to captive distribution.

[60] In 1987, for example, Coca-Cola sold nearly twice the volume of Pepsi-Cola through fountain sales. See Muris, Scheffman, and Spiller (1993).

[61] Another disadvantage for Pepsi-Cola is that parent PepsiCo is the country's largest fast-food franchisor (Pizza Hut, Taco Bell, and Kentucky Fried Chicken), which provides some disincentive for other franchisors to sell Pepsi products. Before PepsiCo purchased these firms, however, Coke's lead in fountain was even larger than today.

Coca-Cola's fountain distribution system is consistent with our hypothesis that independent bottling arose because it was impossible to have a captive distribution system involving hundreds of geographically dispersed local manufacturing and delivery operations. Because fountain distribution did not place these demands on a captive system, Coca-Cola retained fountain rights and has dominated this channel ever since.[62]

Today, fountain is an increasingly important distribution channel. For example, Coca-Cola sold in McDonald's restaurants represents about 5 percent of all Coca-Cola sales. Because Pepsi bottlers have had more control over fountain distribution than their Coke competitors, Pepsi-Cola has been at a significant disadvantage to Coca-Cola in fountain distribution. Coca-Cola can arrange fountain distribution in any manner it deems appropriate, and can deal directly with a large fountain account on all terms of a deal.[63] The rise of large fast-food franchisors in the past few decades increased the disadvantages of Pepsi-Cola relative to its main rival in competing for large fountain accounts. For example, some large accounts want syrup delivered through their warehouses rather than via direct "store" delivery, and Coca-Cola has no difficulty in arranging such delivery through its fountain distribution system. During the last two decades, Pepsi's contract with its bottlers was modified in a manner that *apparently* gave the CM the right to organize fountain sales to multiterritory accounts; however, it took years for Pepsi and its bottlers to negotiate an interpretation of this clause that could be implemented.[64]

Although these changes in Pepsi's fountain distribution have allowed it to make some headway against its main rival, Pepsi-Cola still does not have the flexibility of Coca-Cola's controlled fountain distribution. Coca-Cola has complete freedom to adjust its fountain distribution to the needs and preferences of fountain customers. About one-half of the top 50 chains that sell Coca-Cola are serviced through warehouses owned by independent wholesalers. Unlike the warehouses covered by Pepsi's Syrup Appointment contracts, these warehouses are free to sell to *any* customers with whom they reach agreement. These so-called open commissaries are not possible in Pepsi's fountain distribution system because of its contracts with bottlers. Unless bottler support is achieved for allowing sales through open

---

[62] The reason for Pepsi's decision to grant fountain rights to its bottlers is unclear. Pepsi-Cola's initial disadvantage vis-à-vis Coca-Cola may have prompted Pepsi to give up the rights to its fountain business in order to entice potential bottlers.

[63] Although a Coke bottler may distribute fountain syrup to some customers in its territory, this is done under the direction and control of parent Coca-Cola.

[64] Paragraph 10 of Pepsi's Syrup Appointment provided: "That the company reserves the right to sell Beverage Company Syrup to chain or multiple-outlet operations and vending machine operations in the Territory. Except as above provided in this paragraph, the Bottler's right to sell Beverage Syrup in Territory shall be exclusive." The bottlers feared that they would lose control over not only fountain, but also supermarket sales. Moreover, fountain sales involve spillovers that make it difficult to assess the relative contributions of the participants to the sales. In 1984 a new paragraph 10 of the Syrup Appointment was issued, covering 62 lines of small print, compared to the three of the previous version.

commissaries, the Pepsi system will continue to be at a disadvantage to the Coca-Cola system.

Another disadvantage in fountain distribution for Pepsi relative to Coca-Cola is Pepsi's difficulty in offering a single national fountain account the same set of products across all that account's outlets. Cocal-Cola, for example, can offer Sprite across the country, even if all its bottlers do not handle Sprite (as a few do not), because Coca-Cola does not have to use its bottlers for fountain distribution. Pepsi-Cola, on the other hand, must arrange fountain distribution through its bottlers, which differ in the brand of lemon-lime flavored soft drink they carry.

In summary, the fact that from the start Coca-Cola had a captive fountain distribution system is consistent with our hypothesis that independent bottling resulted from the impossibility of operating a captive distribution system with hundreds of geographically dispersed manufacturing and delivery operations. Although Pepsi eventually caught its rival in supermarket sales, Pepsi still lags far behind in fountain sales. This result supports our hypothesis that the independent distribution systems are less efficient than captive distribution. The greater flexibility afforded Coca-Cola in fountain by its captive distribution system, the increased requirements for flexibility dictated by current market realities, and Coca-Cola's superior performance in fountain, all support the hypotheses that the increased complexity of the competitive environment and the new strategies of the major CMs create significant advantages for captive distribution.[65]

6.2. The Price Effects of Bottler Acquisitions[66]

If the recent move to captive distribution is indeed driven by the need to cope with increased transaction costs in an efficent manner, and if the relative efficiency of captive distribution is significant, we would expect this relative efficiency to be reflected in lower prices. This section presents statistical estimates of how retail prices (or their rate of change) vary between markets

[65] The practices of other grocery manufacturers provide additional proof of the superiority of captive distribution. As discussed in Muris, Scheffman, and Spiller (1993), most major branded grocery products are distributed through captive distribution systems. Almost all of the rest of the products are distributed through food brokers, who do not take title, do not determine prices or promotions, and are terminable at will, usually on a 30-day basis. (Like Pepsi and Coke, several of the products involved are distributed directly to the customers' stores, rather than to warehouses.) There are virtually no other major branded, nationally advertised grocery products whose distributors have the independence and protections of the independent bottlers of Pepsi and Coke. In addition, virtually no other branded, nationally advertised product requires the number of geographically diffuse production and distribution systems required in the soft drink industry. In recent years, however, the soft-drink industry has become much more like other grocery product categories in product and marketing strategies. And the costs of captive distribution have fallen as the increase in economies of scale in bottling has resulted in a much smaller number of bottlers being able to handle most of the distribution of Coca-Cola and Pepsi-Cola.

[66] The data for this section were obtained from accessing Pepsi-Cola's Nielsen Scantract data set.

where Pepsi has an ownership interest in the bottling operation (company owned, COBO, or joint venture, JV) and markets where a purely independent (franchise) bottler (FOBO) handles Pepsi. Although retailers determine retail prices, if the move to captive distribution has lowered costs and increased agressiveness at wholesale, the price on the supermarket shelf should reflect these changes.

Our estimates are based on data covering the period from February 1987 to September 1989 derived from the Nielsen Scantrack data base, which are aggregated from supermarket scanner data into Nielsen Scantrack Market Areas.[67] To provide estimates of the effects of captive distribution on prices, we use these data to contrast FOBO, COBO, and JV markets, and markets in which ownership recently changed hands. To contrast the different Pepsi markets, the total set of 48 Scantrack markets was divided into four categories:

1. Markets that had COBO or JV bottlers well before and after September 1987: Boston, Dallas, Detroit, Houston, Indianapolis, Los Angeles, Orlando, Philadelphia, Phoenix, Pittsburgh.

2. Markets that had FOBO bottlers well before and after September 1987: Birmingham, Buffalo, Columbus, Nashville, Raleigh.

3. Markets that had COBO or JV bottlers by September 1987 but had FOBO bottlers during part of the previous two years: Atlanta, Cleveland, Jacksonville, Miami, Minneapolis, Salt Lake City, St. Louis, San Francisco, Tulsa/Oklahoma City.

4. Markets that changed from FOBO to COBO or JV bottlers after September 1987: the remaining 24 cities. (Table 13.1 provides a list of all Scantrack markets.)

The next section presents estimates of the effect of a change in bottler ownership status during the study period. We find that the effect of a change of a FOBO Pepsi bottler to a COBO or to a JV is a statistically significant reduction in the bottler's prices of about 3–5 percent, consistent with our hypothesis that a captive bottler is more efficient and/or aggressive. We then analyze the price effects of a Pepsi (or Coke) COBO in a market on its Coke (or Pepsi) competitor's prices. We find that the presence of either a Coke or Pepsi COBO in a market leads to a statistically significant reduction in competitor prices of about 6 percent. These results suggest that the presence of a COBO bottler in a local market, either Pepsi or Coke, results in more aggressive pricing.

In the last part of this section, we compare markets that had stable ownership of the Pepsi bottler (either COBO or FOBO) before and during

---

[67] Thus, when we discuss particular cities later, we are using Nielsen's Scantrack Market concept of the city. Scantrack Market Areas are usually similar in scope to SMSAs, but in some cases they encompass more than a city. This creates the additional problem that soft drink bottlers' areas may not be identical to Scantrack's.

TABLE 13.1
Single-Equation Estimation for All 48 Cities[a]

CONSTANT	−0.0134603	−0.0133853
	(−1.3892776)	(−1.3805158)
DLPEPUS	0.9019304	0.8977921
	(7.8277168)	(7.7443406)
DOWNERSHIP	−0.0416335	—
	(−2.3207277)	—
DPBG	—	−0.0493543
	—	(−1.6966927)
DJOINT	—	−0.0375882
	—	(−1.7412573)
DTEMP	0.0015810	0.0015785
	(2.7815530)	(2.7754874)
DUNEMP	−0.0009936	−0.0009074
	(−0.2036061)	(−0.1855984)
FM87	−0.0236469	−0.0237705
	(−1.2153333)	(−1.2208861)
AM87	−0.0014629	−0.0015590
	(−0.0975842)	(−0.1039253)
JJ87	0.0006872	0.0006307
	(0.0478478)	(0.0438946)
AS87	0.0227241	0.0226470
	(1.4929710)	(1.4870288)
ON87	0.0183102	0.0181765
	(1.0768975)	(1.0682300)
DJ88	0.0356514	0.0351306
	(2.1348320)	(2.0937192)
FM88	0.0120354	0.0122868
	(0.8780512)	(0.8946507)
AM88	−0.0070504	−0.0071898
	(−0.5234681)	(−0.5333123)
JJ88	−0.0038752	−0.0039459
	(−0.2951386)	(−0.3003398)
AS88	0.0412732	0.0410983
	(2.7639551)	(2.7492663)
ON88	0.0039303	0.0039248
	(0.2405906)	(0.2401368)
DJ89	0.0203857	0.0202745
	(1.2744523)	(1.2666226)
FM89	0.0031849	0.0031576
	(0.2283620)	(0.2262959)
R^2	0.083924	0.084036
S.E. of regression	0.086730	0.086772
F statistic	5.000937	4.724917
Log-likelihood	976.6937	979.7518

Dependent variable: DLPEPRICE: period: 2/87–6/89; Number of observations: 946.
Variable definitions for all tables are provided in the appendix.

[a] All references to the sample cities or Scantrack markets encompassed by this study include the following: Albany, Atlanta, Baltimore/Washington, Birmingham, Boston, Buffalo/Rochester, Charlotte, Chicago, Cincinnati, Cleveland, Columbus, Dallas, Denver, Des Moines, Detroit, Grand Rapids, Hartford, Houston, Indianapolis, Jacksonville, Kansas City, Little Rock, Los Angeles, Louisville, Memphis, Miami, Milwaukee, Minneapolis, Nashville, Norfolk/Mobile, New York, Metro Oklahoma City/Tulsa, Omaha, Philadeplphia, Phoenix, Pittsburg, Portland, Raleigh/Durham, Richmond/Norfolk, Sacramento, St. Louis, Salt Lake City/Boise, San Antonio, San Diego, San Francisco, Seattle, Svracuse, and Tampa.

the sample period to markets where the bottler changed from FOBO to COBO shortly before the beginning of the sample period. Some bottlers had experienced problems before being acquired by PepsiCo, such as small territories, disputes among the owners, or difficulties in (or reluctance to) adjusting to the new competitive environment. Thus, one would expect that the FOBO bottlers that PepsiCo acquired first were, on average, less efficient and/or less cooperative than other independent Pepsi bottlers. A bottler's inefficiency and uncooperativeness would be expected to be refected in higher prices[68] and, therefore, lower sales, other things equal.

Other research on the conversion of bottlers to captive operations indicates that conversion of a FOBO to an efficient, integrated COBO takes some time (Muris, Scheffman, and Spiller, 1993). Given the brevity of our data's time span (31 months), bottlers that were recently acquired and converted to COBOs would be expected, therefore, to be inefficient relative to older COBOs.[69] Our analysis below finds that recently acquired Pepsi-Cola bottlers indeed do have higher prices, suggesting that those bottlers, as FOBOs, had higher costs or less aggressive pricing strategies, and that the Pepsi-Cola captive bottling organization may have had insufficient time to implement all the required cost reductions. That cost reductions are in fact made is confirmed by our analysis of the former Denver and St. Louis FOBOs (Muris, Scheffman, and Spiller, 1993), and by the lower prices in markets with a well-established Pepsi-Cola COBO. Finally, we also find that recently formed COBOs show a markedly lower degree of coordination with the rest of the Pepsi-Cola bottling system (FOBO and COBO). This result is consistent with the hypothesis that acquired bottlers are those that were relatively inefficient or uncooperative,[70] and that implementing changes in the bottling operation takes time.

To summarize, the overall results of this analysis of price effects are consistent with our hypothesis that Pepsi-Cola has acquired, on average, high-cost, high-price bottlers that were insufficiently cooperative with Pepsi-Cola. Although improving such bottler operations requires time, Pepsi-Cola has ultimately made them more efficient and competitive. In particular, the results indicate that the presence of an established Pepsi-Cola or Coca-Cola COBO in a local market leads to more aggressive pricing in that market.

---

[68] One significant problem typical of uncooperative bottlers was their disinterest in aggressive price promotions.

[69] To the extent that Pepsi-Cola and Coca-Cola purchased relatively ineffieient FOBOs, recently acquired FOBOs might also be less efficient, on average, than other FOBOs. This issue will be discussed later.

[70] Recall that the cooperation of bottlers is needed not just in coordinating promotions with national chains (e.g., McDonald's, Kmart), but also with regional chains (e.g., supermarkets), as well as in the introduction of new products and packages. Retail prices are affected by all these activities, in particular, supermarket prices. Thus, the prices in our data set, which are obtained from supermarket retail transactions, should reflect the differences in coordination across bottlers and markets.

Price Determination in 48 Scantrack Markets

In this section we present estimates of the retail price effects of a change of a bottler's status from FOBO to COBO or to a joint venture with Pepsi-Cola. The whole applicable Scantrack data set for the 48 cities studied is used in this analysis, yielding a total of 31 monthly price observations across the 48 cities.[71] We estimate pooled cross-section time-series equations of the following form:

$$DLPEPRICE = \alpha_1 + \alpha_2 * DOWNERSHIP + \alpha_3 * DTEMP$$
$$+ \alpha_4 * DUNEMP + \alpha_5 * DLPEPUS + \alpha_6 * SEASONAL$$

$$(1)$$

This equation measures the (percentage) change in price in a local bottling market as a function of any period-to-period variation in ownership status, of period-to-period and over-cities changes in temperature and unemployment, of the period-to-period change in national average Pepsi-Cola (regular brand) price, plus some seasonal dummies to reflect variations in demand. The dummy variable DOWNERSHIP takes a value of 1 if a market changed from FOBO to COBO or JV, a value of zero if it had no change, and a value of -1 if it moved from JV or COBO to FOBO. The α_i's are the parameters to be estimated. DLPEPRICE and DLPEPUS are the first differences of the logarithms of Pepsi-Cola price in the bottling territory and the whole United States, respectively. DTEMP and DUNEMP are the first differences of temperature and unempolyment rates, respectively, and SEASONAL is a set of seasonal dummy variables.

A first-difference equation such as eq. (1) allows us to eliminate some types of market-specific unobservable factors that affect prices. For example, local or national economic factors affecting soft drink prices that do not change significantly over the period "drop out" of an equation in first differences. Finally, to perform this estimation the observations are stacked so that the first N observations (where N reflects the number of cities in the particular sample) reflect the values of the variable for each city for the first time period, the next N observations are for each city for the second time period, and so on.

The results are presented in Table 13.1. The first column of Table 13.1 explores the effects of a change in ownership away from FOBO. The estimated effect of a change in a bottler's status from FOBO to COBO or JV (captured by the estimated coefficient for DOWNERSHIP) is a reduction in the Pepsi-Cola price in that bottling territory of approximately 4 percent. This result is statistically significant at standard levels. The second column

---

[71] As discussed previously, these data cover the period February 1987 to September 1989. Weekly Scantrack data are available, but the other data required for our estimations are only available monthly. Therefore, we created a monthly Scantrack series by choosing the retail price for the middle week of the month.

of Table 13.1 explores whether the effect of a price reduction differs when the FOBO's ownership change is to a JV rather than to a COBO. While the point estimate of a move to COBO ownership (represented by the estimated coefficient for the variable DPBG) is larger in absolute value than that representing a change to JV ownership (JV) (-5 percent compared to -4 percent), this difference is not statistically significant.

These results, then, are consistent with our hypothesis that Pepsi-Cola has chosen inefficient, high-cost, high-price bottlers to acquire or to join in a joint venture. The result of Pepsi-Cola's taking an ownership interest in such bottlers has been a reduction in retail prices.

The Effect of COBOS on Competitor Prices

We now analyze the effect of the presence of a Pepsi-Cola or Coca-Cola COBO in a market on its Coke or Pepsi-Cola competitor's prices. Our analysis in section 5 indicates that the factors driving Coca-Cola and Pepsi-Cola to captive distribution are the same. Thus, either a Pepsi-Cola or Coca-Cola COBO in an area should make a market more competitive, other things equal. The analysis is divided into three parts: the effect of changes in Pepsi-Cola bottler ownership on Coca-Cola prices, the effect of Coca-Cola and Pepsi-Cola COBOs on Coca-Cola prices, and the effect of Coca-Cola and Pepsi-Cola COBOs on Pepsi-Cola prices. The methodology developed in section 6.1 is used for each of these analyses.

Effect of a Change in Pepsi-Cola Bottler Ownership on Coca-Cola Prices. Table 13.2 presents the results of estimating, for the 48 Scantrack cities, equations that attempt to explain the percentage change in the price of Coke as a function of the percentage change in U.S. Coke price, of temperature and unemployment rates, and of dummy variables representing changes in the ownership structure of the associated Pepsi-Cola bottler.

Column 1 of Table 13.2 reports an equation that estimates the effect of a change in Pepsi-Cola ownership (the Pepsi-Cola ownership dummy variable, DOWNERSHIP, is represented by the change in Pepsi-Cola bottler status from FOBO to COBO or JV) on the price of Coke in the area. The effect of such change is about a 5 percent reduction in Coke price. This effect, however, is only statistically significant at 11 percent. Column 2 of Table 13.2 explores whether the type of ownership change matters, by breaking the ownership change into joint venture (DJOINT) or COBO (DPBG). We find that the effect of changing a FOBO Pepsi-Cola bottler to a JV (the coefficient of the variable DJOINT) implies a reduction of 6 percent in the price of Coke (statistically significant at 10 percent). Second, the change of a Pepsi-Cola FOBO to a COBO (the coefficient of the variable DPBG) implies a 3 percent reduction in the price of Coke. That effect, however, is not statistically significant. One reason, perhaps, for these statistically inconclusive results is that it takes time for Pepsi-Cola to turn around an inefficient bottling operation, and the data period available was not yet long enough for this change to have occurred. Another possible reason is that the

TABLE 13.2
Single-Equation Estimation for 48 Cities

CONSTANT	−0.0020604	−0.0023316
	(−0.1252892)	(−0.1416687)
DLCKUS	0.4582924	0.4563552
	(4.2362904)	(4.2147634)
DPBG	—	−0.0251311
	—	(−0.5197309)
DJOINT	—	−0.0579097
	—	(−1.6466645)
DOWNERSHIP	−0.0469641	—
	(−1.5955224)	—
DTEMP	0.0003545	0.0003578
	(0.3765278)	(0.3798565)
DUNEMP	0.0102640	0.0100916
	(1.2727414)	(1.2500223)
FM87	−0.0156020	−0.0152655
	(−0.4655562)	(−0.4552797)
AM87	−0.043562	−0.0041400
	(−0.1742542)	(−0.1655270)
JJ87	−0.0041366	−0.0039643
	(−0.1733350)	(−0.1660411)
AS87	−0.0067031	−0.0063950
	(−0.2551248)	(−0.2432615)
ON87	−0.0063063	−0.0060702
	(−0.2242953)	(−0.2157937)
DJ88	0.0354598	0.0372026
	(1.2520063)	(1.3054620)
FM88	−0.007799	−0.0015076
	(−0.0339082)	(−0.0654245)
AM88	−0.0199539	−0.0194374
	(−0.8899466)	(−0.8658867)
JJ88	−0.0083451	−0.0081291
	(−0.3819304)	(−0.3718558)
AS88	0.0059893	0.0061223
	(0.2427905)	(0.2480774)
ON88	0.0009431	0.0013321
	(0.0329045)	(0.0464466)
DJ89	−0.0006296	−0.0003170
	(−0.0234342)	(−0.0117905)
FM89	0.0060268	0.0062795
	(0.2537168)	(0.2642145)
R^2	0.042468	0.042804
S.E. of regression	0.143917	0.143970
F statistic	2.421160	2.302988
Log-likelihood	500.6067	500.7720

Dependent variable: DLCKPR Period: 2/87–6/89; Number of observations: 946.
Notes to Table 13.1 apply to Table 13.2.

most inefficient operations are acquired first rather than becoming joint ventures.

COBO Effects on Coca-Cola and Pepsi-Cola Prices in 24 Cities.

In this section we explore the effect of bottler ownership on competition in the 24 cities in which ownership was stable during the sample period. As discussed in the introduction to this section, these 24 sample cities were placed into three groups: those with stable COBO ownership, those with stable FOBO ownership, and those that changed from FOBO to COBO within two years prior to the beginning of the sample period (February 1987).

Table 13.3 presents estimates of pooled cross-sectional time series equations relating the local retail prices of Coca-Cola or Pepsi-Cola (in logs) to exogenous variables (the U.S. price of Coca-Cola and Pepsi-Cola, respectively, and local temperature, unemployment, and population growth) and to the ownership status of the Coca-Cola and Pepsi-Cola bottler in the area. Column 1 of Table 13.3 presents the determinants of the Coke price without any ownership variable. The terms AR(1) and AR(2) represent autoregressive parameters of order 1 and 2, respectively. Column 2 introduces two variables: INDEP, representing a city served by an independent Pepsi-Cola bottler; and FOCO, representing a city served by a bottler that changed ownership just prior to the same period. The omitted dummy variable, then, represents cities served by Pepsi-Cola COBOs. The results indicate that cities with an independent Pepsi-Cola bottler are estimated to have Coke prices that are 8 percent higher than cities that have a COBO Pepsi-Cola bottler (the estimated coefficient for the variable INDEP). The result is consistent with established Pepsi-Cola COBOs being more aggressive competitors than Pepsi-Cola FOBOs.

In Column 3 of Table 13.3 the variable ATLONC is introduced to represent the presence of at least one Pepsi-Cola or Coca-Cola COBO in the market. The purpose is to see whether markets with at least one such COBO are more competitive, in the sense of having lower Coke prices, than markets with no COBO. The estimated effect of the presence of at least one COBO in a market leads to a statistically significant fall of about 7 percent in the price of Coke (the estimated coefficient for the variable ATLONC).

Finally, column 4 of Table 13.3 measures whether Pepsi-Cola prices are affected by having at least one COBO (whether Pepsi-Cola, Coca-Cola, or both) in the territory. As in the case of the Coke price regression, the ATLONC variable is introduced. Column 4 shows that the presence of a Pepsi-Cola or Coca-Cola COBO (or both) in a market is estimated to reduce Pepsi-Cola prices by nearly 7 percent (the estimated coefficient for the variable ATLONC). Thus, the analysis of this section provides evidence that captive bottling not only reduces a bottler's own prices, but also reduces those of the main competitor as well.

Characteristics of Bottling Operations Converted to COBOs.

This section reports results of estimating the determinants of prices in the 24 cities

TABLE 13.3
Single-Equation Estimation for 24 Cities[a]

Dependent Variable	LCKPR	LCKPR	LCKPR	LPEPPR
CONSTANT	2.6267730	2.6142392	2.747182	0.3405347
	(2.0098857)	(2.0716130)	(2.158214)	(0.4539078)
LPEPUS	—	—	—	0.9486517
	—	—	—	(8.9611286)
LCKUS	0.6876479	0.6281807	0.686039	—
	(5.4704053)	(4.9126982)	(5.460208)	—
LAHE	0.6099864	0.6255123	0.645168	0.2076127
	(1.5332917)	(1.6888638)	(1.668559)	(0.9466228)
LAWE	−0.5973785	−0.6198060	−0.653977	−0.1469858
	(−1.7469074)	(−1.8754722)	(−1.952892)	(−0.8468377)
LTEM	0.0161467	0.0091528	0.020139	0.0216972
	(0.6951246)	(0.3545609)	(0.869825)	(2.0518892)
LUNEMP	0.0069461	−0.0235330	0.000172	−0.0171905
	(0.1818553)	(−0.6807776)	(0.004669)	(−0.8458989)
POPGR	0.0050804	0.0105613	0.009373	0.0069539
	(0.3923380)	(1.0804696)	(0.766198)	(0.5769918)
LPOPUL	−0.0137008	0.0161570	0.010050	0.0149885
	(−0.6160903)	(0.8247766)	(0.434389)	(0.6477876)
INDEP	—	0.0802165	—	—
	—	(2.2310759)	—	—
FOCO	—	0.0333282	—	—
	—	(1.1871640)	—	—
ATLONC	—	—	−0.070946	−0.0667725
	—	—	(−2.205933)	(−2.0698820)
AR(1)	0.3451983	0.4587028	0.331598	0.5700039
	(7.4911435)	(10.774556)	(7.157049)	(12.866924)
AR(2)	0.2829820	—	0.269488	0.2619086
	(6.0812256)	—	(5.77705)	(6.0157784)
R^2	0.356949	0.312612	0.363465	0.742492
S.E. of regression	0.115411	0.119457	0.114954	0.048888
F statistic	27.50760	20.23786	25.40973	128.3102
Log-likelihood	342.6395	327.4378	344.9616	734.8434

Period: 9/87–5/89; number of observations: 456.

Note: Observations were stacked so that, for example, the first period represents the first 24 observations, and so on. The autoregressive parameter is estimated as an autoregressive parameter of order 24, so that it relates the residual of a given city at a particular time period with its correspondent city at the immediately preceding period.

[a] These sample cities were composed of three groups, as follows: Acquisitions just prior to the period covered by the data: Atlanta, Cleveland, Jacksonville, Miami, Minnesota, Salt Lake City, San Francisco, Tulsa/Oklahoma City; FOBOs: Birmingham, Buffalo, Columbus, Nashville, Raleigh; COBOs: Boston, Dallas, Detroit, Houston, Indianapolis, Los Angeles, Orlando, Philadelphia, Phoenix, Pittsburgh.

that did not change ownership structure during the period September 1987 to May 1989. As in the previous section, these sample cities composed three categories: COBO cities well before and after September 1987; FOBO cities well before and after September 1987; and those that were COBO cities by

September 1987, but which had changed from FOBO to COBO during the previous two years. The last group of markets revealed characteristics of bottlers that recently became COBOs.

Here we attempt to ascertain whether particular characteristics are associated with bottlers that changed from FOBO to COBO. The main implications of section 5 are that bottler inefficiencies and CM problems with bottler contracting and coordination form the main rationale for the movement to captive bottling. As explained above, markets where bottlers recently changed from FOBO to COBO (FOCOs) would be expected to be those with significant contracting inefficiencies. Because such inefficiencies take time to eliminate after a bottler is acquired,[72] the shortness of our data series is likely to lead to the most recently acquired bottlers still exhibiting evidence of inefficiency that captive ownership has not yet fully eliminated.

Bottler inefficiency has multiple dimensions. One is the higher costs of the bottling operation. A second dimension of inefficiency is a bottler's weak coordination with its CM's bottling system as a whole. As a proxy for coordination we use the responsiveness of a Pepsi-Cola bottler's prices with respect to Pepsi-Cola's national average prices, while controlling for other factors affecting the bottler's prices. This is an admittedly crude proxy for coordination, but it conforms with the intuition that if, for example, a fall in national Pepsi-Cola prices caused by a national promotional campaign is only partially matched by a particular bottler, that bottler is exhibiting a below-average degree of cooperativeness with its CM.

We hypothesize that bottlers that have been acquired by Pepsi-Cola were, on average, less efficient and cooperative than other FOBOs. Both expectations are borne out by the data: markets in which FOBOs recently changed to COBOs (FOCOs) have higher Pepsi-Cola prices (reflecting, presumably, higher costs or short-run maximizing decisions), and prices in those markets did not track average Pepsi-Cola bottling prices (COBO and FOBO) as did prices in markets with stable FOBO and COBO Pepsi-Cola bottlers.

A model of the determinants of Pepsi-Cola prices across cities is postulated. In general form, the Pepsi-Cola retail price level in a city is assumed to be a function of the market's population and population growth (general determinants of potential demand), the market's level of unemployment (the business-cycle component of the demand), the market's average temperature for that month (the time-of-the-year component of demand), the average level of Pepsi-Cola price in the United States (to represent aggregate Pepsi-Cola behavior), and a time trend.

---

[72] An expectation that was borne out by interviews with Pepsi-Cola bottling officials and our analysis of the conversion of Pepsi-Cola's St. Louis and Denver FOBOs to COBOs. See Muris, Scheffman, and Spiller (1993).

The actual pooled cross-sectional time-series specification is as follows:

$$LOGPEPRICE_{jt} = \beta_1 + \beta_2 * POPULATION_{jt}$$
$$+ \beta_3 * POPULATION\ GROWTH_{jt}$$
$$+ \beta_4 * TIME_j + \beta_5 * LPEUSPRICE_t$$
$$+ \beta_6 * LOG\ TEMPERATURE_{jt}$$
$$+ \beta_7 * LOGUNEMPLOYMENT_{jt}$$
$$+ AR(1) \qquad \text{for } j = 1, \ldots, N \text{ and } t = 1, \ldots, 21 \qquad (2)$$

The expressions β_i are constants to be estimated, and AR(1) represents an autoregressive error term common to all cities in the estimation.

Equations like eq. (2) were estimated for all cities in the sample, imposing the restriction that all coefficients are the same across cities. If each equation had been estimated separately, the scarcity of observations for each city would have made any inference from these results quite unreliable. The imposition of the restriction that all parameters across cities be the same allows us to estimate more precisely the impact of ownership on prices.[73]

The results of different estimates of eq. (2) are shown in Table 13.4. Column 1 of Table 13.4 presents those estimates for only the 10 COBO markets in the 24-city sample. It is interesting to observe that the elasticity of Pepsi-Cola price in those markets to the U.S. average Pepsi-Cola price (the coefficient for the variable LOG US PRICE) is not statistically different from 1, indicating a close cooperation with the whole Pepsi-Cola bottling system. Also, our estimates of this elasticity are statistically precise. Thus, COBO markets track U.S. prices quite well. The second column of Table 13.4 presents the estimation of eq. (2) for the nine cities in which FOBOs were acquired just prior to the time period under analysis (FOCOs). It can be observed that the intercept is significantly higher, and the coefficient of the logarithm of Pepsi-Cola's US price is significantly lower than their respective estimates for COBO markets—reflecting, in this admittedly crude equation, the lower coordination of these bottling operations. The third column presents an estimate of eq. (2) for only the FOBO markets. Neither the intercept nor the coefficient of log of U.S. Pepsi-Cola price is statistically different from that estimated for the COBO markets.

Finally, the last column of Table 13.4 presents the joint estimation of eq. (2) for FOBO and COBO markets. This estimation imposes the restriction that all parameters be the same for both FOBO and COBO markets.

---

[73] We model eq. (2) as a single equation, in which the observations for each city are stacked as described in the previous section. When estimating eq. (2), we must be sure that the autoregressive parameter is properly relating the errors corresponding to each city, rather than across cities. For that purpose, while the error structure is of a first-order nature, in the actual estimation it is made of order N, where N is the number of cities, so that only errors from observations corresponding to the same city are related by a first-order autoregressive structure.

TABLE 13.4

Joint Estimation Dependent Variable: Log of Pepsi-Cola Price Method: Iterative Seemingly Unrelated Equations; All Parameters Constrained to be Equal Across City Equations

	COBOs [a]	FOCOs[b]	FOBOs[c]	FOBOs AND COBOs[d]
CONSTANT	−0.0656886	0.5088290	0.1146658	−0.0138833
	(−0.5379672)	(3.8605286)	(0.4965330)	(−0.283773)
POPULATION	0.0000131	−0.0000134	−0.0001298	5.942E-06
	(3.7319943)	(−0.9126834)	(−1.4966883)	(1.9574447)
POPUL GROWTH	0.0128958	0.0421300	−0.0729017	−0.0024307
	(4.3811820)	(2.1252919)	(−4.5287007)	(−1.0933881)
TIME	0.0010371	0.0026246	−0.0.0012462	0.0015648
	(1.6591345)	(1.1151669)	(−0.5658721)	(4.6952917)
LOG US PRICE	1.0839973	0.6736598	0.9857895	1.0154619
	(12.0567600)	(7.0052195)	(6.5937797)	(28.948712)
LOG TEMPER	−0.0062899	−0.0022390	0.0325259	−0.0119128
	(−0.6367655)	(−0.3431929)	(1.5236163)	(−2.3926549)
LOG UNEMP	−0.0718762	−0.0517812	−0.0120800	−0.0004882
	(−4.5876145)	(−3.0549734)	(−0.3963310)	(−0.0560534)
AR(1)	0.4735584	0.8400226	0.7401559	0.6112888
	(9.1180110)	(20.3082810)	(11.9558600)	(16.532464)

Number of observations per equation: 21; period: 9/87–5/89; system point estimates and standard errors.

Note: Observations were stacked so that, for example, the first period represents the first N observations, and so on, where N represents the number of cities in each sample. The autoregressive parameter is estimated as an autoregressive parameter of order N, so that it relates the residual of a given city at a particular time period with its correspondent city at the immediately preceding period.

[a] These sample cities were: Boston, Dallas, Detroit, Houston, Indianaplis, Los Angeles, Orlando, Philadelphia, Phoenix, and Pittsburgh, $N = 10$.

[b] These sample cities were: Atlanta, Cleveland, Jacksonville, Miami, Minneapolis, Salt Lake City, San Francisco, St. Louis, and Tulsa/Okahoma, $N = 9$.

[c] These sample cities were: Birmingham, Buffalo, Columbus, Nashville, and Raleigh. $N = 5$.

[d] These cities were: Boston, Dallas, Detroit, Houston, Indianaplis, Los Angeles, Orlando, Philadelphia, Phoenix, Pittsburgh, Birmingham, Buffalo, Columbus, Nashville, Raleigh, $N = 15$.

Comparison of the last column with column 2 reveals important differences. First, markets in which bottler ownership changed seem to have been laggard markets, in the sence that the elasticity of their prices with respect to U.S. Pepsi-Cola price is well below 1 (the point estimate is 0.67, which is almost four standard deviations away from 1). Second, at the same values for the independent variables, markets in which ownership changed had higher prices than those in which ownership persisted.

This last result is further examined in Table 13.5. The two columns of Table 13.5 explore the determinants of Pepsi-Cola prices across the 24 cities. The first column presents the result of estimating an equation like eq. (2) for all 24 cities. The second column, however, allows the intercept and the coefficient for the U.S. Pepsi-Cola price to differ across the three types of markets. This is done by introducing two dummies, one for cities that had a FOBO during the period (FOBO), and one for cities in which a FOBO

TABLE 13.5
Single-Equation Estimation for 24 Cities[a]

CONSTANT	0.2554572	−0.020620
	(0.3307110)	(−0.027863)
LOG US PRICE	0.9571296	1.224181
	(9.0616352)	(7.834380)
FOBO	—	0.160459
	—	(0.492296)
FOCO	—	0.959603
	—	(3.504488)
LUSIN	—	−0.080868
	—	(−0.313103)
LUSFOCO	—	−0.705829
	—	(−3.250393)
LAHE	0.1748505	0.307915
	(0.7670778)	(1.481116)
LAWE	−0.1019656	−0.175169
	(−0.5839745)	(−1.013527)
LTEM	0.0217700	0.016907
	(2.0647398)	(1.348472)
LUNEMP	−0.0132011	−0.031528
	(−0.6409026)	(−1.535411)
POPGR	0.0020069	0.008977
	(0.1472621)	(0.907154)
LPOPUL	−0.0069261	6.635E-0
	(−0.2902919)	(0.849249)
AR(1)	0.5812595	0.780148
	(13.191911)	(27.110271)
AR(2)	0.2732849	—
	(6.3171135)	—
R^2	0.740433	0.728153
S.E. of regression	0.049028	0.050344
F statistic	141.3603	98.88301
Log-likelihood	733.0272	722.4888

Period: 9/87–5/89, dependent variable: LPEPPRICE; number of observations: 456.
[a] Notes to Table 13.3 apply to this table.

changed to a COBO (FOCO) just before the period. Those two dummies are introduced separately and also interactively with the U.S. Pepsi-Cola price (LUSIN for cities with an independent FOBO, and LUSFOCO for cities with a FOCO). Again, we find that those bottlers that changed ownership just before September 1987 behave differently than those that remained either FOBO or COBO. From Table 13.5, we see that, everything else the same, bottling operations that changed ownership (FOCOs) tend to have higher prices, and the elasticity of their prices with U.S. prices is substantially smaller than that for FOBOs or COBOs. Furthermore, FOBOs and COBOs are approximately the same in average Pepsi-Cola prices and in the elasticity of their prices with respect to U.S. Pepsi-Cola prices.

We have postulated that transaction cost and strategic factors have been the stimulus of the move to captive distribution. However, some of our results are also consistent with the "double-marginalization" hypothesis. This hypothesis focuses on market-power-based motivations for vertical integration, suggesting that a move toward captive distribution should be observed in those markets where the independent bottlers had significant market power. There is some support for this hypothesis, in that some of the bottlers acquired by Pepsi-Cola and Coca-Cola had been engaged in price fixing. Under the double-marginalization theory, recently acquired COBOs should show higher prices than long-standing COBOs and FOBOs, because Pepsi should have purchased only those bottlers who were exercising significant market power. While our finding that the recently acquired COBOs tend to have higher prices than long-standing COBOs and FOBOs is consistent with the double-marginalization hypothesis, we believe we have provided a number of transaction cost- and strategy-based reasons for vertical integration that dominate that hypothesis. In particular, the double-marginalization hypothesis cannot explain the *general* move toward captive distribution, unless there was a sudden significant increase in market power across bottlers. This possibility is inconsistent with the competitive conditions of the Cola Wars, particularly aggressive price discounting, that have led to more price competition at the bottler level than ever before. Bottler price fixing may have been one factor in some cases of poor bottler performance, but most bottlers apparently have not been engaged in price fixing.

To summarize, this section analyzed the extent by which the determinants of CSD retail prices in cities in which bottlers were recently acquired differ from those determinants in cities where bottler ownership remained stable. The following hypothesis received some empirical support: For cities where ownership changed shortly before our data period, Pepsi-Cola prices were higher than in cities with ownership stability, and Pepsi-Cola prices were not as closely related to U.S. Pepsi-Cola prices as in the latter cities. These results are consistent with our hypothesis that Pepsi-Cola has acquired bottlers that were relatively inefficient and relatively uncooperative among its independent bottlers. These results suggest, then, that the acquisition process was triggered by contracting and coordination needs.

7. CONCLUSIONS

In recent years Coca-Cola and Pepsi-Cola have begun a shift from independent to captive distribution. Following Chandler, we postulated that this change in organization was driven by changes in competitive conditions and the new strategies of Coke and Pepsi. The new strategies dramatically increased the need for close cooperation with bottlers. The independent bottling systems, protected by exclusive, perpetual territories, could only provide such cooperation at significant costs—costs that could be reduced through moving to captive distribution. Our statistical evidence, both of the competitive edge that captive distribution has given Coca-Cola in fountain sales and of the increased competition and lower prices of packaged soft drinks resulting from captive distribution, supports our basic hypothesis.

Our analysis also is relevant to the concern of the antitrust agencies about the movement by the two leading cola manufacturers to captive distribution Our results indicate that this change in distribution systems is driven not by the desire to raise prices, but by a need to economize on transactions costs in light of the new competitive environment and the new competitive strategies of Coca-Cola and Pepsi-Cola. The statistical evidence indicates that the move to captive distribution has lowered prices for Coca-Cola and Pepsi-Cola.

APPENDIX: VARIABLE DEFINITIONS

DLPERPRICE Change in the natural logarithm of Pepsi price in a given city.

DLPEPUS Change in the natural logarithm of Pepsi price in the United States.

DLCKPR Change in the natural logarithm of Coke price in a given city

DLCKUS Change in the natural logarithm of Coke price in the United States.

DOWNERSHIP Dummy variable equals 1 if there is a change in Pepsi's bottler ownership from FOBO to COBO or JV, equals −1 if there is a change from JV or COBO to FOBO.

DPBG Dummy variable equals 1 if there is a change in Pepsi's bottler ownership from FOBO to COBO.

DJOINT Dummy variable equals 1 if there is a change in Pepsi's bottler ownership from FOBO to JV.

DTEMP Change in the city's temperature.

DUNEMP Change in the city's unemployment.

FM87..FM89 Set of dummy variable equal to 1 for a pair of months. Thus, FM87 equal 1 for February and March 1987.

LCKPR Natural logarithm of Coke price in a particular city.

LCKUS Natural logarithm of Coke price in the United States.

LPEPPR Natural logarithm of Pepsi price in a particular city.

LPEPUS Natural logarithm of Pepsi price in the United States.

LAHE Natural logarithm of average hourly earnings in a particular city.

LAWE Natural logarithm of average weekly earnings in a particular city.

LTEM Natural logarithm of average monthly temperature in a particular city.

LUNEMP	Natural logarithm of monthly unemployment in a particular city.
INDEP	Dummy variable equal to 1 if the Pepsi bottler is franchise-owned.
FOCO	Dummy variable equal to 1 if the Pepsi bottler ownership changed from franchise to company.
ATLONC	Dummy variable equal to 1 if either the Pepsi or Coke bottlers are company-owned.
POPULATION	Population of the city in latest census.
POPUL GROWTH	Rate of growth of the city's population.
TIME	Trend variable.
FOBO	Dummy equal to 1 if the Pepsi bottler is franchise-owned.
COBO	Dummy equal to 1 if the Pepsi bottler is company-owned.
LUSIN	Natural logarithm of Pepsi price in the United States times INDEP.
LUSFOCO	Natural logarithm of Pepsi price in the United States times FOCO.

COSTS OF CONTROL: THE SOURCE OF ECONOMIC RENTS FOR McDONALD'S FRANCHISEES

Patrick J. Kaufmann and Francine Lafontaine

1. INTRODUCTION

Franchising, and more precisely business format franchising, is an important and growing phenomenon in the U.S. economy.[1] The Department of Commerce estimates that the number of business format franchisors

Patrick Kaufmann is Associate Professor of Marketing, Georgia State University; Francine Lafontaine is Associate Professor of Business Economics and Public Policy, the University of Michigan. This article could not have been written without the cooperation of the McDonald's Corporation. It has also benefited greatly from the comments of Jerold Cohen, Paul Joskow, Nancy Lutz, Scott Masten, Steve Michael, Wallace Mullin, Russell Pittman, Marius Schwartz, Kathryn Shaw, Margaret Slade, an anonymous referee, and Alan Sykes. We also thank participants in the Business Economics Workshop at the University of Michigan, the Department of Economics Workshop at Dalhousie University, the Economic and Legal Organization Workshop at the University of Chicago, the Marketing Workshop at the Harvard Business School, the Marketing Research Workshop at the University of Alabama, and the 1992 Industrial Organization Program Meeting at the National Bureau of Economic Research for their comments. Finally, we thank Robert Picard for his assistance. The usual caveat applies. Also, the analyses contained in this article are for academic purposes only and are not earning claims by the company or the authors.

[1] The U.S. Department of Commerce, *Franchising in the Economy: 1986–1988* (1988), classifies franchises according to the main component of the transaction: "Product and Trade Name Franchising" (or "Traditional Franchising") involves franchised dealers who "concentrate on one company's product line and to some extent identify their business with that company" (1)
(continued)

increased from 909 in 1972 to 2,177 in 1986.[2] Total nominal sales through outlets of business format franchisors grew by 442 percent between 1972 and 1986, with the number of outlets growing by 65 percent in the same period, from 189,640 to 312,810.

Touted success stories of both franchisors and franchisees have certainly contributed to this growth. Franchises such as McDonald's, which Justis and Judd (1989) describe as blue-chip franchises, are recognized as safe and lucrative investment opportunities. This might explain why one finds queues of potential franchisees for these franchises: according to the *Wall Street Journal*, "[W]ell over 2000 people apply to become McDonald's franchisees in the U.S. each year, but ... most years, only about 150 applicants gain admission to the Golden Arches" (March, 1989: 131). In other words, in any given year, the admission rate is only about 7.5 percent. Other sources, such as Noren (1990), estimate this rate to be even lower, at about 2–3 percent. Some authors, notably Mathewson and Winter (1985), have interpreted the existence of these queues as evidence that franchisees of these franchise systems may earn expected rents ex ante. Also, Banerji and Simon (1992) and Lafontaine (1992a) have both argued that there might be ex ante rents left with franchisees because they find no significant negative correlation between royalty rates and franchise fees in their data on individual franchisors.

While several authors have hinted at the possibility of downstream rents in franchising, almost no evidence is available on this issue. The main purpose of this article is therefore to establish empirically, using financial data, that there are both ex ante and ex post rents left downstream at McDonald's. We focus on McDonald's in part because it is the ultimate franchise, at least in most people's minds. Interestingly, however, McDonald's is not a typical franchise. In fact, in most respects, including the amount of training required, the success rate, and the amount of control the franchisor exerts over franchisees, McDonald's is quite atypical. However, in terms of the issues of interest in this paper, McDonald's sophistication in dealing with its more that 12,000 outlets worldwide is a major asset: it leads us to believe that most of what McDonald's Corp. does is done on purpose. In particular, if any franchise chain was able technically to extract all rents, ex ante or ex post, McDonald's certainly would be. Thus the existence of significant amounts of rents downstream at McDonald's suggests that this company purposefully chooses to leave rents downstream. The next question then is why.

This type of franchising is limited to car dealerships, soft-drink bottlers, and gasoline service stations. In "Business Format Franchising," the franchise relationship "includes not only the product, service, and trademark, but the entire business concept itself—a marketing strategy and plan, operating manuals and standards, quality control, and a continuing process of assistance and guidance" (3). Examples include restaurants, business and employment services, and real estate agencies. Together, these two forms of franchising were expected to account for about 34 percent of all retail sales in the United States in 1988 (14). In this article, the term "franchising" refers to Business Format Franchising only.

[2] U.S. Dept. of Commerce (1988: 5). This publication was suspended by the Department of Commerce (DOC) as part of its privatization program, and 1986 is the last year for which this information is available from the DOC.

To provide some perspective on our main empirical result, we note that the presence of ex post rents is consistent with most incentive theories of franchising.[3] In these models, ex post rents can serve as an incentive mechanism or coordination device that complements, from an incentive perspective, the profit-sharing rights granted to franchisees. In other words, because of these ex post rents, the cost to a franchisee of reducing effort is composed not only of the induced reduction in the franchisee's share of profits for the period over which effort is reduced but also of the increased risk of termination and consequent loss of the entire future stream of ex post rents of the outlet (see Mathewson and Winter, 1985). Our showing that there are such rents downstream at McDonald's hence supports the incentives-based theories of franchising.

The existence of ex ante rents is more puzzling from a theoretical perspective: most incentive theories of franchising assume that the franchisor, whenever there is competition among franchisees, can obtain the net present value of the ex post rents from the franchisees via an up-front franchise fee. Following Mathewson and Winter (1985), we propose that the ex ante rents represent the costs that McDonald's must incur to maintain the stream of ex post rents necessary to achieve strict control over its system in the face of down stream liquidity constraints. In other words, ex ante rents arise here because the franchisor needs to leave a stream of ex post rents downstream to create franchisee incentives, and franchisees' wealth constraints prevent the up-front extraction of the full net present value of these ex post rents. Finally, we argue that McDonald's desire for a particular type of individual to operate its franchises, namely, owner-operators whose livelihoods will be tied to the success of their outlet(s), increases the likelihood that downstream operators will face liquidity constraints. This in turn contributes to the need for McDonald's to leave ex ante rents downstream.

The article is organized as follows. In the next section, we assess whether or not there are rents, ex post and ex ante, left downstream at McDonald's by calculating the net present value of typical franchises. In section 3, we verify results obtained in section 2 using a different method, namely, by examining the prices at which some existing franchises have been transferred to new franchisees. Under both approaches, we find that the present value of the amount of ex ante rents that the owner of a new McDonald's franchise can expect to earn, after taxes, over the 20-year period covered by the franchise contract is between $300K and $455K in 1982 dollars. The amount of ex post rents is, of course, even larger as it includes not only the above amounts but also all up-front fees and specific investments. In section 4, we discuss various theoretical arguments found in the literature that can explain the existence of rents, namely, the incentive-based arguments noted above and theories focusing on informational asymmetries, on the franchisor's or the franchisee's side. Although the data in this article do not allow us to discriminate

---

[3] See, for example, Rubin (1978); Klien (1980); Telser (1980); Klein and Saft (1985); Mathewson and Winter (1985); Lal (1990); and Bhattacharyya and Lafontaine (1992).

among the theories directly, we present arguments based on the existing literature, on our knowledge of franchising, and on conversations with company officials as to why we find explanations for rents based on incentive theories to be especially compelling. Section 5 contains concluding remarks.

2. ANALYZING THE RETURNS FROM A McDONALD'S FRANCHISE

This section uses data on the yearly returns of McDonald's restaurants to ascertain whether McDonald's franchisees can expect to earn economic rents ex post, that is, once they are operating, and/or ex ante, namely, before they become involved in the franchise relationship. Table 14-1 shows in some detail how one can calculate franchisees' yearly earnings from data provided by the McDonald's company as part of its disclosure documents.[4] The information we use relates to 1982. (See the appendix for an analysis of the 1989 data.) As stated in the disclosure documents, the cost data used in Table 14.1 are based on observed costs for the 1,283 U.S. company-owned McDonald's restaurants open at least 13 months by the end of 1982. Table 14.1 gives information for three levels of sales, namely, $900K, $1,100K, and $1,300K. According to the disclosure documents, of the more than 5,400 McDonald's restaurants (franchised and company owned) opened 13 months or more in the United States as of December 1982, 76 percent had sales over $900K, 49 percent had sales above $1,100K, and 24 percent had sales greater than $1,300K. The average sales of U.S. McDonald's restaurants that year were $1,123K.[5]

In deriving the estimates shown in Table 14.1, we make use of some information obtained directly from the disclosure documents and from company officials:

1. At McDonald's, it is the franchisor, and not the franchisee, who chooses the location of any given outlet. In fact, McDonald's often asks individuals

---

[4] In 1978, the Federal Trade Commission (FTC) enacted a rule requiring franchisors to divulge specific information about their franchise to potential franchisees, 16 CFR 436 (1978). One way to satisfy this requirement, and various state disclosure requirements, is to provide a Uniform Franchise Offering Circular to potential franchisees. See Justis and Judd (1989) for more on these documents, which may include earning claims. Most franchisors (89 percent of them in the early 1980's, according to Warren L. Lewis (1991)) choose not to include earning claims because of the level of accuracy required: such claims must be relevant to the location of the prospective franchisee, all assumptions used must be disclosed, and the franchisor must retain and produce on request to the prospective franchisee, the FTC, and the state administrators all the data necessary to substantiate them. Fortunately, McDonald's does provide this information.

[5] The lowest sales level was $360K, and the highest was $3,223K. We presume throughout this article that the distribution of sales levels is the same for company-owned stores and for franchised stores. This assumption is supported by data describing the average sales levels of all the 178 MacDonald's restaurants operating in three television markets (as defined and used by the A. C. Nielsen company in its rating of television stations) between 1983 and 1985 (see Irving H. Plotkin, On the Nature of Intangible Assets in a McDonald's Franchise, Expert's Report, in *Canterbury* v. *Commissioner*, No. 38037-87 (U.S. Tax Ct. 1991)). In these data, the means of average yearly sales for the 148 franchised and 30 company-owned restaurants were $1,430.4K and $1,447.2K, respectively.

TABLE 14.1

Yearly Economic Rents ($) for a McDonald's Franchise in 1982

	Level of sales		
	Low	**Mid**	**High**
Yearly sales	900,000	1,100,000	1,300,000
Cost of sales			
Food cost	292,636	356,116	419,596
Paper cost	38,455	47,655	56,855
Total	331,091	403,771	476,451
Gross profits	568,909	696,229	823,549
Controllable expenses			
Crew labor	158,174	182,134	206,094
Management labor[a]	41,488	44,668	47,848
Ads and promotions	58,708	69,368	80,028
Utilities	35,833	38,633	41,433
Others	53,673	60,973	68,273
Total	347,876	395,776	443,676
Gross profits less controllables	221,033	300,453	379,873
Other expenses			
Royalty/rent[b]	112,416	126,500	149,500
Others	38,155	39,075	39,995
Total	150,571	165,575	189,495
Yearly income from operations	70,462	134,878	190,378
Opportunity costs:			
Interest (5% per year)[c]	20,550	22,600	30,150
Franchisee labor[d]	48,000	48,000	48,000
Total	68,550	70,600	78,150
Yearly economic rents	1,912	64,278	112,228

Source: McDonald's Corp., Franchise Offering Circular (1983).

Note: Based on data for approximately 1,283 U.S. company-owned units open 13 months or more in 1982. That year, about 76 percent of the more than 5,400 domestic McDonald's restaurants open for at least 13 months had sales above $900K, 49 percent were above $1,100K, and 24 percent were above $1,300K. The average level of sales was $1,123K.

[a] The management labor figures here differ from those in McDonald's company-owned units' profit and loss statements by the amount of the store manager's salary ($19K, $22K, and $25K, respectively, for the three types of stores), whose position is assumed to be taken over by the franchisee.

[b] Royalties, including rents, are 11.5 percent of gross sales except for stores with monthly sales below $83,741. Those pay a minimum rent of $7,118 monthly plus 3 percent of gross sales. For a restaurant with yearly sales of $900K, this amounts to $112,416, that is, about 12.5 percent of sales.

[c] Includes the forgone interest on the security deposit. Also, since the franchisee contributes 40 percent or more of the initial capital and borrows the rest, real interest payments are part of this cost. For the median outlet, the initial investment is taken to be $452K ($310K initially, and $220K spread over the next 20 years for reequipment; assuming a lag of 10 years before these expenses take place on average, this is worth $142K in 1982, given a 5 percent discount rate). For the lower sales outlet, the total investment is taken to be $411 ($282 + $129), and for the high sales outlet, $603 ($410K + $193K).

[d] A 1992 proprietary survey shows prior earnings of new McDonald's franchisees previously unaffiliated with the company at $72K, amounting to about $48K in 1982 dollars.

interested in becoming franchisees to relocate. Franchisees do not buy the land or the building in which their business is housed: McDonald's typically owns these, and it leases the others from third parties.[6] It then rents these properties to its franchisees. The required royalty payments, which were 11.5 percent of sales in 1982, are inclusive of rent.

2. The initial investment required from the franchisee includes the franchise fee of $12.5K, a security deposit of $15K (returned without interest to the franchisee at the end of the 20-year contract if performance was satisfactory), as well as some amount of initial inventory, which the company says varies between $10K and $18K, and some prepaid expenses and working capital worth $45K–$65K. The franchisee is also responsible for buying all the equipment: The cost of this equipment varies from $200K to $300K.[7] Presumably the variation in all these figures is a function of the size of the restaurant. Hence the total investment required for a smaller restaurant would be around $282K, while for a larger outlet, it would be about $410K. Furthermore, since the profit and loss statements provided by the company all assume a total investment of $310K, we take this to be a typical amount, and we use this estimate in our calculations involving the median size restaurant. We estimate that the equipment component of this last figure is about $220K.

3. The management labor figure in the profit and loss statements includes a salary for the store manager. Based on figures provided to us by company officials for 1990, we estimate that in 1982, the amount of salary included in this figure for the store manager of a median size outlet was about $22K.[8] For the smaller restaurants, the salary could be as low as $19K, while it might go up to about $25K in the larger restaurants.[9]

We also make the following assumptions:

1. Franchisees must regularly invest to update and maintain their equipment. According to company officials, over the duration of the contract, franchisees can expect this investment to be equivalent to a complete reequipping of the outlet. Hence we take the present value of an investment of $220K of 1982 dollars to be spent in 1992 as the cost of maintaining and updating the equipment in the median sales outlet. Assuming a real discount rate of 5 percent, this amounts to a present value of $142K in 1982 dollars.

[6] According to Noren (1990: 61), McDonald's owns 60 percent of its locations and is acquiring more.

[7] See McDonald's Corp., Franchise Offering Circular (1983).

[8] The figures for the costs of labor (management and crew labor) in the 1989 profit and loss statements are about 1.5 times those in the 1982 versions. Throughout the article, we use 1.5 to deflate labor costs across these 2 periods. This corresponds to the change in the CPI for services between 1982 and 1991 according to the U.S. President, *The Economic Report of the President Transmitted to the Congress* (1991).

[9] According to company officials, in 1990, store managers earned anywhere from about $28K to $38K. In addition, they were paid a profit-sharing bonus representing approximately 14 percent of their base salary, and benefits—health care coverage and life insurance—not included in the management labor figure. Together, these added probably about 40 percent of the base salary to the total compensation of managers in company-owned outlets.

For the smaller (larger) outlet, we use the lower (upper) limit of $200K ($300K), which once discounted back to 1982 is worth $129K ($193K).

2. To calculate the interest cost, we assume a real interest rate of 5 percent. This we believe is an appropriate rate, given that the disclosure document for 1982 stipulates a borrowing rate of 13 percent for the investment in equipment, despite inflation rates of 13.5 percent and 10.7 percent in the previous 2 years. This 13 percent rate is comparable to the interest rate on Aaa corporate bonds.[10] This is a low rate for a small business, reflecting the comparatively low risk associated with investing in a McDonald's franchise.[11] For comparison purposes, in subsequent analyses, we examine the effect of using a high real interest rate of 7.5 percent (see Table 14.2 below).[12]

3. A proprietary survey conducted in 1992 revealed that the salary of new franchisees previously unaffiliated with McDonald's prior to their becoming franchisees, was about $72K, which in 1982 would amount to roughly $48K. We use this figure as our estimate of the opportunity cost of franchisees' labor. We do this despite the fact that according to company officials, this figure is much higher than the average compensation of all new franchisees: only about one-third of the new franchisees in 1991 were previously unaffiliated with the company.[13] Another third were recruited from among company employees, and the last third were employees of franchisees. Their earnings prior to becoming franchisees were not surveyed, but as noted earlier, the average compensation of store managers, who among the managers are the most likely to be granted a franchise, was around $31K in 1982 dollars ($22K times 1.4 to reflect benefits). This fairly large gap in prior compensation levels among the two main types of franchisees might be explained by risk and effort differentials, as most of the previously un-affiliated recruits had been self-employed. We come back to these issues later.

From Table 14.1, we find that most McDonald's franchisees can expect to earn some amount of economic rents ex post, that is, once they have become a part of the system. Assuming sales are completely flat over the life of the agreement, all franchisees whose restaurants achieve sales of $900K or more yearly (in 1982 dollars), that is, owners of more than 75 percent of the restaurants, would earn enough each year to cover the opportunity cost of their labor and capital. Before taxes, the level of ex post rents franchisees can expect to obtain, or the level of rents at the average (which here is the same as the median) level of sales, is around $64K per year. Given the intricacies of the U.S. tax system, it is impossible to generate a good estimate

---

[10] See U.S. President, *Economic Report of the President* (1991).

[11] One contributing factor to this low risk from the lender's perspective is McDonald's "rent relief" policy, where the company imposes a moratorium on rent and royalty payments for franchisees that do not do well through no fault of their own.

[12] Note that franchisees must provide 40 percent of the initial $310K investment themselves. These savings would likely earn less than a 5 percent real rate in their best alternative uses.

[13] In 1982, the proportion of unaffiliated recruits was higher, but we do not know by how much.

TABLE 14.2

Present Discounted Value Calculations for a Single McDonald's Restaurant (thousands of 1982 dollars)

	Interest cost calculated at a real interest rate of 5 percent			Interest cost calculated at a real interest rate of 7.5 percent		
	Low	Mid	High	Low	Mid	High
Yearly sales	900	1,100	1,300	900	1,100	1,300
Yearly rents	1.9	64.3	112.2	(8.4)	53.0	97.2
Present discounted value of rents	24.9	841.4	1,468.4	(109.9)	693.5	1,271.9
Ex ante costs[a]						
Equipment[b]	329	362	493	329	362	493
Franchise fee	12.5	12.5	12.5	12.5	12.5	12.5
Training[c]	50	50	50	50	50	50
Total	391.5	424.5	555.5	391.5	424.5	555.5
Ex ante rents						
Before taxes	(366.6)	416.9	912.9	(501.4)	269.0	716.4
After taxes[d]	(366.6)	291.8	639.0	(501.4)	188.3	501.5

Note: Numbers in parentheses denote losses.

[a] The security deposit is not included as an ex ante cost since it is usually refunded.

[b] All investments in equipment are assumed to be worthless at the end of the 20-year contract. The total investment in equipment for the median size outlet is taken to be $220K (out of total initial investment of $310K). The reequipment expenditures over the course of the contract are assumed to be worth the same amount. Once discounted back 10 years (the average lag before reequipment), they are worth $142K, for a total investment in equipment of $362 over the duration of the contract. For the low (high) sales outlet, the initial investment in equipment is worth $200K ($300K). Assuming the same amounts are spent over the duration of the contrat for reequipment, the present values of the reequipment are $129K and $193K, respectively. Hence the total cost of equipment for the low (high) sales outlet is $329K ($493K).

[c] This estimate assumes a value of time for the franchisee of about $25/hour, consistent with our estimate of yearly earnings at $48K. The results are not sensitive to reasonable changes in these amounts. Note that no tuition is paid for training and that a large number of new franchisees who are ex-employees of a franchisee or the company do not incur any training cost.

[d] Assuming a 30 percent tax rate to be applied to both the profits of the franchise and the revenues the franchisee would obtain from his labor and his capital under their best alternative uses. Clearly, this is very "naive," not allowing for different tax rates for businesses and individuals, nor for the fact that some costs (acclerated depreciation, car expenses, etc.) reduce firms' tax liabilities. Hence, the results reported on this line should be interpreted as very coarse approximations.

of after-tax rents. But assuming a tax rate of about 30 percent, and assuming that franchisees' labor revenues and revenues from investing their capital in their best alternative uses would be taxed at about the same level, the after-tax amount of economic rents ex post from the average McDonald's restaurant would be $45K each year.[14] Given that, on average, McDonald's

[14] Of course, this analysis is very naive. Not only does it not deal with differences in tax rates for businesses and individuals, but it also abstracts from the fact that some costs (accelerated depreciation, car expenses, etc.) reduce firms' tax liabilities compared to individuals. Still, in 1982, the actual average tax rate for a single individual earning around $40K of taxable income (salary plus investment income) was 29 percent. The rate for a firm showing a taxable income between $50K and $75K was 30 percent. See Commerce Clearing House, 1983 *U.S. Master Tax Guide* (66th ed. 1982).

franchisees own and operate about three stores, franchisees can in fact expect to earn at least three times this amount.[15] However, only "good" franchisees will have access to these larger amounts of rent as McDonald's only grants the rights to buy new restaurants to franchisees who are performing well within the system.

While the data in Table 14.1 show that McDonald's franchisees can expect to earn economic rents ex post, they say nothing about whether or not franchisees earn rents ex ante. Franchisees might be required to post bonds or bear costs such that they in fact pay for the expected stream of ex post rents up front, in which case they would not be earning any ex ante rents. Table 14.2 addresses this issue. It shows the present value of the expected stream of ex post rents along with the various ex ante costs that franchisees must bear. In the first three columns of Table 14.2, we assume a 5 percent real interest rate, as we did in Table 14.1. Since we believe that this rate is appropriate for our purposes, our discussion of results relies mostly on those shown in these three columns. However, for comparison purposes, the next three columns in the table show the estimates of rents one obtains under the assumption of a real interest rate of 7.5 percent.

Additional assumptions used in constructing Table 14.2 include (1) that real sales and costs will remain constant for the duration of the 20-year contract; (2) that the equipment the franchisee must buy is worth nothing at the end of the contract; and (3) that franchisees' time is worth about $25/hour, which is consistent with our estimate of their labor opportunity cost. Franchisees are required to spend about 2,000 uncompensated hours in training to become McDonald's frachisees, most of which is spent working in different capacities in existing restaurants, while the rest is spent in classrooms (see Noren, 1990). Because franchisees pay no tuition, the total cost of this training to the franchisee thus amounts to about $50K.

Table 14.2 shows that the majority of McDonald's franchisees can expect to earn rents even on an ex ante basis. On average, the present value of the stream of ex ante rents to be earned over the 20-year contract before taxes will be more than $400K per outlet. Interpolating between the $900K and $1,100K levels of sales to find the level of sales at which franchisees begin to earn rents ex ante, we find that all restaurants with sales levels above $1,000K earn some positive amount of ex ante rents.[16] Assuming a normal distribution, or using the data from Plotkin (see note 5) to generate an

---

[15] The average number is 3.1 according to Bertagnoli (1989: 33). Note that multiplying the rents from one restaurant by three to get the rents from three outlets assumes that the cost of managing three of them will be three times the opportunity cost of the franchisee's labor. But franchisees can probably pay store managers less than what we assessed as their opportunity cost, as we saw above. Hence the rents from owning three restaurants would be more than three times those one gets from owning only one.

[16] As noted at the bottom of Table 14.1, restaurants with sales below a certain level must pay a higher proportion of their sales in rent than what is standard for McDonald's. While this probably reflects McDonald's perception of the real estate value, it also says that McDonald's in a sense expected the restaurant to perform better than it does, or it would not have established a restaurant there. Hence, minimum rental fees at McDonald's in fact punish those franchisees

(continued)

empirical distribution of McDonald's restaurant sales, we find that despite our very conservative estimates of rents, about 65 percent of all new McDonald's restaurants earn rents ex ante.[17] Note that this percentage would be even greater if we assumed that sales are only highly correlated over time for a given restaurant instead of assuming, as is done here, that they are perfectly correlated from year to year.[18] Finally, owning the average number of stores implies that "good" franchisees—as only good franchisees are given permission to buy additional restaurants—can expect to earn more than $1,200K in ex ante rents before taxes.

This conclusion, that the majority of franchisees earn ex ante rents, is not sensitive to reasonable changes in our assumptions. Moreover, while the amounts of ex ante rents found in Table 14.2 are nontrivial, there are a number of reasons to believe that our calculations understate the actual amounts of rent significantly.

First, as stated above, we assumed that sales and costs would remain constant over the next 20 years. But given McDonald's track record, and especially its track record up to 1982, it is unlikely that the franchisor or the franchisee was functioning under this assumption in 1982. Table 14.3 shows that between 1964 and 1988, the growth rate of nominal sales per restaurant has typically been greater than increases in the consumer price index (CPI). If, as the data in Table 14.1 suggest, costs increase less than proportionately with increases in sales, and if sales are growing in real terms, our forecasts of profits from operations will be below the realized values. Thus the amounts of rents would be even greater than we estimate them to be.

Second, we assumed that the equipment is worth absolutely nothing at the end of the 20 years of operation. It is likely in fact that this capital will have some positive value at the end of the contract.

Third, we assumed that the investment in human capital is completely specific, that the training is worth nothing to the franchisee outside of the McDonald's system. In reality, it is likely to increase the value of the franchisee's labor, so that it should not all be treated as a cost. Further, we are assuming that every individual must go through the same training to become a franchisee. But most of the new franchisees who were employees of

whose restaurants are not performing well relative to expectations. The lack of profits we find for these are therefore a matter of company policy to some extent. And in fact, as noted above, the company has a "rent relief" policy for franchisees whose restaurants are unprofitable through no fault of their own.

[17] To obtain these percentages, we use a normal distribution with a mean of $1,100K and a standard deviation of $300K, which approximates quite well the quartile data described at the bottom of Table 14.1. As for Plotkin (see note 5), as noted earlier, he provides data on monthly sales for 178 McDonald's restaurants. The average sales level in his data is $1,433K, not $1,123K. Part of this is explained by a difference in time periods, as his data are averaged over the 1983–85 period. The other part apparently is just sampling error. We adjust these data by multiplying the sales levels by (1,123/1,433), so that the distribution centers on $1,123 (and the variance is reduced accordingly), before calculating the proportion of stores with sales above $1,000K. If we adjust the sales data only for the change in the CPI, we find that 90 percent of all restaurants generate rents.

[18] We thank Lars Osberg for making this point.

TABLE 14.3
Growth in Nominal Sales per Restaurant Compared to Inflation Rates, 1964/65–1987/88

Year	Number of outlets	Sales per outlet[a]	Growth rate, year to year (% change)	Changes in CPI[b] (% change)
1964	688	188,372		
1965	760	224,868	19.4	1.6
1966	862	253,480	12.7	2.9
1967	967	275,491	8.7	3.1
1968	1,125	297,778	8.1	4.2
1969	1,345	335,167	12.6	5.5
1970	1,592	368,719	10.0	5.7
1971	1,944	403,344	9.4	4.4
1972	2,272	514,877	27.7	3.2
1973	2,784	563,218	9.4	6.2
1974	3,037	677,642	20.3	11.0
1975	3,756	696,619	2.8	9.1
1976	4,225	724,970	4.1	5.8
1977	4,736	789,274	8.9	6.5
1978	5,185	882,353	11.8	7.6
1979	5,747	936,837	6.2	11.3
1980	6,262	994,251	6.1	13.5
1981	6,739	1,057,872	6.4	10.3
1982	7,259	1,075,768	1.7	6.2
1983	7,778	1,116,804	4.5	3.2
1984	8,304	1,205,034	8.3	4.3
1985	8,901	1,235,917	3.5	3.6
1986	9,410	1,317,747	2.7	1.9
1987	9,911	1,445,909	6.7	3.6
1988	10,513	1,528,013	3.7	4.1
Mean			9.0	5.8

[a] Number of McDonald's restaurants and average sales per restaurant, worldwide. *Source:* Lisa Bertagnoli, McDonald's: Company of the Quarter Century, *Restaurants and Institutions* 32 (July 1989).
[b] From U.S. President, *The Economic Report of the President to the Congress* (1991).

McDonald's or of franchisees (approximately two-thirds of the franchisees recruited in 1991) had to go through this training to qualify for their previous positions. For most of them, the incremental cost to become qualified as franchisees is basically zero.[19]

Fourth, the cost estimates used in Table 14.1 are based on data obtained from company-owned restaurants. There is some evidence in the literature

[19] According to company officials, the employees of franchisees who apply to become franchisees are at the level of store managers or above, and they require no additional training to become qualified as franchise buyers. The same is true for employees of McDonald's who work in the field. For those who worked in the field, but have not dealt with operations for a while, a customized refresher course is required. Only company employees who have never worked in the field are required to go through the kind of training discussed above.

suggesting that costs are higher in company-owned than in franchised outlets of the same chain.[20]

Fifth, our estimate of the opportunity cost of the franchisee's labor is very generous. As stated earlier, this estimate reflects the previous earnings of the one-third of new franchisees with the highest level of compensation. We could have used one of two alternative measures for the franchisee's cost of labor, namely, a weighted average of the earnings of all new franchisees, previously affiliated or not, or a measure of the compensation of company-owned store managers, given that franchisees are the managers in their own restaurants. Both of these would have led to a lower assessment of this cost.[21] We chose to use the $48K figure instead for a number of reasons. First, as noted earlier, given that this estimate is derived from a group of mostly self-employed individuals, it likely includes compensation for the greater amount of risk involved in running an independent business. Since running a franchised business is more risky than being a company manager (though owning a McDonald's franchise is likely to be less risky than owning an independent business), we wanted a figure that incorporated an amount of compensation for risk.[22] Second, franchisees, like independent business owners, may work longer hours than company managers. We wanted a compensation figure that reflected that, although according to company officials, McDonald's franchisees do not work significantly more hours than managers of company-owned stores.[23]

Finally, the last important benefit that our estimates do not include arises from the fact that McDonald's typically allows its franchisees to rewrite their franchise contract at the termination of the original agreement, at the terms offered to new franchisees at that time.[24] Noren (1990: 61) notes that 92 percent of contracts up for renewal are rewritten at McDonald's. So while rewriting is not a franchisee right, it is a likely outcome for "good" franchisees. Hence rents will typically be available to the "good" franchisee for more than 20 years. Assuming for example that the contract is renewed once, and that the franchisee must make the same total investment in equipment in the second 20-year period as in the first contract period, the discounted stream of rents for the median outlet would be $593K before taxes (assuming a 5 percent discount rate), and $415K after taxes. Equivalently,

---

[20] See Shelton (1967); and Krueger (1991).

[21] In the first case, with an average compensation of about $31K for two-thirds of the new franchisees, and $48K for one-third, the estimate would have been $36K. In the second case, it would have been $31K.

[22] Note that a McDonald's franchise is a fairly safe investment as evidenced by the low failure rates (see note 31 below). And the franchisee's exposure to this risk is quite limited: even in cases of failures, franchisees only lose a fraction of their initial investment.

[23] Comapny officials told us that McDonald's must provide a certain quality of life to its franchisees that is incompatible with 7-day weeks. On average, franchisees supposedly work 5.5–6 days a week, as company store managers do, and put in a similar number of hours.

[24] Thus franchisees rewriting their contract in 1982 would pay a franchise fee of $12.5K and royalties of 11.5 percent of sales in exchange for franchise rights for a new 20-year period.

because franchise rights are usually renewed, franchisees leaving the industry can sell their outlet at a higher price than what the remaining length of the contract would warrant (see Table 14.4 below).

All of the above arguments suggest that there are benefits from owning a franchise that are excluded from our calculations in Table 14.2, leading us to conclude that our estimates of ex post and ex ante rents are very conservative. Furthermore, though the analysis of the 1989 data reported in the appendix reveals somewhat smaller amounts of rents, it nevertheless indicates that rents are not a transitory phenomenon at McDonald's. Overall, we conclude that significant amounts of ex post and ex ante rents are left downstream at McDonald's.

There are several possible reasons why McDonald's might choose to leave these rents with its franchisees. We discuss these in Section 4. For now, as a way to verify the results above, we turn to a different method for assessing the existence and extent of downstream rents at McDonald's.

3. EXAMINING THE SALE PRICES OF EXISTING McDONALD'S RESTAURANTS

In this section, we use data on the prices at which existing McDonald's franchises are sold as another way to address the issue of whether or not McDonald's franchisees earn economic rents ex post or ex ante, and if so, how much. Table 14.4 provides data on the sale prices and other characteristics of 11 existing McDonald's franchises that were sold by franchisees to franchisees between 1975 and 1983 (all dollar values are in 1982 dollars). Though the restaurants covered in this table represent only a very small proportion of franchise sales by franchisees to franchisees, according to company officials, these sales are representative of the overall population.[25] Those included in Table 14.4 represent cases where the new franchisees were denied the right to amortize, for tax purposes, their total investment in their unit, namely, the total sale price.[26] Hence they decided to sue the Internal Revenue Service (IRS), giving us access, through court records, to these data. The last column in Table 14.4 gives the difference between the prices paid for the restaurants and the value of the tangible assets included in the transaction, as noted in company records.[27] In all cases, franchise buyers were willing to pay an amount significantly above the value of the tangibles: on average, they

---

[25] Company records show that in 1981, 1982, and 1983, there were 99, 83, and 149 such sales, respectively.

[26] In other words, the amount they paid over and above the value of the tangible assets plus the franchise fee of $12.5K was not allowed as part of their amortizable capital by the IRS, and the franchisees were contesting this. They won. See *Canterbury* v. *Commissioner*, 160 Tax Decisions & Rulings K-2 (U.S. Tax Ct. 1992, hereafter cited as Canterbury).

[27] Using our own assessment of the value of the tangibles, based on the initial investment requirements and a linear depreciation rate of 10 percent, led to equivalent results.

TABLE 14.4
Sale Prices for Existing McDonald's Restaurants (all dollar values in 1982 dollars)

Site number	Date opened	Date of sale	Remaining franchise life (in months)	Trailing 12 months sales	Sale price	Value of tangibles	Value of franchise
1	June 17, 1974	December 22, 1980	162	1,132,614	466,599	86,666	379,833
2	June 15, 1973	September 30, 1978	178	931,724	503,221	118,405	384,816
3	September 15, 1970	January 21, 1983	92	860,485	346,180	93,781	252,399
4	June 17, 1974	January 31, 1983	136	1,207,528	734,743	53,000	681,743
5	June 15, 1973	January 23, 1983	125	868,754	473,605	76,629	396,976
6	October 1, 1969	October 31, 1978	131	884,634	347,814	0	347,814
7	December 9, 1975	December 29, 1981	179	925,944	387,486	132,701	254,785
8	February 2, 1971	April 15, 1978	153	1,370,207	671,086	78,371	592,715
9	March 28, 1961	July 1, 1979	21	1,782,306	611,433	95,835	515,598
10	October 2, 1969	November 21, 1975	161	1,577,752	714,514	140,694	573,820
11	December 9, 1974	November 21, 1975	230	1,383,627	1,013,162	228,084	785,078
Mean			142	1,175,052	569,986	100,379	469,597

Source: Canterbury v. Commissioner, Stipulations of Fact, U.S. Tax Court No. 38037-87 (1991).

paid $470K above the value of the tangible assets for their franchise, as compared to the $12.5K that buyers of new restaurants pay as a franchise fee.

Interestingly, the price paid for an existing McDonald's restaurant is likely to understate the buyer's valuation of the unit because of the constraints that McDonald's purposely imposed on the sales process. At the time of these sales, McDonald's would allow *one and only one* buyer from its list of preapproved individuals to make an offer to the seller of an existing restaurant at any given time. This list of preapproved buyers included only those individuals who had successfully completed McDonald's training program (or who were already McDonald's franchisees and had been given permission to buy an additional unit).[28] If the two parties successfully negotiated an agreement, the sale took place at the price they had agreed on. Otherwise, this buyer withdrew and McDonald's allowed a new candidate to go through the same process. Thus McDonald's eliminated all direct competition among buyers, while allowing each individual bidder to adjust his or her bid during negotiations with the seller. As a result, the agreed-on price did not necessarily represent the full amount of the buyer's valuation. Hence the buyer of an existing restaurant could still expect to derive some ex ante rents from the outlet, though these would be much lower than those that accrue to a first-time buyer.[29]

The fact that the buyer of a new outlet can expect rather large amounts of ex ante rents, as described in Table 14.2, while the buyer of an existing restaurant pays for most of these up front, raises the issue as to why an "approved" buyer would ever choose to buy an existing outlet rather than wait for a new one. The answer hinges on questions of availability, both in terms of location and time: it is not clear when or whether new outlets will be opened in the area where the franchisee wants to be. This will be especially important for established franchisees who may want to consolidate their holdings in a particular geographical area. For these franchisees, who are prevented by contract from doing anything besides operating their McDonald's franchises, expanding is the only way to spread the opportunity cost of their labor across more units. For new franchisees buying an existing outlet affords them the opportunity to bid on other outlets later on, if they are successful in operating their first one. The earlier

---

[28] McDonald's determines which buyers are appropriate for existing outlets in part on the basis of location. The company tries to limit the intermingling of different franchisees' restaurants because it feels that this leads to too much intrachain competition.

[29] If this process implies that franchisees are unable to obtain from buyers the full value of the stream of rents to come, it would reduce franchisees' tendency to sell their units, leading to less turnover in the management of restaurants, a side effect the company would clearly value as this implies lower costs. This is not to say, however, that McDonald's actively discourages franchisee turnover—company officials know that franchisees who are no longer interested in being with the comapny are not likely to perform well the kind of work that McDonald's needs them to do. However, McDonald's is generally interested in keeping franchisees, and especially good franchisees, for long periods of time. Trying to keep franchisees happy in various ways and using a 20-year franchise contract are just two aspects of this commitment.

they can begin this process, the better off they are likely to be in the end.[30]

There are a number of factors that might explain the level of prices paid for existing franchises in Table 14.4. First, the price premia, which we define here as the difference between the prices paid and the value of the tangibles included in the transaction, could be explained by differences in requirements imposed by McDonald's on buyers of existing restaurants compared to buyers of new outlets. But in fact the requirements are the same for the buyers of both types of outlets, thereby refuting this explanation.

Alternatively, buyers of existing McDonald's restaurants may pay more than the value of tangible assets because the information that becomes available about the sales and profit potential of the unit after it has been operating for some time can be used to better forecast the future performance of the outlet. Since the buyer of a new outlet pays an amount equal to the value of the tangible assets plus the franchise fee of $12.5K for the franchise rights, the buyer of an existing outlet may be willing to pay an amount above that total to account for the value of this informational asset.

While we recognize the value of this type of information, we do not believe it warrants the level of price premia found in Table 14.4. For one thing, McDonald's is well recognized in the industry for its technical sophistication and resulting capacity to forecast accurately the sales potential at new locations. Its incentives to perform these tasks well have become especially strong as a result of its policy of owning and developing the real estate of its franchised as well as its company-owned restaurants. Empirically, McDonald's strength in these activities is supported by the fact that a new store typically "will meet its projected annualized volume level within the first week of operation" (Canterbury: K-12) and by the very low discontinuation rates of restaurants in the McDonald's system.[31] In addition, we find in Table 14.4 that buyers are willing to pay fairly large price premia ($300K and more) for stores that have recorded sales placing them in the lower quartile of the distribution of sales levels (below $900K). It is difficult to believe that buyers would pay these price premia to learn that their outlet is so much below average. In fact, buyers of such units are willing to pay these price premia apparently because they believe that the unit is badly run,

---

[30] Between 1980 and 1990, new franchisees obtained 12.9 percent of the newly opened McDonald's restaurants, existing franchisees bought 61.5 percent of them, and McOpCo, the company-owned side of the corporation, controlled 25.6 percent of them. As for sales of existing restaurants, the breakdown over the same period was 29.4 percent for new franchisees, 63.3 percent for existing franchisees, and 7.3 percent for McOpCo.

[31] Though accurately forecasting sales and accurately forecasting that a store will not go bankrupt are two different things, it is noteworthy that from 1980 to 1982, only 47 of the 4,478 franchised units were either canceled or not renewed by McDonald's for a yearly discontinuation rate of about 0.3 percent. Including franchisor buybacks among the failures increases this rate to only 1.8 percent. Given that buybacks, and in fact nonrenewals, are not all equivalent to failures (in fact, buybacks and nonrenewals often suggest that the company expects the outlet to become more profitable under new management), the discontinuation rates are very small, suggesting a very low rate of error in assessing the market potential of new locations.

and so they disregard the current sales and profit information in favor of some notion of what the intrinsic value of the unit is.[32]

Buyers of existing restaurants might also pay higher prices because of the goodwill attached to these restaurants. Goodwill is generally understood as the value of an established reputation, of a well-respected business name, and of good customer relations. To include goodwill in the determination of the price of an operating outlet implies that consumers must associate positive value to this outlet that is distinct from the value they associate with the franchise system or with its specific location (given that McDonald's typically controls it). But McDonald's specifically prohibits its franchisees from identifying their franchise in any way to distinguish them from the system. As a result, most customers do not even know to whom a restaurant belongs, whether it is a franchisee or the company itself. Hence, any goodwill that is generated by a franchisee, who does a good job, for example, of keeping the premises clean, is likely to revert to the chain as a whole at least as much as to the individual outlet. And though the actual price of the unit is likely to include some compensation for the franchisee's good work, it will again mostly be a function of what is perceived to be the intrinsic value of the restaurant. Finally, even if consumers knew the franchisee, and even if they had positive feelings toward him or her, this could not be included in the price of the outlet. To increase the price of the outlet, goodwill must be transferable: value that is due to positive feelings toward the person of the original franchisee is not. Hence we conclude that in the McDonald's system, there is very little franchisee goodwill, so that goodwill cannot account for the price premia found in Table 14.4.[33]

Finally, going-concern value, which is usually defined as the added value associated with the fact that a business is already operating, might explain the price premia paid by buyers of existing restaurants. While it is sometimes considered to include goodwill, we define going-concern value as resulting from the fact that a variety of start-up costs, such as assembling and training

---

[32] Restaurants in the McDonald's system typically sell for some percentage of their yearly sales. But this percentage varies: the pristine units sell at a lower percentage because the company and the buyer find there is not much they can improve upon. Units that are not so well run sell for a price that is a higher percentage of the sales level because the buyer can do things to improve performance. This suggests that the units have some intrinsic value based on what can be achieved when operated according to specifications.

[33] In a rare case where a McDonald's lost its arches, that is, where a restaurant was operated very similarly by the same individuals in the same place after terminating its relationship with the McDonald's system, its sales fell by 60 percent immediately. Sales continued to go down after the initial shock, and never again exceeded 35 percent of the level they achieved as part of the McDonald's system. The restaurant closed down some 12–18 months later. (See Affidavit of David Atkins, exhibit 51 in *Canterbury* v. *Commissioner*, No. 38037-87 (U.S. Tax Ct. 1991).) That the sales levels of a restaurant would fall this much as a result of losing its connection to McDonald's supports our conclusion that there is very little franchisee goodwill at McDonald's. (The tax court agreed: see *Canterbury*.) In fact, the series of events described above suggest that there is not much location-specific goodwill either. Note that very few such "disconnections" exist at McDonald's given that the company owns the land and buildings in the majority of cases and that convenants not to compete are now included in its contracts. Both of these policies prevent franchisees from continuing to operate in the same location after termination.

a new work force, developing supplier relationships, and setting up equipment, have already been incurred. However, because franchised outlets are not really new businesses but rather clones of established businesses in new locations, we argue that the going-concern value attached to an existing outlet, beyond that provided by the franchise system is minimal. This is especially true in a finely tuned system such as McDonald's, where most, if not all, of the types of costs mentioned above have already been incurred by the frachisor. In fact, expertise in these matters is a major component of what franchisors sell to their franchisees. As a result, we conclude that going-concern value cannot account for the price premia found in Table 14.4.

In summary, we find that going-concern value, goodwill, and the informational advantage of existing restaurants cannot account for the level of price premia paid for these. Thus we conclude that buyers are willing to pay prices that are significantly above the value of the tangibles included in the transaction because they expect to earn economic rents. In other words, we believe that the data found in the last column of Table 14.4 represent estimates of the present value of expected rents for these restaurants. Given that buyers of existing restaurants pay for these up front, these are only ex post rents. However, from Table 14.2, we know that franchisees buying new outlets pay only $12.5K more than the value of the tangibles for their franchise rights. If the buyers of existing restaurants were allowed to do the same, the price premia found in Table 14.4, minus $12.5K, would provide a measure of the amount of ex ante rents that they would expect to earn from these units. In that sense, these figures (minus $12.5K) are comparable to the amounts of ex ante rents found in Table 14.2.[34] On average, we find rents of $470K minus $12.5K, or about $455K in our sample. And these are after-tax rents since buyers should only be willing to pay up front for the after-tax benefit they obtain from owning a franchise.[35]

The $455K estimate obtained here is somewhat larger than, but still consistent with, those estimates obtained in section 2 (especially those that we calculated over 40 rather than 20 years, to include the value of renewal). The fact that the price premia are positive in all 11 cases in Table 14.4 supports the notion that the majority of franchisees earn, or expect to earn rents. Here, even some restaurants with trailing sales of $900K or less apparently allow their owners to capture some rents, even though our analyses in section 2 suggest that there should be no ex ante rents attached to such stores. This is consistent with our contention that the estimates in

---

[34] There is no need to reduce this amount further by the cost of training as buyers of existing restaurants incur this cost as well as buyers of new ones. Hence the amount they are willing to pay for the restaurants must already have been reduced by the cost of training.

[35] Assigning a positive but low value to the available information, or to goodwill and going-concern value, could reduce our estimate of rents somewhat. For example, we could say that these account for 10–20 percent of the price premia. However, given that we have no good basis for choosing a percentage value of this type, and that such an assumption would not alter our conclusions, we chose to use the full $455K as our estimate of rents, especially since we believe that the prices paid for restaurants are not inclusive of all the rents given the sales process described above.

section 2 were conservative. In fact, the data in Table 14.4 support our previous estimates even further: arguments suggesting that our estimates of some of the costs in Tables 14.1 or 14.2 would be too low, and hence that the rents found there are too high, can be countered using the data in Table 14.4. The rents found there simply cannot be accounted for based on such arguments. For example, if the buyers are risk averse, or expect to have to put a lot of effort into their franchise, requiring an even higher estimate of the opportunity cost of their labor than the one we used, the prices they will pay for existing franchises will reflect that. In other words, they will have reduced their offers by an amount sufficient to compensate themselves for the risk involved, for the expected level of effort, and generally for what they perceive to be the value of their labor. Hence the data found in Table 14.4 strongly support our estimates from section 2, and our conclusion that there are ex ante rents left downstream at McDonald's. We conclude that McDonald's franchisees can expect to earn at least $300K to $455K in ex ante rents after taxes, in 1982 dollars, for each new restaurant they own. These estimates are consistent with others from the literature: for example, Noren (1990: 62) notes that "[a] McDonald's franchise is a very lucrative investment, and owning several has made many people millionaires."

4. WHY DOES McDONALD'S LEAVE RENTS WITH ITS FRANCHISEES?

Having established that McDonald's leaves both ex post and ex ante rents downstream, the next question to address is why. Given McDonald's reputation, and its capacity to develop a very precise and well-managed system, we do not believe that the rents we have found are "accidental." It is our contention that McDonald's actually chooses to leave these rents with its franchisees. For one thing, we believe this because the expected value of the ex ante rents is positive, implying that McDonald's does not set its contract terms, royalty rate, and franchise fee to extract all the ex ante rents from even the median (or in this case average) outlet. Furthermore, there are fairly costless mechanisms that McDonald's could use to extract more rents from higher-volume or promising restaurants. For example, it could use an increasing scale for its royalty rate, as some franchisors do, and thus reduce both ex post and ex ante rents.[36] Or it could use a formula to define its franchise fee, making it dependent on some measure of market potential, for example, as a number of franchisors do, thereby reducing ex ante rents.[37] But it does neither. In fact, not only does it not tailor its franchise fee, it

[36] See Lafontaine (1992b: 18), who found that 2 of 118 franchisors in her survey asked for such increasing royalty payments. Most franchisors who used a nonlinear scheme, however, relied on a decreasing scale (18 cases in her data).

[37] See Bhattacharyya and Lafontaine (1992). They found that out of a total of 54 franchisors, 10 used this type of market potential formula to define their franchise fee.

rarely adjusts it over time: in 1987, the franchise fee was increased to \$22.5K from \$12.5K, where it had been since 1960.[38]

There are a number of existing theories of franchising that could lead to downstream rents. Most emphasize incentive problems on the part of the franchisee and sometimes the franchisor. Others are based on informational asymmetries on the franchisor's or the franchisee's side. To date, the empirical literature on franchising has generally been supportive of the idea that incentive issues are important both in terms of the extent to which firms rely on franchising as opposed to company ownership[39] and in terms of the extent to which they rely on royalty rates.[40] Hence we focus first and foremost on incentive arguments below. We come back to some other explanations for franchising that can lead to downstream rents at the end of this section.

4.1. Incentive Arguments for Rents

As noted in the introduction, the existence of ex post rents is quite consistent with much of the existing incentive-based literature on franchising. In fact, ex post rents have been the explicit focus of one branch of this literature, where authors have argued that contracts can and should be made privately enforceable by making sure that the party (parties) subject to incentive problems in a relationship will lose something valuable if the relationship is terminated.[41] This argument is very similar to that found in the efficiency-wage literature in labor economics.[42] To provide incentives in these models, franchisors can either ask franchisees to post a forfeitable bond that, given the probability of perfect or non-noisy monitoring, exceeds in value their expected gains from shirking. Or they can provide franchisees with a stream of rents that they lose if the franchise relationship is terminated because they were found shirking. Note that there is no reason to rely on profit sharing

---

[38] And when McDonald's did increase this fee, it did so in what appears to be a very ad hoc fashion. According to company officials, this increase was brought about by complaints among management that the fee was now too low and that it no longer covered the costs that McDonald's had to bear to open a new restaurant. Someone suggested increasing it to \$22.5K, and others simply agreed. Note that McDonald's resembles most franchisors in this respect: franchise fees generally appear to be dictated mostly by the costs of opening new outlets. At Wendy's, the up-front franchise fee is called a "technical assistance fee," which "is used to defray the cost to the Company of providing to its franchise owners site selection assistance, standard construction plans, specifications and layouts, review of specific restaurant site plans, certain training in the Company's restaurant systems, and certain bulletins, brochures and reports." Wendy's Corp., 10K report, April 5, 1993, at 5. See Lafontaine (1992a); and Dnes (1992), for evidence related to this issue.

[39] See, for example, Brickley and Dark (1987); Norton (1988); Brickley, Dark, and Weisbach (1991); Minkler (1990); Banerji & Simon (1992); Lafontaine (1992a).

[40] See Lafontaine (1992a); and Sen (1993).

[41] See Klein (1980); Telser (1980); Klein and Saft (1985); Williamson (1985); and Klein and Murphy (1988).

[42] See, for example, Becker and Stigler (1974); and Shapiro and Stiglitz (1984). Akerlof and Yellen (1986) provide a collection of important contributions in this area.

for franchisee incentives in this type of model: the threat of termination and resulting potential losses are sufficient to induce the desired level of effort from franchisees. Also, rents and bonds are efficient as self-enforcing mechanisms only if franchisors possess the right to terminate franchisees. The existing evidence suggests that franchisors can and do exercise this right, at least under current legislation. There is also evidence that franchisors in general, and McDonald's in particular, value this right.[43]

Another more static stream of the literature has focused not on rents but on profit sharing as the main incentive mechanism for both franchisees.[44] The ex post rents themselves are not usually focused on as an incentive mechanism in this literature; they arise because the royalty rate, which is chosen to align incentives (and possibly to insure the franchisee), is not designed to and will not by itself extract all the profits of franchisees. One exception is Mathewson and Winter (1985), who discuss the potential incentive effect of rents in a profit-sharing model. They note that in a model where a franchisee earns rents ex post, the cost of shirking includes not only the direct losses in the franchisee's share of profits during the period over which effort is reduced but also the increased probability that the franchisee will lose access to the stream of ex post rents that he can expect to earn if he remains within the franchise relationship.

In most of the models that focus on profit sharing, if there is competition among franchisees, franchisors are assumed to use the up-front fee in the contract to capture the net present value of the stream of ex post rents left downstream by the royalty rate. Similarly, in the self-enforcing contract literature, franchisors can minimize the cost of using rents to generate incentives by getting franchisees to pay up front for the stream of rents to come. In both sets of models then, one expects to observe ex post rents, but no ex ante rents. In other words, asking why we observe ex ante rents here is equivalent to asking why McDonald's does not require franchisees to pay up front for the net present value of this stream of rents. The literature suggests two reasons why it may not be possible for franchisors to extract large fees such as these up front. The first is franchisor opportunism, and the second, franchisee liquidity constraints.

Franchisor opportunism refers to the possibility that franchisors might use the threat of termination to appropriate franchisees' investments unfairly. As a result, franchisees would not agree to post large bonds. According to

---

[43] See Hadfield (1990) for a discussion of some termination cases and their treatment by the courts. Brickley, Dark, and Weisbach, (1991) find that state laws requiring good cause for the termination of franchised outlets reduce the extent of franchising and have an adverse effect on the stock returns of franchised companies. Presumably, this occurs in part because of the chilling effect of the law, even on termination for good cause. Franchisors typically oppose the passage of laws imposing constraints on their termination rights, and the International Franchise Association lobbies heavily against them. Most recently, McDonald's filed a suit to have a new Iowa franchise law declared unconstitutional. This law, among other things, imposes conditions under which franchisors can terminate franchisees.

[44] See, for example, Rubin (1978); Mathewson and Winter (1985); Lal (1990) and Bhattacharyya and Lafontaine (1992).

Mathewson and Winter (1985), franchisor opportunism is likely to constrain the franchise fee and up-front payment required by new franchisors, but not by those that have an established reputation. Klein and Saft (1985) also note that the reputational cost of such behavior to a firm like McDonald's, and the increased cost of running the whole chain as a vertically integrated rather than a franchised system, would likely be greater than the benefits the firm would obtain from behaving opportunistically, thus deterring such a firm from doing so. Hence we conclude that franchisor opportunism does not explain why McDonald's does not require large up-front fees.

Franchisee liquidity contraints, in contrast, are likely to play an important role here. Many of the individuals that McDonald's wants to have as franchisees face these types of constraints. In selecting its franchisees, early in its history, McDonald's decided that for incentive purposes, it was important not to separate the management of the unit from its ownership.[45] The company established policies against passive investors and absentee owners, and also against partnerships, real-estate developers, and corporations. It also developed a pretty good idea of the "types" of individuals that were suited to become franchisees: "McDonald's also thinks twice about applications from doctors, lawyers, accountants, or any other experts used to having customers come to them. The fear is that somebody like that might be reluctant to circulate during the lunch crunch with a pot of coffee and a ready smile. People most likely to get interviews are those with 'ketchup in their veins'—a McDonald's expression for outgoing, high-energy types who will devote their lives to the Golden Arches" (Marsh, 1989: B1).

All McDonald's franchisees are required to be owner-operators. In fact, McDonald's consistently refers to these individuals as owner-operators and not franchisees. When buying a new franchise, franchisees are required to provide 40 percent of the initial capital requirement themselves. This ensures that the franchisee-managers have a large personal stake in their franchise. Finally, they are not allowed to continue to hold another job when they begin operations or to own any franchises from any other chain during their involvement with McDonald's.

Under these conditions, requiring a large bond or fee up front would prevent individuals with the right qualifications, but with limited wealth, from becoming McDonald's franchisees. Even if McDonald's allowed these individuals to borrow much of the up-front bond, they would probably not be able to find a lender. Borrowing makes the lender bear the risk of their misbehavior: if they shirk and the relationship is terminated as a result, given the individual's limited liability and wealth, the lender loses his or her investment. Knowing this, the lender would refuse to lend (or would lend at an unacceptably high price).

Three of McDonald's management policies suggest that the company is mindful of franchisees' liquidity problems. The first was the creation of the BFL (for Business Facilities Lease), a special leasing arrangement that the

[45] See Love (1986, ch. 4). Wendy's has a similar attitude toward investors.

company has developed to allow promising individuals with especially limited wealth to buy a McDonald's franchise.[46] The existence and use of this program, in a context where a large number of individuals apply each year to become franchisees and get turned down, suggests that the company has determined that liquidity constraints are an issue for at least some proportion of the population of people it wants to attract as franchisees. The second policy established by McDonald's relates to sales of existing restaurants: while buyers of new restaurants are required to provide 40 percent of their total investment from unencumbered cash, buyers of existing restaurants need only provide 25 percent (Noren, 1990: 60, 61). Clearly, this acknowledges the difference in the amounts that the two types of buyers are required to pay. But it also relaxes the cash constraint for buyers of existing restaurants, making it possible for more people to become franchisees. Third, and finally, McDonald's has a policy requiring that buyers of new and existing restaurants be able to "survive" on their cash flow. According to company officials, this policy bears directly on the price at which the company sells new restaurants. It also influences the price of existing restaurants in that McDonald's assists potential buyers in determining the price they can pay for a restaurant as a function of the revenue stream it can generate. These notions, that franchisees must be able to survive on their cash flow from the first year onward, and that franchised units must provide a reasonable return for their owners whose investments are not diversified, were recurring themes in conversations with company officials.

Still, since buyers of existing restaurants are willing and able to pay amounts up to $1M, liquidity contraints must not apply to all potential franchisees. Hence McDonald's could require at least some of its franchisees to pay for their rents up front. In fact it does, indirectly, for buyers of existing outlets. Since McDonald's does not control the prices at which existing restaurants are sold on the market, these prices will internalize most of the expected ex post rents. We would argue that from McDonald's perspective, however, requiring all potential buyers to pay such amounts up front would reduce the number of qualified franchise applicants too much. Hence if the company wishes to allow less wealthy individuals to become McDonald's franchisees, it must do so via its pricing of new restaurants. But then the question is why would it not at least tailor its franchise fee to reflect the varying degress of liquidity constraints of the new franchisees? The answer might lie in the potential for franchisor opportunism on renewal. As McAfee and Schwartz (1994) have noted, contract-term unformity is an important source of protection from opportunism for franchisees.

---

[46] This program allows individuals to lease the equipment as well as the building from McDonald's. The program includes an option to purchase the franchise at a price that is set according to a prespecified formula, based on trailing sales, at some point during the 3 years of the BFL contract. In 1982, 77 company-operated stores were "sold" to franchisees under a BFL arrangement, while 59 such stores were sold "normally" to franchisees. According to Dnes (1992: 89), Ford operates a program similar to the BFL in England.

HYBRIDS

This conclusion, that franchisee liquidity constraints play a significant role in generating ex ante rents at McDonald's, basically by preventing McDonald's from extracting the ex post rents up front, raises some interesting issues. In the type of incentive model that focuses on profit sharing, ex post rents are in some sense incidental: they arise because the royalty rate is designed to align incentives, not to extract all of the franchisees' ex post profits. Rent extraction is then supposed to be carried out by the franchise fee. One way to state our result therefore is to say that the franchise fee chosen by McDonald's is simply too low. But if, as we argued above, this is because McDonald's faces franchisee liquidity constraints, then it should try to minimize the amount that it requires franchisees to pay up front. One alternative to an up-front franchise fee extracting the next 20 years worth of franchisee profits would be to require franchisees to pay a fixed amount per shorter time period (year or month) in addition to their royalties. As long as the unit does well some of the time, the liquidity constrained franchisee will be able to pay these smaller but recurring amounts. On average, and over time, the franchisor could extract more from franchisees if it "financed" the fee this way.[47] Moreover, if franchisor opportunism was an issue, this type of ongoing fixed payment would not really be subject to it, again allowing franchisors to extract more rents from downstream firms.

This, of course, raised the issue as to why we do not observe ongoing fixed payments in franchising in general, and at McDonald's in particular. Consistent with the self-enforcement literature, we would argue that this is because franchisors care about maintaining a high level of ongoing ex post rents with franchisees during the contract period for incentive purposes. With these rents, franchisees' incentives will be affected not only by the effect their shirking might have on their current income but also by the effect it might have on the probability that they will continue to earn the ex post rents available to them within the franchise relationship. Maybe even more important, in a dynamic and long-term context such as the one in which the franchise relationship operates, the existence of a stream of ex post rents will likely reduce the free-riding and policy-contesting problems that arise when the franchisee is compensated via revenue or profit sharing.

We conclude that the ex post rents found in this article represent an incentive mechanism that complements the use of profit-sharing rights at McDonald's, as in Mathewson and Winter (1985). Given that both buyers of existing and buyers of new restaurants can expect to earn similar amounts of ex post rents, we can conclude that all franchisees face similar incentives despite the difference in the amount of ex ante rents that they earn. Ex ante rents, however, arise here from the combination of the need for ex post rents and the presence of franchisee wealth constraints. The type of individuals

---

[47] This possibility of ongoing fixed payments does not arise in the profit-sharing literature because the models have been mostly static, so that there is no difference there between an up-front fee and ongoing fixed payments.

that McDonald's wants to recruit as franchisees, namely, owner-operators whose livelihoods are dependent on their units, are especially likely to face liquidity constraints. This in turn increases the need for McDonald's to leave ex ante rents with some of its franchisees. Finally, we note that the potential for contract renewal after each 20-year period guarantees that there is never a time in the relationship when franchisees feel that they no longer have anything to lose from misbehaving. Hence the contract continuously satisfies the conditions for self-enforcement.

4.2. Explanations for Rents Based on Information Asymmetries

Two other types of explanations for franchising, both of which rely on some form of information asymmetry, can lead to rents being left downstream. While our data do not allow us to "test" competing theories for rents, we discuss here reasons why we believe these models do not provide good explanations for the rents found in this article.

The first type of model is based on franchisors' need to signal their type, which is known only to themselves (Gallini and Lutz, 1992). This model leads to downstream rents if the franchisor uses strictly its royalty rate to signal its type. When a firm uses both the company ownership of outlets and a positive royalty rate, as is the case at McDonald's, franchisees earn no rents. Because of this, and the fact that it does not seem reasonable to expect a well-known firm such as McDonald's to have to signal its type, and the lack of empirical support for this model (Lafontaine, 1993), we do not believe that it offers a reasonable explanation for the rents found here.

The second type of model focusses on franchisee adverse selection or screening.[48] There are also a number of reasons why we do not believe that this model provides a good explantion for the rents found here. First, the screening model implies that franchisors should offer a menu of contracts to franchisees to allow them to self-select and thereby reveal their type. But such menus are never observed in practice. Second, under the screening model, franchisors must leave rents with all but the lowest-ability franchisees in order to get franchisees to self-select, which would be very costly, given the 20-year duration of the contract. We believe that franchisors can gather information on individual franchisees' ability levels in more efficient ways than those implied by this model. For example, during the 2 years of training, McDonald's is certainly able to evaluate each potential franchisee's performance at a number of different tasks and in terms of a variety of criteria.[49] Through these processes, McDonald's learns about individuals, and it is able to identify those who have potential as McDonald's franchisees and those

---

[48] See for example, Hallagan (1978) for a screening model of sharecropping; and Lafontaine (1988) for a franchising application.

[49] Of the 300 or so hopefuls involved in the training program at any one time, about one-third do not make it through. See Noren (1990: 60).

who do not.[50] Finally, the screening model is not very appealing in a dynamic context such as this one. Once the contracts have led franchisees to reveal information about themselves, franchisors will want to offer new contracts that no longer allocate rents to them. Knowing this, franchisees will have an incentive not to reveal their information to start with, so that no screening or separation in fact would occur.[51]

An alternative and more interesting way to think about the informational asymmetry relative to franchisees' ability level is to note that ex ante rents increase the size of the applicant pool to include more people with high potential earnings, and thus presumably more high-quality individuals. We believe that this is a nice side effect of these rents, one that franchisors will certainly value, at least to some extent. However, ex ante rents do not necessarily attract only the kind of people the firm wants: doctors and lawyers are a case in point. What McDonald's wants is to attract the best people among the set of those who will want to be owner-operators rather than simply investors or people whose main interest would remain elsewhere. But again, these people will tend to be liquidity constrained: the fact that the company has devised the BFL in the face of large queues of potential franchisees attests to the fact that it still does not find "enough" qualified people among the "unconstrained" set. This in turn leads back to our original argument as to why ex ante rents exist at McDonald's.[52]

5. CONCLUSION

The goal of this article was to show that there are important amounts of downstream rents, both ex post and ex ante, at McDonald's. The conclusion that there are ex ante rents is especially interesting given that most incentive-based theories of franchising, which we find are the most promising explanations for this organizational form, predict that there should not be such rents. Yet we arrived at this conclusion from two different approaches, first by looking at the returns of individual units, and second through an examination of the prices at which franchises are sold. Furthermore, our conclusion is supported by the fact that (1) qualified franchisees wait up to 2 years to get their franchise, supporting once again the notion that these are very valuable to them; (2) according to company officials, there are investors who would be willing to buy McDonald's franchises at higher prices if they were allowed to do so; and (3) there are two devices that are used at McDonald's to provide incentives to franchisees, both of which were mentioned in section 2, that critically depend on the existence of ex ante rents

[50] In fact, it is able to gather enough information about applicants that, according to Burton Cohen, senior vice president of franchising at McDonald's, the percentage of franchisees "that drops out after the store opens is a 'statistical zero.'" Bertagnoli (1989: 44).

[51] See Freixas, Guesnerie, and Tirole (1985); and Laffont and Tirole (1988) on this issue.

[52] See Love (1986, ch. 4) for an account of how the first "owner operator" showed Kroc how successful a McDonald's franchise could be compared to franchises operated by investors.

downstream to function, the first is contract renewal: only franchisees who have performed well are granted a new franchise contract at the expiration of their current contract. The second is the granting of additional restaurants: franchisees are granted the right to buy additonal McDonald's restaurants one at a time, and only if they have performed well in their current ones.[53] Neither one of these policies would be effective in terms of franchisee incentives if there were no ex ante rents left downstream.

We believe that our result, that there are ex ante rents left downstream in franchising, is not limited to McDonald's. This, we would argue, is supported by the existence of queues of potential franchisees in various chains, as noted by Mathewson and Winter (1985).[54] It is also consistent with Smith, who argues that car dealerships are "awarded at below market-clearing prices."[55] Finally, the notion that there are ex ante rents in other franchised chains is consistent with the lack of negative correlation between franchise fees and royalty rates reported in Banerji and Simon (1992) and Lafontaine (1992a).

One central question we have not addressed in this article is why the firm chooses to franchise, especially if it means leaving ex ante rents downstream, when it can, and does, operate restaurants directly. In fact, between 1967 and 1976, McDonald's experimented with an increased reliance on company ownership (from 9 to 33 percent) but found that company-owned stores did not do as well as franchised stores, especially in low-volume locations. As a result, a decision was made to limit the proportion of company-owned stores in the chain to the current 25 percent.[56]

McDonald's results in this experiment were consistent with results from the literature suggesting that costs are not controlled as efficiently under company operation as compared to franchisee management (see Shelton, 1967; Krueger, 1991). Furthermore, because franchisees are self-motivated, the amount of company resources devoted to supervising them is much lower than that needed to monitor managers of company-owned stores. Each area supervisor at McOpCo oversees the operations of an average of four company-owned stores, with a maximum of six. On the franchised side of the company, the equivalent "field consultants" are responsible for an average of nine franchisees, who on average control 21 restaurants. Since we assigned the total cost of each franchisee to the management of a single store in our

---

[53] Ray Kroc, who developed the company after buying the rights from the McDonald brothers, clearly recognized the incentive effect of attributing potential additional outlets on the basis of good behavior: "Kroc kept them (franchisees) doubly motivated with the promise of an additional restaurant, doled out one at a time to franchisees who followed his procedures to the letter." Bertagnoli (1989: 38).

[54] See Jeffrey A. Tannenbaum, Franchise Pool Is Drying Up for Some Firms, *Wall St. J.* (November 14, 1989: B1) for evidence that not all franchised chains face queues of potential franchisees.

[55] Smith (1982: 129). Shepard (1993) notes that lessee-dealer licenses in gasoline retailing sell for $100K to $300K and concludes from this that there are ex post rents left downstream in gasoline retailing.

[56] See Love (1986: 61). The expansion far exceeded the initial purpose of the McOpCo (company-owned) system, which had been to groom experienced managers capable of supervising the franchised system.

calculations of rents, this difference in responsibilities represents a direct cost differential to the company between the two organizational forms. Finally, franchising leads to less turnover of store management, which again leads to lower costs for McDonald's. Given all this, it is very possible that despite the need to leave rents with its franchisees, McDonald's still finds that franchising is a more efficient organizational form for the majority of its restaurants.[57]

Although the available data did not allow us to test competing theories of rents directly, having considered various explanations for them, we argue that they result from the need to provide franchisees with a stream of ex post rents for incentive purposes that complements the assignment of profit-sharing rights. In addition, we conclude that McDonald's leaves a stream of ex ante rents with the buyers of new restaurants, by not requiring them to pay for the rents up front, because a number of the individuals who qualify as potential owner-operators have limited wealth. This combination of owner-operators and ex post rents, we believe, provides McDonald's with significant control over its franchisees, with the promise of additional outlets and contract renewal dependent on current performance enhancing this level of control even further.

We have followed much of the existing literature on contractual self-enforcement in assuming that ex post rents are needed for incentive purposes, but ex ante rents are not. In other words, ex post rents paid for in full up front are considered in the literature to be as efficient an incentive mechanism as ex post rents that are not paid for up front. But the latter make people richer, and allowing individuals to "get rich" could generate different incentives, for example, more loyalty and cooperation from them. According to Love (1986: 82), Kroc "believed that McDonald's could only succeed if its franchisees became wealthy." If so, the fact that buyers of existing franchises do not earn as much rents ex ante as buyers of new restaurants would have implications from an incentive point of view. In fact, we might expect that the amount of loyalty and cooperation within the chain will decrease over time or, put differently, as the number of second- and third-time buyers increases. Though this is beyond the scope of the present article, one could potentially test for this effect using data on franchisor-disputes. We believe this would be a promising avenue for future research in the area of self-enforcing contracts.

Finally, the existence of downstream rents in at least some franchised chains suggests that although the static literature on share contracts has been useful in increasing our understanding of various aspects of the franchising relationship, it may not be capturing the whole story. Models that could build on the work of Mathewson and Winter (1985) and explore further the potential for the simultaneous use of profit sharing and ex post rents, and their interaction from an incentive perspective, might provide

---

[57] In general, one does not find much evidence in the literature that franchisors would prefer more company ownership. See Lafontaine (1992b: 9) for some survey results on this issue, and Dant, Kaufmann, and Paswan (1992) for an overview of the empirical literature on this topic.

further insights into the workings of this and similar types of relationships. One possibility might be that profit sharing addresses mostly the more direct problems related to the level of effort put in by the franchisee in each period, while bonding, via up-front fees and/or rents, would address more of the ongoing free-riding and policy-contesting type of issues that arise once the agent is compensated via profit sharing. It is our hope that this article will stimulate research in these directions.

APPENDIX

TABLE A1
Yearly Economic Rents ($) for a McDonald's Franchise in 1989

	Level of sales		
	Low	**Mid**	**High**
Yearly sales	1,300,000	1,500,000	1,700,000
Cost of sales			
Food cost	369,396	423,579	474,187
Paper cost	54,406	62,397	70,464
Total	423,802	485,976	544,651
Gross profits	876,198	1,014,024	1,155,349
Controllable expenses			
Crew labor	222,672	253,832	276,904
Management labor[a]	62,526	67,555	71,655
Ads and promotions	80,809	90,663	100,135
Utilities	43,193	46,582	49,496
Others	76,727	86,129	92,105
Total	485,927	544,761	590,295
Gross profits less controllables	390,271	496,263	565,054
Other expenses			
Royalty/rent[b]	186,200	206,250	233,750
Others	58,152	60,760	62,152
Total	244,352	267,010	295,902
Yearly income from operations	145,919	202,253	269,152
Opportunity costs			
Interest (5% per year)[c]	41,100	45,200	60,300
Franchisee labor[d]	72,000	72,000	72,000
Total	113,100	117,200	132,300
Yearly economic rents	32,819	85,053	136,852

Source: McDonald's Corp., Franchise Offering Circular (1990).

Note: Based on data for approximately 1,592 U.S. company-owned units open thirteen months or more in 1989. That year, about 65 percent of the more than 7,600 domestic McDonald's restaurants open for at least thirteen months had sales above $1,300K, 45 percent had sales above $1,500K, and 28 percent had sales above $1,700K. The average level of sales was $1,505K.

(*Table A1 continued*)

[a] The management labor figures shown here differ from those in the McDonald's profit and loss statements by the amount of the store manager's salary ($28K, $33K, and $38K, respectively, for the three types of stores), whose position is assumed to be taken over by the franchisee.

[b] Royalties, including rents, are 13.75 percent of gross sales except for stores with monthly sales below $114,390. Those pay a minimum rent of $11,725 monthly plus 3.5 percent of gross sales. For a restaurant with yearly sales of $1,300K, this amounts to $186,200, or 14.32 percent of sales.

[c] Includes the forgone interest on the security deposit. Also, since the franchisee contributes 40 percent or more of the initial capital and borrows the rest, real interest payments are part of this cost. The disclosure document calculations are based on an initial investment of $610K, which we take to be the typical outlet investment. Since this is about twice the investment required in 1982, we assume that all investment figures are doubled.

[d] A 1992 proprietary survey shows prior earnings of new McDonald's franchisees previously unaffiliated with the company at $72K.

TABLE A2
Present Discounted Value Calculations for a Single McDonald's Restaurant (thousands of 1989 dollars)

	Interest cost calculated at a real interested rate of 5 percent			Interest cost calculated at a real interest rate of 7.5 percent		
	Low	Mid	High	Low	Mid	High
Yearly sales	1,300	1,500	1,700	1,300	1,500	1,700
Yearly rents	32.8	85.1	136.9	12.3	62.5	106.7
Present discounted value of rents	429.2	1,113.5	1,791.3	161.0	817.8	1,396.2
Ex ante costs[a]						
Equipment[b]	658.0	724.0	986.0	658.0	724.0	986.0
Franchise fee[c]	22.5	22.5	22.5	22.5	22.5	22.5
Training[d]	75.0	75.0	75.0	75.0	75.0	75.0
Total	755.5	821.5	1,083.5	755.5	821.5	1,083.5
Ex ante rents						
Before taxes	(326.3)	292.0	707.8	(594.5)	(3.7)	312.7
After taxes[e]	(326.3)	204.3	495.5	(594.5)	(3.7)	218.9

Note Numbers in parentheses denote losses.

[a] The security deposit is not included as an ex ante cost since it is usually refunded.

[b] All investments in equipment are assumed to be worthless at the end of the twenty-year contract. The disclosure document calculations are based on an initial investment of $610K, which we take to be the typical outlet investment. Since this is about twice the investment required in 1982, we assume that all investment figures, including equipment investment figures, are doubled.

[c] The franchise fee in 1989 was $22.5K.

[d] Since the 1989 management labor figures are about 1.5 times the 1982 figures, we apply this ratio to the 1982 estimates of the cost of training. The results are not sensitive to reasonable changes in these amounts. No tuition is paid for training, and a large number of new franchisees who are ex-employees of franchisees or the company do not have to bear any training cost.

[e] Assuming a 30 percent tax rate to be applied to both the profits of the franchise and the revenues the franchisee would obtain from his labor and his capital under their best alternative uses. Clearly, this is very "naive," not allowing for different tax rates for businesses and individuals, nor for the fact that some costs (accelerated depreciation, car expenses, etc.) reduce firms' tax liabilities. Hence, the results reported on this line should be interpreted as very coarse approximations.

BIBLIOGRAPHY

Acheson, James M. 1988. *The Lobster Gangs of Maine.* Hanover, N.H.: University Press of New England.

Adams, J. W., and Robert Hamlisch. 1952. *Report on Monopolistic Controls in the Tuna Industry.* Bureau of Industrial Economics, U.S. Federal Trade Commission (December 31).

Aghion, Phillipe, and Partick Bolton. 1987. "Contracts as a Barrier to Entry," *American Economic Review* 77: 388–401.

Akerlof, George A., and Janet L. Yellen. 1986. *Efficiency Wage Models of the Labor Market.* New York: Cambridge University Press.

Alchian, Armen A. 1959. "Costs and Outputs," in M. Abramovitz, ed., *The Allocation of Economic Resources.* Stanford: Stanford University Press.

Alchian, Armen A., and Harold Demsetz. 1972. "Production, Information Costs, and Economic Organization," *American Economic Review* 62: 777–95.

Alchian, Armen A., and Susan Woodward. 1987. "Reflections on the Theory of the Firm," *Journal of Institutional and Theoretical Economics* 143: 110–36.

Amemiya, Takeshi. 1981. "Qualitative Response Models: A Survey," *Journal of Economic Literature* 19: 1483–1536.

Anderson, Erin. 1985. "The Sales Person as Outside Agent," *Marketing Science* 4: 234–54.

Anderson, Erin, and David C. Schmittlein. 1984. "Integration of the Sales Force: An Empirical Examination," *Rand Journal of Economics* 15: 385–95.

Armour, H. O., and David J. Teece. 1980. "Vertical Integration and Technological Innovation," *Review of Economics and Statistics,* August: 470–74.

Arrow, Kenneth J. 1962. "The Economic Implications of Learning by Doing," *Review of Economic Studies* 29: 155.

———. 1969. "The Organization of Economic Activity: Issues Pertinent to the Choice of Market versus Nonmarket Allocation," in *The Analysis and Evaluation of Public Expandures: The PPB System,* 59–73. Joint Economic Committee, 91st Congress. Washington, D.C.: U.S. Government Printing Office.

———. 1971. *Essays in the Theory of Risk-Bearing.* Chicago: Markham.

Ashley, Clifford W. 1938. *The Yankee Whaler.* Boston: Houghton Mifflin.

Banerji, Shumeet, and Carol Simon. 1992. "Franchising vs. Ownership: A Contracting Explanation." Manuscript, Graduate School of Business, University of Chicago.

Barton, J. H. 1972. "The Economic Basis of Damages for Breach of Contract," *Journal of Legal Studies* 1: 277–304.

Barzel, Yoram. 1977. "Some Fallacies in the Interpretation of Information Costs," *Journal of Law and Economics* 20: 291–307.

———. 1982. "Measurement Costs and the Organization of Markets," *Journal of Law and Economics* 25: 27–48.

Becker, Gary S., and George J. Stigler. 1974. "Law Enforcement, Malfeasance, and Compensation of Enforcers," *Journal of Legal Studies* 3: 1–18.

Bertagnoli, Lisa. 1989. "McDonald's: Company of the Quarter Century," *Restaurants and Institutions,* July 10, 32–60.

Bhattacharyya, Sugato, and Francine Lafontaine. 1992. "Double-Sided Moral Hazard and the Nature of Share Contracts." University of Michigan, School of Business Administration Working Paper no. 698.

Bittlingmeyer, George. 1993. "The Stock Market and Early Antitrust Enforcement," *Journal of Law and Economics* 36: 1–32.

Bockstoce, John R. 1986. *Whales, Ice, and Men: The History of Whaling in the Western Arctic.* Seattle: University of Washington Press.

Bork, Robert H. 1978. *The Antitrust Paradox.* New York: Basic Books.

Boston Consulting Group. 1986. *The Future of the Soft Drink Industry, 1985–1990.* Boston.

Bowman, Ward S. 1956. "Review of 'United States vs. United Shoe Machinery Corporation, An Economic Analysis' by Carl Kaysen," *Yale Law Journal* 66: 303–14.

Branch, Alan E. 1981. *Elements of Shipping.* New York: Chapman & Hall.

Brickley, James A., and Frederick H. Dark. 1987. "The Choice of Organizational Form: The Case of Franchising," *Journal of Financial Economics* 18: 401–20.

Brickley, James A., Frederick H. Dark, and Michael. S. Weisbach. 1991a. "An Agency Perspective on Franchising," *Financial Management* 20: 27–35.

———. 1991b. "The Economic Effects of Franchise Termination Laws," *Journal of Law and Economics* 34: 101–32.

Broadman, H. G., and M. A. Toman. 1983. "Non-Price Provisions in Long-Term Natural Gas Contracts," Resources for the Future, Washington.

Broderick, Dale G. 1973. *An Industry Study: The Tuna Fishery.* Ph.D. diss., Columbia University.

Business Week. 1982. "The 80's Look in Chips: Custom, Not Standard." January 18, 36D–36L.

Byers, Edward. 1987. *The Nation of Nantucket: Society and Politics in an Early American Commercial Center, 1660–1820.* Boston: Northeastern University Press.

Calabresi, Guido, and A. Douglas Melamed. 1972. "Property Rules, Liability Rules, and Inalienability: One View of the Cathedral," *Harvard Law Review* 85: 1089.

Canes, M. E., and D. A. Norman. 1983. "Analytics of Take-or-Pay Provisions in Natural Gas Contracts." Discussion Paper No. 029. American Petroleum Institute, Washington, D.C.

Carney, E. M. 1978. "Pricing Provisions in Coal Contracts," *Rocky Mountain Mineral Law Institute,* 197–30. New York: Matthew Bender.

Chandler, Alfred D., Jr. 1962. *Strategy and Structure: Chapters in the History of Industrial Enterprise.* Cambridge: MIT Press.

———. 1977. *The Visible Hand: The Managerial Revolution in American Business.* Cambridge: Harvard University Press.

Chapman, Kenneth, and Michael J. Meuer. 1989. "Efficient Remedies for Breach of Warranty," *Law and Contemporary Problems* 52: 107–31.

Chatterton, Edward Keble. 1926. *Whalers and Whaling.* Philadelphia: J. B. Lippincott.

Cheung, Steven N. S. 1969. "Transaction Costs, Risk Aversion, and the Choice of Contractual Arrangements," *Journal of Law and Economics* 12: 23–46.

Clark, Robert C. 1985. "Agency Costs versus Fiduciary Duties," in J. Pratt and R. Zeckhauser, eds., *Principles and Agents: The Structure of Business.* Boston: Harvard Business School Press.

Coase, Ronald H. 1937. "The Nature of the Firm," *Economica* 4: 386–405.

———. 1972. "Durability and Monopoly," *Journal of Law and Economics* 15: 143–49.

———. 1988. "The Nature of the Firm: Origins, Meaning, Influence," *Journal of Law, Economics, and Organization* 4: 3–48.

Cooper, Russell, and Thomas W. Ross. 1985. "Product Warranties and Double Moral Hazard," *Rand Journal of Economics* 16: 103–13.

Corey, E. Raymond. 1978. *Procurement Management: Strategy, Organization, and Decision-Making.* Boston: CBI Publishing Co.

Coughlan, A. 1985. "Competition, Cooperative Marketing, and Channel Choice: Theory and Applications," *Marketing Science* 4: 110–29.

Crocker, Keith J., and Scott E. Masten. 1986. "Mitigating Contractual Hazards: Unilateral Options and Contract Length." Working Paper no. 449. Graduate School of Business Administration, University of Michigan.

———. 1988. "Mitigating Contractual Hazards: Unilateral Options and Contract Length," *Rand Journal of Economics* 19: 327–43.

———. 1991. "Pretia ex Machina? Prices and Process in Long-Term Contracts," *Journal of Law and Economics* 34: 69–99.

———. 1995. "Regulation and Administered Contracts Revisited: Lessons from Transaction-Cost Economics for Public Utility Regulation," *Journal of Regulatory Economics.*

Dant, Rajiv P., Patrick J. Kaufmann, and Audesh K. Paswan. 1992. "Ownership Redirection in Franchised Channels," *Journal of Public Policy and Marketing* 11: 33–44.

deGraeve, Emil L., and James H. Forbes, Jr. 1954. *The Impact of Imports on the United States Tuna Industry.* Stanford Research Institute Project 1191, prepared for the Tuna Industry Committee, Stanford, Calif.

Demsetz, Harold. 1964. "The Exchange and Enforcement of Property Rights," *Journal of Law and Economics* 7: 11–26.

———. 1967. "Toward a Theory of Property Rights," *American Economic Review* 57: 34–59.

———. 1995. *Theory of Industrial Organization: Critical Commentaries.* New York: Cambridge University Press.

Dewing, Arthur S. 1914. *Corporate Promotion and Reorganizations.* Cambridge: Harvard University Press.

Director, Aaron, and Edward Levi. 1956. "Law and the Future: Trade Regulation," *Northwestern University Law Review* 51: 281–96.

Diver, Colin S. 1983. "The Optimal Precision of Administrative Rules," *Yale Law Journal* 93: 65.

Dnes, Antony W. 1992. *Franchising: A Case-Study Approach.* Aldershot: Avebury.

Dow, George Francis. 1925. *Whale Ships and Whaling.* Salem, Mass.: Marine Research Society.

Drewry, H. P. 1972–92. *Shipping Statistics and Economics.*

———. 1975–89. *Shipping Studies.*

Dubin, Jeffrey, and R. Douglas Rivers. 1986. *Statistical Software Tools*, Version 1.0. Pasadena, Calif.

Ehrlich, Isaac, and Richard A. Posner. 1974. "An Economic Analysis of Legal Rulemaking," *Journal of Legal Studies* 3: 257.

Ellickson, Robert C. 1986. "Of Coase and Cattle: Dispute Resolution among Neighbors in Shasta County," *Stanford Law Review* 38: 623.

———. 1987. "A Critique of Economic and Sociological Theories of Social Control," *Journal of Legal Studies* 16: 67–99.

———. 1991. *Order without Law: How Neighbors Settle Disputes.* Cambridge: Harvard University Press.

Evans, David, and Sanford Grossman. 1983. "Integration," in D. Evans, ed., *Breaking Up Bell.* New York: North-Holland.

Fasullo, P., T. Tarillion, and J. Matson. 1982. "Price of Dwindling Supply of Better Quality Coke," *Oil and Gas Journal* 198.

Finney, D. J. 1952. *Probit Analysis*, 2d ed. Cambridge: The University Press.

Flath, David. 1980. "The Economics of Short-Term Leasing," *Economic Inquiry* 18: 247–59.

Forbes, Stevenson and Co. 1968. "A Tuna Transshipment Plant in San Diego and Other Ocean-Oriented Facilities." Feasibility study prepared for the Economic Development Administration, U.S. Department of Commerce (Project no. 07-6-09121, June 25).

Freixas, Xavier, Roger Guesnerie, and Jean Tirole. 1985. "Planning under Incomplete Information and the Ratchet Effect," *Review of Economic Studies* 52: 173–91.

Gallini, Nancy T., and Nancy A. Lutz. 1992. "Dual Distribution and Royalty Fees in Franchising," *Journal of Law, Economics, and Organization* 8: 471–501.

Gely, Rafael, and Pablo T. Spiller. 1990. "A Rational Choice Theory of Supreme Court Statutory Decisions with Applications to the *State Farm* and *Grove City* Cases," *Journal of Law, Economics, and Organization* 2: 263–300.

Goetz, Charles J., andd Robert E. Scott. 1981. "Principles of Relational Contracts," *Virginia Law Review* 67: 1089–1150.

———. 1983. "The Mitigation Principle: Toward a General Theory of Contractual Obligation," *Virginia Law Review* 69: 967–1024.

Goldberg, Victor P. 1976. "Regulation and Administered Contracts," *Bell Journal of Economics* 7: 426–48.

————. 1980. "Relational Exchange: Economics and Complex Contracts," *American Behavioral Scientist* 23: 337–52.

————. 1985. "Price Adjustment in Long-Term Contracts," *Wisconsin Law Review* (1985): 527–43.

————. 1990a. "The United Shoe Machinery Leases." Manuscript, Columbia University Law School.

————. 1990b. "Aversion to Risk Aversion in the New Institutional Economics," *Journal of Institutional and Theoretical Economics* 146: 216–22.

Goldberg, Victor P., and John R. Erickson. 1982. "Long-Term Contracts for Petroleum Coke." Working Paper no. 206, University of California, Davis, Department of Economics.

————. 1987. "Quantity and Price Adjustment in Long-Term Contracts: A Case Study in Petroleum Coke," *Journal of Law and Economics* 30: 369–98.

Grossman, Sanford J., and Oliver D. Hart. 1986. "The Costs and Benefits of Ownership: A Theory of Vertical and Lateral Integration," *Journal of Political Economy* 94: 691–719.

Guandolo, John. 1979. *Transportation Law*. 3d ed. Dubuque, Iowa: Brown.

Guide to Coal Contracts. 1981, 1983. Arlington, Va.; Pasha Publications.

Hadfield, Gillian K. 1990. "Problematic Relations: Franchising and the Law of Incomplete Contracts," *Stanford Law Review* 42: 927–92.

Hall, A. D. 1973. "Some Fundamental Concepts of Systems Engineering," in S. L. Optner, ed., *Systems Analysis*. Harmondsworth, U.K.: Penguin.

Hallagan, William. 1978. "Self-Selection by Contractual Choice and the Theory of Share-cropping," *Bell Journal of Economics* 9: 344–54.

Hardin, Garrett. 1968. "The Tragedy of the Commons," *Science* 162: 1243.

Harris, Brian. 1986. "How Direct Product Profit Can Keep Your Supermarket Alive." Speech reprinted in *InterBev86*. Washington, D.C.: InterBev Limited.

Harris, Milton, and Robert Townsend. 1981. "Resource Allocation under Asymmetric Information," *Econometrica* 49: 33–64.

Hart, Oliver, and Bengt Holmstrom. 1986. "The Theory of Contracts," Working Paper no. 418, MIT, Department of Economics. Subsequently published in Truman Bewley, ed., *Advances in Economic Theory: Fifth World Congress*. Cambridge: Cambridge University Press, 1987.

Hawkins, Clark A. 1969. *The Field Price Regulation of Natural Gas*. Tallahassee: Florida State University Press.

Hayek, Friedrich A. 1945. "The Use of Knowledge in Society," *American Economic Review* 35: 519–30.

Heckman, James. 1976. "The Common Structure of Statistical Models of Truncation, Sample Selection and Limited Dependent Variables and a Simple Estimator for Such Models," *Annals of Economic and Social Measurement* 5: 475–92.

————. 1979. "Sample Selection Bias as a Specification Error," *Econometrica* 47: 153–61.

Hobbes, Thomas. 1651. *Leviathan*. Reprint, 1909. Oxford: Clarendon Press.

Hohman, Elmo Paul. 1928. *The American Whaleman: A Study of Life and Labor in the Whaling Industry*. New York: Longmans, Green.

Holmes, Oliver Wendell, Jr. 1881. *The Common Law*. Boston: Little, Brown.

Jackson, Gordon. 1978. *The British Whaling Trade*. London: A. & C. Black.

Japan Iron and Steel Federation. 1989. *The Steel Industry of Japan*. Tokyo: Japan Iron and Steel Federation.

Jensen, Michael C., and William H. Meckling. 1976. "Theory of the Firm: Managerial Behavior, Agency Costs and Ownership Structure," *Journal of Financial Economics* 3: 305–60.

Joskow, Paul L. 1985. "Vertical Integration and Long-Term Contracts: The Case of Coal-Burning Electric Generation Plants," *Journal of Law, Economics, and Organization* 1: 33–80.

————. 1986. "Price Adjustment in Longer Term Contracts: The Case of Coal." Subsequently published as "Price Adjustment in Long-Term Contracts: The Case of Coal," *Journal of Law and Economics* 31 (1988): 47–83.

————. 1987. "Contract Duration and Relationship-Specific Investments: Evidence from Coal Markets," *American Economic Review* 77: 168–85.

——. 1988. "Asset Specificity and the Structure of Vertical Relationships: Empirical Evidence," *Journal of Law, Economics, and Organization* 4: 98–115.

Joskow, Paul, and Frederick Mishkin. 1977. "Electric Utility Fuel Choice Behavior in the United States," *International Economic Review* 18: 719–36.

Joskow, Paul, and Richard Schmalensee. 1985. "The Performance of Steam Electric Generating Plants in the United States: 1960–1989." Working Paper no. 371, MIT, Department of Economics.

Judge, George G., et al. 1985. *The Theory and Practice of Econometrics*, 2d ed. New York: Wiley.

Justis, Robert T., and Richard J. Judd. 1989. *Franchising.* Cincinnati: South-Western Publishing Co.

Kahn, E. J. 1960. *The Big Drink: The Story of Coca-Cola.* New York: Random House.

Kaysen, Carl. 1956. *United States v. United Shoe Machinery Corporation: An Economic Analysis of an Anti-trust Case.* Cambridge: Harvard University Press.

Kennedy, Duncan. 1976. "Form and Substance in Private Law Adjudication," *Harvard Law Review* 89: 1685.

Kenney, R. W., and B. Klein. 1983. "The Economics of Block Booking," *Journal of Law and Economics* 26: 497–540.

——. 1985. "The Law and Economics of Contractual Flexibility." Working Paper no. 388, UCLA, Department of Economics.

Klein, Benjamin. 1980. "Transaction Cost Determinants of 'Unfair' Contractual Arrangements," *American Economic Review* 70: 356–62.

——. 1983. "Contracting Costs and Residual Claims: The Separation of Ownership and Control," *Journal of Law and Economics* 26: 367–74.

——. 1988. "Vertical Integration as Organizational Ownership: The Fisher Body–General Motors Relationship Revisited," *Journal of Law, Economics, and Organization* 4: 199–213.

——. 1992. "Contracts and Incentives: The Role of Contract Terms in Assuring Performance," in Lars Werin and Hans Wijkander, eds., *Contract Economics.* Cambridge, Mass.: Blackwell.

Klein, Benjamin, R. A. Crawford, and A. A. Alchian. 1978. "Vertical Integration, Appropriable Rents, and the Competitive Contracting Process," *Journal of Law and Economics* 21: 297–326.

Klein, Benjamin, and Keith B. Leffler. 1981. "The Role of Market Forces in Assuring Contractual Performance," *Journal of Political Economy* 89: 615–41.

Klein, Benjamin, and Kevin M. Murphy. 1988. "Vertical Restraints as Contract Enforcement Mechanisms," *Journal of Law and Economics* 31: 265–97.

Klein, Benjamin, and Lester F. Saft. 1985. "The Law and Economics of Franchise Tying Contracts," *Journal of Law and Economics* 28: 345–61.

Klein, Peter G., and Howard A. Shelanski. 1994. "Empirical Research in Transaction Cost Economics: A Survey and Assessment." Mimeo, University of California at Berkeley, Department of Economics.

Klevorick, Alvin K. 1991. "Directions and Trends in Industrial Organization: A Review Essay on the *Handbook of Industrial Organization*," *Brookings Papers on Economic Activity: Microeconomics* 1991: 241–64.

Komesar, Neil. 1981. "In Search of a General Approach to Legal Analysis: A Comparative Institutional Alternative." *Michigan Law Review* 79: 1350.

Koopmans, Tjalling, and Martin Beckmann. 1957. "Assignment Problems and the Location of Economic Activity," *Econometrica* 25: 35–76.

Kotler, Philip. 1984. *Marketing Management: Analysis, Planning, and Control*, 5th ed. Englewood Cliffs, N.J.: Prentice-Hall.

Krueger, Alan B. 1991. "Ownership, Agency and Wages: An Examination of the Fast Food Industry," *Quarterly Journal of Economics* 106: 75–101.

Laffont, Jean-Jacques, and Jean Tirole. 1988. "The Dynamics of Incentive Contracts," *Econometrica* 56: 1153–75.

Lafontaine, Francine. 1988. *Franchising as a Share Contract: An Empirical Assessment.* Ph.D. diss., University of British Columbia.

———. 1992a. "Agency Theory and Franchising: Some Empirical Results," *Rand Journal of Economics* 23: 263–83.

———. 1992b. "How and Why Do Franchisors Do What They Do: A Survey Report." In *Franchising: Passport for Growth & World of Opportunity*, ed. Patrick J. Kaufmann and Rajiv Dant. Proceedings of the Sixth Conference of the Society of Franchising. The Society.

———. 1993. "Contractual Arrangements as Signaling Devices: Evidence from Franchising," *Journal of Law, Economics, and Organization* 9: 256–89.

Lal, Rajiv. 1990. "Improving Channel Coordination through Franchising," *Marketing Science* 9: 299–318.

Lee, L. S., G. S. Maddala, and R. P. Trost. 1979. "Testing for Structural Change by D-Methods in Switching Simultaneous Equations Models," *Proceedings of the American Statistical Association* (Business and Economics Section), 461–66.

Leffler, Keith B., and Randal R. Rucker. 1991. "Transaction Costs and the Efficient Organization of Production: A Study of Timber-Harvesting Contracts," *Journal of Political Economy* 99: 1060–87.

Levy, Brian, and Pablo T. Spiller. 1994. "The Institutional Foundations of Regulatory Commitment: A Comparative Analysis of Telecommunications Regulation," *Journal of Law, Economics, and Organiztion* 10: 201–46.

Levy, David T. 1988. "Short-Term Leasing and Monopoly Power: The Case of IBM," *Journal of Institutional and Theoretical Economics* 144: 611–34.

Lewis, Warren L. 1991. "Earnings Claims Gain Favor," *Franchising World* 23: 5–9.

Libecap, Gary D., and Steven N. Wiggins. 1984. "Contractual Responses to the Common Pool: Prorationing of Crude Oil Production," *American Economic Review* 74: 87–98.

Lindahl, Martin L., and William A. Carter. 1959. *Corporate Concentration and Public Policy*, 3d ed. Englewood Cliffs, N.J.: Prentice-Hall.

Louis, J. C., and Harvey, Yazijian. 1980. *The Cola Wars*. New York: Everest House.

Love, John F. 1986. *McDonald's: Behind the Arches*. New York: Bantam Books.

Macaulay, Stewart. 1963. "Non-Contractual Relations in Business: A Preliminary Study," *American Sociological Review* 28: 55–70.

MacAvoy, Paul W., and Robert S. Pindyck. 1975. *The Economics of the Natural Gas Shortage (1960–1980)*. New York: American Elsevier.

Macneil, Ian R. 1974. "The Many Futures of Contracts," *South California Law Review* 47: 691–816.

———. 1992. "Efficient Breach of Contract: Circles in the Sky," *Virginia Law Review* 68: 947–69.

Maddala, G. S. 1983. *Limited-Dependent and Qualitative Variables in Economics*. Cambridge: Cambridge University Press.

Manski, Charles F., and Steven R. Lerman. 1977. "Estimation of Choice Probabilities from Choice Based Samples," *Econometrica* 45: 1977–88.

Marasco, Richard J. 1970. *The Organization of the California Tuna Industry: An Economic Analysis of the Relations between Market Performance and Conservation in the Fisheries*. Ph.D. diss., University of California at Berkeley.

Marsh, Barbara. 1989. "Going for the Golden Arches," *The Wall Street Journal*. May 1, B1.

Martin, Milward W. 1962. *Twelve Full Ounces*. New York: Holt, Rinehart and Winston.

Marvel, Howard P. 1982. "Exclusive Dealing," *Journal of Law and Economics* 25: 1–25.

Masten, Scott E. 1982. *Transaction Costs, Institutional Choice, and the Theory of the Firm*. Ph.D. diss., University of Pennsylvania.

———. 1984. "The Organization of Production: Evidence from the Aerospace Industry," *Journal of Law and Economics* 27: 403–17.

———. 1988a. "Minimum Bill Contracts: Theory and Policy," *Journal of Industrial Economics* 37: 85–97.

———. 1988b. "A Legal Basis for the Firm," *Journal of Law, Economics, and Organization* 4: 181–98.

———. 1988c. "Equity, Opportunism, and the Design of Contractual Relations," *Journal of Institutional and Theoretical Economics* 144: 180–95.

Masten Scott E., and Keith J. Crocker. 1984. "Regulation and Nonprice Competition in Long-Term Contracts for Natural Gas." Working Paper, University of Virginia, Department of Economics.

———. 1985. "Efficient Adaptation in Long-Term Contracts: Take-or-Pay Provisions for Natural Gas," *American Economic Review* 75: 1083–93.

Masten, Scott E., James W. Meehan, and Edward A. Snyder. 1989. "Vertical Integration in the U.S. Auto Industry: A Note on the Influence of Transaction-Specific Assets," *Journal of Economic Behavior and Organization* 12: 265–73.

———. 1991. "The Costs of Organization," *Journal of Law, Economics, and Organization* 7: 1–25.

Masten, Scott E., and Edward A. Snyder. 1989. "The Design and Duration of Contracts: Strategic and Efficiency Considerations," *Law and Contemporary Problems* 52: 63–85.

Mathewson, G. Frank, and Ralph A. Winter. 1985. "The Economics of Franchise Contracts," *Journal of Law and Economics* 28: 503–26.

Mayers, David, and Clifford W. Smith. 1982. "On the Corporate Demand for Insurance," *Journal of Business* 55: 281–96.

McAfee, R. Preston, and Marius Schwartz. 1994. "Multilateral Vertical Contracting: Opportunism, Nondiscrimination, and Exclusivity," *American Economic Review* 84: 210–30.

McDonald, Stephen L. 1971. *Petroleum Conservation in the United States: An Economic Analysis.* Baltimore: Johns Hopkins University Press.

McNeely, Richard L. 1961. "Purse Seine Revolution in Tuna Fishing," *Pacific Fisherman* 59: 27–58.

Melville, Herman. 1851. *Moby-Dick.* Reprint, 1972. Harmondsworth, U.K.: Penguin.

Merring, F. E. 1982. "Oil Futures Trading: Successes in New York and London," *Petroleum Economist* 49: 9–12.

———. 1984. "The Spot Market: The Oil Industry's Changing Structure," *Petroleum Economist* 51: 9–14.

Milgrom, Paul, and John Roberts. 1992. *Economics, Organization, and Management.* Englewood Cliffs, N.J.: Prentice-Hall.

Mining Information Services. 1981. *Keystone Coal Industry Manual.* New York: McGraw-Hill.

Minkler, Alanson P. 1990. "An Empirical Analysis of a Firm's Decision to Franchise," *Economics Letters* 34: 77–82.

Mohnfeld, J. H. 1982. "World Oil Markets: Implications of Structural Change," *Petroleum Economist* 49: 269–72.

Monteverde, Kirk, and David J. Teece. 1982a. "Supplier Switching Costs and Vertical Integration in the Automobile Industry," *Bell Journal of Economics* 13: 206–13.

———. 1982b. "Appropriable Rents and Quasi-Vertical Integration," *Journal of Law and Economics* 25: 321–27.

Morison, Samuel Eliot. 1921. *The Maritime History of Massachusetts, 1783–1860.* Boston: Houghton Mifflin.

Mulherin, J. Harold. 1986. "Complexity in Long-Term Contracts: An Analysis of Natural Gas Contract Provisions," *Journal of Law, Economics, and Organization* 2: 105–17.

Muris, Timothy J. 1981. "Opportunistic Behavior and the Law of Contracts," *Minnesota Law Review* 65: 575–80.

Muris, Timothy J., David T. Scheffman, and Pablo T. Spiller. 1993. *Strategy, Structure, and Antitrust in the Carbonated Soft-Drink Industry.* New York: Quorum Books.

National Coal Association. (various years) *Steam Electric Plant Factors.* Washington, D.C.

Nelson, Richard R. 1981. "Assessing Private Enterprise: An Exegesis of Tangled Doctrine," *Bell Journal of Economics* 12: 93–111.

Nelson, Richard R., and Sidney G. Winter. 1982. *An Evolutionary Theory of Economic Change.* Cambridge: Belknap Press of Harvard University Press.

Noren, D. L. 1990. "The Economics of the Golden Arches: A Case Study of the McDonald's System," *The American Economist* 34: 60–64.

Norman, Donald A. 1984. "Indefinite Pricing Provisions in Natural Gas Contracts." Discussion Paper no. 034, American Petroleum Institute, Washington, D.C.

North, Douglas C., and Barry R. Weingast. 1989. "Constitutions and Commitment: The Evolution of Institutions Governing Public Choice in Seventeenth-Century England," *Journal of Economic History* 49: 803–32.

Norton, Seth W. 1988. "An Empirical Look at Franchising as an Organizational Form," *Journal of Business* 61: 197–217.

Orbach, Michael K. 1977. *Hunters, Seamen, and Entrepreneurs: The Tuna Seinermen of San Diego.* Berkeley: University of California Press.

Ouchi, William G. 1981. *Theory Z: How American Business Can Meet the Japanese Challenge.* Reading, Mass.: Addison-Wesley.

Palay, Thomas M. 1981. *The Governance of Rail-Freight Contracts: A Comparative Institutional Approach.* Ph.D. diss., University of Pennsylvania.

———. 1984. "Comparative Institutional Economics: The Governance of Rail Freight Contracting," *Journal of Legal Studies* 13: 265–87.

———. 1985. "Avoiding Regulatory Constraints: Contracting Safeguards and the Role of Informal Agreements," *Journal of Law, Economics, and Organization* 1: 155–76.

Peltzman, Sam. 1991. "*The Handbook of Industrial Organization*: A Review Article," *Journal of Political Economy* 99: 201–17.

Pierce, Richard J. 1983. "Natural Gas Regulation, Deregulation, and Contracts," *Virginia Law Review* 68: 63–115.

Plotkin, Irving H. 1991. "On the Nature of Intangible Assets in a McDonald's Franchise." Expert's report in *Canterbury v. Commissioner*, no. 38037-87, U.S. Tax Ct.

Porter, Glenn, and Harold C. Livesay. 1971. *Merchants and Manufacturers: Studies in the Changing Structure of Nineteenth-Century Marketing.* Baltimore: Johns Hopkins Press.

Posner, Richard A. 1976. *Antitrust Law: An Economic Perspective.* Chicago: University of Chicago Press.

Prescott, Edward C., and Michael Visscher. 1980. "Organizational Capital," *Journal of Political Economy* 88: 446–61.

Priest, George L. 1981. "A Theory of the Consumer Product Warranty," *Yale Law Journal* 90: 1297–1352.

Putterman, Louis, ed. 1986. *The Economic Nature of the Firm: A Reader.* Cambridge: Cambridge University Press.

Rasmusen, Eric. 1991. "Recent Developments in the Economics of Exclusionary Contracts," in R. S. Khemani and W. T. Stanbury, eds., *Canadian Competition Law and Policy at the Centenary.* Halifax, N.S.: The Institute for Research on Public Policy.

Roeber, J. 1979. "The Dynamics of the Rotterdam Market," *Petroleum Economist* 46: 49–52.

———. 1982. "The Rotterdam Oil Market: What Determines World Oil Prices?" *Petroleum Economist* 49: 181–83.

Roesti, Robert M. 1960. *Economic Analysis of Factors Underlying Pricing in the Southern California Tuna Canning Industry.* Ph.D. diss., University of Southern California.

Rogerson, William P. 1989. "Profit Regulation of Defense Contractors and Prizes for Innovation," *Journal of Political Economy* 97: 1284–1305.

Rosen, Sherwin. 1972. "Learning by Experience as Joint Production," *Quarterly Journal of Economics* 86: 366.

———. 1988. "Transactions Costs and Internal Labor Markets," *Journal of Law, Economics, and Organization* 4: 49–64.

Rubin, Paul H. 1978. "The Theory of the Firm and the Structure of the Franchise Contract," *Journal of Law and Economics* 21: 223–33.

Scherer, F. M. 1980. *Industrial Market Structure and Economic Performance*, 2d ed. Chicago: Rand McNally.

Schmalensee, Richard, and Paul L. Joskow. 1986. "Estimated Parameters as Independent Variables: An Application to the Costs of Steam Electric Generating Units," *Journal of Econometrics* 31: 275–305.

Sen, Kabir C. 1993. "The Use of Initial Fees and Royalties in Business Format Franchising," *Managerial and Decision Economics* 14: 175–90.

Shapiro, Carl, and Joseph E. Stiglitz. 1984. "Equilibrium Unemployment as a Worker Discipline Device," *American Economic Review* 74: 433–44.

Shavell, Steven. 1980. "Damage Measures for Breach of Contract," *Bell Journal of Economics* 11: 466–90.

Shelton, John P. 1967. "Allocative Efficiency vs. 'X-Efficiency': Comment," *American Economic Review* 57: 1252–58.

Shepard, Andrea. 1993. "Contractual Form, Retail Price, and Asset Characteristics in Gasoline Retailing," *Rand Journal of Economics* 24: 58–77.

Simon, Herbert A. 1957. *Models of Man, Social and Rational.* New York: Wiley.

———. 1961. *Administrative Behavior,* 2d ed. New York: Macmillan.

———. 1978. "Rationality as Process and Product of Thought," *American Economic Review* 68: 1–16.

———. 1991. "Organizations and Markets," *Journal of Economic Perspectives* 5: 25–44.

Smith, Richard L., II. 1982. "Franchise Regulation: An Economic Analysis of State Restrictions on Automobile Distribution," *Journal of Law and Economics* 25: 125–57.

Snyder, Edward A., and Thomas E. Kauper. 1991. "Misuse of the Antitrust Laws: The Competitor Plaintiff," *Michigan Law Review* 90: 551–603.

Stackpole, Edouard A. 1953. *The Sea-Hunters: The New England Whalemen during Two Centuries, 1635–1835.* Philadelphia: Lippincott.

Stigler, George. 1951. "The Division of Labor Is Limited by the Extent of the Market," *Journal of Political Economy* 59: 185–93.

Stuckey, John A. 1983. *Vertical Integration and Joint Ventures in the Aluminum Industry.* Cambridge: Harvard University Press.

Sullivan, Robert E. 1955. *Handbook of Oil and Gas Law.* New York: Prentice-Hall.

Sun Oil Co. 1956–72. *Tanker Market Review.*

Teece, David J. 1977. "Technology Transfer by Multinational Firms: The Resource Costs of Transferring Technological Know-How," *Economic Journal* 87: 242–61.

———. 1980. "Economies of Scope and the Scope of the Enterprise," *Journal of Economic Behavior and Organization* 1: 223–47.

Telser, Lester G. 1980. "A Theory of Self-Enforcing Agreements," *Journal of Business* 53: 27–44.

Tollison, Robert, David Kaplan, and Richard Higgins. 1991. *Competition and Concentration: The Economics of the Carbonated Soft Drink Industry.* Lexington, Mass.: Lexington Books.

Umbeck, John. 1977. "A Theory of Contract Choice and the California Gold Rush," *Journal of Law and Economics* 20: 421–37.

U.S. Department of Commerce. 1988. *Franchising in the Economy,* by Andrew Kostecka. Washington D.C.: U.S. Department of Commerce.

U.S. Department of Energy, Energy Information Administration (EIA). 1982a. *Natural Gas Producer/Purchaser Contracts and Their Potential Impacts on the Natural Gas Market.* Part 2 of *An Analysis of the Natural Gas Policy Act and Several Alternatives.* DOE/EIA-0330. Washington D.C.: U.S. Government Printing Office.

———. 1982b. *Gas Supplies of Interstate Natural Gas Pipeline Companies—1980.* DOE/EIA-0167 (80). Washington D.C.: U.S. Government Printing Office.

———. (various years). *Cost and Quality of Fuels for Electric Utility Plants.* DOE/EIA-0191. Washington D.C.: U.S. Government Printing Office.

U.S. Department of the Interior, Fish and Wildlife Service. 1953. *Survey of the Domestic Tuna Industry,* by A. W. Anderson and W. S. Stolting. Washington, D.C.: U.S. Government Printing Office.

U.S. President. 1991. *The Economic Report of the President Transmitted to the Congress.* Washington D.C.: U.S. Government Printing Office.

Wachter, Michael L., and Oliver E. Williamson. 1978. "Obligational Markets and the Mechanics of Inflation," *Bell Journal of Economics* 9: 549–71.

Walker, Gordon, and David Weber. 1984. "A Transaction Cost Approach to Make-or-Buy Decisions," *Administrative Science Quarterly* 29: 373–91.

————. 1987. "Supplier Competition, Uncertainty and Make-or-Buy Decisions," *Academy of Management Journal* 30: 589–96.

Weingast, Barry R., and William J. Marshall. 1988. "The Industrial Organization of Congress; or Why Legislatures, Like Firms, Are Not Organized as Markets," *Journal of Political Economy* 96: 132–63.

White, L. J. 1971. *The Automobile Industry since 1945*. Cambridge: Harvard University Press.

Wiley, John S., Eric Rasmusen, and J. Mark Ramseyer. 1990. "The Monopolist That Leases," *UCLA Law Review* 37: 693–731.

Williams, William Fish. 1964. "The Voyage of the *Florence*, 1973–1874," in H. Williams, ed., *One Whaling Family*. Boston: Houghton Mifflin.

Williamson, Oliver E. 1971. "The Vertical Integration of Production: Market Failure Considerations," *American Economic Review* 61: 112–23.

————. 1975. *Markets and Hierarchies: Analysis and Antitrust Implications*. New York: Free Press.

————. 1979a. "Transaction Costs Economics: The Governance of Contractual Relations," *Journal of Law and Economics* 22: 233–62.

————. 1979b. "The Economics of Defense Contracting: Incentives and Performance," in Roland N. McKean, ed., *Issues in Defense Economics*, 229–32. New York: NBER.

————. 1983. "Credible Commitments: Using Hostages to Support Exchange," *American Economic Review* 73: 519–40.

————. 1985. *The Economic Institutions of Capitalism*. New York: Free Press.

————. 1988. "The Logic of Economic Organization," *Journal of Law, Economics and Organization* 4: 65–93.

————. 1989. "Transaction Cost Economics," in R. Schmalensee and R. Willig, eds., *Handbook of Industrial Organization*, vol. 1. Amsterdam: North-Holland: 135–82.

————. 1991. "Comparative Economic Organization: The Analysis of Discrete Structural Alternatives," *Administrative Science Quarterly* 36: 269–96.

Winter, S. G. 1980. "An Essay on the Theory of Production." Working Paper Series A no. 39, Yale School of Organization and Management.

Zimmerman, Martin. 1981. *The U.S. Coal Industry: The Economics of Policy Choice*. Cambridge: MIT Press.

INDEX